iTOEFL iBT® LISTENING
New Edition

LinguaForum

New Edition TOEFL iBT® i Listening

Contents Development	LinguaForum
Project Director	Issac Kim
Project Managers	Selene Joo, Sharon SB Cho, Sue Lee
Project Assistants	Brantley Smith, Chris Newton
Main Author	Craig Michael Smith
Authors	Arthur Koo, Yuri Yi, Josephine Chung, Esther Nam, Carrie Jang, Noah Williams
Proofreaders	Kyle Wilson, Aidan Hammond, Will Winchester, Susan Kim, Paul Lee
Editing & Design	Design Yeon, Hyun Jung Cho
Audio Recording	109Sound
Publisher	Gil Ho Lee

Tel 02)590-6900 **Fax** 02)590-6901
ISBN 978-89-286-3728-7 [13740]   **Price** ₩22,000

TIME Education Co. Ltd
5F Peugeot Biz Tower, 310, Gwangnaru-ro, Seongdong-gu, Seoul, 04799, Republic of KOREA

Copyright © 2017 by LinguaForum

No unauthorized photocopying
All rights reserved. No part of this book may be reproduced or transmitted in any form or by any means, electronic or mechanical, including photocopying, recording, or any other information storage and retrieval system without the written permission of the publisher.

Printed in the Republic of Korea

iTOEFL iBT LISTENING
New Edition

LinguaForum

Contents

i Listening Structure   6
TOEFL iBT   8
TOEFL iBT Listening   9
Note-taking for iBT Listening   10
Study Plan   12
Diagnostic Test   14

PART A. Question Types

Chapter 01 Main Idea   24

Chapter 02 Detail   30

Chapter 03 Function   36

Chapter 04 Attitude   42

Chapter 05 Organization   48

Chapter 06 Connecting Content   54

Chapter 07 Inference   62

New Edition TOEFL iBT i Listening

PART B. Approaching Themes

Chapter 08 Office Hours — 70

Chapter 09 Service Encounters — 84

Chapter 10 Humanities — 98

Chapter 11 Life Science — 112

Chapter 12 Physical Science — 126

Chapter 13 Social Science — 140

Actual Test 1 — 156

Actual Test 2 — 162

Answer Key & Explanations A2 ~ A146

i Listening Structure

Diagnostic Test

실제 시험의 구성 및 난이도로 제작된 Diagnostic Test를 통하여 자신의 실력을 스스로 점검할 수 있도록 하였으며, 이 결과에 따라 수준에 맞는 학습을 진행할 수 있도록 하였다.

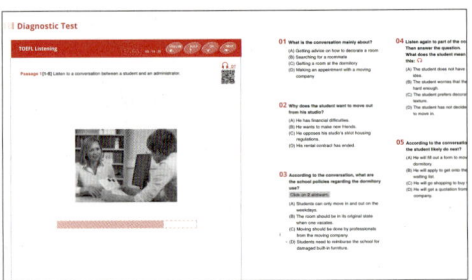

PART A _ Question Types

Keys to Solution
각 문제 유형의 문제 풀이 전략을 상세하게 학습할 수 있다.

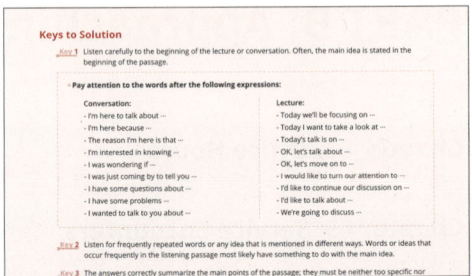

Sample Question
예시 문제를 통해 문제 풀이 전략을 구체적으로 활용해 보고 연습할 수 있다.

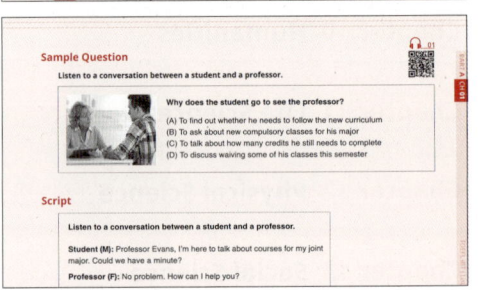

Basic Drill
각 문제 유형에 필요한 기초 스킬을 익히고 난 후, 단문 길이의 지문 및 문제를 통해 각 문제 유형을 집중적으로 연습할 수 있다.

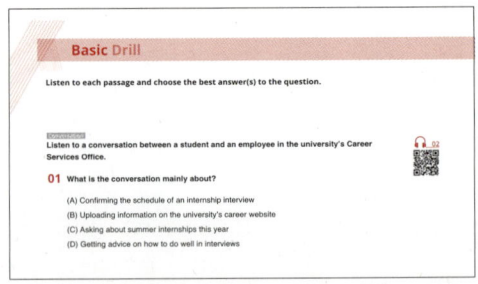

Listening Practice
실제 TOEFL iBT에서 출제되는 다양한 주제의 청취 지문들을 통해 본격적으로 듣기 연습을 해 볼 수 있다.

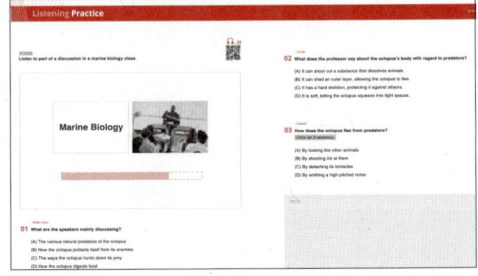

PART B _ Approaching Themes

Listening Preview

Chapter에 수록된 지문을 학습하기에 앞서, 각 지문의 주제에 대한 배경지식을 관련 사진과 함께 제시하여, 타 시험에 비해 수준이 높은 TOEFL 지문 주제들에 대한 배경지식을 쉽게 이해할 수 있도록 하였다.

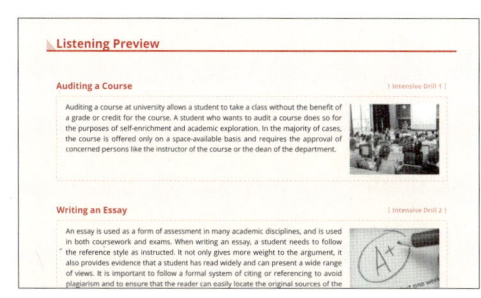

Intensive Drill

실제 TOEFL iBT에서 출제되는 주제별로 구성된 다양한 지문을 통해 충분히 청취 연습을 할 수 있도록 하였다. 각 Chapter에 3개의 세트가 수록되어 있다.

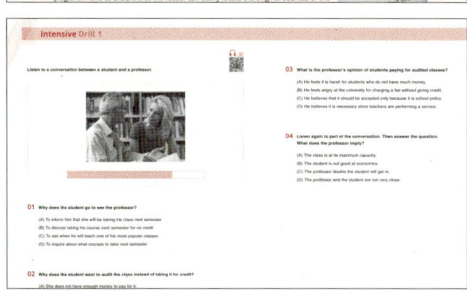

Mini Test

Intensive Drill보다 난이도가 높은 지문을 통해 여러 가지 문제 유형을 골고루 접하고 TOEFL iBT를 학습할 기회를 마련하였다. 각 Chapter에 2개의 세트가 수록되어 있다.

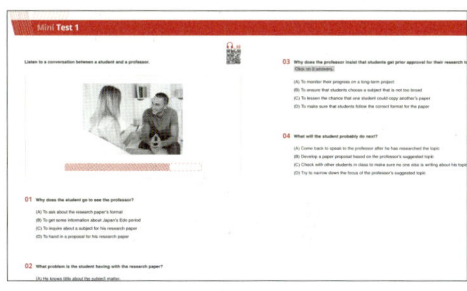

iBT Practice

실제 TOEFL iBT에서 자주 출제되는 주제의 지문을 실전과 동일한 길이와 문제로 구성하여, 실전 감각을 키울 수 있도록 하였다.

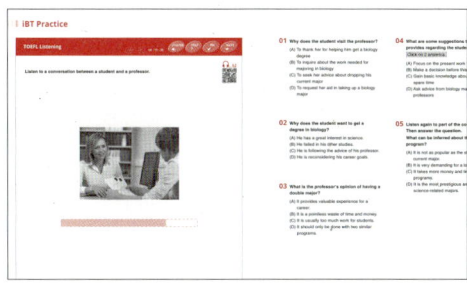

Actual Test

2회분의 Actual Test를 수록하여, 실전에서의 자신의 예상 점수를 가늠해 보고 실전 적응력을 높일 수 있도록 하였다.

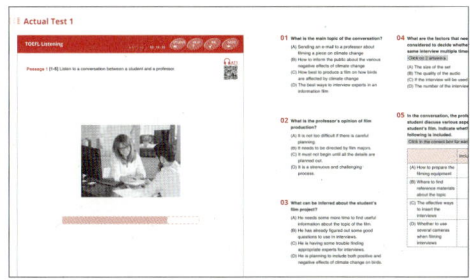

TOEFL iBT

New Edition **TOEFL iBT i Listening**

TOEFL iBT 시험은 대학 수준의 영어를 사용하고 이해할 수 있는 능력을 측정한다. 그리고 학술적 주제의 과제를 수행하는 데 듣기, 읽기, 말하기 및 쓰기 실력을 얼마나 잘 결합하는지를 평가한다.

■ 한국 내 응시

- **실시 일자**: 1년에 50회 정도 실시, 각 나라와 지역별로 시험일에 차이가 있음
- **시험 장소**: ETS Test Center
- **접수 방법**: 인터넷 접수: 시험일로부터 최소 7일전 인터넷으로 등록 (www.ets.org/toefl)
  전화 접수: 시험일로부터 최소 7일전 전화로 등록
- **응시료**: $185(USD)
- **지불 형식**: 신용/직불카드 – American Express®, Discover®, JCB®, MasterCard®, VISA®
  전자 수표(e-수표) 또는 PayPal® 계정
- **유효 신분증**: 여권 (유효기간, 서명 확인 필수), 주민등록증, 운전면허증, 군인신분증
- **소요 시간**: 약 4시간 30분 소요
- **성적 확인**: 시험일로부터 약 10일 후에 온라인상에서 확인 가능
  성적표 유효기간: 2년

■ 시험 영역

영역	제한 시간	지문 및 문항 수	과제
Reading	60~80분	3~4개 지문 - 지문당 12~14문항 (총 36~56문항)	대학 교재 글을 읽고 질문에 답하기
Listening	60~90분	2~3개 대화 - 대화당 5문항 4~6개 강의 - 강의당 6문항 (총 34~51문항)	강의, 교실 토론 및 대화를 듣고 질문에 답하기
휴식	10분		
Speaking	20분	독립형 2개 통합형 4개	익숙한 주제에 대한 의견을 표현하기, 읽기와 듣기 과제를 바탕으로 말하기
Writing	55분	통합형 1개 독립형 1개	읽기 및 듣기 과제를 바탕으로 글쓰기, 특정 주제에 대한 글쓰기

TOEFL iBT Listening

New Edition TOEFL iBT i Listening

▰ Listening 구성

2개 혹은 3개의 세트로 구성되며, 각 세트는 1개의 대화와 2개의 강의로 구성된다.

- **대화**   총 2~3개 대화, 각각 5문항 출제, 대화당 길이 약 3분
- **강의**   총 4~6개 강의, 각각 6문항 출제, 강의당 길이 약 3~5분

▰ 화면 구성

 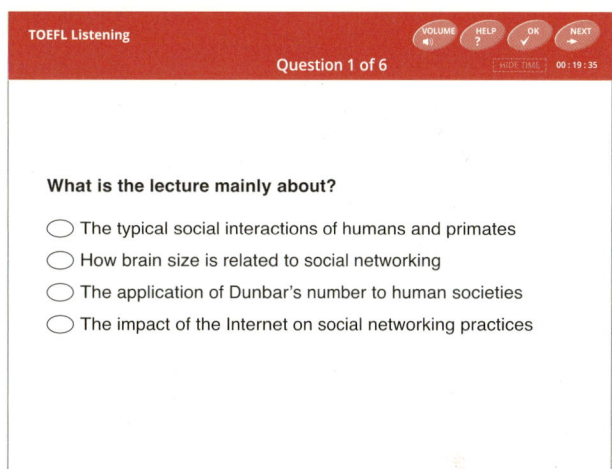

▰ 문제 유형: 총 7가지 유형의 문제 출제

- **Main Idea**   포괄적으로 주제를 묻는 유형
- **Detail**   세부 정보를 묻는 유형
- **Function**   지문의 일부를 다시 듣고 화자의 숨은 의도를 묻는 유형
- **Attitude**   화자의 말하는 태도나 의견을 묻는 유형
- **Organization**   전개 구조를 묻는 유형
- **Connecting Content** 주어진 내용들 간의 관계를 묻는 유형
- **Inference**   제시된 정보로 유추 가능한 내용을 묻는 유형

Note-taking for iBT Listening

The key to effective note-taking is being quick and concise. Familiarize yourself with the following symbols and abbreviations, and find the most effective note-taking method for you.

Symbols

Using symbols will not only save your time, but it will also make your notes easier to read.

Symbol	Meaning	Example
→	lead to, cause, mean	smoking → cancer
←	come from, because of	field trip canceled ← rain
↓	decrease	unemployment ↓ labor market
↑	increase	profit ↑ April
@	at	dinner @ French restaurant
&	and	Smith & Jones Attorneys
/	per	2 hours / day
∴	therefore, so	I think ∴ I am
∵	because	actions ∵ policy
+	plus, in addition, also	ride bike + skateboard
=	is equal to, to be	Seoul = largest city in Korea
≠	is not the same, not to be, false	results ≠ data
#	number (numbers)	Q4 answer → #2
x	times	5 x increase
〉	greater than, more important	5 > π
〈	less than	my salary < Tony's
~	approximately, more or less	sum ~ 300
$	cost, price, dollars	Price = $50,000
≐	almost same	a ≐ b

Abbreviations

Writing the shortened form of a word when taking notes will save your valuable time. However, you must be careful not to make the word unrecognizable. There are many ways to make an abbreviation. (e.g. leave out the vowels, just write the beginning of a long word, etc.) There is no specific rule to it, and the only thing you need to remember is to make it recognizable to you.

Abbreviation	Meaning	Example
w/	with	disagree w/ distinction
w/o	without	available w/o charge
s.th	something	s.th happens
i.e.	that is, in other words	courses, i.e. studies
e.g.	example	mammals e.g. whales
etc.	et cetera, and so on	insects, scorpions, etc.
b/c	because	high prices b/c high wages
esp.	especially	employees esp. clerks
min.	minimum	yield min. 100 units
max.	maximum	max. 1,000 units
ASAP	as soon as possible	send data ASAP
ref.	reference	ref. August sales figures
b/4	before	work b/4 leisure
Co.	company	the firm of Smith & Co.
comm.	communication	refer comm. department
gov't	government	gov't offices
prof.	professor	Prof. Wilson
btw	between	btw 15 & 30 kg
info.	information	info. society

Study Plan

■ 나에게 맞는 Study Plan 고르는 방법

방법 1

Diagnostic Test(p.14) 점수 결과에 따라 본인에게 맞는 Study Plan 사용
- 맞은 개수 12개 이상 ➡ **4-Week Study Plan**
- 맞은 개수 11개 이하 ➡ **6-Week Study Plan**

방법 2

본인에게 해당하는 항목을 골라 체크(✔)한 후, 체크 개수에 따른 Study Plan 사용
- ☐ 토플 시험을 본 적이 있다.
- ☐ 토플 점수가 80점 이상이다.
- ☐ 토플 문제 유형에 대한 기본 지식이 있다.
- ☐ 한 번 들은 영어 문장을 받아 쓸 수 있다.
- ☐ 지문을 듣고 핵심 내용을 주요 단어로 정리할 수 있다.
- ☐ 토플 Listening 문제집 한 권을 끝낸 경험이 있다.

- 체크 4개 이상 ➡ **4-Week Study Plan**
- 체크 3개 이하 ➡ **6-Week Study Plan**

■ Study Plan 100% 활용하기

4 Week Study Plan
문제 유형에 따른 문제 풀이 전략을 빠르게 파악하고 연습한 후, 실전 대비용 지문들과 실전 모의고사(Actual Test)를 통해 청해 실력을 탄탄하게 다질 수 있다. 문제 유형에 대한 기본 지식이 있는 학생들을 위한 한 달짜리 속성 과정이다.

6 Week Study Plan
하루에 문제 유형 하나씩 학습하며 유형에 따른 문제 풀이 방법을 탄탄히 익힌다. 그 후, 짧은 지문(Intensive Drill) → 중간 지문(Mini Test) → 긴 지문(iBT Practice) 순으로 단계적인 학습을 거쳐 실전에 대한 부담감을 줄이고, 차근차근히 대비해 갈 수 있도록 구성된 과정이다.

1. Study Plan에 제시된 학습 분량을 공부한다. 최대한 Study Plan을 지키고 미루지 않도록 한다.
2. 링구아포럼 홈페이지(www.linguaforum.com)에서 제공하는 Dictation 자료를 활용하여 정확한 영어 발음과 억양을 익힌다.
3. 정해진 학습 분량을 공부한 후, 해설집을 통해 틀린 문제의 문제 유형과 정답 관련 문장을 분석하여 오답 노트를 작성한다.
4. 학습 분량이 없는 요일을 활용하여, 한 주 동안 작성한 오답 노트를 복습한다. 자주 틀리는 문제 유형을 파악하고 PART A(Ch. 01~07)의 관련 유형을 찾아 복습한다.
5. PART B(Ch. 08~13) 학습 시, 목차를 통해 관심 있는 배경지식 분야를 우선으로 학습할 수도 있다.

4-Week Study Plan

	Day 1	Day 2	Day 3	Day 4	Day 5
WEEK 1	Diagnostic Test	Ch. 01-02 & Ch. 01-02 Dictation	Ch. 03-04 & Ch. 03-04 Dictation	Ch. 05-06 & Ch. 05-06 Dictation	Ch. 07 & Ch. 08 Intensive Drill
	Day 6	Day 7	Day 8	Day 9	Day 10
WEEK 2	Ch. 08 Mini Test & iBT Practice	Ch. 09 Intensive Drill	Ch. 09 Mini Test & iBT Practice	Ch. 10 Intensive Drill	Ch. 10 Mini Test & iBT Practice
	Day 11	Day 12	Day 13	Day 14	Day 15
WEEK 3	Ch. 07-10 Dictation	Ch. 11 Intensive Drill	Ch. 11 Mini Test & iBT Practice	Ch. 12 Intensive Drill	Ch. 12 Mini Test & iBT Practice
	Day 16	Day 17	Day 18	Day 19	Day 20
WEEK 4	Ch. 13 Intensive Drill	Ch. 13 Mini Test & iBT Practice	Ch. 11-13 Dictation	Actual Test1 & Dictation	Actual Test 2 & Dictation

6-Week Study Plan

	Day 1	Day 2	Day 3	Day 4	Day 5
WEEK 1	Diagnostic Test	Ch. 01	Ch. 02	Ch. 03	Ch. 04 & Ch. 01-04 Dictation
	Day 6	Day 7	Day 8	Day 9	Day 10
WEEK 2	Ch. 05	Ch. 06	Ch. 07	Ch. 05-07 Dictation	Ch. 08 Intensive Drill
	Day 11	Day 12	Day 13	Day 14	Day 15
WEEK 3	Ch. 08 Mini Test	Ch. 08 iBT Practice & Ch. 08 Dictation	Ch. 09 Intensive Drill	Ch. 09 Mini Test	Ch. 09 iBT Practice & Ch. 09 Dictation
	Day 16	Day 17	Day 18	Day 19	Day 20
WEEK 4	Ch. 10 Intensive Drill	Ch. 10 Mini Test	Ch. 10 iBT Practice & Ch. 10 Dictation	Ch. 11 Intensive Drill	Ch. 11 Mini Test
	Day 21	Day 22	Day 23	Day 24	Day 25
WEEK 5	Ch. 11 iBT Practice & Ch. 11 Dictation	Ch. 12 Intensive Drill	Ch. 12 Mini Test	Ch. 12 iBT Practice & Ch. 12 Dictation	Ch. 13 Intensive Drill
	Day 26	Day 27	Day 28	Day 29	Day 30
WEEK 6	Ch. 13 Mini Test	Ch. 13 iBT Practice & Ch. 13 Dictation	Actual Test 1	Actual Test 2	Actual Test 1-2 Dictation

* 링구아포럼 홈페이지(www.linguaforum.com)에서 제공하는 Dictation 자료, 단어장, 단어테스트를 이용하여 청해 실력 및 어휘 실력을 향상시킬 수 있습니다.

TOEFL iBT i Listening   www.linguaforum.com

Diagnostic Test

Diagnostic Test

TOEFL Listening

Passage 1 [1-5] Listen to a conversation between a student and an administrator.

01 What is the conversation mainly about?

(A) Getting advice on how to decorate a room
(B) Searching for a roommate
(C) Getting a room at the dormitory
(D) Making an appointment with a moving company

02 Why does the student want to move out from his studio?

(A) He has financial difficulties.
(B) He wants to make new friends.
(C) He opposes his studio's strict housing regulations.
(D) His rental contract has ended.

03 According to the conversation, what are the school policies regarding the dormitory use?

Click on 2 answers.

(A) Students can only move in and out on the weekdays.
(B) The room should be in its original state when one vacates.
(C) Moving should be done by professionals from the moving company.
(D) Students need to reimburse the school for damaged built-in furniture.

04 Listen again to part of the conversation. Then answer the question.
What does the student mean when he says this:

(A) The student does not have any specific idea.
(B) The student worries that the wall is not hard enough.
(C) The student prefers decorations with a soft texture.
(D) The student has not decided on what date to move in.

05 According to the conversation, what will the student likely do next?

(A) He will fill out a form to move into the dormitory.
(B) He will apply to get onto the dormitory's waiting list.
(C) He will go shopping to buy wall hangings.
(D) He will get a quotation from the moving company.

Passage 2 [6-11] Listen to part of a lecture in a zoology class.

06 Why does the professor discuss the habitat of the vervet monkey?

(A) To explain why the alarm calls vary
(B) To compare it to that of predators
(C) To emphasize its geographical advantage
(D) To describe the reason altruistic behavior is needed

07 According to the lecture, what are mentioned as vervet monkey's reactions to the alarm call?
Click on 2 answers.

(A) Standing on both legs and looking down
(B) Hiding in a bush
(C) Clinging to another vervet monkey
(D) Swimming in the closest river

08 Why does the professor mention the vervet monkey's altruistic behavior?

(A) To describe vervet monkey's newly discovered behavior
(B) To explain its advantage through evolution
(C) To compare two different viewpoints about alarm calls
(D) To highlight the vervet monkey's high moral code

09 What can be inferred about young vervet monkeys?

(A) They are willing to sacrifice themselves on behalf of other monkeys.
(B) They often confuse the alarm calls they should make.
(C) They take years to fully develop alarm calls.
(D) They retain strong emotional connections with their mother.

10 What is the professor's attitude toward the vervet monkeys?

(A) He questions their place between apes and humans.
(B) He mocks their moral level.
(C) He thinks they are worthy of careful study.
(D) He agrees they are the most evolved primates.

11 In the lecture, the professor describes several different alarm calls made by the vervet monkey. Indicate which alarm call is related to which predator.
Click in the correct box for each phrase.

	Leopard	Eagle	Snake
(A) Tonal alarm			
(B) Low-pitched grunt			
(C) High-pitched chutter			
(D) Short alarm			

Passage 3 [12-17] Listen to part of a lecture in a U.S. history class.

12 What is the main idea of this lecture?

(A) The development of the railroad in the 1800s
(B) The role the railroad plays in the U.S. economy
(C) Social and economic problems caused by the railway
(D) How to secure employment in the railway sector

13 Why does the professor mention the commuter train?

(A) To appreciate its role in daily life
(B) To contrast its structure to that of the freight train
(C) To differentiate the role of the freight train
(D) To illustrate extended roles of the train in the nineteenth century

14 According to the lecture, how did the railway help the American West?

(A) By promoting local business growth
(B) By convincing people to enter the transportation industry
(C) By transporting early European-American settlers
(D) By producing a number of high-paying jobs

15 Listen again to part of the lecture. Then answer the question.
What does the professor mean when she says this: 🎧

(A) She believes there should be more benefits from working in the railway industry.
(B) She considers that the railway industry is a relatively easy field to get a job in.
(C) She thinks the railway industry is a profitable industry to work in.
(D) She feels the workers in the railway sector are overpaid.

16 According to the professor, what are the public benefits of freight trains?
Click on 2 answers.

(A) They are more fuel efficient.
(B) They catalyze the real estate boom.
(C) They relieve highway congestion.
(D) They provide faster shipment of goods.

17 What can be inferred about the railroad system in the U.S.?

(A) It assures high salaries and benefits.
(B) It was a mostly used means of transportation in the past.
(C) It guarantees unemployment problem solving.
(D) It stretches throughout the mainland of the U.S.

TOEFL iBT i Listening   www.linguaforum.com

PART A
Question Types

Chapter 01 Main Idea
Chapter 02 Detail
Chapter 03 Function
Chapter 04 Attitude
Chapter 05 Organization
Chapter 06 Connecting Content
Chapter 07 Inference

Chapter 01   Main Idea

Main Idea questions ask you about the overall topic, main idea, or purpose of the listening passage. The main idea of the passage may be directly stated, or it may be implied. The Main Idea question will always be the first question after each listening passage.

How the Question is Worded

Main Topic
- ☐ What is the main topic of the conversation/lecture?
- ☐ What are the speakers mainly discussing?
- ☐ What is the conversation/lecture mainly about?
- ☐ What problem does the student have?

Main Purpose
- ☐ Why does the student go to see the professor?
- ☐ Why does the student visit the registrar's office/library/student office?
- ☐ Why did the professor ask to see the student?

Keys to Solution

Key 1 Listen carefully to the beginning of the lecture or conversation. Often, the main idea is stated in the beginning of the passage.

> **+ Pay attention to the words after the following expressions:**
>
> Conversation:
> - I'm here to talk about …
> - I'm here because …
> - The reason I'm here is that …
> - I'm interested in knowing …
> - I was wondering if …
> - I was just coming by to tell you …
> - I have some questions about …
> - I have some problems …
> - I wanted to talk to you about …
>
> Lecture:
> - Today we'll be focusing on …
> - Today I want to take a look at …
> - Today's talk is on …
> - OK, let's talk about …
> - OK, let's move on to …
> - I would like to turn our attention to …
> - I'd like to continue our discussion on …
> - I'd like to talk about …
> - We're going to discuss …

Key 2 Listen for frequently repeated words or any idea that is mentioned in different ways. Words or ideas that occur frequently in the listening passage most likely have something to do with the main idea.

Key 3 The answers correctly summarize the main points of the passage; they must be neither too specific nor too broad.

Sample Question

Listen to a conversation between a student and a professor.

Why does the student go to see the professor?

(A) To find out whether he needs to follow the new curriculum
(B) To ask about new compulsory classes for his major
(C) To talk about how many credits he still needs to complete
(D) To discuss waiving some of his classes this semester

Script

Listen to a conversation between a student and a professor.

Student (M): Professor Evans, I'm here to talk about courses for my joint major. Could we have a minute?

Professor (F): No problem. How can I help you?

Student: I'll be in my third year of a joint major in math and physics next semester. I was wondering if I can keep following the old curriculum for the joint major instead of taking those compulsory courses listed on the new curriculum.

Professor: Students who have completed their second year can stick to the old curriculum. So, if you're in your third year next semester, I don't think you need to worry about the new curriculum.

Student: Oh, that's a relief. If I follow the new curriculum, I should take eight more classes including prerequisites. It would be a complete waste of a semester.

Professor: We don't certainly want that kind of problem to happen.

Student: Great. I pay for my own tuition and, as you know, it is quite hard to manage studies and work at the same time.

Professor: I know. I appreciate your sincere effort.

Student: Thank you for saying that. Have a great day, Professor Evans.

> **Key 1** Listen carefully when the student says "I was wondering if ..." as he is going to say why he came to the professor.
>
> **Key 2** Listen for frequently repeated words.

Answer & Explanations

Answer Book p. A4

(A)

The student says he wants to know if he can keep following the old curriculum, and according to the professor, he does not need to worry about the new curriculum. That is, he came to the professor to find out whether he needs to follow the new curriculum.

Basic Drill

Listen to each passage and choose the best answer(s) to the question.

Conversation
Listen to a conversation between a student and an employee in the university's Career Services Office.

01 What is the conversation mainly about?

(A) Confirming the schedule of an internship interview
(B) Uploading information on the university's career website
(C) Asking about summer internships this year
(D) Getting advice on how to do well in interviews

Lecture
Listen to part of a lecture in an American history class.

02 What is the lecture mainly about?
Click on 2 answers.

(A) The causes of the American Civil War
(B) The similarities between the North and the South
(C) The consequences of the American Civil War
(D) The abolition of slavery in the North and the South

Lecture
Listen to part of a lecture in a medical science class.

03 What is the main topic of the lecture?

(A) The ways to properly use antibiotics
(B) The downsides of antibiotics
(C) The discovery of antibiotics
(D) The rise of antibiotic-resistant bacteria

Answer Book p. A4

Conversation

Listen to a conversation between a student and a professor.

04 Why does the student visit the professor?

(A) To discuss a possible topic for his paper
(B) To ask about the way to document sources for his paper
(C) To ask about where to find resources for his paper
(D) To discuss the charts included in his paper

Lecture

Listen to part of a lecture in an anthropology class.

05 What is the main purpose of the lecture?

(A) To talk about images of deforestation in the Amazon
(B) To discuss the discovery of Amazonian earth mounds
(C) To give an example of a modern Amazonian civilization
(D) To explain the uses of ancient Amazonian structures

Lecture

Listen to part of a discussion in a philosophy class.

06 What are the speakers mainly discussing?

(A) Activists influenced by Henry David Thoreau
(B) Henry David Thoreau's protest against slavery
(C) Henry David Thoreau's life in nature
(D) The beliefs of Henry David Thoreau

Chapter 01 Main Idea 27

Listening Practice

Lecture
Listen to part of a discussion in a marine biology class.

|Main Idea|

01 What are the speakers mainly discussing?

(A) The various natural predators of the octopus

(B) How the octopus protects itself from its enemies

(C) The ways the octopus hunts down its prey

(D) How the octopus digests food

|Detail|

02 What does the professor say about the octopus's body with regard to predators?

(A) It can shoot out a substance that dissolves animals.
(B) It can shed an outer layer, allowing the octopus to flee.
(C) It has a hard skeleton, protecting it against attacks.
(D) It is soft, letting the octopus squeeze into tight spaces.

|Detail|

03 How does the octopus flee from predators?
Click on 2 answers.

(A) By looking like other animals
(B) By shooting ink at them
(C) By detaching its tentacles
(D) By emitting a high-pitched noise

NOTE

Chapter 02 Detail

Detail questions ask you about explicit facts and details given in the listening passage. They generally ask about the important details related to the gist of a lecture or conversation. Typically, there will be 1-3 Detail questions. Sometimes these questions ask you to select more than 1 correct answer.

How the Question is Worded

- According to the conversation/professor, who/when/where/what/why/how ~?
- What does the student/professor say about ~?
- What are ~?
- What does the professor suggest to the man?
- Which of the following are true about ~?

Keys to Solution

Key 1 Take notes on major points and important details while you listen. Detail questions ask about the important details of a conversation or lecture, not minor ones.

> **+ Major details often include:**
>
> - Definitions of new terms/concepts/ideas
> - Important features of things or concepts
> - Causes or effects of specific events
> - New facts, reasons, results, examples, etc.

Key 2 The answer is often paraphrased. Do not simply choose the answer choices that have the same words or phrases from the listening passage. To answer these questions, you need to understand the essential ideas from the passage and make sure that the answer accurately conveys the information from the listening passage.

Sample Question

Listen to part of a discussion in an American history class.

Which remains of La Venta depict a god of the Olmecs?

(A) The large head statues
(B) The central clay mound
(C) The giant mosaics found in the city
(D) The carvings on the stone altars

Script

Listen to part of a discussion in an American history class.

Professor (F): Now, in Central America between two to three thousand years ago, there existed an ancient civilization known as the Olmec. Much of what we know about them comes from the excavation of an ancient city known as La Venta, located on the southern coast of Mexico on the Gulf of Mexico and first excavated in the 1940s. Who can tell me some things we've found there?

Student 1 (M): Well, there are those giant stone head monuments, right?

Professor: Yes, that's the most famous discovery. These statues of rulers are nine feet high and weigh about 18 tons, but they are just one amazing find. There's also a large central clay mound that resembles a volcano, large mosaics representing jaguar masks, and elaborate stone altars. Now, these altars contain some interesting features. What might those be?

Student 2 (F): Are you talking about the images of their gods, the weird jaguar-babies?

Professor: Right. Some of them have carved figures that look like a mixture of a jaguar and a human infant. Most people believe that these depict some kind of divine being that was worshipped. This has been found in Olmec monuments from other locations, too.

> **Key 1** Take notes on major points and important details. The important feature of the stone altars is the carved figures believed to be some kind of divine being.
>
> **Key 2** The answer is often paraphrased. "Carved figures" is paraphrased to "The carvings."

Answer & Explanations

Answer Book p. A12

(D)
The professor mentions stone altars as one of the Olmec remains and says most people believe their carved figures are some kind of divine being that was worshipped, which also means they depict a god of the Olmecs.

Basic Drill

Listen to each passage and choose the best answer(s) to the question.

Conversation
Listen to a conversation between a student and a professor.

01 Why does the student need a letter of recommendation?

(A) To get into an engineering program
(B) To apply for a teaching position
(C) To go to graduate school
(D) To work as a summer intern

Lecture
Listen to part of a lecture in an earth science class.

02 What are two reasons early humans favored the use of obsidian?
Click on 2 answers.

(A) It is easily broken into pieces to make tools.
(B) It is readily collected from areas around volcanoes.
(C) Its multiple colors are useful for decorative purposes.
(D) Its surface is very reflective.

Lecture
Listen to part of a lecture in a psychology class.

03 What was the Milgram experiment meant to test?

(A) The effective way to guard concentration camps
(B) Whether people obey immoral commands
(C) The amount of electricity people can handle
(D) The capacity to provide the correct answers when punished

Answer Book p. A12

Conversation

Listen to a conversation between a student and a university administrator.

04 What is the reason that the student cannot put the poster on the bulletin boards at faculty buildings?

(A) He needs to be on the waiting list for two weeks.

(B) The size of the poster that the student brought is too big.

(C) The boards at faculty buildings are for notices from the faculties only.

(D) The student did not get permission from the faculties.

Lecture

Listen to part of a discussion in a zoology class.

05 Which of the following are true about spotted hyenas?
Click on 3 answers.

(A) Females are physically smaller than males.

(B) Males have less social power than females.

(C) They only hunt weak and sick animals.

(D) They have powerful stomach acids.

(E) Females choose mates for reproduction.

Lecture

Listen to part of a lecture in an art history class.

06 Why did Picasso paint *Guernica*?

(A) To condemn Spain's destruction of a town

(B) To create an artwork best reflecting Cubism

(C) To stage a protest against World War II

(D) To celebrate the military might of Spain

Listening Practice

Conversation
Listen to a conversation between a student and a professor.

| Main Idea |

01 Why does the student go to see the professor?

(A) To get information about local libraries

(B) To ask about the syllabus for her class

(C) To discuss different versions of a textbook

(D) To talk about ways to save money for class

|Detail|

02 **According to the professor, why does the student need the newer version of the short story anthology?**

(A) It includes some new exercises.

(B) Its structure has been changed.

(C) It has new analyses.

(D) It discusses British history.

|Detail|

03 **Which of the following does the professor say about the book of critical essays?**
Click on 2 answers.

(A) It is released online for free.

(B) It is not available in the school library.

(C) The critical essays are newly written.

(D) The student does not need to buy a new version of it.

NOTE

Chapter 03 Function

Function questions ask about the speaker's purpose or the implied meaning of a specific statement. To answer these questions, you need to understand *why* the speaker says something as well as *what* the speaker means by what he or she says. These types of questions always replay a specific statement from the listening passage. Typically, there will be 1-2 Function questions for each passage.

How the Question is Worded

- Why does the Professor/student say this: 🎧 (replay)
- What does the Professor/student mean when he/she says this: 🎧 (replay)

Keys to Solution

Key 1 Pay close attention to the context in which the statement is made. In spoken language, a single statement can have different meanings depending on the situation.

Key 2 Listen to the tone of the speakers. Function questions test your understanding of certain features of spoken English. Understand that the speaker's statement can have an intended meaning that is very different from the literal meaning of the statement.

Key 3 The following words are likely to appear in answer choices for the questions asking the purpose of the speaker's statement.

- To ask / inquire / urge / request / encourage
- To indicate / suggest / imply
- To point out / remind / correct / clarify / verify / check
- To explain / introduce / emphasize / give an example / illustrate
- To complain / criticize / apologize / praise

Sample Question

Listen to a conversation between a student and a professor.

Listen again to part of the conversation. Then answer the question. Why does the professor say this: 🎧

(A) To ask the student to come later to continue the discussion
(B) To indicate that he does not have much left to explain to the student
(C) To stop the conversation with the student in a polite way
(D) To check if the student understands what he is talking about

Script

Listen to a conversation between a student and a professor.

Student (F): Professor Johnson, I'd like to ask some quick questions about the presentation on the local public art project.

Professor (M): Sure, come on in.

Student: Basically, you asked us to find local public arts that contain instrumental value rather than intrinsic value. I understand that I should look beyond mere aesthetic value, but isn't it too broad? I'm not really sure where to focus.

Professor: Good question. 🎧 When looking for instrumental value, it doesn't mean simply looking for functions and other aspects completely detached from the aesthetic perspective. But rather, through the artwork, there should be something educative, something that could create convenience, boost local and tourist attendance, and provide employment . . . Do you follow me?

Student: Yes, I get it. So there should be benefits resulting from the artwork, but they can manifest in a variety of ways, either from its artistic meaning or its function.

Professor: Exactly. So what was your topic for the presentation?

Student: I was going to talk about the big traffic light tree in Canary Wharf, but now that I think of it, I need to find a better example.

> **Key 1** Pay close attention to the context in which the statement is made.
> "Do you follow me?" means "Do you understand me?" in this context.

Answer & Explanations

(D)

The professor wants to check if the student understands what he is talking about by saying "Do you follow me?" because he has been explaining to the student what instrumental value is.

Basic Drill

Listen to each passage and choose the best answer to the question.

Conversation
Listen to a conversation between a student and a clerk at the Student Health Center.

01 Listen again to part of the conversation. Then answer the question.
Why does the student say this:

(A) To request the clerk to provide more details
(B) To get the clerk to change his group
(C) To indicate his displeasure about the arrangement
(D) To remind the clerk of his medical needs

Lecture
Listen to part of a discussion in an entomology class.

02 Listen again to part of the lecture. Then answer the question.
What does the professor mean when he says this:

(A) He urges the student to describe symbiosis in more detail.
(B) The student does not understand the concept of symbiosis.
(C) He praises the student for giving a relevant example.
(D) The student's example of symbiosis is incorrect.

Lecture
Listen to part of a lecture in a political science class.

03 Listen again to part of the lecture. Then answer the question.
What does the professor mean when she says this:

(A) She cannot accurately describe the country's emotions.
(B) Nixon's actions created very negative opinions of him among Americans.
(C) Most people in America had different opinions about Nixon's actions.
(D) The students will never really know how Americans felt.

Answer Book p. A19

Conversation

Listen to a conversation between a student and a professor.

04 Listen again to part of the conversation. Then answer the question.
Why does the professor say this: 🎧

(A) To imply the student has already missed the test
(B) To clarify that he and the student are talking about the same test
(C) To point out that he could not have possibly graded the test yet
(D) To show his reluctance to discuss the test with the student

Lecture

Listen to part of a lecture in an environmental science class.

05 Listen again to part of the lecture. Then answer the question.
What does the professor mean when she says this: 🎧

(A) Sound can actually travel much faster and farther than expected.
(B) The speed that sound travels in water is the most significant factor.
(C) The range and loudness of sound also contribute to the problem.
(D) It is not important that sound travels very fast in water.

Lecture

Listen to part of a discussion in a literature class.

06 Listen again to part of the lecture. Then answer the question.
Why does the professor say this: 🎧

(A) To suggest that he will provide some more information
(B) To point out that the student is not entirely correct
(C) To express his dissatisfaction that not everyone knows the subject
(D) To apologize for not teaching more about Biblical lore

Chapter **03** Function 39

Listening **Practice**

Lecture
Listen to part of a discussion in an American history class.

|Main Idea|

01 What is the discussion mainly about?

(A) The battles of the American Revolution

(B) The Boston Massacre as an inciting incident

(C) The British troops' cruel acts

(D) How to use political agendas effectively

|Function|

02 **Listen again to part of the lecture. Then answer the question.**
What does the student mean when he says this: 🎧

(A) The British troops deserve to be blamed for their brutality.

(B) It is obvious why the Americans rebelled.

(C) He wishes that he could share the colonists' perspective.

(D) There should be more debate about the rebellion's causes.

|Function|

03 **Listen again to part of the lecture. Then answer the question.**
Why does the professor say this: 🎧

(A) To encourage the students to express their opinions about the subject

(B) To remind the class that no one knows all the facts about the events

(C) To return the class's focus to how colonists viewed the events

(D) To praise Alex's correct understanding of the subject

NOTE

Chapter 04   Attitude

Attitude questions ask about a speaker's attitude or opinion toward a particular topic, which is not directly stated in the listening passage. Some of these questions also ask about a speaker's degree of certainty. There will be 0-1 Attitude question for each passage.

How the Question is Worded

- ☐ What is the student's/professor's attitude toward ~?
- ☐ What is the student's/professor's opinion of ~?
- ☐ How does the student/professor seem to feel about ~?

Keys to Solution

Key 1   Learn to interpret the speaker's tone of voice (positive, negative, certain, uncertain, encouraging, critical, etc). A single expression, "Are you OK?" for example, can indicate very different attitudes depending on how it is said. The speaker's tone can help you answer this type of question.

Key 2   Pay attention to the words or phrases that indicate the speaker's attitude or opinion. These will give you important clues regarding how he or she feels about a particular topic.

+ **Examples of words or phrases that indicate the speaker's attitude:**

• Likes	want, prefer, enjoy, interested, excited, look forward to
• Dislikes	hate, detest, can't stand
• Certainty	apparently, possibly, bound to doubt, there's no way
• Positive	brilliant, admirable, revolutionary, reasonable, valuable
• Negative	tough, ridiculous, absurd, annoyed, a waste of time

Sample Question

Listen to part of a discussion in a marine biology class.

What is the professor's attitude toward zooplankton?

(A) He thinks the impact of pollution on them is not very significant.
(B) He argues more attention be paid to their role in the marine food chain.
(C) He suggests more research be needed on them.
(D) He believes their increasing numbers affect the marine food chain.

Script

Listen to part of a discussion in a marine biology class.

Professor (M): We are going to take a look today at the diet of one of the marine food chain's lowest species, zooplankton. Zooplankton are extremely small organisms found in bodies of water, usually at the surface.

Student (F): I guess their small size doesn't allow them to escape easily from predators.

Professor: Well, not exactly. While it is true that they normally drift along with water currents, marine biologists have noticed that zooplankton do migrate to lower depths of water to avoid predators during the day and then go up closer to the surface of the water at night to feed on phytoplankton.

Student: So are phytoplankton their main source of food?

Professor: Umm, phytoplankton make up a large portion of their diet, but they also feed on other organic material that flows into the water from the surrounding environment. The problem is greater amounts of pollution in the environment mean that zooplankton are digesting high levels of toxins. *[Resolutely]* We urgently need more measures in place to minimize the pollutants ingested by zooplankton, as they form the base structure of marine food chain and ecosystem. The pollution has a detrimental impact on the entire food chain that will only get worse if we do nothing about it.

> **Key 1** Learn to interpret the speaker's tone of voice. The professor's tone of voice indicates he is giving his opinion resolutely and firmly.

Answer & Explanations

Answer Book p. A27

(B)

By saying "We urgently need more measures in place ... as they form the base structure of marine food chain and ecosystem," the professor argues more attention be paid to their role in the marine food chain.

Basic Drill

Listen to each passage and choose the best answer to the question.

Conversation

Listen to a conversation between a student and a professor.

01 What is the professor's opinion of the student getting a job?

(A) It is not as necessary for him as taking her seminar is.
(B) It shows the student is being responsible by saving up money.
(C) It will interfere with his other classes.
(D) It will provide him with helpful work experience.

Lecture

Listen to part of a lecture in an anthropology class.

02 What is the professor's attitude toward the Maori youth?

(A) He wishes that they would not leave their rural homelands.
(B) He admires that they have embraced their traditional culture.
(C) He regrets that so many have forgotten their traditions.
(D) He hopes that they accept urban culture more.

Lecture

Listen to part of a discussion in a music history class.

03 What is the professor's opinion of Franz Liszt's works?

(A) She thinks they are better than Frédéric Chopin's works.
(B) She believes that they sound like most nineteenth-century compositions.
(C) She thinks that they show off his playing ability but are not very moving.
(D) She feels that they should be more famous among listeners.

Answer Book p. A27

Conversation

Listen to a conversation between a student and a clerk at the Student Service Center.

04 How does the student seem to feel about the special outreach program in the business school?

(A) It helps encourage more freshmen to pursue a business degree.
(B) It is reasonable that only qualified students should participate in it.
(C) It would be more effective if it allowed more students to join.
(D) It would be better if it helped out more curious high school students.

Lecture

Listen to part of a lecture in a geology class.

05 What is the professor's attitude toward the science of predicting volcanic eruptions?

(A) She thinks predicting volcanic eruptions will save few lives.
(B) She feels safer methods of predicting eruptions are required.
(C) She believes the methods for predicting eruptions do not need further development.
(D) She suggests satellite imagery will allow for greater prediction of eruptions.

Lecture

Listen to part of a discussion in a history class.

06 What is the student's opinion of Frederick the Great?

(A) He was not an effective political leader.
(B) Napoleon was a better military strategist than he was.
(C) His attempts at political reforms are very respectable.
(D) His abilities as a military leader deserve to be admired.

Chapter 04 Attitude

Listening **Practice**

Conversation
Listen to a conversation between a student and a university administrator.

|Attitude|

01 **What is the student's opinion of the current support system for student information?**

(A) It is satisfactory enough for first-year students.

(B) It is not at all up to basic standards.

(C) It does not provide enough services for students.

(D) It can be perfect if it goes through a few adjustments.

|Detail|

02 **What is an example the student gives of a way to cut costs in implementing the one-stop information center?**

(A) Erecting a temporary center

(B) Holding a fundraising event

(C) Creating an online information center

(D) Hiring volunteer workers

|Attitude|

03 **What is the administrator's attitude toward the student's proposal by the end of the conversation?**

(A) She thinks it deserves to be considered.

(B) She does not consider it as a viable option.

(C) She feels that it is the best way to provide information.

(D) She believes it is a huge waste of money.

NOTE

Chapter 05 Organization

Organization questions ask you to identify the organizational structure of a listening passage. There are generally two types for these questions: Organization questions asking how a speaker presents his or her ideas, and Purpose questions asking why the speaker mentions a particular piece of information. There will be 0-1 Organization question for each passage, and Organization questions appear mostly with lectures.

How the Question is Worded

Organization
- ☐ How does the professor introduce the topic?
- ☐ How does the professor explain ~?

Purpose
- ☐ Why does the student mention ~?
- ☐ Why does the professor discuss ~?

Keys to Solution

Key 1 Recognize how a speaker organizes information in the listening passage through signal words/phrases associated with patterns of organization. In general, there are some typical patterns of organization that are used frequently. Being aware of these patterns will help you understand and remember what you hear.

+ Signal words and phrases associated with patterns of organization:

• List / Example	first, second, third one, another, other first of all, in addition, moreover, finally for example/instance, in this case, among them is/are, such as, like
• Chronology	first, next, then, finally, when before, earlier than, previously, prior to, sooner than afterwards, later, subsequent, following that
• Cause / Effect	because (of), may be due to, as a result of, have an effect on therefore, consequently, for this reason, thus
• Comparison / Contrast	similarly, likewise, same as, both, compared to in contrast, however, different from, as opposed to, on the other hand

Key 2 Understand why a particular piece of information is mentioned in the listening passage.
"What is the relation to the main idea?"
"Is it an example or an explanation of a prior statement?"
These kinds of questions will help you understand the connection between specific information and the passage as a whole.

Sample Question

Listen to part of a lecture in a literature class.

How does the professor explain Victor Hugo?

(A) By providing examples of his novels
(B) By describing some of his influences
(C) By comparing him to other French writers
(D) By providing a brief biography of him

Script

Listen to part of a lecture in a literature class.

Professor (F): Today we're going to discuss one of my favorite authors of all time: Victor Hugo, a great nineteenth-century French novelist. Many of you are probably familiar with some of his famous works, even if you don't realize it. A lot of them have been made into successful movies or plays you've most likely seen. For example, here's a very good one for you: Notre-Dame de Paris, more famously known in English as *The Hunchback of Notre Dame*. I'm pretty sure all of you have heard of this title. This novel tells the tragic story of a deformed but kind man who tries to save the woman he loves from an unruly mob in Renaissance France. The novel is an excellent examination of religious hypocrisy and social justice. My personal favorite, though, is probably Les Misérables, or *The Miserables*, which is now also a famous musical. This is an epic story of love and war set right before the French Revolution. In it, Hugo offers some of his most powerful criticism of Paris's social conditions and the problems of its poorer residents.

▶ **Key 1** Recognize how a speaker organizes information through signal words/phrases. "For example" is one of the signal phrases indicating that the pattern of the organization will provide examples.

▶ **Key 2** Understand why a particular piece of information is mentioned. Notre-Dame de Paris and Les Misérables are Victor Hugo's novels.

Answer & Explanations

Answer Book p. A34

(A)

The professor discusses Victor Hugo by listing/providing some familiar examples of his novels, such as *Notre-Dame de Paris* and *Les Misérables*.

Basic Drill

Listen to each passage and choose the best answer to the question.

Conversation
Listen to a conversation between a student and a professor.

01 Why does the professor talk about John Cage's music?

(A) To give an example that demonstrates harmonious modern music
(B) To indicate the student's definition of music is too limited
(C) To help the student understand birdsong via a piece of human music
(D) To compare the music to birdsongs with regard to harmonic series

Lecture
Listen to part of a lecture in an archaeology class.

02 Why does the professor discuss Hindu epic poems?

(A) To explain why Angkor Wat was originally built
(B) To show how Khmer's religious art and poetry changed
(C) To illustrate the myths surrounding Angkor Wat
(D) To describe the subjects of Angkor Wat's sculptures

Lecture
Listen to part of a discussion in a physics class.

03 How does the professor introduce the concept of Newtonian physics and rockets?

(A) By illustrating how the third law occurs in everyday life
(B) By asking a student for an example of Newton's third law
(C) By detailing the forces acting against each other in a rocket
(D) By describing each of the three laws of motion

Conversation

Listen to a conversation between a student and a registrar.

04 Why does the registrar mention the computer lab?

(A) To remind the student of an omitted course for his graduation
(B) To provide an example of an extra graduation requirement
(C) To describe the process of registering for graduation
(D) To compare the studies of different departments

Lecture

Listen to part of a lecture in a zoology class.

05 How does the professor explain the king cobra?

(A) By comparing them with two other venomous snakes
(B) By showing how fatal their venom is to their prey
(C) By discussing their distinct features and traits
(D) By classifying their species according to the location of their habitats

Lecture

Listen to part of a discussion in a psychology class.

06 Why does the professor discuss repression?

(A) To contrast the methods of different defense mechanisms
(B) To explain the operations of defense mechanisms more clearly
(C) To give a definition of what a defense mechanism is
(D) To emphasize how much psychological damage defense mechanisms cause

Listening Practice

Conversation

Listen to a conversation between a student and a professor.

| Main Idea |

01 What is the conversation mainly about?

Click on 2 answers.

(A) The topics that the U.S. history course will discuss throughout the semester

(B) The content that will be covered on the upcoming midterm

(C) Information about the extra classes for review

(D) The Great Depression and President Franklin Delano Roosevelt's role

|Organization|

02 **Why does the professor talk about the Roaring Twenties and the Great Depression?**

(A) To give examples of important time periods

(B) To explain why he is including the New Deal on the midterm

(C) To let the student know that each review session will cover one topic

(D) To warn the student about how much she will have to prepare for the exam

|Function|

03 **Listen again to part of the conversation. Then answer the question.
What does the professor mean when he says this:** 🎧

(A) The student suggested offering review sessions that were already planned.

(B) The student arrived at his office just before he did.

(C) The student already finished reviewing the chapters for the upcoming midterm.

(D) The student guessed correctly that the midterm will include one more chapter.

NOTE

Chapter 06 Connecting Content

Connecting Content questions ask about the relationships among pieces of information in a listening passage. There are three types for these questions: List questions determining whether a certain detail is Yes (or Included) or No (or Not Included), Matching questions classifying information into categories, and Ordering questions putting events or steps in the correct order. There will be 0-1 Connecting Content question for each passage.

How the Question is Worded

☐ **[List]** In the conversation/lecture, the professor ~. Indicate whether each of the following is ~.
Click in the correct box for each phrase.

	Yes (or Included)	No (or Not Included)
Statement A		
Statement B		
Statement C		

☐ **[Matching]** The professor explains/discusses examples of ~. Indicate for each example what type of ~.
Click in the correct box for each phrase.

	Type A	Type B	Type C
Example 1			
Example 2			
Example 3			

☐ **[Ordering]** The professor explains/discusses the steps in the process of ~. Put these steps in order.
Drag each sentence to the space where it belongs.

Step 1	
Step 2	
Step 3	

Keys to Solution

Key 1 Connecting Content questions are most likely to appear when a speaker mentions several pieces of information in relation to the main topic (ex: definitions, examples, or characteristics). In these cases, take careful notes on how these pieces of information relate to one another.

Key 2 Pay special attention to any sections of the listening passages that deal with comparisons and contrasts, classified information, or steps in a process.

Sample Question

Listen to part of a lecture in a chemistry class.

In the lecture, the professor describes some properties of mercury. Indicate whether each of the following is included.

Click in the correct box for each phrase.

	Included	Not Included
(A) Reacts well with acids		
(B) Has the lowest freezing point		
(C) Has a liquid form at standard room temperature		
(D) Easily combines with metals		

Script

Listen to part of a lecture in a chemistry class.

Professor (M): Mercury is a chemical element that has several unique properties. Today though, we're only going to focus on two of its properties, its temperature and its ability to alloy with other metals. OK, mercury is the only common metal that has a liquid form at ordinary room temperature. This is actually the main reason mercury is used in devices such as thermometers, since the liquid will expand or contract based on changes in temperature. This is because it has quite a low boiling point for a metal.

The second property I'd like to look at is mercury's ability to combine fairly easily with almost all metals, except for iron, platinum, and tungsten. These metal alloys are referred to as amalgams. One of the most common amalgams is the silver-mercury amalgam, which is generally used in dentistry to fill cavities. Another common amalgam is the gold-mercury amalgam, which is used in the extraction of gold from ore. The gold particles from the ore dissolve into the mercury part of the alloy, facilitating the collection of very small particles of gold.

Key 1 Connecting Content questions are most likely to appear when a speaker mentions several pieces of information in relation to the main topic.
The professor discusses several unique properties of mercury, its temperature, and its ability to alloy with other metals.

Answer & Explanations

Answer Book p. A41

[Included – (C), (D)], [Not Included – (A), (B)]

The professor discusses some of mercury's properties, specifically that it has a liquid form at ordinary room temperature and that it easily combines with almost all metals. The answer choices (A) and (B) are either untrue or not included in the lecture.

Basic Drill

Listen to each passage and choose the best answer(s) to the question.

Conversation

Listen to a conversation between a student and a professor.

01 In the conversation, the student and professor discuss tasks that the student still has to make up. Indicate whether each of the following is a task.
Click in the correct box for each phrase.

	Yes	No
(A) Test on several chapters from the textbook		
(B) Explanation about the research paper		
(C) Writing on a certain era of South Africa		
(D) Oral presentation about the book report		

Lecture

Listen to part of a discussion in an art history class.

02 The professor and students discuss the lives of Leonardo and Michelangelo. Indicate the features of each artist's life.
Click in the correct box for each phrase.

	Leonardo	Michelangelo
(A) Worked on Medici family's tombs		
(B) Spent his last years in France		
(C) Spent a short time sculpting in Bologna		
(D) Worked for the Duke of Milan		

Lecture

Listen to part of a lecture in a sociology class.

03 In the lecture, the professor discusses areas based on income in the multiple nuclei model. Indicate for each area a defining characteristic.

Click in the correct box for each phrase.

	Upper-class Areas	Middle-class Areas	Lower-class Areas
(A) Provide higher security			
(B) Located in suburbs			
(C) Proximity to factories			
(D) High housing density			

Conversation

Listen to a conversation between a student and an employee at the office of student affairs.

04 The employee explains some special events that will be held for freshmen. Put these events in the correct order.

Drag each phrase to the space where it belongs.

1	
2	
3	
4	

(A) Movie viewing in the auditorium

(B) Welcoming assembly distributing a bunch of useful items

(C) Campus fair at free of charge

(D) Meal with the school community members

Basic Drill

Lecture
Listen to part of a discussion in a botany class.

05 The professor discusses three types of plant tissue systems. Indicate which type of tissue system the following phrases are a description of.
Click in the correct box for each phrase.

	Dermal	Vascular	Ground
(A) Made up of plant cells offering a support function in plants			
(B) Contains tissues that help with the transport of water and nutrients			
(C) Includes two layers covering and protecting plants			
(D) Consists of plant cells that are responsible for photosynthesis			

Answer Book p. A41

Lecture
Listen to part of a lecture in an American history class.

06 The professor describes the events that led up to the Civil War. Put these events in the correct order.

Drag each sentence to the space where it belongs.

1	
2	
3	
4	

(A) The nation was divided into free states and slave states.

(B) The Missouri Compromise was passed.

(C) Supporters and opponents of slavery battled each other.

(D) The Kansas-Nebraska Act was enacted.

Listening **Practice**

Conversation

Listen to a conversation between a student and a counselor at the university counseling center.

|Connecting Content|

01 In the conversation, the counselor and student discuss the student's academic schedule next semester. Indicate whether each of the following is suggested by the counselor or not. Click in the correct box for each phrase.

	Suggested	Not Suggested
(A) Complete the remaining prerequisite courses first		
(B) Enroll in a total of four courses		
(C) Enroll in a prerequisite course and upper division courses together		
(D) Skip one of the general education courses		

|Attitude|

02 **What is the counselor's attitude toward the student's situation?**

(A) She is indifferent to the student's extracurricular commitments.

(B) She firmly recommends that the student take more courses.

(C) She is sympathetic toward the student's struggles.

(D) She is disappointed that the student does not want to handle a greater workload.

|Function|

03 **Listen again to part of the conversation. Then answer the question.**
Why does the counselor say this: 🎧

(A) To challenge the student to take more courses

(B) To claim that all students can excel academically

(C) To provide another appropriate option for the student

(D) To show that it is not impossible to manage five courses

NOTE

Chapter 07   Inference

Inference questions ask about the information that is implied in a listening passage rather than directly stated. These questions test your ability to draw logical information/conclusions based on the facts provided in the listening passage.

Some Inference questions may be Replay questions. Others may ask you to make predictions about the action that will follow. Typically, there will be 0-1 question for each passage.

How the Question is Worded

- What does the professor imply about ~?
- What can be inferred about ~?
- What can be concluded about ~?
- [Conversation] What will the student probably do next?

Keys to Solution

Key 1 Make sure your answer is based on the listening passage. Do not answer the questions based on information that is not addressed by the passage or based on your own knowledge. You must be able to connect your answer choice with supporting evidence directly stated in the passage.

Key 2 Inference questions often ask you to use information from more than one place in the listening passage. To answer these questions, you need to identify the facts correctly first and synthesize them to reach a logical conclusion.

Key 3 Pay close attention to the end of the listening passage. Take special note of ideas that seem incomplete, or, in the conversations, things that the speakers have not yet done. These incomplete details are often the basis of Inference questions.

Sample Question

Listen to a conversation between a student and an employee at the university library.

What can be inferred about the student?

(A) He plans to get some credits during summer vacation.
(B) He prefers the inventory assistant position to the other positions.
(C) He needs to earn money for his tuition fee.
(D) He has experience working as a circulation assistant.

Script

Listen to a conversation between a student and an employee at the university library.

Student (M): Hi, I'm looking for a part-time job at the library.

Employee (F): OK. Do you have a particular area you'd like to work in?

Student: I'm not sure. What kinds of jobs are available?

Employee: There are several positions available. One is a circulation assistant who checks out and renews books.

Student: Oh, so it's for sorting books, handing out, and accepting returned materials. How much is the hourly wage?

Employee: It's $7.50.

Student: That's not a lot of money. Hmm . . . is there any temporary full-time work for the summer semester?

Employee: Two positions are available at the moment. One is an inventory assistant. It pays $8.50 per hour. You need to monitor all the printers in the university libraries. Basically, your job will be refilling paper and toner supplies and picking up supplies from the business office.

Student: That doesn't sound too hard. What about the other one?

Employee: The other one is a teaching assistant at the library.

Student: Um, I don't have any teaching experience, so I think the former position fits me better.

Key 1 Make sure your answer is based on the passage.
Based on what the student says about the job positions, we can infer which position the student prefers.

Key 2 Inference questions often ask you to use information from more than one place.
We need to identify the facts about what the student thinks about the positions, and synthesize them to conclude which position the student prefers.

Answer & Explanations

Answer Book p. A49

(B)
The employee mentions three job positions available. The student indicates he does not want the circulation assistant job and the teaching assistant job. Also, he says the former position(the inventory assistant job) fits him better, so it can be inferred that the student prefers the inventory assistant position to the other ones.

Basic Drill

Listen to each passage and choose the best answer to the question.

Conversation
Listen to a conversation between a student and a campus bookstore clerk.

01 What will the student probably do next?

(A) Find a computer that runs the software
(B) Buy a different program for her computer
(C) Sell the software back to the bookstore
(D) Try to find a student who wants the software

Lecture
Listen to part of a discussion in a biology class.

02 What does the professor imply about calcium?

(A) It is most successfully absorbed when one gets sufficient vitamin D.
(B) A person must consume large amounts of it just to absorb a little.
(C) A person does not need it if he gets plenty of vitamin D in his diet.
(D) It is the most important nutrient for keeping the heart healthy.

Lecture
Listen to part of a lecture in a history class.

03 What does the professor imply about the British fleet?

(A) It was eager to fight the Spanish to further England's colonial interests.
(B) It actually possessed a number of advantages over the Spanish Armada.
(C) It was the dominant sea power long before the defeat of the Spanish Armada.
(D) It could defeat the Spanish Armada due to its numerical superiority.

Answer Book p. A49

Conversation

Listen to a conversation between a student and a professor.

04 Listen again to part of the conversation. Then answer the question.
What can be inferred about the student's textbook?

(A) It can be finished in a short time.
(B) It discusses complex material.
(C) It contains very long chapters.
(D) It is not informative enough for students.

Lecture

Listen to part of a discussion in an art class.

05 What can be inferred about Louis Comfort Tiffany?

(A) He put great effort into the lighting effect when making his stained-glass lamps.
(B) He used gemstones to achieve the lighting effect of his stained-glass works.
(C) He tried to evoke a religious experience as in churches with his lamps.
(D) He failed to achieve a functional purpose with his stained-glass lamps.

Lecture

Listen to part of a lecture in a zoology class.

06 Listen again to part of the lecture. Then answer the question.
What can be inferred about the Grand Canyon?

(A) Its physical barriers managed to alter the gene flow of surrounding bird populations.
(B) It is occupied by various bird species because of its formation.
(C) It did not isolate the bird populations enough for allopatric speciation to occur.
(D) Its physical barriers did not affect the gene flow of squirrel and bird populations.

Chapter 07 Inference 65

Listening Practice

Lecture
Listen to part of a lecture in an environmental science class.

| Detail |

01 According to the professor, which of the following are true about the Everglades?
Click on 2 answers.

(A) It has a wide variety of wildlife.
(B) It does not receive much rainfall.
(C) It is located throughout the U.S.
(D) It has constantly warm weather.

|Organization|

02 **How does the professor discuss the development of the Everglades?**

(A) By providing a history of development in the area

(B) By describing the harmful effects of development

(C) By discussing the reasons for development there

(D) By giving examples of products from the area

|Inference|

03 **According to the professor, what can be concluded about the Everglades?**

(A) The environment in that area is not very hospitable for people to live in.

(B) The efforts of the U.S. government to conserve the area have been very effectual.

(C) More effective measures need to be drawn up to remove the threat to the area.

(D) The canals and dams made the region more habitable for animals.

NOTE

TOEFL iBT i Listening   www.linguaforum.com

PART B
Approaching Themes

Chapter 08 Office Hours
Chapter 09 Service Encounters
Chapter 10 Humanities
Chapter 11 Life Science
Chapter 12 Physical Science
Chapter 13 Social Science

Chapter 08 Office Hours

University professors have *office hours*, which are usually listed on their course syllabus. A professor may ask a student to come to visit his or her office during office hours to discuss something regarding an assignment or lecture. Also, when a student has any questions or problems with an assignment or lecture, the student can visit his or her professor's office. For example, a student can go to seek advice on a topic for a research paper, ask something about a lecture, request an extension on an assignment or a reference letter, discuss choosing a major, etc.

Listening Preview

Auditing a Course | Intensive Drill 1 |

Auditing a course at university allows a student to take a class without the benefit of a grade or credit for the course. A student who wants to audit a course does so for the purposes of self-enrichment and academic exploration. In the majority of cases, the course is offered only on a space-available basis and requires the approval of concerned persons like the instructor of the course or the dean of the department.

Writing an Essay | Intensive Drill 2 |

An essay is used as a form of assessment in many academic disciplines, and is used in both coursework and exams. When writing an essay, a student needs to follow the reference style as instructed. It not only gives more weight to the argument, it also provides evidence that a student has read widely and can present a wide range of views. It is important to follow a formal system of citing or referencing to avoid plagiarism and to ensure that the reader can easily locate the original sources of the citation.

Field Trip

| Intensive Drill 3 |

A field trip is defined as a course-related activity that serves educational purposes and occurs outside of the classroom at a location other than the campus at which the course is regularly taught.

If can be an important—and enjoyable—element of education in that it often significantly enhance the content of a course by providing a type of information not easy to convey in the classroom.

Research Paper

| Mini Test 1 |

Most university courses involve some kind of extended writing assignment, usually in the form of a research paper. Many instructors give specific requirements for research papers, detailing topics, word limit, use of sources, and documentation methods. A student may visit the professor's office to discuss the research paper regarding its topic, reference materials, deadline, or writing tips.

Research Proposal

| Mini Test 2 |

Professors may assign the task of writing a research proposal before conducting the research. The goal of a research proposal is to present and justify the need to study a research problem and to present the practical ways in which this research should be conducted. A proposal should contain all the key elements involved in designing a completed research study, with sufficient information that allows readers to assess the validity and usefulness of your proposed study.

Double Major

| iBT Practice |

Having or doing a double major usually means that you complete two college majors. For example, a student may double major in psychology and sociology. Students may double major because they are so passionate about two fields of study that they want to do both and they are willing to take on the extra workload.

Intensive Drill 1

Listen to a conversation between a student and a professor.

01 Why does the student go to see the professor?

(A) To inform him that she will be taking his class next semester
(B) To discuss taking his course next semester for no credit
(C) To ask when he will teach one of his most popular classes
(D) To inquire about what courses to take next semester

02 Why does the student want to audit the class instead of taking it for credit?

(A) She does not have enough money to pay for it.
(B) She is afraid of doing poorly in the class.
(C) She already registered too many classes.
(D) She needs the information for her graduation thesis.

03 What is the professor's opinion of students paying for audited classes?

(A) He feels it is harsh for students who do not have much money.

(B) He feels angry at the university for charging a fee without giving credit.

(C) He believes that it should be accepted only because it is school policy.

(D) He believes it is necessary since teachers are performing a service.

04 Listen again to part of the conversation. Then answer the question.
What does the professor imply?

(A) The class is at its maximum capacity.

(B) The student is not good at economics.

(C) The professor doubts the student will get in.

(D) The professor and the student are not very close.

Intensive Drill 2

Listen to a conversation between a student and a professor.

01 What problem does the student have?

(A) He does not fully understand the content of his essay.

(B) His grade on the essay was reduced due to late submission.

(C) He is likely to get a poor grade on his essay.

(D) He cannot pass the course, as he failed both essay and final exam.

02 According to the professor, what are the problems the student's essay has?
Click on 3 answers.

(A) Being unable to meet the word limit

(B) Not using enough references

(C) Using obsolete references

(D) Citing a disproved idea

(E) Failing to follow a reference style

74   PART B Approaching Themes

03 **Why does the professor mention the final exam?**

(A) To tell that the student is not eligible to take the exam

(B) To remind the student about final exam schedule

(C) To warn the student to do well on the exam to pass the course

(D) To say that it would be very difficult to get a perfect score on the exam

04 **Listen again to part of the conversation. Then answer the question. What does the student mean when he says this:** 🎧

(A) He does not remember what he was going to say.

(B) He feels offended that the professor pointed out his problem.

(C) He feels embarrassed for not doing well on his essay.

(D) He does not know whether contents or references are more important.

Intensive Drill 3

Listen to a conversation between a student and a professor.

01 What is the conversation mainly about?
Click on 2 answers.

(A) How to plan a practical field trip for students
(B) Information about the alumni participating in the field trip
(C) The reasons why the student did not want to go on the field trip
(D) Detailed information about the field trip

02 What does the professor imply about the field trip next week?

(A) It has been improved in a way to be more helpful to students.
(B) It needs to be improved to satisfy as many students as possible.
(C) It focuses heavily on the business management field.
(D) It will allow for more participants than last year's field trip.

03 The professor explains the activities of the field trip. Put these activities in the correct order.
Drag each sentence to the space where it belongs.

1	
2	
3	
4	

(A) A workshop will be held for preparing résumés and career plans.

(B) There will be a Q&A session with alumni at their workplace.

(C) Students will be categorized into groups based on their career interests.

(D) Students will visit alumni's workplaces for hands-on experience of the work.

04 Listen again to part of the conversation. Then answer the question.
Why does the professor say this: 🎧

(A) To indicate that the student is asking too many questions

(B) To imply that the student's question is very difficult to answer

(C) To mention details that will be very helpful to the student

(D) To incorporate the student's suggestions into the field trip

Mini Test 1

Listen to a conversation between a student and a professor.

01 Why does the student go to see the professor?

(A) To ask about the research paper's format

(B) To get some information about Japan's Edo period

(C) To inquire about a subject for his research paper

(D) To hand in a proposal for his research paper

02 What problem is the student having with the research paper?

(A) He knows little about the subject matter.

(B) He needs the professor to extend the deadline.

(C) He cannot find enough information on the topic.

(D) He could not find a topic to write about.

03 Why does the professor insist that students get prior approval for their research topics?
Click on 2 answers.

(A) To monitor their progress on a long-term project
(B) To ensure that students choose a subject that is not too broad
(C) To lessen the chance that one student could copy another's paper
(D) To make sure that students follow the correct format for the paper

04 What will the student probably do next?

(A) Come back to speak to the professor after he has researched the topic
(B) Develop a paper proposal based on the professor's suggested topic
(C) Check with other students in class to make sure no one else is writing about his topic
(D) Try to narrow down the focus of the professor's suggested topic

Mini Test 2

Listen to a conversation between a student and a professor.

01 What is the reason the student gives for being excited about going to Spain?

(A) She loves the scenery.

(B) She speaks the language very well.

(C) She has been there before and enjoyed her time there.

(D) She is attracted to its culture.

02 Why does the professor mention the number of years that the Pintia site has been extensively studied?

(A) To show that the Pollentia civilization has been around for a lot longer than that of Pintia

(B) To point out that there may not be plenty of research on Pintia

(C) To indicate whether the excavation site meets the time requirement for the research project

(D) To emphasize that it has been studied and analyzed long enough

Answer Book p. A63

03 In the conversation, the student and professor discuss the differences between the two archaeological sites. Indicate whether each of the following is related to Pintia or Pollentia.
Click in the correct box for each phrase.

	Pintia	Pollentia
(A) Roman culture		
(B) Inland location		
(C) Coastal area		
(D) Burial site		

04 What is the student's attitude toward the professor's suggestions about her research site?

(A) She thinks they are worth considering carefully.

(B) She is ready to accept them and change her choice.

(C) She believes they are not appropriate for her situation.

(D) She is convinced that they are not better than her first choice.

Chapter 08 Office Hours 81

iBT Practice

TOEFL Listening

Listen to a conversation between a student and a professor.

01 Why does the student visit the professor?

(A) To thank her for helping him get a biology degree
(B) To inquire about the work needed for majoring in biology
(C) To seek her advice about dropping his current major
(D) To request her aid in taking up a biology major

02 Why does the student want to get a degree in biology?

(A) He has a great interest in science.
(B) He failed in his other studies.
(C) He is following the advice of his professor.
(D) He is reconsidering his career goals.

03 What is the professor's opinion of having a double major?

(A) It provides valuable experience for a career.
(B) It is a pointless waste of time and money.
(C) It is usually too much work for students.
(D) It should only be done with two similar programs.

04 What are some suggestions the professor provides regarding the student's situation?
Click on 2 answers.

(A) Focus on the present work this semester
(B) Make a decision before this semester ends
(C) Gain basic knowledge about biology in his spare time
(D) Ask advice from biology majors and professors

05 Listen again to part of the conversation. Then answer the question.
What can be inferred about the biology program?

(A) It is not as popular as the student's current major.
(B) It is very demanding for a lot of students.
(C) It takes more money and time than other programs.
(D) It is the most prestigious among science-related majors.

Chapter 09 Service Encounters

There are a variety of facilities offering services for students at universities, such as libraries, bookstores, the registrar's office, the finance office, computer labs, etc. Students may visit them when they have an inquiry or problem about the services they offer.

In TOEFL listening, in general, a student visits a facility to ask some questions and an employee there provides answers to the questions or information about what the student wants to know.

Listening Preview

Registering for Classes
| Intensive Drill 1 |

At the beginning of every semester is an enrollment period. This is when students select the courses they wish to take during that semester. Each course has a limited number of seats available, and registration for the class is on a first-come-first-served basis. Once all the seats have been filled, students who still wish to take the course are put on the wait list. Also, in general there is a limit on the number of credit hours students can enroll in a semester. If they want to take more courses, they need to take a special step, such as getting a permit from the course professor.

Using Libraries
| Intensive Drill 2 |

Universities have at least one main library. Students may need their student ID card to check out books. In many cases, to find a specific book at the university libraries, students should start with the library catalog. The catalog is the list of books in the library, and it will show students the location and call number needed to find the books on the shelves. Students may ask librarians for help when they have a problem finding books, using the computers at the libraries, booking study rooms, etc.

The Student Career Center

| Intensive Drill 3 |

Almost every university has the Student Career Center on campus. It provides a variety of services to help students pursue careers (full-time jobs, part-time jobs, volunteer experiences, internships, etc.) with regard to career decision making and career exploration. It also helps students with their résumés, cover letters, and job interview preparation through individual advisors as well as workshops.

Campus Parking Lot

| Mini Test 1 |

Universities provide parking spaces on campus for students, visitors, and faculty members. There are normally regulations they need to follow when using the parking lots, and they may get fined or their cars may get towed away if they violate those regulations. Students can file an appeal if they feel that they have been wrongly fined or if extenuating circumstances exist.

Campus Housing

| Mini Test 2 |

At most universities, students can choose to either live off or on campus. Students who live off campus live in apartments or houses that are not owned or associated with the university. Students who live on campus generally live in dormitories, which are owned and operated by the university. There is usually a facilities department that is in charge of maintaining the dormitories, and students who have problems with their rooms can go to this department to resolve their problems.

University Clubs

| iBT Practice |

There are clubs for nearly all types of hobbies and interests at universities. There are also social groups, called fraternities and sororities. To start a club, there is usually a process to follow. For example, students need to submit a proposal including information about the club, such as the club's goals, activities, constitution, etc. Then they will meet with staff members to discuss their proposal. Also, in general, they need approval from the school committee.

Intensive Drill 1

Listen to a conversation between a student and a clerk at the registrar's office.

01 What does the clerk think about the student's plan to take 18 credit hours?

(A) It shows that she is a very ambitious student.

(B) She will probably have difficulty with that many classes.

(C) She will be allowed to do so if her grades are good.

(D) She should have talked to him about it earlier.

02 Why does the university require students to get permission to take 18 or more credit hours?

(A) To prevent students from creating an unrealistic workload for themselves

(B) To encourage students to only take courses that are relevant to their major

(C) To ensure that there are enough course spaces available for other students

(D) To make sure students take courses and pay tuition for four full years

03 Which courses does the clerk suggest the student register for immediately?

(A) The courses most relevant to her major
(B) The courses that fill up most quickly
(C) The courses that she is most likely to do well in
(D) The courses that are only offered once a year

04 Listen again to part of the conversation. Then answer the question.
What does the student mean when she says this: 🎧

(A) She does not have time to register for her courses now.
(B) She does not see the point of the clerk's suggestion.
(C) She needs more time to consider which courses to sign up for.
(D) She needs to speak to her department head before registering for her classes.

Intensive Drill 2

Listen to a conversation between a student and a librarian.

01 What is the topic of the conversation?

(A) Reading reference numbers
(B) Searching catalog through library website
(C) Returning books to the school library
(D) Finding books for an assignment

02 Why does the librarian mention 'O?'

(A) To provide information which could be helpful later on
(B) To show the critical difference between the 'A' and 'O'
(C) To explain the reason why the student cannot find some books
(D) To indicate where to find the books the student needs for his assignment

03 What will the student do next?

(A) Find the book he needs from the library archive
(B) Wait for the librarian to get the book from the archive
(C) Collect the book he needs from the 'just returned' section
(D) Go to the 900s section to find the book he needs

04 Listen again to part of the conversation. Then answer the question.
What does the librarian mean when she says this: 🎧

(A) She wants to make sure that she searched for the right book.
(B) She indicates that the student said the wrong title of the book.
(C) She does not understand why the student wants the book.
(D) She blames the student for not naming the author of the book.

Intensive Drill 3

Listen to a conversation between a student and an employee at the Student Career Center.

01 What is the conversation mainly about?

Click on 2 answers.

(A) Finding out if the student can register for an interview workshop

(B) Comparing the interview workshop and the interview preparation course

(C) Providing suggestions to improve the interview workshops

(D) Getting information about an interview preparation course

02 Why does the student mention that she got an interview offer?

(A) To boast that she has won an opportunity

(B) To point out how effective Professor Williams's workshop was

(C) To ask for advice on how to do well in the interview

(D) To explain why she should take Professor Williams's workshop

03 In the conversation, the employee explains about the interview preparation course during the summer session. Indicate whether each of the following is included.
Click in the correct box for each phrase.

	Included	Not Included
(A) Provides a simple oral interview		
(B) Includes digital recordings of mock interviews		
(C) Offers feedback from professors about mock interviews		
(D) Led by Professor Williams		

04 What can be inferred about the interview preparation course?

(A) The employee prefers it to the interview workshop by Professor Williams.

(B) It is the best alternative solution to the interview workshop.

(C) It does not contain as many programs as the interview workshop.

(D) It has a good reputation among job applicants.

Mini Test 1

 66

Listen to a conversation between a student and a clerk at the Campus Security Department.

01 Why does the student visit the Campus Security Department?

(A) To pay off a parking ticket that he received
(B) To contest a parking ticket that he received
(C) To request that visitors be given parking tickets
(D) To complain about the strict parking regulations

02 What does the clerk suggest that the student do?
Click on 2 answers.

(A) Follow the rules of parking at other dorms
(B) Park at the basketball stadium
(C) Ignore the fine until her boss reviews the tickets
(D) Report any parking violations

92 PART B Approaching Themes

03 How does the student feel about the ticketing of visitors in his parking lot?

(A) The policy has not been effective so far.
(B) The university should address the problem immediately.
(C) The amount of the fines should be increased.
(D) The university should give more warnings before issuing tickets.

04 Listen again to part of the conversation. Then answer the question.
Why does the student say this: 🎧

(A) To indicate that it should not matter where he parked
(B) To explain exactly where he parked
(C) To emphasize that he had no choice in the matter
(D) To express his surprise at receiving a ticket

Mini Test 2

Listen to a conversation between a student and a housing coordinator.

01 Which of the following are true about summer housing for full-time students?
Click on 2 answers.

(A) It is cheaper than housing for part-time students.
(B) Full-time students have roommates, while part-time students do not.
(C) Only full-time students are allowed to stay in suites during the summer.
(D) Full-time students get preferential treatment in housing placements.

02 What is the student's opinion of the suites?

(A) They offer better living conditions than the dormitories.
(B) It is unfair that they are only available to upperclassmen.
(C) They are not much different from the dormitories.
(D) All the dormitories should be converted to suites.

03 What does the coordinator imply about on-campus housing during the summer?

(A) It is more expensive than during the fall and spring semesters.

(B) There are more housing options available to students.

(C) Housing rules are relaxed because there are fewer students living on campus.

(D) Generally, only upperclassmen are allowed to stay on campus during the summer.

04 Which of the following are food options during the summer term?
Click on 2 answers.

(A) Campus dining halls

(B) Restaurants in the student center

(C) Student meal plan

(D) Local restaurants off-campus

iBT Practice

TOEFL Listening

Listen to a conversation between a student and a clerk at the Student Union Office.

01 Why does the student go to the Student Union Office?

(A) To inquire about the process for creating a club
(B) To submit an application for an activity club
(C) To find a student senator to sponsor his club
(D) To look at examples of activity club constitutions

02 What is the difference between activity clubs and other groups?

(A) Activity clubs must pay a fee to the school.
(B) Activity clubs cannot use money from the Student Government Association.
(C) Activity clubs must have at least ten members.
(D) Activity clubs cannot use any campus facilities.

03 What are the documents that must be submitted by a club before being approved?

Click on 2 answers.

(A) A request for funds
(B) A description of guidelines
(C) A list of members
(D) A recommendation from an adviser

04 In the conversation, the clerk describes the steps of creating an activity club.
Put these steps in the correct order.

Drag each sentence to where it belongs.

1	
2	
3	
4	

(A) A student senator sponsors the club.
(B) All paperwork is submitted to the director.
(C) An adviser is selected for the club.
(D) The Student Government Association decides whether to approve the club.

05 Listen again to part of the conversation. Then answer the question.
Why does the clerk say this?

(A) To get the student to be careful with the complex paperwork
(B) To remind the student that all clubs must fill out paperwork
(C) To warn the student that the Student Government may reject the paperwork
(D) To urge the student to submit the paperwork as soon as possible

Chapter 10 Humanities

- **Humanities**
  A study of how people process and document the human experience
- **Related fields**
  History, Art, Literature, Religion, Music, Philosophy, Linguistics, Languages, etc.

Listening Preview

Art History – Ancient Greek & Roman Sculpture | Intensive Drill 1 |

Greek Sculpture
Around 2,600 years ago, the Greeks were already able to build life-size, freestanding statues in an attempt to mimic the human form based on values in Greek culture. Their techniques for creating realistic and idealistic representations improved over the centuries, and the Greek sculptures became widely influential to those of later civilizations.

Roman Sculpture
In the earliest days of Roman history, when a Roman man died, his family created a wax sculpture of his face, which they kept in a special shrine at home. Yet Roman sculpture was not just about revering the dead, but also about honoring the living. Important Romans were rewarded for their valor or greatness by having statues of themselves put on public display.

History – Leonardo da Vinci's Flying Machines: Ornithopter | Intensive Drill 2 |

Leonardo da Vinci, born in Vinci, Italy, was probably the first European interested in a practical solution to the problem of flight. Leonardo designed a multitude of mechanical devices, including parachutes, and studied the flight of birds and bats as well as their structure. Around the year 1485 he drew detailed plans for a human-powered ornithopter, a wing-flapping device intended to fly. Even though there is no evidence that he actually attempted to build such a device, the notion of a human-powered mechanical flight device, patterned after birds or bats, would resurface again and again over the next few centuries.

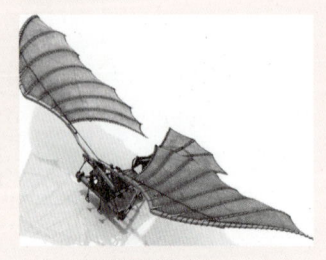

Architecture - Suspension Bridge

| Intensive Drill 3 |

A suspension bridge is a type of bridge that suspends the roadway, also called the deck, by cables, ropes, or chains from several tall towers. A typical example of this kind of bridge is the Golden Gate Bridge, which is one of the most internationally recognized symbols of San Francisco, California, and the United States.

Literature - Rubén Darío

| Mini Test 1 |

Rubén Darío was an influential Nicaraguan poet, journalist, and diplomat who started the Spanish-American literary movement known as modernism that flourished at the end of the nineteenth century. Darío developed a highly original poetic style that founded a tradition, and has had a great and lasting influence on twentieth-century Spanish literature and journalism.

Art – Participatory Art

| Mini Test 2 |

Participatory art is an approach to making art in which the audience is engaged directly in the artistic process, allowing them to become co-authors, editors, and observers of the work. Therefore, this type of art can be completed with the viewers' physical interaction. Public, folk, and tribal art are considered to be types of participatory art.

American History – John D. Rockefeller & Andrew Carnegie

| iBT Practice |

John D. Rockefeller was the head of the Standard Oil Company and one of the world's richest men. By 1882 he had a near-monopoly of the oil business in the U.S., but his business practices led to the passing of antitrust laws. It is also believed that he, late in his life, devoted himself to philanthropy, using his fortune to fund ongoing philanthropic causes.

Andrew Carnegie was one of the wealthiest businessmen in the nineteenth-century U.S. as a self-made steel tycoon. By 1889 he owned Carnegie Steel Corporation, which was the largest of its kind in the world. Late in life, he sold his business and devoted his time to philanthropic work, especially to education.

Intensive Drill 1

Listen to part of a lecture in an art history class.

01 What is the main topic of the lecture?

(A) The purposes behind Roman sculpture
(B) The typical statues of Greek and Roman sculpture
(C) The influence of Greek techniques on Roman sculpture
(D) The differences between Greek and Roman sculpture

02 How does the professor discuss the topic?

(A) By comparing the sculptures' subjects and the portrayal of those subjects
(B) By discussing the sculpting techniques of the Greeks and those of the Romans
(C) By explaining the origins of Roman sculpture and showing examples of it
(D) By discussing Greek myths and how they were portrayed in sculptures

03 What was the purpose of most Roman sculptures?

(A) To recount tales from Roman mythology

(B) To glorify powerful individuals

(C) To present the beauty of the human body

(D) To decorate the exteriors of buildings

04 Why do many Roman statues have less captivating features?

(A) The artists were rebelling against Greek influences.

(B) The artists used exaggeration to express certain ideals.

(C) The statues realistically reflected their subjects.

(D) The patrons hired inexperienced sculptors.

05 Listen again to part of the lecture. Then answer the question.
What does the professor mean when he says this: 🎧

(A) Roman sculptors occasionally went back to correct their previous mistakes.

(B) Roman sculptors did make some attempts to improve the appearance of their subjects.

(C) Roman sculptors were dissatisfied with the appearance of many of their subjects.

(D) Roman sculptors were careful to only choose attractive subjects.

Intensive Drill 2

Listen to part of a discussion in a history class.

01 What is the purpose of the lecture?

(A) To introduce a new approach to understanding biomimicry

(B) To illustrate an example of biomimicry in human history

(C) To demonstrate how early inventors turned to nature

(D) To show the importance of biomimicry in early technology

02 What can be inferred about Leonardo da Vinci's flying machines?

(A) They did not necessarily reflect his keen observations of birds and bats.

(B) They probably remained only in the conceptualization stage.

(C) Whether they qualify as an approach to flight is a subject of debate.

(D) Many historians regard them as true innovations in flight technology.

03 Which of the following is true about what Borelli found out?

(A) Humans cannot generate sufficient power from their chest muscles for flying.

(B) The way human muscles are built requires more complicated bird-like wings.

(C) Early inventors did not have a proper understanding of bird pectoral muscles.

(D) Leonardo's flying machines could have succeeded since he studied human muscles.

04 What is the professor's opinion of some of the early inventors of flight?

(A) They were stubborn but not determined enough to fly successfully.

(B) They ended up impeding the advancement of aviation technology.

(C) Their works should be revisited and evaluated for further studies.

(D) They failed to become inspirations to their later successors.

05 The professor explains the events that led to creating human-powered flight in history. Put these events in the correct order.

Drag each sentence to the space where it belongs.

1	
2	
3	
4	

(A) Leonardo da Vinci made numerous notes and sketches of flying machines.

(B) Bladud from Troja Nova crashed after he tried to fly with imitation wings.

(C) The Wright brothers turned to nature for inspiration by observing birds.

(D) Borelli made his conclusions on the wing-flapping theory.

Intensive Drill 3

Listen to part of a discussion in an architecture class.

01 What is the discussion mainly about?

(A) The design challenges of suspension bridges

(B) The reasons for building suspension bridges

(C) The advantages and drawbacks of suspension bridges

(D) The most famous examples of suspension bridges

02 Why do suspension bridges require fewer pylons than other bridges?

(A) The road decks they support are lighter.

(B) They use less concrete in their designs.

(C) They do not only rely on pylons to support their road decks.

(D) They are designed to swing with the wind.

03 What are the advantages of suspension bridges over other types of bridges?
Click on 2 answers.

(A) They can sometimes be built at a lower cost.

(B) They interfere less with sea traffic.

(C) They can cross wider bodies of water.

(D) They are inherently stronger.

04 Why does the professor mention the Tacoma Narrows Bridge?

(A) To illustrate a basic design weakness of suspension bridges

(B) To discuss an alternative design for suspension bridges

(C) To show how engineers improved the design of the Golden Gate Bridge

(D) To introduce the next topic of discussion

05 Listen again to part of the lecture. Then answer the question.
Why does the professor say this: 🎧

(A) To remind students of the topic of discussion

(B) To guide the students' thinking in regard to his question

(C) To encourage students to focus on their previous discussion

(D) To emphasize the importance of the question to the discussion

Mini Test 1

Listen to part of a lecture in a literature class.

01 What is the main topic of the lecture?

(A) The style of Darío's poetry
(B) The factors that shaped Darío's writings
(C) The political beliefs of Darío
(D) The way Darío influenced Spanish literature

02 Why does the professor discuss the French Parnassian Poets?

(A) To explain the origins of modern literature
(B) To compare the styles of French and Spanish literature
(C) To explain the qualities of Darío's early writings
(D) To contrast modern literature with Darío's writings

03 Why was the book *Azul* important to Darío's career?

(A) It featured Darío's new style of Spanish writing.

(B) It featured poetry that inspired Darío.

(C) It featured Darío's first political poems.

(D) It featured Darío's notes from his time in Europe.

04 What can be inferred about Darío's feelings toward the United States?

(A) He was pleased with its cultural developments.

(B) He was angry that it had defeated Spain.

(C) He was relieved that it would help Latin America.

(D) He was afraid it would dominate Latin America.

05 How did Darío's later work differ from his earlier work?

(A) It used more complex sentence structures.

(B) It was more popular in Latin America.

(C) It discussed more realistic subject matter.

(D) It was more influenced by European literature.

Mini Test 2

Listen to part of a discussion in an art class.

01 What is the main purpose of the discussion?

(A) To introduce controversial works by participatory artists

(B) To discuss the concepts and effects of a new artistic trend

(C) To criticize the current status of established art museums

(D) To underline the importance of social approaches in art

02 What is the professor's opinion of visitors contributing things requested by Paul Ramirez?

(A) It shows how people may look for social values in artistic performances.

(B) It encourages many museums to reevaluate their traditional exhibitions.

(C) It demonstrates trust and social bonds between the visitors and the artist.

(D) It exemplifies the individual's creativity and their expectations for art.

Answer Book p. A86

03 The professor illustrates the ideas and examples of participatory art. Indicate whether each of the following is mentioned as part of participatory art.
Click in the correct box for each sentence.

	Yes	No
(A) It challenges established art and traditional exhibitions.		
(B) Many of its works became popular on the Internet.		
(C) Visitors are required to engage with its artwork without any prior understanding.		
(D) Its artists try to create social and cultural experiences that include people.		

04 What does the student say she felt about Abramovic's work she saw in London?

(A) She felt alienated from her art.
(B) She felt more engaged with the visitors.
(C) She felt pressured to understand the artwork.
(D) She felt confused with the difficult instructions.

05 Listen again to part of the lecture. Then answer the question.
What does the professor imply about established museums adopting participatory art?

(A) They have been more open with participatory art in order to avoid criticism.
(B) They try to be less judgmental in order to provide different forms of art.
(C) They want to make access to art available for diverse groups of visitors.
(D) They hope to connect with people by restoring the basic philosophy of art.

iBT Practice

TOEFL Listening

Listen to part of a discussion in an American history class.

01 What is the main topic of the discussion?

(A) Rockefeller and Carnegie's relationship with the Progressive movement
(B) Rockefeller and Carnegie's methods of becoming immensely wealthy
(C) The labor unrest caused by Carnegie and Rockefeller's management
(D) The many charities to which Carnegie and Rockefeller donated money

02 How does the professor organize the discussion?

(A) By discussing Carnegie's rise to power and then Rockefeller's rise to power
(B) By discussing Carnegie and Rockefeller's charity work and then Progressives' criticism
(C) By discussing the causes of the Progressive movement and then its effects
(D) By discussing America's transition to industry and then how Carnegie and Rockefeller enabled this change

03 Why did Progressives criticize Rockefeller and Carnegie?

(A) Progressives opposed the spread of industry in the United States.
(B) Progressives were angry that neither man donated to a good cause.
(C) Progressives felt that their business practices were immoral.
(D) Progressives thought that they undermined the government's authority.

04 What is the professor's opinion of Andrew Carnegie?

(A) He cared more about business than charity.
(B) He is too harshly judged for his business practices.
(C) He was not as charitable as Rockefeller was.
(D) He was too kind to his employees.

05 What are the examples indicating that Carnegie and Rockefeller were ruthless businessmen?
Click on 2 answers.

(A) They used violent measures to call off strikes.
(B) They did not care at all about social issues, only their business.
(C) They fired a number of laborers without any given reasons.
(D) They caused poverty and inequity by monopolizing the markets.

06 Listen again to part of the lecture. Then answer the question.
What does the student mean when she says this: 🎧

(A) She has never heard of Carnegie and Rockefeller.
(B) She does not believe the claim being made by the professor.
(C) She does not follow the professor's lecture on this topic.
(D) She viewed Carnegie and Rockefeller from a different perspective.

Chapter 11 Life Science

- **Life Science**
  A scientific study of all types of living organisms such as microorganisms, plants, animals, and human beings
- **Related Fields**
  Microbiology, Botany, Entomology, Marine Biology, Zoology, Physiology, etc.

Listening Preview

Zoology – Animal Altruism | Intensive Drill 1 |

Some wildlife researchers believe that altruism — defined as an act in which an animal sacrifices its own wellbeing for the benefit of another animal — is a well-documented behavior. Those who say animal altruism exists cite examples such as dolphins helping others in need or a leopard caring for a baby baboon.

Other researchers point out that emphasizing selflessness as an organizing principle of animal behavior is dishonest. Animals are only altruistic when it promotes their survival. They say that it's quite a stretch to believe that animals are capable of the complex thinking required to save a life.

Biology – Keystone Species | Intensive Drill 2 |

A keystone species is a plant or animal that plays a unique and crucial role in the way an ecosystem functions. Without the keystone species, the ecosystem would be dramatically different or cease to exist altogether. Its disappearance could affect other species that rely on it for survival. Also, without the keystone species, new plants or animals could come into the habitat and push out native species.

Physiology – Aging

| Intensive Drill 3 |

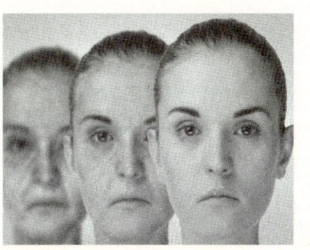

In humans, aging represents the accumulation of changes in a human being over time, including physical, psychological, and social changes.

The causes of aging are as yet unknown, but there are two currently convincing theories. The first one is the damage concept, in which the accumulation of internally or externally induced damage, such as oxidized bases or DNA breaks, can cause biological systems to fail. The other one is the programmed aging concept, whereby internal processes, such as DNA telomere shortening, may cause aging.

Microbiology – Cyanobacteria

| Mini Test 1 |

Cyanobacteria are a type of bacteria that are aquatic and photosynthetic. In other words, they live in the water and can produce their own food. They are quite small and usually unicellular, although they often grow in large colonies. They are also found in the oldest known fossils, more than 3.5 billion years old.

Botany - Spotted Knapweed

| Mini Test 2 |

Spotted knapweed is an exotic invasive plant that has become widespread in the United States. It is considered the number one weed problem in many areas in the U.S. This species reproduces via seeds which can remain dormant for five years, waiting to germinate when conditions are favorable.

Marine Biology - Dolphins

| iBT Practice |

Dolphins are one of the most intelligent marine mammals and part of the family of toothed whales. Dolphins are found worldwide, mostly in the shallow seas of the continental shelves. They are carnivores, consuming a variety of prey including fish, squid, and crustaceans. Their coloration varies, but they are generally gray in color with darker backs than the rest of their bodies.

Intensive Drill 1

Listen to part of a discussion in a zoology class.

01 What is the main purpose of the discussion?

(A) To criticize a theory on the humanlike characteristics of chimpanzees

(B) To explain the latest approach to observing captured animals

(C) To discuss how a new study verified a contradicting theory

(D) To emphasize the critical role of fieldworkers in zoology

02 According to the professor, what was the disputed view among the chimpanzee experts?

(A) Whether chimpanzees can use tools for sharing food

(B) Whether chimpanzees should be captured for observation

(C) Whether chimpanzees mourn when others die in their group

(D) Whether chimpanzees demonstrate any regard for others

03 What is the professor's attitude toward the fieldworkers?

(A) She thinks their argument over chimpanzees deserves some credit.

(B) She argues they often make exaggerated and unscientific claims.

(C) She believes they have a great workload in supporting scientists.

(D) She criticizes them for monitoring the chimpanzees too heavily.

04 In the discussion, the professor mentions how the approach of the new study was different from that of the past experiments. Indicate whether each of the following is related to the new approach or the old one.
Click in the correct box for each sentence.

	New Approach	Old Approach
(A) Chimpanzees were given complex tools to deliver food.		
(B) Chimpanzees were trained to choose between two options.		
(C) Chimpanzees were unable to realize the consequence of their behavior.		
(D) Chimpanzees were placed next to each other.		

05 Listen again to part of the lecture. Then answer the question.
What does the professor imply about the past studies on chimpanzees?

(A) They failed to consider the rather unique nature of chimpanzees.

(B) The researchers should not have tried to control the evidence.

(C) There could have been a better way to control their outcomes.

(D) The fact that they had many restrictions resulted in failure.

Intensive Drill 2

Listen to part of a lecture in a biology class.

01 What is the lecture mainly about?
Click on 2 answers.

(A) The ecological significance of keystone species
(B) Benefits and harm caused by keystone species
(C) The general classification of keystone species
(D) Ways to conserve endangered keystone species

02 Why does the professor mention keystones in architecture?

(A) To highlight the critical link between two academic fields
(B) To draw a parallel between its role and a biological concept
(C) To look at a biological key concept from a new perspective
(D) To emphasize the importance of interdisciplinary studies

03 According to the professor, which of the following are true about keystone species?
Click on 3 answers.

(A) Their absence may cause the destruction of an ecosystem.

(B) They can prevent crowding out of certain species in a habitat.

(C) Their effect on other species is limited due to their small population.

(D) They are mostly carnivorous animals with some exceptions.

(E) They can change or maintain the physical conditions of a habitat.

04 Why is elephants' feeding behavior important in African plains?

(A) It maintains the grassland that supports various grazing animals.

(B) It promotes the expansion of trees which protect small animals.

(C) It disperses a wide range of seeds and helps plant diversity.

(D) It gradually decreases the population of dominant predators.

05 What is the professor's opinion of conserving the environment by targeting keystone species?

(A) Its overall influence on the environment is still uncertain.

(B) It should be regarded as being of great importance and urgency.

(C) It is ineffective in some cases because of its lengthy process.

(D) It may neglect the need to protect a wider range of species.

Intensive Drill 3

Listen to part of a lecture in a botany class.

01 What is the main topic of the lecture?

(A) Ways of controlling the spotted knapweed
(B) The history of the spotted knapweed in North America
(C) The reasons why the spotted knapweed is a threat
(D) The life cycle of the spotted knapweed

02 Which of the following are true about spotted knapweed seeds?
Click on 2 answers.

(A) They are frequently consumed by cows and sheep.
(B) They are produced in large numbers at one time.
(C) They can survive in the soil for a long time.
(D) They are very heavy and have thick shells.

03 What is one reason why the spotted knapweed is difficult to kill?

(A) It contains certain chemicals that help it grow quickly.
(B) It is too deeply rooted to dig out of the ground.
(C) It is highly resistant to chemical pesticides.
(D) It is not consumed by many animals.

04 How does the professor feel about using chemical pesticides?

(A) It is too risky for treating some pests.
(B) It is the most effective way to kill pests.
(C) They should be used with other methods.
(D) Most people do not properly understand them.

05 Listen again to part of the lecture. Then answer the question.
Why does the professor say this: 🎧

(A) To warn the students about an upcoming assignment
(B) To promise the students that he will not grade harshly
(C) To alert the students that he is about to start his lecture
(D) To assure the students they will get their grades soon

Mini Test 1

Listen to part of a discussion in a microbiology class.

01 What is the main topic being discussed?

(A) How cyanobacteria perform photosynthesis
(B) The ways other life forms benefit from cyanobacteria
(C) The role of cyanobacteria in plant evolution
(D) The importance of cyanobacteria in agriculture

02 Why does the professor discuss the chloroplasts in plant cells?

(A) To describe the complex structure of plant cells
(B) To explain how cyanobacteria helped create plants
(C) To compare the parts of plant cells to cyanobacteria cells
(D) To show how photosynthesis works

03 What can be inferred about cyanobacteria?

(A) They were first nourished by the Earth's atmosphere.

(B) They produce more oxygen than plants.

(C) They are no longer found in the oceans.

(D) They are older than animal and plant life.

04 Which processes are cyanobacteria able to perform?
Click on 2 answers.

(A) Establish nitrogen compounds in soil

(B) Discharge nitrogen into the atmosphere

(C) Release oxygen-rich compounds into the soil

(D) Create their own food with sunlight

05 Listen again to part of the lecture. Then answer the question.
Why does the professor say this: 🎧

(A) To involve the students in the discussion

(B) To shame the students for not studying enough

(C) To indicate to the students that the topic needs more research

(D) To dismiss any questions from the students so she can continue

Mini Test 2

Listen to part of a lecture in a physiology class.

01 What is the main purpose of the lecture?

(A) To explain the process of oxidative damage in a cell
(B) To distinguish DNA damage from mutation
(C) To support theories about aging with relevant experiments
(D) To describe current leading theories about aging

02 How does the professor introduce DNA damage theory?

(A) By clarifying how DNA damage differs from DNA mutation
(B) By reviewing the previous discussion about how to maximize lifespans
(C) By comparing it to some other popular theories
(D) By outlining the course overview regarding the theories of aging

03 Which of the following is true about DNA damage theory?

(A) Enzymes accumulate in the system and attack DNA.

(B) DNA damage prohibits the formation of proteins.

(C) DNA damage in slowly replicating cells can lead to mutation.

(D) Cells with DNA damage are removed from the system.

04 The professor explains the steps in the process of oxidative damage. Put these steps in the correct order.

Drag each sentence to the space where it belongs.
One of the answer choices will not be used.

1	
2	
3	
4	

(A) ROS accumulates in the cell.

(B) DNA mutation occurs during respiration.

(C) Reactive oxygen species are produced in mitochondria.

(D) Oxidative stress damages macromolecules and promotes disease.

(E) Enzymes are unable to break down all ROS.

05 Listen again to part of the lecture. Then answer the question.
What does the professor mean when he says this: 🎧

(A) Anti-oxidant enzymes do not completely convert ROS to benign molecules.

(B) Some ROS can become harmless without an aid of enzymes.

(C) Mitochondrial respiration allows ROS to remain in our system safely.

(D) Not all ROS cause dangerous effects when reacting with proteins.

iBT Practice

TOEFL Listening

Listen to part of a discussion in a marine biology class.

01 What are the speakers mainly discussing?

(A) The way that dolphins communicate with each other
(B) Experiments that train dolphins to perform actions
(C) Dolphins' capacity for abstract and creative thought
(D) New behaviors dolphins develop for rewards

02 According to the discussion, what do dolphins use most of their brains for?

(A) Developing new kinds of behavior
(B) Dealing with visual information
(C) Keeping track of audio information
(D) Communicating with their species

03 What was the significance of the dolphin tearing off small bits of garbage?

(A) Dolphins can distinguish between food and waste.
(B) Dolphins can understand consequences and future events.
(C) Dolphins can communicate ideas to one another.
(D) Dolphins can follow commands even when grammar is reversed.

04 What does the professor imply about dolphin and human language?

(A) Dolphins do not have their own language but understand human language concepts.
(B) Dolphins use their own language when communicating with each other.
(C) Dolphins understand human language by analyzing the structure of sentences.
(D) It depends on each species whether dolphins have their own language or not.

05 How does the professor discuss the intelligence of dolphins?

(A) By describing the unique structure of their brains
(B) By comparing their behavior with that of other mammals
(C) By explaining the evolution of dolphins from land mammals
(D) By providing examples from experiments and observations

06 Listen again to part of the lecture. Then answer the question.
What does the professor mean when she says this: 🎧

(A) She is embarrassed because she does not know the answer.
(B) She is cautious because the answer to the question is complex.
(C) She admits that dolphins use a very difficult language.
(D) She is confused because she does not understand the question.

Chapter 12 Physical Science

- **Physical Science**
  An area of science that deals with materials that are not alive and the ways in which nonliving things work
- **Related Fields**
  Physics, Astronomy, Chemistry, Earth Science, Chemistry, Environmental Science, Geology, etc.

Listening Preview

Earth Science – Ice Age
| Intensive Drill 1 |

An ice age is a period of long-term reduction in the temperature of the Earth's surface and atmosphere, resulting in the presence or expansion of continental and polar ice sheets and alpine glaciers.

Scientists have determined that variations in the Earth's orbit and shifting plate tectonics spur the waxing and waning of these periods. There have been at least five significant ice ages in the Earth's history, with approximately a dozen epochs of glacial expansion occurring in the past one million years.

Physics – Albert Einstein
| Intensive Drill 2 |

In 1950, Albert Einstein determined that the laws of physics are the same for all non-accelerating observers, and that the speed of light in a vacuum acts independently of the motion of all observers. This was the theory of special relativity.

He then spent 10 years trying to include acceleration in the theory and published his theory of general relativity in 1915. In it, he determined that massive objects cause a distortion in space-time, which is felt as gravity.

Environmental Science – Waste-to-Energy (WtE)

| Intensive Drill 3 |

Some alternative energy companies are developing new ways to recycle waste by generating electricity from landfill waste and pollution. This process of generating energy in the form of electricity and heat from the primary treatment of waste is called Waste-to-Energy or WtE. Most WtE processes produce electricity and/or heat directly through combustion, or produce a combustible fuel commodity, such as methanol, methane, ethanol, or synthetic fuels.

Astronomy – A Star's Spectrum

| Mini Test 1 |

A spectrum is a term for the different colors of light that comes from a star. The light that comes to us from stars is very similar and looks to our eyes as if it is just one color, but it is actually made up of many different colors. Astronomers can break up the light and measure how much light comes from each color, and they use this information to find information about the star, like its temperature, size, and distance from the Earth.

Geology – Glaciers

| Mini Test 2 |

Glaciers are large, thickened ice masses made up of snow that has accumulated over many years. Glaciers form when snow remains in one location long enough to transform into ice. Presently, glaciers occupy about 10 percent of the world's total land area, and are mostly located in polar regions like Antarctica, Greenland, and the Canadian Arctic. Due to sheer mass, glaciers move, or flow, like very slow rivers.

Astronomy – Late Heavy Bombardment

| iBT Practice |

The Late Heavy Bombardment, also known as the LHB or lunar cataclysm, is an event that occurred approximately 4.1 to 3.8 billion years ago, after the Earth and other rocky planets had formed and accrued most of their mass. It is believed that a large number of asteroids collided with the early terrestrial planets in the inner Solar System, such as Mercury, Venus, Earth, and Mars.

Intensive Drill 1

Listen to part of a discussion in an earth science class.

01 What is the lecture mainly about?

(A) Predicting when and how the next ice age will happen
(B) The clues and factors involved in the study of ice ages
(C) The impact of various human activities on glacial cycles
(D) The causes and development process of the last ice age

02 What is the professor's opinion of the prediction of a mini ice age based on the solar cycle?

(A) He disagrees with it since it ignores crucial factors.
(B) He agrees with it and its study process.
(C) He thinks it needs to be done very carefully.
(D) He does not think such prediction is necessary.

03 What did paleoclimatologists discover after they unveiled the evidence of glacial cycles in the past?

(A) Ice ages on the Earth took place with regular pattern.
(B) The previous notions of ice ages were surprisingly incorrect.
(C) Human activity did not play a regular part in causing ice ages.
(D) The last glacial cycle occurred much more recently.

04 What are the possible consequences of plate movement that may lead to the development of ice ages?
Click on 2 answers.

(A) Changes in the shape of continental boundaries
(B) The emission of ash particles from volcanic eruptions
(C) The formation of patterns in volcanic eruptions
(D) Shifts in oceanic and atmospheric circulation

05 In the lecture, the professor explains the factors involved in the Milankovitch cycle to speculate about ice ages. Indicate whether each of the following statement is related to the speculation.
Click in the correct box for each sentence.

	Yes	No
(A) The apex of ice ages occurs every 100,000 years.		
(B) The tilted orbital axis of the Earth affects the amount of sunlight that reaches the Earth.		
(C) The Sun's temperature has been cooling down over the last century.		
(D) The variation in the shape of the Earth's orbit changes its orbital position.		

Intensive Drill 2

Listen to part of a lecture in a physics class.

01 What is the main topic of the lecture?

(A) Einstein's greatest failure
(B) Einstein's most influential theories
(C) Einstein's attitudes towards science
(D) Einstein's disproved theories

02 How does the professor explain Einstein's approach to science?

(A) By telling a couple of anecdotal stories about Einstein
(B) By contrasting it with the approaches of other great scientists
(C) By explaining how it helped him avoid the wrong theories
(D) By discussing the origins of Einstein's approach

03 How did Einstein judge quantum mechanics?

(A) According to the evidence confirming or denying its accuracy

(B) According to how it fit into his own theories

(C) According to how completely it explained the universe

(D) According to his own gut feelings of how the world worked

04 What does the professor say about scientists?

(A) They would do well to follow Einstein's example.

(B) They should not allow personal feelings to cloud their scientific judgment.

(C) They should only rely on intuition when firm evidence is unavailable.

(D) They should focus on developing new theories rather than disproving existing ones.

05 What is the professor's opinion of Einstein's attempt to disprove the theory of quantum mechanics?

(A) It was a noble effort that led to different discoveries.

(B) It was a pointless distraction that kept Einstein from greater achievements.

(C) It was a logical effort given the lack of evidence for quantum mechanics.

(D) It failed because he did not rely on his intuition this time.

Intensive Drill 3

Listen to part of a lecture in an environmental science class.

01 What is the main purpose of the lecture?

(A) To examine several implications of WtE processes

(B) To explain some advantages of WtE production

(C) To describe diverse efforts to utilize human wastes

(D) To compare thermal and non-thermal treatments in WtE

02 According to the professor, which of the following factors contribute to the debate of using incineration technology?
Click on 3 answers.

(A) Safety of the procedure

(B) Speed and cost effectiveness

(C) Conflicting technology

(D) Procedural residues

(E) Environmental complications

03 In the lecture, the professor describes pyrolysis and gasification as types of thermal treatment of waste. Indicate whether each of the following processes is related to pyrolysis or gasification. Click in the correct box for each phrase.

	Pyrolysis	Gasification
(A) Uses bio-mass and plastic as main ingredients		
(B) Involves heating in a low-oxygen atmosphere		
(C) Uses carbonaceous substances from waste		
(D) Leaves potentially toxic charcoal as a byproduct		

04 What does the professor imply about the use of anaerobic digestion?

(A) Its slow process can increase the production of energy.

(B) The biogas created from its process has inconsistent quality.

(C) The use of energy as a result of its process may be limited.

(D) The use of microorganisms can speed up the digestion process.

05 Listen again to part of the lecture. Then answer the question.
What does the professor mean when he says this: 🎧

(A) Incineration is gradually losing its popularity as a WtE process.

(B) Other WtE technologies have advanced only with regard to cost.

(C) The byproducts of incineration can improve its cost effectiveness.

(D) Incineration technology features much higher cost effectiveness.

Mini Test 1

Listen to part of a discussion in an astronomy class.

01 What are the speakers mainly discussing?

(A) How to observe a distant star's spectrum

(B) Differentiating star classes by their spectrums

(C) Determining the temperature of a star from its color

(D) What can be learned about a star from its spectrum

02 Why do larger stars emit more blue light?

(A) They burn more nuclear fuel.

(B) They travel at greater speeds.

(C) They have higher internal temperatures.

(D) They have large diameters.

03 What is the professor's opinion of the student confused about a big and red star?

(A) His confusion is her fault due to her inappropriate terminology.
(B) He lacks an understanding of standard terminology.
(C) He was not paying enough attention earlier in the discussion.
(D) He should be praised for his courage to bring up a problem.

04 What does the professor compare between blue super giants and red giants?

(A) Their respective ages
(B) Their internal chemistry
(C) Their distribution in the universe
(D) Their overall mass

05 What can be inferred about stars?

(A) Blue stars are always closer than red stars.
(B) Red stars are more common in the universe than blue stars.
(C) There is more than one factor that affects the color of a star's spectrum.
(D) A star's spectrum only provides valuable information if its size is already known.

Mini Test 2

Listen to part of a lecture in a geology class.

01 How does the professor introduce his discussion of glacier movement?

(A) By explaining recent discoveries concerning the topic
(B) By reviewing what the students have already learned about glaciers
(C) By outlining the basic forces involved in glacier movement
(D) By emphasizing why understanding glacier movement is beneficial

02 Which part of a glacier moves the fastest?

(A) The sides
(B) The core
(C) The top middle
(D) The bottom

03 What does the professor imply about the movement of glaciers?

(A) The force of gravity makes it easier for the glaciers to slide down towards the bottom despite their weight.
(B) The melting of the ice in a glacier decreases the frictional force between the bedrock and the glacier and eases the movement.
(C) The movement of glaciers cannot be compared with that of ice cubes because their properties are different from each other.
(D) The ice at the bottom of a glacier moves the fastest due to the effects of the melting of its ice.

04 Why does the professor mention an ice cube?

(A) To illustrate how melting water facilitates glacier movement
(B) To describe the structure of a glacier
(C) To indicate why glaciers follow the path of least resistance
(D) To explain how glaciers crack and split as they move

05 Listen again to part of the lecture. Then answer the question.
Why does the professor say this: 🎧

(A) To suggest a connection between glaciers and bodies of free-flowing water
(B) To emphasize the complexities of glacier movement
(C) To clarify the principle that determines how glaciers move
(D) To point out the role of gravity in glacier movement

iBT Practice

TOEFL Listening

Listen to part of a lecture in an astronomy class.

01 What is the lecture mainly about?

(A) The possible causes of the Late Heavy Bombardment
(B) The evidence for the Late Heavy Bombardment
(C) The severity of the Late Heavy Bombardment
(D) The effects of the Late Heavy Bombardment

02 How does the professor demonstrate the severity of the Late Heavy Bombardment?

(A) By explaining how it prevented life on other planets
(B) By describing how it changed the landscape on the Earth
(C) By comparing it to other astronomical events
(D) By giving information on the frequency of asteroid impacts on the Earth

03 What is the professor's opinion of the planetary migration scenario?

(A) It has nothing to do with the Late Heavy Bombardment.
(B) It is the most likely explanation for the Late Heavy Bombardment.
(C) It most likely occurred as a result of the Late Heavy Bombardment.
(D) It was once considered the most convincing cause of the Late Heavy Bombardment.

04 What does the professor say about the asteroid belt before the start of the Late Heavy Bombardment?

(A) It orbited much more closely to the Sun.
(B) It contained much more material.
(C) It rarely sent objects towards the inner planets.
(D) It frequently involved collisions with Neptune and Uranus.

05 The professor describes the history of the Late Heavy Bombardment. Put the following events in the correct order.

Drag each sentence to the space where it belongs.

1	
2	
3	
4	

(A) The orbits of Uranus and Neptune became unstable.
(B) The inner planets experienced increased asteroid bombardment.
(C) Neptune and Uranus passed through the asteroid belt.
(D) Saturn and Jupiter migrated to orbits more distant from the Sun.

06 Listen again to part of the lecture. Then answer the question.
What does the professor imply about astronomers?

(A) They are unsure when the Late Heavy Bombardment actually occurred.
(B) They believe that the early solar system may have been much larger.
(C) They know more about the effects of the Late Heavy Bombardment than about its causes.
(D) They are reluctant to speculate about the Late Heavy Bombardment due to lack of information.

Chapter 13 Social Science

- **Social Science**
  A branch of science that deals with the institutions and functioning of human society and with the interpersonal relationships of individuals as members of society
- **Related Fields**
  Archaeology, Anthropology, Psychology, Economics, Sociology, Political Science, etc.

Listening Preview

Archaeology – Mohenjo-Daro
| Intensive Drill 1 |

Mohenjo-daro is widely recognized as one of the largest and most important early settlements of South Asia and the Indus Valley Civilization, which flourished between 2600 and 1900 BCE. Significant excavation has been conducted at the site of the city, and it was designated a UNESCO World Heritage Site in 1980.

Anthropology – Maya Civilization
| Intensive Drill 2 |

The Maya civilization was a Mesoamerican civilization indigenous to Mexico and Central America. The civilization is well known for its art, architecture, mathematics, calendar, and astronomical system.

The fall of the Maya is one of history's great mysteries. One of the mightiest civilizations in the ancient Americas simply fell into ruin in a very short period of time. There are many theories as to what happened to the Maya, such as the warfare theory, the famine theory, and the environmental change theory, but there is little consensus among experts.

Archaeology – Ancient Egyptian Writings

| Intensive Drill 3 |

The ancient Egyptians believed that it was important to record and communicate information about religion and government. Thus, they invented written scripts that could be used to record this information. The most famous of all ancient Egyptian scripts is hieroglyphs. Most remaining texts in the Egyptian language are primarily written in hieroglyphic script.

Psychology – Conformity

| Mini Test 1 |

Conformity is a type of social influence involving a change in belief or behavior in order to fit in with a group. This change results from real or imagined group pressure. The term "conformity" is often used to indicate an agreement with the majority position, brought about either by a desire to fit in or be liked, or because of a desire to be correct, or simply to conform to a social role.

Economics – Bretton Woods Agreement

| Mini Test 2 |

The Bretton Woods Agreement established the landmark system for monetary and exchange rate management in 1944. It was developed at the United Nations Monetary and Financial Conference held in Bretton Woods, New Hampshire, from July 1 to July 22, 1944. A major objective of the Bretton Woods Agreement was to promote financial stability and to lay the foundation for free trade.

Sociology – Dunbar's Number

| iBT Practice |

Robin Dunbar is a British anthropologist and evolutionary psychologist and a specialist in primate behavior. He hypothesized that there is a cognitive limit to the number of individuals with whom any one person can maintain stable relationships. He proposed that humans can only comfortably maintain 150 stable relationships. This number is referred to as Dunbar's number.

Intensive Drill 1

Listen to part of a discussion in an archaeology class.

01 What are the speakers mainly discussing?

(A) How Mohenjo-Daro was first discovered in the 1920s
(B) What Mohenjo-Daro reveals about the Indus Valley Civilization
(C) The artistic value of artifacts found in Mohenjo-Daro
(D) The technological developments of Mohenjo-Daro society

02 What does the professor imply about the city's gridded layout?

(A) It is not used any more as a means of city planning.
(B) It made it easier to establish the city's sanitation system.
(C) It was invented mainly for religious and political purposes.
(D) It has been commonly used in regular city planning.

03 What is one of the interesting features about the houses of Mohenjo-Daro?

(A) They were connected to the city granary.
(B) They all featured large courtyards and gardens.
(C) They tended to contain statues for decoration.
(D) They had bathrooms with pipes for waste disposal.

04 What do the stone seals found in Mohenjo-Daro show?

(A) How the society practiced commerce
(B) How the society had upper and lower classes
(C) What each animal species carved in the seals stood for
(D) How its carving technology developed

05 Listen again to part of the lecture. Then answer the question.
Why does the professor say this: 🎧

(A) To encourage the students to research the subject
(B) To elicit a response from the students
(C) To indicate her disappointment about the students' passiveness
(D) To obtain information she currently lacks

Intensive Drill 2

Listen to part of a lecture in an anthropology class.

01 What is the main purpose of the lecture?

(A) To discuss a possible theory for the decline of the Maya civilization

(B) To give an overview of the technological and architectural achievements of the Maya

(C) To prove that the Maya did not abandon their cities

(D) To show how deforestation can lead to prolonged droughts

02 How does the professor introduce his description of the Maya empire?

(A) By comparing it with one of the other civilizations from that era

(B) By reminding the students what he discussed during the last lecture

(C) By providing examples that show its superiority in various aspects

(D) By emphasizing its advancement due to the favorable surrounding environment

03 What is the professor's opinion of the various accomplishments of the Maya?

(A) No other civilization in history can rival the achievements of the Maya.
(B) Their accomplishments are remarkable and significant.
(C) They should not receive sole credit for their inventions.
(D) The Maya achievements were a result of receiving help from foreigners.

04 According to the lecture, what are some theories that attempt to explain the decline of the Maya empire?
Click on 3 answers.

(A) The Maya had to leave their habitat due to lack of food.
(B) A civil war weakened its army and hindered its control of the Maya social order.
(C) The area in which the Maya settled was too tropical.
(D) A long drought was made worse by the continuous cutting of trees.
(E) A foreign society invaded and took over the Maya.

05 The professor explains the steps in the process of the latest theory about the decline of the Maya. Put these steps in the correct order.
Drag each phrase to the space where it belongs.
One of the answer choices will not be used.

1	
2	
3	
4	

(A) Less evaporation of water to form rainclouds
(B) Lack of food
(C) Lack of rainfall
(D) Aggression by foreign people
(E) Continued clearing of trees

Intensive Drill 3

Listen to part of a discussion in an archaeology class.

01 What is the main purpose of the discussion?

(A) To compare the growths and changes of two ancient cultures
(B) To study the development of an ancient written language
(C) To examine various purposes of ancient Egyptian scripts
(D) To illustrate the difference between ancient symbols and alphabets

02 What is the professor's attitude toward hieratic and demotic scripts?

(A) She regards them as other forms of hieroglyphic script.
(B) She thinks each should be given a separate category.
(C) She is reluctant to treat them as symbolic writings.
(D) She regrets the lack of attention given to them.

03 In the discussion, the students and professor talk about various ancient Egyptian writing systems. Indicate whether each of the following is included as part of the descriptions.
Click in the correct box for each sentence.

	Included	Not Included
(A) Hieroglyphs are the oldest and the primary writing system of ancient Egypt.		
(B) Hieratic was mainly used for sacred writings in temples and tombs.		
(C) Demotic is highly cursive in order to document people's everyday affairs.		
(D) The ancient Egyptians had to use the modified Greek letters for their writing.		

04 Why does the professor mention Alexander the Great?

(A) To mention the background influence of Greek culture on ancient Egypt
(B) To explain the political significance of the ancient Egyptian language
(C) To describe the advancement of the Greek alphabet during his reign
(D) To indicate how he promoted the general use of Coptic script

05 According to the professor, what are the significant aspects of Coptic script?
Click on 2 answers.

(A) It has become the principal writing system of the Egyptian language.
(B) It used vowels for the first time in the history of Egypt.
(C) It managed to survive for many years under Greek occupation.
(D) It made written language become more publically available.

Mini Test 1

Listen to part of a discussion in a psychology class.

01 What are the speakers mainly discussing?

(A) Ways to resolve disagreements of opinion in a group
(B) The tendency for people to follow the majority's opinion
(C) The tendency of people to obey authority figures
(D) What makes each person perceive an illusion differently

02 According to the discussion, what are essential elements of conformity?
Click on 2 answers.

(A) It only occurs in very large groups.
(B) It is a way of resolving differences in perception.
(C) It involves the altering of opinions or actions.
(D) It is undertaken in the absence of physical danger.

03 What can be inferred about the results of Muzafer Sherif's experiment?

(A) People have a tendency to conform to reach a general agreement in a group.

(B) Conformity only occurs when social groups exist for long periods.

(C) People choose to conform when they lack reliable evidence to form their own opinions.

(D) Conformity relies on a leader who guides the group's opinions.

04 What does the professor find interesting about Sherif's experiment?

(A) That people disregarded their own perceptions to conform to the group

(B) That people tended to form an agreement even when there was no obvious threat

(C) That people conformed to draw a consensus even without any group discussion

(D) That people changed their opinions slowly over a period of time rather than instantly

05 Listen again to part of the lecture. Then answer the question.
Why does the professor say this: 🎧

(A) To suggest that the student's definition is not acceptable

(B) To correct the student's definition through mild criticism

(C) To imply the definition is a good one

(D) To seek another opinion using a light-hearted joke

Mini Test 2

Listen to part of a lecture in an economics class.

01 What is the lecture mainly about?

(A) The economic problems the Bretton Woods Agreement was meant to solve

(B) The structure of the financial system created in the Bretton Woods Agreement

(C) How the United States was able to solve the financial crisis of the 1930s

(D) The role of the IMF in hosting the Bretton Woods Conference

02 Which of the following institutions are mentioned as being products of the Bretton Woods Agreement?
Click on 2 answers.

(A) The IMF

(B) The Stock Exchange

(C) The World Bank

(D) APEC

03 What caused currency devaluation in the 1930s?

(A) The stock market crash of 1929

(B) The onset of World War II

(C) The lack of capital for foreign investment

(D) The self-interested policies of individual nations

04 What was the ultimate result of the development of trading blocs in the 1930s?

(A) The gradual improvement of the world economy

(B) The development of international financial systems

(C) The hindrance of general economic recovery

(D) Increased levels of hatred between nations

05 Listen again to part of the lecture. Then answer the question.
What can be inferred about the United States?

(A) It had to borrow extensively to pay for the reconstruction after the war.

(B) It was the main beneficiary of the Bretton Woods Agreement.

(C) It had played a relatively minor part in World War II.

(D) It was tricked into signing the Bretton Woods Agreement.

TOEFL Listening

Listen to part of a lecture in a sociology class.

01 What is the lecture mainly about?
Click on 2 answers.

(A) The typical social interactions of humans and primates
(B) How brain size is related to social networking
(C) The application of Dunbar's number to human societies
(D) The impact of the Internet on social networking practices

02 How did Dunbar first develop his theory?

(A) By studying the structure of the human brain
(B) By researching the sizes of armies throughout history
(C) By recognizing patterns in the size of social networking websites
(D) By observing the sizes of different primate groups

03 According to Dunbar, why can humans have a larger number of intimate relationships than primates can?

(A) Humans have the capacity for language.
(B) Humans have to form larger groups to survive.
(C) Humans have more time for social interaction.
(D) Humans do not fight as much as primates.

04 Why does the professor mention the organization of militaries throughout history?

(A) To disprove the validity of Dunbar's number
(B) To explain how language plays different roles in different groups
(C) To show how survival groups reach a similar maximum limit
(D) To compare Dunbar's theory with later theories

05 What can be inferred about social groups based on Dunbar's theory?

(A) If a group contains less than 150 people, more effective communication is available.
(B) The more desperate a situation a group is in, the more effectively the group functions.
(C) If a group is composed of over 200 people, disharmony prevents it from working well.
(D) People tend to minimize their number of relationships when they face a severe threat.

06 Listen again to part of the lecture. Then answer the question.
Why does the professor say this:

(A) To emphasize that Dunbar's theory has flaws
(B) To elaborate on the point he just made
(C) To get the students' opinions on the subject
(D) To prevent the students from asking any similar questions

TOEFL iBT i Listening   www.linguaforum.com

Actual Test

Actual Test 1
Actual Test 2

Actual Test 1

Passage 1 [1-5] Listen to a conversation between a student and a professor.

01 What is the main topic of the conversation?

(A) Sending an e-mail to a professor about filming a piece on climate change
(B) How to inform the public about the various negative effects of climate change
(C) How best to produce a film on how birds are affected by climate change
(D) The best ways to interview experts in an information film

02 What is the professor's opinion of film production?

(A) It is not too difficult if there is careful planning.
(B) It needs to be directed by film majors.
(C) It must not begin until all the details are planned out.
(D) It is a strenuous and challenging process.

03 What can be inferred about the student's film project?

(A) He needs some more time to find useful information about the topic of the film.
(B) He has already figured out some good questions to use in interviews.
(C) He is having some trouble finding appropriate experts for interviews.
(D) He is planning to include both positive and negative effects of climate change on birds.

04 What are the factors that need to be considered to decide whether to film the same interview multiple times?

Click on 2 answers.

(A) The size of the set
(B) The quality of the audio
(C) If the interview will be used in snippets
(D) The number of the interviewees

05 In the conversation, the professor and student discuss various aspects of the student's film. Indicate whether each of the following is included.

Click in the correct box for each phrase.

	Included	Not Included
(A) How to prepare the filming equipment		
(B) Where to find reference materials about the topic		
(C) The effective ways to insert the interviews		
(D) Whether to use several cameras when filming interviews		

Passage 2 [6-11] Listen to part of a lecture in a linguistics class.

06 What is the lecture mainly about?

(A) The pronunciation of words in Middle English
(B) The changes that occurred with the rise of Modern English
(C) The printing press's effect on Middle English spelling
(D) The Great Vowel Shift's effect on Modern English

07 What are diphthongs?

(A) Vowels in English that changed during the Great Vowel Shift
(B) Spellings of a word based on its pronunciation in certain dialects
(C) Different ways of pronouncing a word with a single spelling
(D) Vowels formed from the combination of two other vowels

08 What does the professor imply about Middle English?

(A) It had a closer resemblance to French than Modern English does.
(B) It survived many changes due to the invention of the printing press.
(C) It featured very few dialects and regional variations among speakers.
(D) Its words had more confusing spellings than those in Modern English.

09 Why does the professor discuss William Caxton?

(A) To explain how England's government helped standardize English
(B) To show how the Renaissance introduced printing to England
(C) To compare the different English dialects used in publishing
(D) To demonstrate why printers felt it necessary to standardize English

10 What is the professor's attitude toward William Caxton?

(A) She thinks he was the most influential publisher in England.
(B) She appreciates his role in establishing standardized spelling.
(C) She believes his efforts to settle on a standard spelling caused many problems.
(D) She denies his influence on decreasing the confusion of various dialects.

11 Listen again to part of the lecture. Then answer the question.
Why does the professor say this: 🎧

(A) To elicit responses from the students
(B) To emphasize the severity of the problem
(C) To point out the problems of standardized spelling
(D) To encourage students to experiment with alternate spellings

Passage 3 **[12-17]** Listen to part of a discussion in an environmental science class.

12 What are the speakers mainly discussing?

(A) The use of low pressure in desalinization
(B) The development of heat exchange technology
(C) Desalinization techniques that save energy
(D) Desalinization's effect on the environment

13 What is the professor's stance on desalinization?

(A) He thinks that it should not be heavily relied on.
(B) He doubts that it will have a positive effect on the environment.
(C) He regrets that it is not more efficient.
(D) He feels that it is becoming more necessary.

14 How does the professor introduce the modern desalinization process?

(A) By comparing it to earlier desalinization methods
(B) By listing areas in which it is frequently used
(C) By describing the natural phenomenon on which it is based
(D) By criticizing the problems of traditional desalinization methods

15 What makes flash generators useful for desalinization?

(A) They help fresh water condense from vapor more quickly.
(B) They remove larger amounts of salt from the water.
(C) They preheat salt water so it dissolves more easily.
(D) They cause water to evaporate at lower temperatures.

16 What does the professor say about heat exchange technology and flash generators?

(A) They are frequently used in combination.
(B) They are technologies that still need to be perfected.
(C) They require greater amounts of energy than traditional desalinization.
(D) They cause a number of environmental problems.

17 Listen again to part of the lecture. Then answer the question.
What does the professor mean when he says this: 🎧

(A) Heat exchange is especially beneficial to the environment.
(B) Heat exchange solves more than one problem.
(C) Heat exchange works twice as fast as other methods.
(D) Heat exchange relies on two energy sources.

Actual Test 2

TOEFL Listening

Passage 1 [1-5] Listen to a conversation between a student and an employee at the Housing Department.

01 Why does the student go to the Housing Department?

(A) To ask for a switch to a new dorm room
(B) To comply with one of their investigations
(C) To request that other students be removed from his dorm
(D) To make a complaint about his dorm life

02 Why does the RA allow misbehavior in his dorm?

(A) He has no authority to stop it.
(B) He is not aware that it bothers anyone.
(C) He is friends with many of the people misbehaving.
(D) He is afraid of the people misbehaving.

03 How does the employee try to deal with the student's situation?

(A) By insisting that the RA is competent
(B) By going over the rules for dorms
(C) By promising to look into the problem
(D) By offering to refund part of his tuition

04 What is the student most likely to do next?

(A) Try to change his dorm room
(B) Ask his RA to control the dorm residents
(C) Call campus security on the dorm residents
(D) Wait for his RA to be investigated

05 Listen again to part of the conversation. Then answer the question.
What does the employee mean when she says this: 🎧

(A) She suspects that there have been many similar instances.
(B) She is unimpressed with just one instance of misbehavior.
(C) She wants the student to give a more detailed explanation.
(D) She is upset that the student has had a bad experience.

Passage 2 **[6-11]** Listen to part of a discussion in a drama class.

06 What is the lecture mainly about?
Click on 2 answers.

(A) Significant figures in the history of method acting
(B) The emergence of method acting in America
(C) Differences among styles of method acting
(D) The historical development of method acting

07 Why did Stanislavsky develop his methods?

(A) He felt that actors were not physical enough.
(B) He thought that actors did not fully understand their characters.
(C) He wanted to improve his reputation in the Moscow theater.
(D) He did not think that actors were influenced by the audience.

08 How is Chekhov's technique different from Stanislavsky's method?

(A) It focuses on delivering lines with precision.
(B) It uses more stage settings for dramatic effect.
(C) It requires that an actor use more of his or her mind and body.
(D) It requires that an actor be moderate in expressing emotions.

09 What is the professor's opinion of Michael Chekhov?

(A) He thinks that he is one of the most important teachers of method acting.
(B) He feels that unfortunate circumstances made him relatively unknown.
(C) He believes that his interpretation of method acting is superior to others.
(D) He hopes that more acting teachers will use his theories in their classes.

10 In the lecture, the professor discusses the history of method acting. Put the following events in order.
Drag each sentence to the space where it belongs.

1	
2	
3	
4	

(A) Michael Chekhov set up his school in London.
(B) Lee Strasberg joined the Actors' Studio.
(C) Stanislavsky put on a production of *The Seagull*.
(D) *Respect for Acting* by Uta Hagen was published.

11 Listen again to part of the lecture. Then answer the question.
What does the professor mean when he says this: 🎧

(A) Providing these names is a waste of time.
(B) There are so many examples available.
(C) He is eager to show off his knowledge.
(D) He has covered all the material in his lecture.

Passage 3 [12-17] Listen to part of a lecture in a biology class.

12 What is the main topic of the lecture?

(A) Environmental competition between K-strategists and r-strategists
(B) The reproductive strategies of various marine species
(C) How environmental influences affect the chances of survival
(D) Energy allocation in reproduction and the factors that influence it

13 How does the professor explain why various species have evolved to be r-strategists or K-strategists?

(A) By discussing the environmental pressures they face
(B) By explaining the life cycles of r-strategists and K-strategists
(C) By discussing the evolutionary origins of several species
(D) By comparing the chances of survival between r-strategists and K-strategists

14 Which of the following are true of K-strategists?
Click on 2 answers.

(A) They are generally large predators that prey on smaller species.
(B) They invest most of their energy in a small number of offspring.
(C) They generally have a high chance of survival once they reach maturity.
(D) They are usually found in habitats with plentiful food resources.

15 In the lecture, the professor mentions several characteristics of blue whales and American shad. Indicate which characteristics belong to each species.
Click in the correct box for each phrase.

	Blue Whale	American Shad
(A) Reaches sexual maturity quickly		
(B) Low rate of reproduction		
(C) No natural enemies		
(D) Subject to rapid population declines		
(E) Does not spend energy raising its young		

16 According to the lecture, which of the following species is an r-strategist?

(A) The mice
(B) The birds
(C) The alligators
(D) The elephants

17 Listen again to part of the lecture. Then answer the question.
Why does the professor say this:

(A) To introduce a discussion of how humans impact animal reproduction
(B) To illustrate the harmful effects that human development has had on the world environment
(C) To emphasize the role humans have played in the evolution of K-strategist species
(D) To acknowledge that external factors can affect the normal stability of the blue whale population

MEMO

New Edition
i TOEFL iBT® LISTENING

Answer Key & Explanations

LinguaForum

New Edition
i TOEFL iBT® LISTENING

Answer Key & Explanations

Diagnostic Test	A2
Part A Question Types	A4
Part B Approaching Themes	A56
Actual Test	A131

Diagnostic Test

Passage 1
01 (C) **02** (B) **03** (B), (D) **04** (A) **05** (A)

Passage 2
06 (A) **07** (A), (B) **08** (C) **09** (D) **10** (C) **11** [Leopard – (A), (D)], [Eagle – (B)], [Snake – (C)]

Passage 3
12 (B) **13** (C) **14** (A) **15** (C) **16** (A), (C) **17** (D)

Passage 1 p.16

01 (C) **02** (B) **03** (B), (D) **04** (A) **05** (A)

Listen to a conversation between a student and an administrator.

Administrator (F): Good morning. How may I help you?

Student (M): Hi. I'm here because I want to know if it's possible to move into the dormitory. Do you know who I could speak to for the information?

Administrator: I can actually help you with that, although I must say at this point in the semester, the rooms are pretty much filled up. Is there any particular reason you want to move?

Student: Well, I'm actually renting a studio apartment across from the university because I thought it would be great to have some personal space. But now I realize that living in a dormitory will be a great chance to meet others and make some friends since I'm a freshman from out of town.

Administrator: I see. Well, if you feel so, let me see what I can do . . . Oh! You're in luck. Someone will be moving out next week, so it looks like we will have a vacancy. Hmm . . . But the elevators are all booked for the weekend. It seems like you'll have to move during the weekday. Is that alright for you?

Student: Oh, really? There's no way to move on the weekend? My school schedule is pretty hectic, so it's going to be hard to move on a weekday.

Administrator: I'm afraid it's already all taken. Do you have a lot of things to move?

Student: Not exactly. Just my clothes and some small personal things. I do have a lot of books, though, which I'll need to bring. Oh, and a desk, which is kind of heavy. Does the school have any kind of moving services to help students?

Administrator: Generally, no. That's up to the student. However, if you think you'll have trouble finding one, I could look that up for you and see what I can find.

Student: That would be extremely helpful. I'm still pretty clueless about everything around here.

Administrator: Sure. We'll help you. Your room will be a decent size, so everything should fit in quite well.

Student: That's great to know. I was wondering if I am allowed to add some personal touches to the room.

Administrator: What kinds of décor are you thinking?

Student: Nothing concrete. I just want to know the regulation before I decorate the room.

Administrator: We don't allow room modifications such as wall paintings but you can put up wall hangings if you want to. Just make sure to mount them firmly. The school's policy is that students can change their room, as long as they return the room to its original state when they leave. Also be careful not to cause any damage to the built-in furniture, otherwise it will cost you a fine. Any other questions?

Student: No, that answers everything for now, I guess.

Administrator: Alright, well why don't we get started on your paper work and get your move underway?

Passage 2

p.18

06 (A)　　07 (A), (B)　　08 (C)　　09 (D)　　10 (C)　　11 [Leopard – (A), (D)], [Eagle – (B)], [Snake – (C)]

Listen to part of a lecture in a zoology class.

Professor (M): Good morning, everyone. As I mentioned last class, today we're going to look at a form of communication animals use to share information. This form is called "alarm calling" and it's used by animals to alert others of predators which may be nearby. One of the most well-known species of animals who use this communication technique is the vervet monkey which has evolved different alarm calls for different predators. You see, the vervet monkey's habitat is known for having predators attacking them from all sides: leopards and snakes on the ground, as well as eagles in the air. The sight of each kind of predator elicits an acoustically distinct alarm call. The alarm calls are also high frequency sounds. They make these higher-pitched sounds because they are harder to be localized by predators. The alarm call for a leopard is short and tonal, produced in a series of inhalations and exhalations. On the other hand, the alarm call for an eagle is a low-pitched grunt. Finally, snake alarm calls are high-pitched "chutters." Now, alarm calls for each predator are distinct and different, because the reaction of the vervet monkey depends on the call. For example, if the vervet monkeys interpret a leopard alarm call, it would try to run up into a tree to avoid being ambushed by the leopard. The vervet monkeys would then sit on the branches furthest away from the tree trunk. They do this because leopards can climb trees, but those farther, smaller branches can't support their weight. Now, how will the vervet monkey react when an eagle alarm call is given?

Student (F): I guess the exact opposite from a leopard alarm call?

Professor: Yes, that's correct. They will immediately look up and then find the nearest bush to run for cover to avoid an overhead aerial attack. Lastly, if a vervet monkey hears a snake alarm call, it would stand on both legs and instantly look down at the ground. As I just said, vervet monkey is a really interesting primate to understand the communication skills in animals. In addition to their communication skills, they are valuable subjects since their behavior also resembles certain social behavior of humans. One of the controversies among scholars is whether or not these alarm calls represent a selfless act or a selfish act. What I mean by this is that if a vervet monkey raises an alarm call for others to hear, it risks identifying its location to the predator, thus the self-sacrificing behavior. Scientists refer to this kind of selfless act as altruistic behavior. However, other research into this animal behavior indicates that vervet monkeys will only raise alarm calls if they know an immediate family member is near. Young monkeys, for example, would probably only cry out to warn their mother, rather than a monkey who is not related to them. This line of thought falls into the notion that alarm calls are simply an instinctual response to ensure the continuation of the family gene pool.

Passage 2

p.20

12 (B)　　13 (C)　　14 (A)　　15 (C)　　16 (A), (C)　　17 (D)

Listen to part of a lecture in a U.S. history class.

Professor (F): As I mentioned last class, we're going to go over today how essential the railroad system is to the economy of the United States. When we think of various products, like the food on our table, the shoes on our feet or even the cars we drive, the first thing that comes to mind might not necessarily be trains. But, the fact is, in the United States, a very large percentage of products are transported around the country by train. Now, of course when I say "train" I'm not talking about commuter trains, but rather freight trains. Commuter trains or "passenger trains" now play a very limited role, especially compared to other countries who rely on commuter trains to move their populations around their country. On the other hand, in the U.S. freight trains are still heavily used for shipments and account for almost 40 percent of all shipments of products. Does anyone want to guess the role of the trains in U.S. history?

Student (M): I heard it not only fostered industry growth but also lowered transportation costs.

Professor: You're right. As you said, railroads have always played a crucial role in the economic growth of our country. But there are some other roles, too. Engineering and natural resource industries took off to fuel the development of the railroad in the nineteenth century, providing a ton of jobs for Americans. The railroad was also a key factor in the development of the American West, not only by transporting investors and laborers across the country from the East coast to the center and West coast, but also by stimulating the growth of business in these areas that were beginning to be settled by European-Americans. Now, if we fast forward to the present year, we'll see that American freight railroads have become some of the best in the world. They support about 1.2 million jobs in various industries, including almost 200,000 high-paying jobs in the freight rail industry. These workers are some of America's most highly compensated workers with wages and benefits earned totaling around $114,000. Not a bad industry to be working in, huh? To put this into perspective, the average wage of a full-time U.S. employee including benefits is $70,000. Finally, there are a lot of other public benefits the freight system provides, which we might not always think about. First, compared to trucks, freight trains are more fuel efficient and emit less harmful gases into the atmosphere. Most importantly, they relieve traffic congestion on the highways. According to the Texas Transportation Institute, in 2011 highway congestion cost Americans $121 billion, a figure which is possibly even more today. Freight trains, however, can carry the same freight as several hundred trucks, reducing highway gridlock and the pressure to build costly new highways. Okay, let's take a look at some of the main products shipped by freight trains.

PART A | Question Types

Chapter 01 Main Idea

Sample Question
p.25

Listen to a conversation between a student and a professor.

Student (M): Professor Evans, I'm here to talk about courses for my joint major. Could we have a minute?

Professor (F): No problem. How can I help you?

Student: I'll be in my third year of a joint major in math and physics next semester. I was wondering if I can keep following the old curriculum for the joint major instead of taking those compulsory courses listed on the new curriculum.

Professor: Students who have completed their second year can stick to the old curriculum. So, if you're in your third year next semester, I don't think you need to worry about the new curriculum.

Student: Oh, that's a relief. If I follow the new curriculum, I should take eight more classes including prerequisites. It would be a complete waste of a semester.

Professor: We don't certainly want that kind of problem to happen.

Student: Great. I pay for my own tuition and, as you know, it is quite hard to manage studies and work at the same time.

Professor: I know. I appreciate your sincere effort.

Student: Thank you for saying that. Have a great day, Professor Evans.

학생과 교수의 대화를 들으시오.

학생 (남): Evans 교수님, 제 복수 전공에 필요한 강좌들에 대해 상의하려고 왔습니다. 잠깐 말씀 좀 나눌 수 있을까요?

교수 (여): 그럼. 어떻게 도와줄까?

학생: 다음 학기가 되면 제가 수학과 물리학을 복수 전공한 지 3년 차가 되거든요. 제가 새 커리큘럼에 나와 있는 필수 과목들 대신 예전 커리큘럼을 따라서 복수 전공을 계속할 수 있는지 궁금해서요.

교수: 2학년을 마친 학생들은 예전 커리큘럼을 계속 따를 수 있어. 그러니 자네가 다음 학기에 3학년이 된다면 새 커리큘럼에 대해서는 걱정할 필요가 없을 것 같은데.

학생: 아, 그거 다행이네요. 새 커리큘럼을 따르면, 저는 선수 과목들을 포함해서 여덟 과목을 더 수강해야 하거든요. 한 학기 전체가 낭비되는 거죠.

교수: 우리는 당연히 그런 문제가 생기지 않기를 바라지.

학생: 잘됐어요. 저는 스스로 학비를 대는데요, 교수님도 아시다시피 공부와 일을 동시에 병행하는 것은 너무 힘들어요.

교수: 나도 알지. 자네의 성실한 노력이 가상하네.

학생: 그렇게 말씀해 주셔서 고맙습니다. 안녕히 계세요, Evans 교수님.

학생이 교수를 찾아간 이유는?

(A) 새 커리큘럼을 준수해야 하는지 알아보기 위해
(B) 전공에 필요한 새 필수 과목들에 대해 물어보기 위해
(C) 과정을 이수하려면 아직 몇 학점이 필요한지에 대해 상의하기 위해
(D) 이번 학기에 일부 과목들을 보류하는 문제를 의논하기 위해

어휘 | **prerequisite** 선수 과목 (상급 과목을 신청하기 전에 학생들이 필수적으로 들어야 하는 과목)   **tuition** (특히 대학의) 수업료, 등록금

Basic Drill
p.26

01 (C)   02 (A), (C)   03 (B)   04 (C)   05 (B)   06 (D)

01

Listen to a conversation between a student and an employee in the university's Career Services Office.

Student (F): Good afternoon. I have some questions about which summer internships I can apply for this year.

학생과 대학교 진로상담소 직원의 대화를 들으시오.

학생 (여): 안녕하세요. 올해에 제가 어떤 여름 인턴 자리에 지원할 수 있는지 문의드리려고요.

Employee (M): OK. What's your major?

Student: I'm majoring in accounting.

Employee: All right. Have you had any particular internship experiences before?

Student: Yes, I had an internship at a big accounting firm. It was last year, and at the end of it my performance was assessed and credited. I'm looking for a similar internship experience for this summer as well.

Employee: Luckily, a lot of accounting firms are looking for interns this summer. You can find the information of the firms on our website. I think you might make a great candidate because some of the firms, well, mostly big international firms, are looking for only those with internship experiences.

Student: Wonderful. How do I apply for these international firms? Is it different from applying for local firms? Last year, I sent my résumé directly to the company.

Employee: For the international firms, students can just upload their résumés to a candidate pool through our university's career website. Then the companies will review the résumés.

Student: OK. Then when should I hear whether I've been accepted?

Employee: Once you are chosen, the companies will contact you to arrange for an in-depth interview in person. It should take about ten working days until you're contacted.

직원 (남): 네. 전공이 뭐죠?

학생: 회계학을 전공하고 있어요.

직원: 좋아요. 전에 인턴 일을 해 본 적이 있나요?

학생: 네, 큰 회계 사무소에서 인턴으로 일한 적이 있어요. 작년이었는데, 인턴직 말에는 근무 성적 평가를 받았고 학점도 받았어요. 이번 여름에도 비슷한 인턴 경험을 할 만한 자리를 찾고 있어요.

직원: 다행스럽게도 이번 여름에는 많은 회계 사무소에서 인턴들을 찾고 있어요. 우리 웹사이트에서 그 회사들에 대한 정보를 얻을 수 있어요. 학생은 아주 훌륭한 인턴 후보자가 될 것 같은데요. 일부 회사가, 그러니까, 주로 큰 다국적 기업들은 인턴 경험이 있는 사람들만 찾고 있으니까요.

학생: 잘됐네요. 이런 다국적 기업들에는 어떻게 지원하나요? 지역 회사들에 지원하는 것과 다른가요? 저는 작년에 회사에 직접 이력서를 보냈거든요.

직원: 다국적 기업들의 경우에는 학생들이 우리 대학의 진로 웹사이트를 통해 이력서를 지원자 풀에 올리기만 하면 돼요. 그러면 그 회사들이 그 이력서들을 검토할 겁니다.

학생: 알겠습니다. 그러면 합격 여부는 언제 들을 수 있나요?

직원: 일단 선발이 되면, 회사 측에서 연락을 해서 심층 면접 일정을 준비할 거예요. 연락이 오기까지 근무일 기준으로 약 열흘 정도 걸릴 거예요.

대화의 주된 내용은?
(A) 인턴직을 위한 면접 일정 확인하기
(B) 대학교 진로 웹사이트에 정보 올리기
(C) 올해 여름 인턴직에 대해 문의하기
(D) 면접을 잘 보는 방법에 대한 조언 구하기

해설 | 여름 인턴 자리를 문의하러 온 학생과 진로 상담 직원의 대화이다.

어휘 | **apply for** ~에 지원하다   **major** (대학생의) 전공   **at the end of** ~의 말에   **as well** 또한, 역시   **candidate** 후보자   **local** 지역의, 현지의   **contact** 연락하다   **arrange for** 준비하다, 계획을 짜다   **in-depth** 심층적인, 심도 있는

02

Listen to part of a lecture in an American history class.

Professor (F): Now, we all know that the Civil War, fought from 1861 to 1865, was a major turning point for the United States. For one thing, it brought about the release of the slaves when President Abraham Lincoln issued the Emancipation Proclamation.

Student (M): Only the slaves in the "enemy territory" were freed, right?

Professor: Yes, Sam. Unfortunately, those in the Border States of Delaware, Maryland, Kentucky, and Missouri were not included. Also, the American Civil War is regarded as the deadliest war in the history of the United States. Both sides lost thousands of young men in just a few years. More than 600,000 people died not only from injuries in battle, but also from diseases.

미국 역사학 강의 중 일부를 들으시오.

교수 (여): 자, 우리 모두 1861년에서 1865년까지 벌어졌던 남북전쟁이 미국에 커다란 전환점이 되었다는 점을 알고 있어요. 우선 첫째로, Abraham Lincoln 대통령이 노예 해방 선언을 발표하여 노예들의 해방을 이루었어요.

학생 (남): "적지"에 살던 노예들만 해방되었어요, 맞죠?

교수: 맞아요, Sam. 안타깝게도 델라웨어, 메릴랜드, 켄터키, 미주리 같은 경계 주들에 살던 노예들은 여기에 포함되지 않았어요. 또한, 남북전쟁은 미국 역사상 가장 치명적인 전쟁으로 간주됩니다. 불과 수년 사이에 양측에서 수천 명의 젊은이가 목숨을 잃었으니까요. 60만 명 이상의 사람들이 전투에서 입은 부상뿐 아니라 질병으로도 죽었어요.

So . . . what exactly caused this destructive conflict? Well, a lot of things. Tension had been building up for a long time between the Southern States, which permitted slavery, and the Northern States, which prohibited it. Beyond that, there were many cultural differences between the two regions. The North was primarily industrial and politically progressive, while the South relied on farming and was politically conservative. These issues were exacerbated by America's expansion westward. People debated a lot about how to create new states, whether the new states should allow slavery or not, and so on. But the final spark was the South's decision to secede, or break away from the Union in 1861. This would trigger the destructive confrontation between the North and the South.

그러면… 이런 파괴적인 싸움을 일으킨 정확한 원인이 무엇이었을까요? 글쎄요, 많은 것들이 있어요. 노예제를 허용했던 남부 주들과 이를 금지했던 북부 주들 사이에는 오랫동안 긴장이 쌓여오고 있었습니다. 그 외에도 두 지역 사이에는 많은 문화적 차이가 존재했어요. 북부는 주로 산업 시설이 많고 정치적으로 진보적인 성향을 보였던 반면, 남부는 농업에 의지했고 정치적으로 보수적이었습니다. 이러한 문제는 미국이 서부 지역으로 확장해 가면서 더욱 악화되었어요. 사람들은 어떻게 새로운 주들을 만들지, 그리고 그 새로운 주들은 노예제를 허용해야 하는지 말아야 하는지 등에 대한 많은 논쟁을 벌였습니다. 그러나 최후의 도화선은 남부가 1861년 분리 독립, 즉 연방에서 탈퇴하기로 결정한 사건이었죠. 이는 북부와 남부 간에 파괴적인 대립을 일으켰습니다.

강의의 주된 내용은?
2개의 답을 고르시오.

(A) 남북전쟁의 원인
(B) 북부와 남부의 유사점
(C) 남북전쟁의 결과
(D) 북부와 남부에서의 노예제 폐지

해설 | 교수는 초반에 남북전쟁이 미국에 커다란 전환점이 되었다면서 남북전쟁의 결과들에 대해 설명한 후, "So . . . what exactly caused this destructive conflict?"라고 질문하며 미국 남북전쟁을 일으킨 원인에 대해 설명한다.

어휘 | **Emancipation Proclamation** 노예 해방 선언[해방령] (1862년 Lincoln 대통령이 선언) **bring about** 일으키다, 초래하다
Border State 경계주 (남북전쟁 전에 노예 제도를 인정하던 남부의 주 중에 북부의 노예 금지 지역에 인접해 있던 주) **industrial** 산업 시설이 많은
exacerbate 악화시키다

03

Listen to part of a lecture in a medical science class.

Professor (M): Now, if you all remember from the previous class, we discussed one of the most important medical breakthroughs in history — the discovery of antibiotic in 1928, used to wipe out infestations of bacteria. Now, despite their importance, I would like to turn our attention to some severe drawbacks to the use of antibiotics.

One of the most important ones is the rise of bacteria that are resistant to such medicine. As you all know, bacteria reproduce at a far greater rate than larger organisms. In the course of this, they tend to mutate more quickly too, and certain strains can develop that are resistant to antibiotic drugs. Well, this is made worse if antibiotic drugs kill off all other kinds of bacteria within a host. This eliminates competition for the mutated strain, which can quickly cause an infection within a host. This infection can't be effectively treated by antibiotic medicine.

In addition, though, there can be other difficulties. For one thing, some people are allergic to some types of antibiotics. While mild allergic reactions might only cause a skin rash, more severe ones can include shortness of breath, hives, and swelling of the face, lips, or tongue. Some types of antibiotics can also contribute to the formation of kidney stones and various blood and bowel disorders.

의학 강의 중 일부를 들으시오.

교수 (남): 자, 모두 이전 시간에 했던 내용을 기억한다면, 우리는 역사상 가장 중요한 의학적 발견에 대해 이야기했었죠. 바로 1928년에 체내에 침입한 박테리아를 없애기 위해 쓰이는 항생제를 발견한 것이었죠. 자, 항생제는 중요하지만, 그 사용에 따르는 몇 가지 심각한 결점에 주의를 돌려보죠.

가장 중요한 결점 중 하나는 이러한 약물에 저항력이 있는 박테리아의 출현이에요. 알다시피 박테리아는 더 큰 생물체보다 훨씬 더 빠른 속도로 번식해요. 이 과정에서 박테리아는 더 빨리 돌연변이가 되기도 하는데, 항생제에 저항력이 있는 특정 변종이 생길 수도 있습니다. 자, 만약 항생제가 숙주 내의 다른 모든 종류의 박테리아를 죽이면 문제는 더욱 심각해져요. 이는 변종의 경쟁을 없애므로, 숙주 내에서 빠르게 감염을 일으킬 수 있거든요. 이런 감염은 항생제로 효과적으로 치료할 수 없어요.

게다가, 다른 문제점들도 있을 수 있어요. 우선 특정 종류의 항생제에 알레르기가 있는 사람들이 있어요. 가벼운 알레르기 반응은 피부 발진을 일으키는 정도에 그치지만, 더 심각한 반응으로 숨가쁨, 두드러기, 얼굴, 입술 또는 혀의 부기 등이 올 수 있어요. 어떤 종류의 항생제는 신장 결석의 형성 및 다양한 혈액 질환이나 장 질환을 일으킬 수도 있어요.

강의의 주제는?

(A) 항생제를 올바르게 사용하는 방법
(B) 항생제의 부정적인 면
(C) 항생제의 발견
(D) 항생 물질 내성균의 출현

해설 | 교수는 항생제의 발견과 함께 나타난 항생제 사용의 여러 가지 문제점들을 나열해가며 설명하고 있다.

어휘 | **breakthrough** (귀중한) 발견, 큰 발전   **antibiotic** 항생제   **wipe out** 없애다, 쓸어 내다   **infestation** (기생충 등의) 체내 침입   **drawback** 결점, 단점   **resistant** 저항력이 있는, 끄떡없는   **reproduce** 번식하다   **mutate** 돌연변이가 되다   **strain** 변종   **host** (기생 동식물의) 숙주   **eliminate** 없애다   **infection** 감염   **shortness of breath** 숨가쁨   **hives** 두드러기   **kidney stone** 신장 결석   **bowel** 장, 내장

04

Listen to a conversation between a student and a professor.

Student (M): Oh, Dr. Brown. Do you have a moment?

Professor (F): Well, yes, but I have a class in about half an hour. Uh, will that be enough time to talk?

Student: Yeah. I was just coming by to talk about the paper I'm doing for psychology class. I've already written most of the paper and everything, but I'd still like to find some more resources to help with my topic.

Professor: Oh, what is it?

Student: I'm writing about the effect of television on adolescents and teenagers. So do you know any books I can use?

Professor: Well, I think that the best place to start would actually be some psychology journals we have in the library. I mean, you can use any good books you can find, but you must remember that, in the sciences, these topics are being studied all the time. You need to have the most up-to-date research, and that is going to be in the most recent journals.

Student: Yeah, that's a good point. This whole field is just so new to me. I was having a hard time figuring out how to document the sources, but I'm pretty sure I have that down pat now.

Professor: That's good to hear. Remember that I want to see some charts supporting your evidence, too.

Student: Right, I know. I just need to get some more information from those journals first.

학생과 교수의 대화를 들으시오.

학생 (남): 어, Brown 박사님. 잠깐 시간 좀 있으세요?

교수 (여): 음, 그래. 그런데 내가 30분 정도 후에 수업이 있단다. 어, 그 정도 시간이면 얘기하기 충분하겠니?

학생: 네. 제가 심리학 수업에 낼 보고서 때문에 의논을 드리려고 들렀어요. 보고서를 거의 다 쓴 상태이긴 한데, 주제에 도움이 될 만한 자료를 좀 더 찾고 싶어서요.

교수: 오, 주제가 뭐니?

학생: 텔레비전이 청소년들과 십대들에게 미치는 영향에 대해 쓰고 있는데요. 제가 이용할 만한 책을 알고 계시나요?

교수: 글쎄, 우선은 도서관에 있는 심리학 학술지부터 찾아보는 것이 가장 좋을 것 같구나. 그러니까, 네가 찾을 수 있는 좋은 책을 사용해도 되지만, 기억해야 할 것은 이 주제가 과학에서 항상 연구되고 있다는 거야. 너는 가장 최신의 연구가 필요하고 그건 가장 최신 학술지에 있을 거야.

학생: 네, 좋은 지적이세요. 이 분야 전체가 정말 저에게 새롭기만 해요. 전에는 출처를 기록하는 방법을 파악하느라 고생했는데, 지금은 완전히 이해한 것 같아요.

교수: 잘됐구나. 네 증거를 뒷받침해줄 도표도 좀 넣었으면 좋겠다는 사실도 기억해두렴.

학생: 그렇죠, 알아요. 우선은 말씀하신 학술지들에서 정보를 더 얻어야겠어요.

학생이 교수를 찾아간 이유는?

(A) 보고서에 쓸 만한 주제에 대해 논의하기 위해
(B) 보고서에 출처 표시하는 방법을 묻기 위해
(C) 보고서에 필요한 자료를 어디서 찾을지 묻기 위해
(D) 보고서에 포함된 도표에 대해 논의하기 위해

해설 | 학생은 보고서 작성에 더 많은 자료가 필요하여 도움을 얻으러 교수를 찾아 왔다.

어휘 | **come by** (잠깐) 들르다   **journal** 학술지, 저널   **adolescent** (사춘기의) 청소년   **up-to-date** 최신의   **document** (상세한 내용을) 기록하다   **have something down pat** 완전히 이해하다

05

Listen to part of a lecture in an anthropology class.

Professor (M): Today I'd like to continue our discussion on recent anthropological discoveries in South America by looking at an area of the Amazon that researchers have named El Dorado. The discovery was made possible by using satellite imagery of deforested areas of the Amazon. These images depict over 200 geometric earthworks, or "earth mounds" as some researchers refer to them. The earth mounds are made from soils rich in clay, and preliminary dating of the structures places them to be from as early as 200 A.D. The aerial images show structures that were massive in their expanse, with walls over three feet in height.

Now, one of the reasons this is an exciting discovery is that it was once believed the harsh conditions of the Amazon jungle could not support the foundation of an advanced civilization. However, as researchers continue to analyze these large buildings and monuments, they believe these structures point to the existence of a once very complex and sophisticated civilization that thrived in the Amazon before the arrival of Columbus to the Americas. Researchers are still unsure as to what exactly the earthworks were made for, but speculation is that they may have been used for ceremonial, defensive, or even astronomical purposes.

Another reason that researchers are excited about this discovery is the location of the earthworks in the Amazon area itself. While civilizations generally thrive near bodies of water, these earthworks point to a civilization that existed in the plateaus of mountainous regions away from the Amazon River.

인류학 강의 중 일부를 들으시오.

교수 (남): 오늘은 학자들이 엘도라도라고 이름 붙인 아마존 지역을 살펴봄으로써 최근 남아메리카에서 이루어진 인류학적 발견에 대한 논의를 계속하고자 합니다. 이 발견은 아마존의 벌채된 지역의 위성 사진 덕분에 이루어졌습니다. 이 이미지들에는 200개가 넘는 기하학적 토루, 또는 일부 학자들이 지칭하듯이 '흙더미'들이 묘사되어 있어요. 이 흙더미들은 진흙이 풍부하게 함유된 흙으로 만들어졌는데, 이 구조물들에 대한 예비 연대 결정 결과, 이것들의 기원은 무려 서기 200년까지 올라갑니다. 이 항공 사진들은 광대한 지역에 있고, 높이 3피트 이상의 담으로 둘러싸인 거대한 구조물들을 보여 주고 있습니다.

자, 이번 발견이 놀라운 이유 중 하나는 한때 아마존 정글의 혹독한 환경은 고등 문명의 수립을 가능하지 않게 한다고 믿었기 때문입니다. 하지만 이 거대한 건물들과 기념물들을 계속 분석하면서 학자들은 이 구조물들이 Columbus가 아메리카 대륙에 도착하기 전에 아마존 지역에서 한때 번영을 구가했던 매우 복잡하고 수준 높은 문명이 존재했음을 시사한다고 믿게 되었습니다. 학자들은 지금도 그 토루들이 정확히 무엇을 위해 만들어졌는지에 관해서는 확실히 알지 못하지만, 그것들이 아마도 의식, 방어 또는 천문학적 목적으로 사용되었을지 모른다고 추측합니다.

학자들이 이번 발견에 흥분하는 또 하나의 이유는 아마존 지역 내에서 이 토루들이 발견된 장소 자체 때문입니다. 문명들은 일반적으로 수역 근처에서 번영하는데, 이 토루들은 아마존 강에서 떨어져 있는 고원 산악 지대에 존재했던 한 문명을 시사합니다.

강의의 주된 목적은?
(A) 아마존의 삼림 파괴를 보여 주는 이미지에 대해 논의하기 위해
(B) 아마존 흙더미의 발견에 대해 논의하기 위해
(C) 근대 아마존 문명의 사례를 제시하기 위해
(D) 고대 아마존의 구조물들의 용도를 설명하기 위해

해설 | 삼림이 파괴된 아마존 지역에서 위성 사진을 통해 발견된 의문의 흙더미에 대한 강의이다.

어휘 | **anthropology** 인류학 **satellite imagery** 위성 사진 **deforested** 벌채된, 벌거숭이의 **depict** 묘사하다 **geometric** 기하학적인 **earthwork** 토루(土壘), 둑 **earth mound** 흙더미, 토제(土堤) **refer to** 지칭하다, 묘사하다 **preliminary** 예비의, 임시의 **dating** (고고학 등에서의) 연대 결정[측정] **aerial** 항공 **harsh** 혹독한 **point to** ~을 시사하다 **as to** ~에 관해서 **speculation** 추측 **astronomical** 천문학적인 **plateau** 고원

06

Listen to part of a discussion in a philosophy class.

Professor (F): OK, everyone. Today we are going to discuss one of the most influential thinkers in American history. Who has ever heard of Henry David Thoreau?

Student 1 (M): Um, I read a play based on his life one time. Didn't he spend a night in jail once for refusing to pay taxes?

철학 수업 중 토론의 일부를 들으시오.

교수 (여): 좋아요, 여러분. 오늘은 미국 역사에서 가장 영향력 있는 사상가 중 한 명에 대해 알아볼 것입니다. Henry David Thoreau에 대해 들어본 사람 있나요?

학생 1 (남): 음, 언젠가 그의 인생을 바탕으로 한 희곡을 읽은 적 있어요. 세금 내기를 거부해서 감옥에서 하룻밤 지낸 적이 있지 않나요?

Professor: Uh, yes, but we're getting a little ahead of ourselves. Let's start off with discussing Thoreau's philosophy. See, Thoreau subscribed to a belief system called Transcendentalism. It basically says that an individual can achieve a spiritual understanding that moves beyond, or transcends, the physical world. People can reach this understanding through intuition and meditation rather than through designated social methods.

This is important because it shaped many of Thoreau's attitudes toward society. He was outraged at much of the injustice he saw, like slavery and the Mexican-American War, which lasted from 1846 to 1848. He sensed that his common humanity with the victims of these atrocities transcended the laws of society, and he protested slavery and the war by refusing to pay his taxes. In fact, his theories about resisting injustice would later influence peaceful activists like Mahatma Gandhi and Martin Luther King Jr.

Student 2 (F): Didn't Thoreau live in the woods for a while, like a hermit?

Professor: Ah, yes, he built a hut in the woods behind a friend's house because he wanted to become closer to nature. He argued that this was the best way for people to live: away from society, which tends to corrupt people.

교수: 네, 맞아요, 그렇지만 우리가 좀 앞서 나갔네요. Thoreau의 철학에 대한 논의로부터 시작하죠. 자, Thoreau는 초월주의라고 불리는 신념 체계를 지지했어요. 이것은 기본적으로 사람이 물리적 세계를 넘는, 혹은 초월하는 정신적 깨달음을 이룰 수 있다는 신념입니다. 사람들은 정해진 사회적 방식보다 직관과 명상을 통해 이러한 깨달음에 도달할 수 있다고 하였죠.

이 점이 중요한 이유는 이 사상이 Thoreau가 사회를 보는 태도를 형성했기 때문입니다. 그는 1846년에서 1848년까지 지속된 멕시코–미국 전쟁이나 노예제 같은 불의에 격노하였습니다. 그는 이러한 잔학한 행위들의 피해자들에 대한 그의 공동 인류애가 사회 법규를 초월한다고 느꼈고, 세금 내기를 거부하는 방법으로 노예제와 전쟁에 반대했습니다. 사실, 불의에 저항하는 그의 이론은 훗날 Mahatma Gandhi와 Martin Luther King 2세 같은 평화 운동가에게 영향을 주게 됩니다.

학생 2 (여): Thoreau는 오랫동안 은둔자처럼 숲에서 살지 않았었나요?

교수: 아, 맞아요. 그는 자연에 더 가까워지고 싶다는 이유로 한 친구의 집 뒤에 있는 숲에 오두막을 지었습니다. 그는 이것이 사람이 사는 최고의 방법이라고 주장했어요. 사람을 부패시키는 경향이 있는 사회에서 벗어나서 말이죠.

화자들이 논의하고 있는 주된 내용은?
(A) Henry David Thoreau의 영향을 받은 사회 운동가들
(B) 노예제에 대한 Henry David Thoreau의 항의
(C) 자연 속에서의 Henry David Thoreau의 삶
(D) Henry David Thoreau의 신념

해설 | 교수는 강의 초반에서 "Let's start off with discussing Thoreau's philosophy"라고 말한 뒤, Thoreau가 지지했던 초월주의라는 신념과 이로 인해 형성된 Thoreau의 사회에 대한 태도에 대해 설명하고 있다.

어휘 | **be ahead of oneself** 앞서 나가다   **start off with** ~하는 것으로 시작하다   **subscribe to** (의견·이론 등을) 지지하다
Transcendentalism 초월주의   **intuition** 직관, 직감   **meditation** 명상   **atrocity** 잔학한 행위   **hermit** (보통 종교적 이유에 의한) 은둔자

Listening Practice

p.28

01 (B)   **02** (D)   **03** (B), (C)

Listen to part of a discussion in a marine biology class.

Professor (M): OK, today we are continuing our discussion about the octopus. Now, we all know it can be a fearsome predator, due to its lethal combination of strength and intelligence. However, the octopus also has a lot of natural enemies that it must defend itself against. Q01 As a result, it has several ways of evading, escaping, and even defending itself against these enemies. Um, who can describe some of these methods for me?

Student 1 (M): Q03(B) Well, I know that they have ink sacs that let them spray ink at an attacker.

Professor: Yes, this darkens the water and hides the octopus from view, allowing it to escape.

해양 생물학 수업 중 토론의 일부를 들으시오.

교수 (남): 좋아요, 오늘 우리는 문어에 대한 논의를 계속하도록 하겠습니다. 자, 문어는 힘과 지능의 치명적 조합으로 무시무시한 포식자가 될 수 있다는 사실은 모두가 알고 있죠. 하지만 문어 역시 천적이 많으므로 그 천적으로부터 자신을 지켜야 합니다. 그 결과, 문어는 이런 적으로부터 피하거나, 도망치거나, 심지어 방어하는 여러 가지 방법들을 갖고 있어요. 음, 누가 이러한 방법 중 몇 가지를 설명해 줄 수 있나요?

학생 1 (남): 글쎄요, 공격자에게 먹물을 쏠 수 있게 하는 먹물 주머니를 갖고 있다고 알고 있어요.

교수: 맞아요. 이것은 물을 흐려서 문어를 시야에서 숨기고, 그러면 도망칠 수 있게 되죠.

Let's, uh, take a broad look at the body of the octopus. Q02 There is no skeleton in an octopus, so it can easily squeeze itself through small, constricted spaces while fleeing from predators. It also has a propulsion method in its body cavity that allows it to fire a jet of water from its main trunk, quickly propelling it out of danger. And then, of course, there are the tentacles. Q03(C) Some octopus species are able to detach their tentacles, allowing the octopus to escape the grasp of a predator. Uh, think of this as being similar to a lizard's tail, which can also detach to allow lizards to escape danger. And one of the most remarkable abilities they have is camouflage. They can change their pigmentation in order to blend into their surroundings, virtually vanishing from sight.

Student 2 (F): Oh, can't it also appear as some other animals and trick predators, scaring them away?

Professor: Yes, it can puff itself up like a jelly fish, twist itself to appear like a sea snake, and adjust pigmentation to look like a lion fish in order to frighten other animals. Also, an octopus can also stand its ground if it absolutely has to. You should also bear in mind that it has a very sharp beak in its trunk, and it is quite strong for its size. In fact, larger species of octopus have been known to win struggles against smaller sharks.

Finally, while talking about the octopus's defenses, we must consider its remarkable intelligence, something that cannot be overemphasized. Remember, this creature is very smart, at least compared to most other invertebrates. It has a fairly complex nervous system, and some of the benefits of this are both long-term and short-term memory, the ability to distinguish between shapes and patterns, and other mental skills useful in problem-solving. So, um, it can figure out any number of ways to neutralize threats from predators and other similar dangers.

어, 좀 더 넓은 시각으로 문어의 몸을 봅시다. 문어는 뼈가 없기 때문에, 포식자로부터 도망갈 때 작고 비좁은 공간도 쉽게 비집고 들어갈 수 있죠. 또한 체강(體腔) 부분의 추진력 방법을 쓰면, 몸통에서 밖으로 물줄기를 분사하여 위험에서 재빨리 빠져나갈 수 있습니다. 거기다 물론 촉수도 있지요. 어떤 문어 종은 촉수를 분리할 수 있어서 포식자가 붙잡을 때 도망칠 수 있습니다. 어, 도마뱀의 꼬리와 비슷하다고 생각하면 돼요. 도마뱀 꼬리도 분리되어 도마뱀이 위험으로부터 도망칠 수 있게 해주잖아요. 그리고 문어가 가진 가장 뛰어난 능력 중 하나는 위장입니다. 주변과 뒤섞일 수 있도록 피부색을 바꾸어, 실질적으로 시야에서 사라지는 것이죠.

학생 2 (여): 아, 문어가 다른 동물처럼 보이게 해서 포식자를 속이고, 겁을 주어 쫓아버릴 수도 있지 않나요?

교수: 맞아요, 문어는 다른 동물들을 겁주기 위해, 자기 몸을 해파리처럼 부풀리고, 바다뱀처럼 보이도록 제 몸을 비틀고, 쏠배감펭처럼 보이려고 피부색을 조절할 수가 있어요. 또한, 문어는 꼭 필요할 때는 대항할 수 있어요. 그리고 문어의 몸통 안에는 매우 날카로운 부리가 있으며, 그것은 크기에 비해 꽤 세다는 사실도 명심하세요. 사실상, 더 큰 문어 종들은 작은 상어 정도는 싸워서 이긴다고 알려져 있어요.

마지막으로, 문어의 방어력에 대해 우리가 생각해야 할 것은 문어의 뛰어난 지능으로, 이것은 아무리 강조해도 지나치지 않아요. 이 생물이, 적어도 대부분의 다른 무척추동물과 비교하였을 때, 매우 영리하다는 사실을 기억해 두세요. 문어는 꽤 복잡한 신경계를 갖고 있는데, 그로 인한 이점은 장기 및 단기 기억력, 형체나 무늬를 구별할 수 있는 능력, 문제 해결에 유용한 다른 정신적 기술들을 갖는다는 점이에요. 그러니까, 음, 문어는 포식자의 위협이나 다른 유사한 위험들을 무효화시킬 방법을 무수히 생각해 낼 수 있지요.

01 화자들이 논의하는 주된 내용은?
(A) 문어를 위협하는 자연계의 다양한 포식자
(B) 문어가 적으로부터 어떻게 자신을 보호하는지
(C) 문어가 먹이를 추적하는 방법
(D) 문어가 어떻게 먹이를 소화하는지

해설 | Main Idea 교수는 문어가 자신을 방어하는 방법을 묻고 학생들은 문어가 포식자의 공격을 피하는 여러 방법을 답하고 있다.

02 교수가 포식자들과 관련하여 문어의 몸에 대해 말하는 것은?
(A) 동물들을 녹이는 물질을 분사할 수 있다.
(B) 외피를 벗겨내 문어가 도망갈 수 있게 한다.
(C) 단단한 골격이 있어 공격으로부터 보호한다.
(D) 몸이 연해서 문어가 비좁은 공간을 비집고 들어갈 수 있게 해 준다.

해설 | Detail 문어는 골격이 없는 무척추동물로서 위험에 처했을 때 작고 비좁은 공간도 쉽게 비집고 들어갈 수 있다.

03 문어는 포식자부터 어떻게 도망가는가?
2개의 답을 고르시오.
(A) 다른 동물처럼 보임으로써
(B) 먹물을 쏨으로써
(C) 촉수를 분리함으로써
(D) 고음의 소리를 냄으로써

해설 | Detail 교수는 문어가 포식자를 만나면 먹물을 분사하여 시야를 흐리게 하거나 촉수를 떼어내어 도망간다고 설명한다.

어휘 | **fearsome** 무시무시한   **predator** 포식자   **due to** ~ 때문에   **lethal** 치명적인   **evade** 피하다
sac (동식물 체내에서 액체·가스가 들어 있는) 주머니   **squeeze through** (억지로) 비집고 들어가다   **constricted** 비좁은, 수축된
propulsion 추진력   **cavity** (해부·동물) 체강(體腔)   **tentacle** 촉수   **detach** 분리하다   **camouflage** 위장
pigmentation [생물] (색조 형성에 의한) 피부색   **vanish** 사라지다   **stand one's ground** 대항하다   **blend into** ~와 뒤섞이다
trick 속이다   **bear in mind** 명심하다   **compared to** ~와 비교하여   **invertebrate** 무척추동물   **neutralize** 무효화시키다

Chapter 02 Detail

Sample Question

p.31

Listen to part of a discussion in an American history class.

Professor (F): Now, in Central America between two to three thousand years ago, there existed an ancient civilization known as the Olmec. Much of what we know about them comes from the excavation of an ancient city known as La Venta, located on the southern coast of Mexico on the Gulf of Mexico and first excavated in the 1940s. Who can tell me some things we've found there?

Student 1 (M): Well, there are those giant stone head monuments, right?

Professor: Yes, that's the most famous discovery. These statues of rulers are 9 feet high and weigh about 18 tons, but they are just one amazing find. There's also a large central clay mound that resembles a volcano, large mosaics representing jaguar masks, and elaborate stone altars. Now, these altars contain some interesting features. What might those be?

Student 2 (F): Are you talking about the images of their gods, the weird jaguar-babies?

Professor: Right. Some of them have carved figures that look like a mixture of a jaguar and a human infant. Most people believe that these depict some kind of divine being that was worshipped. This has been found in Olmec monuments from other locations, too.

미국 역사학 수업 중 토론의 일부를 들으시오.

교수 (여): 자, 2~3천 년 전 중앙아메리카에는 올메크라고 알려진 고대 문명이 있었습니다. 그 문명에 대해 우리가 알고 있는 것의 많은 부분은 멕시코 만의 멕시코 남부 해안에 있고 1940년대에 처음 발굴된 라 벤타라는 고대 도시의 발굴로 알게 된 것입니다. 그곳에서 우리가 발견한 것들에 대해 누가 말해줄 수 있나요?

학생 1 (남): 음, 거대한 돌 두상 유적들이 있지 않나요?

교수: 네, 그것이 가장 유명한 발견물이죠. 이 통치자들의 상은 9피트 높이에 무게가 18톤 정도 나가는 어마어마한 유적이지만, 이것만이 전부가 아니랍니다. 화산을 닮은 커다란 중앙 진흙 고분과 재규어 얼굴을 표현한 거대 모자이크, 그리고 정교한 돌 제단도 있습니다. 자, 이 제단에는 흥미로운 특징들이 있는데요. 그게 무엇일까요?

학생 2 (여): 그 이상하게 생긴 재규어-아기 형상의 그들의 신에 대해 말씀하시는 건가요?

교수: 맞아요. 그중 일부에는 재규어와 인간의 아기를 섞은 듯한 형상의 조각이 있어요. 대다수의 사람들은 이 조각들이 사람들이 숭배했던 일종의 신성한 존재를 묘사한 것이라고 믿고 있습니다. 이것은 다른 지역에 있는 올메크 유적지들에서도 발견되었습니다.

올메크인들의 신을 묘사한 라 벤타의 유물은?
(A) 거대한 두상
(B) 중앙 진흙 고분
(C) 도시에서 발견된 거대한 모자이크
(D) 돌 제단의 조각

어휘 | **excavation** 발굴　**monument** 유적, 기념물　**mound** 고분, 흙무더기　**resemble** ~을 닮다　**represent** 표현하다, 나타내다　**elaborate** 정교한　**altar** 제단　**weird** 이상한, 기묘한　**infant** 아기, 유아　**divine** 신성한, 신의　**worship** 숭배하다

Basic Drill

p.32

01 (D)　**02** (A), (D)　**03** (B)　**04** (B)　**05** (B), (D), (E)　**06** (A)

01

Listen to a conversation between a student and a professor.

Student (F): Hey, Dr. Conway, can I come in for a minute?

Professor (M): Sure, Becky. What is it that you need?

Student: Ah, well, I was coming by because I need your help. See, I'm applying for this internship with a major company over

학생과 교수의 대화를 들으시오.

학생 (여): 안녕하세요, Conway 박사님. 잠깐 들어가도 될까요?

교수 (남): 그럼, Becky. 무슨 일이지?

학생: 아, 그게요. 교수님의 도움이 필요해서 들렀어요. 그러니까, 제가 이번 여름 방학에 대기업 인턴직에 지원하려고요. 한정된 수의 인턴 자리를 놓고 경쟁이

the summer. There's going to be a lot of competition for a limited number of internships, so my résumé needs to be as strong as possible. I was hoping that you could write a letter of recommendation for me.

Professor: Hmm, OK. What will you be doing as an intern?

Student: I'll basically be learning what chemical engineers do. I'm majoring in chemistry because I'd like to go into an engineering program.

Professor: Well, I'd be glad to help, but I'm not sure how much help I'll be. I know lots about history, but not much about chemical engineering. It would probably look better if you got someone from the science department to write a recommendation.

Student: That's true, but many professors there have already written recommendations for other students who asked before I did.

Professor: Well, I'm sure you can find someone. And I'll be happy to help, but my recommendations are more useful for getting into graduate school or getting teaching jobs.

치열할 것 같아요. 그래서 이력서를 최대한 잘 써야 해요. 교수님께서 추천서를 써주시길 바라고 있어요.

교수: 음, 알았다. 인턴으로 무슨 일을 하게 되니?

학생: 주로 화학 공학자들이 하는 일을 배우게 될 거예요. 저는 공학 과정에 들어가고 싶어서 지금 화학을 전공하는 거거든요.

교수: 글쎄, 도와주고는 싶다만, 내가 얼마나 도움이 될지는 잘 모르겠구나. 내가 역사에 대해서는 많이 알지만, 화학 공학 쪽으로는 잘 모르거든. 만약 네가 이학부에서 추천서를 써 줄 사람을 구하면 추천서가 더 좋아질 텐데.

학생: 맞아요. 하지만 그쪽 교수님 중 많은 분들이 이미 저보다 먼저 부탁한 다른 학생들에게 추천서를 써주셨거든요.

교수: 글쎄, 그래도 누군가는 찾을 수 있을 거야. 그리고 나는 기꺼이 도와주겠지만, 내 추천서는 대학원에 들어가거나 교사직을 구하는 데 더 유용할 거란다.

학생에게 추천서가 필요한 이유는?

(A) 공학 과정에 들어가기 위해
(B) 교직에 지원하기 위해
(C) 대학원에 진학하기 위해
(D) 여름 인턴으로 일하기 위해

해설 | 학생은 여름방학 기간에 지원할 인턴 자리의 경쟁이 치열하므로 이력서를 최대한 잘 쓰기 위해 교수의 추천서가 필요하다고 설명하고 있다.

어휘 | limited 한정된   résumé 이력서   major in ~을 전공하다   science department 이학부(理學部)

02

Listen to part of a lecture in an earth science class.

Professor (F): OK, during the Stone Age, humans crafted objects for daily use from a variety of substances. One of the most common substances was obsidian. Obsidian is a material found throughout the world in areas rich in volcanic activity. It is an igneous rock, which means that it is formed when hot molten rock from inside the earth cools as it flows to the surface. This molten rock cools very rapidly, resulting in the smooth, almost glass-like texture of obsidian. It is usually black in color, but if the molten rock mixes with certain minerals while cooling, obsidian can take on other colors, such as brown or green.

Now, let's get back to the use of obsidian by early humans. Early humans found obsidian to be a very versatile substance that could be used in multiple ways. Since it is very brittle, meaning it is hard but easily broken, early humans found it to be an ideal substance to make sharp objects used for cutting, such as knives. Some evidence also points to obsidian having been used in making weapons. And . . . in addition, obsidian was also used for a variety of decorative purposes. Because of its highly reflective glassy surface, it was also polished into mirrors and even combined with other gemstones to create beautiful jewelry, such as earrings and pendants.

지구과학 강의 중 일부를 들으시오.

교수 (여): 좋아요, 석기 시대에 인간들은 다양한 물질로 일상에서 쓸 물건들을 만들었어요. 가장 흔히 사용한 물질 중 하나가 흑요석이에요. 흑요석은 전 세계에 걸쳐서, 화산 활동이 많은 지역에서 발견되는 물질이죠. 이것은 일종의 화성암이에요. 즉, 이것은 지구 내부에서 나온 고열의 녹은 암석이 지표면을 흐르면서 냉각될 때 형성된다는 말이죠. 이 녹은 암석은 급속히 냉각되면서 부드럽고, 거의 유리 같은 질감의 흑요석이 돼요. 이것은 대체로 검은색을 띠지만, 녹은 암석이 냉각되는 과정에서 특정의 광물과 결합하면 다른 색깔, 예를 들면 갈색이나 초록색을 띠기도 하죠.

자, 초기 인류에 의한 흑요석의 사용으로 돌아갑시다. 초기 인류는 흑요석이 다양한 방법으로 사용될 수 있는 매우 다목적의 물질임을 알게 되었습니다. 이 돌은 매우 잘 깨지기 때문에, 즉 단단하지만 쉽게 부서지기 때문에 초기 인류는 이것이 칼처럼 물건을 자르는 데 쓸 수 있는 날카로운 물체를 만드는 데 이상적인 물질임을 알게 되었어요. 몇몇 증거들은 또 흑요석이 무기를 만드는 데에도 쓰였다는 것을 시사해요. 또… 추가로, 흑요석은 다양한 장식적인 목적에도 사용되었어요. 이 돌의 반사력이 큰 유리 같은 표면 때문에, 사람들은 이 돌을 닦아 거울을 만들거나, 다른 원석들과 결합하여 귀걸이와 펜던트 같은 아름다운 보석을 만들기도 했어요.

초기 인류가 흑요석 사용을 선호한 두 가지 이유는?

2개의 답을 고르시오.

(A) 작은 조각으로 쉽게 부서져 도구를 만들 수 있다.
(B) 화산 주변의 지역에서 쉽게 채집할 수 있다.
(C) 이것의 다양한 색깔은 장식 목적에 유용하다.
(D) 이 돌의 표면은 빛을 매우 잘 반사한다.

해설 | 교수는 흑요석이 잘 부서져 도구 만들기에 용이하고, 빛을 잘 반사하여 거울이나 보석을 만드는 데에 쓸모가 많아 초기 인류가 선호하였다고 설명한다.

어휘 | **substance** 물질　**obsidian** 흑요석　**rich in** ~이 많은, ~이 풍부한　**igneous rock** 화성암　**molten** 녹은　**result in** (결과적으로) ~이 되다, 일으키다　**mineral** 광물　**versatile** 다목적의　**multiple** 다양한, 많은　**brittle** 깨지기 쉬운, 부서지기 쉬운　**point to** ~을 시사하다, 나타내다　**reflective** 빛을 반사하는　**gemstone** 보석의 원석(原石)　**pendant** 펜던트(목걸이 줄에 걸게 되어 있는 보석)

03

Listen to part of a lecture in a psychology class.

Professor (M): Let's get started with the lesson. Today we're looking at the fascinating Milgram experiment, set up by psychologist Stanley Milgram during the early 1960s. In this experiment, Milgram told several people that they would be asking a man in another room several questions. They were then instructed to shock the man for giving wrong answers.

Student 1 (F): This sounds pretty harsh.

Professor: Oh, don't worry. The shocks weren't real, and the man himself was a hired actor, reading pre-written answers to the questions. But the questioners didn't know any of this.

Student 2 (M): [Bewildered] Then what was the point of all this?

Professor: Well, Milgram wanted to see if people would compromise their ethics when ordered by an authority figure. So he tested whether people would actually shock the man with increasingly more powerful shocks when ordered to by the lead researcher. Now, many questioners expressed concern about the man's well-being, but they were assured that they would not be held responsible for his fate. Thus, despite their protests, most of them did as instructed. I should point out one of the motivations for this experiment.

After World War II, the Nazis were being put on trial for their horrible crimes, particularly those in the concentration camps. Most of the officers being tried claimed that they were simply following orders. Hearing this, Milgram wondered if people were really capable of doing such things merely because they were ordered to. The results of this controversial experiment indicated that most people are.

심리학 강의 중 일부를 들으시오.

교수 (남): 수업을 시작하도록 하죠. 오늘은 1960년대 초에 심리학자 Stanley Milgram이 고안한 매우 흥미로운 Milgram 실험에 대해 알아보겠습니다. 이 실험에서 Milgram은 몇 명의 사람들을 모아 놓고 그들이 다른 방에 있는 한 남자에게 몇 개의 질문을 할 것이라고 말했어요. 그리고 그들은 만약 그 남자의 대답이 틀리면 충격을 가하라는 지시를 받았죠.

학생 1 (여): 좀 가혹한 것 같은데요.

교수: 오, 걱정하지 마세요. 충격은 실제가 아니었고, 다른 방의 그 남자는 질문에 대해 미리 쓰인 답을 읽도록 고용된 배우였어요. 하지만 질문자들은 이것에 대해서 전혀 몰랐죠.

학생 2 (남): [놀라서] 그러면 이 실험을 하는 게 무슨 소용이죠?

교수: 그게, Milgram은 권위를 가진 사람이 명령을 내리면 사람들이 자신의 윤리와 타협할지에 대해 알아보고자 한 것이에요. 그래서 책임 연구자가 지시하면, 그 지시에 따라 실제로 그 남자에게 점점 강도를 높여 충격을 줄지 안 줄지 실험한 것이죠. 자, 많은 질문자가 남자의 상태에 대해 우려를 표했지만, 그들에게 그 남자의 운명에 대해 책임을 묻지 않을 거라고 확실히 해 두었답니다. 그러자, 반대하면서도, 대부분의 사람은 지시를 받은 대로 실행했어요. 이 실험을 하게 된 동기 중 하나에 대해 짚고 넘어가야겠군요.

제2차 세계 대전 이후 나치는 그들이 저지른 끔찍한 범죄 행위, 특히 포로수용소에서 저지른 행위에 대해 재판에 세워졌습니다. 재판에 세워진 대부분의 장교들은 자신들이 단순히 명령을 따랐을 뿐이라고 주장했죠. 이 말을 들은 Milgram은 사람들이 순전히 그런 명령을 받았다는 이유로 그런 일을 정말 실행할 수 있는지 궁금해했어요. 이 논쟁거리가 된 실험의 결과는 대부분의 사람들이 그렇다는 것을 보여주었죠.

Milgram 실험이 실험하고자 했던 것은?

(A) 포로수용소를 감시하는 효과적인 방법
(B) 사람들이 비도덕적인 명령에 복종하는지 여부
(C) 사람들이 감당할 수 있는 전류의 양
(D) 처벌 시 옳게 대답할 수 있는 능력

해설 | "Then what was the point of all this?"라는 학생의 질문에 대해 교수는 권위를 가진 사람이 명령했을 경우 사람들이 자신의 윤리와 타협할지를 알아보고자 한 것이라고 설명하고 있다.

어휘 | **compromise** 타협하다　**ethics** 윤리, 가치 체계　**authority** 권위　**put on trial** 재판에 세우다　**concentration camp** 포로수용소　**officer** 장교, 공무원

04

Listen to a conversation between a student and a university administrator.

Student (M): Hello, I was wondering if I could put these posters on bulletin boards around the university.

Admin. (F): What are they about?

Student: They're promoting a fundraising event for the Department of Childhood Education.

Admin.: A fundraising event?

Student: Yes. There are six early childhood centers run by our university, and as an event organizer, the head of the Department of Childhood Education will host this fundraising event to seek financial support for the department and to build soft playgrounds at all six centers.

Admin.: You mean like sponge floors, ball pools, and inflatable castles?

Student: Exactly.

Admin.: That sounds wonderful. I hope the event goes successfully.

Student: Thank you.

Admin.: My pleasure. Anyway, how many do you plan to post?

Student: Frankly speaking, as many as I can. Plus, I want to place my posters where students can easily notice them, such as in the Student Learning Center, the main library, and the school cafeteria.

Admin.: There are 14 bulletin boards around the university, including those places you mentioned. So, if you leave the posters with us, we will put them up for you. However, you are not allowed to place posters this big on the bulletin boards at faculty or department buildings, as only A5 format is allowed.

Student: I didn't know there is a size limit. Thank you for the notice.

Admin.: You're welcome. And just to be clear, the posters on bulletin boards will be removed after two weeks, just to be fair to those who are waiting for their turn to put up their own.

학생과 대학교 관리자의 대화를 들으시오.

학생 (남): 안녕하세요. 이 포스터를 대학 구내 게시판에 붙일 수 있는지 알아보러 왔습니다.

관리자 (여): 무슨 포스터인데요?

학생: 아동교육학과에서 하는 모금 행사를 홍보하는 거예요.

관리자: 모금 행사요?

학생: 네. 우리 대학에서 운영하는 유아 센터가 여섯 군데가 있는데요. 행사 조직자인 아동교육학과장님이 이 모금 행사를 주최하여 학과의 재정 지원도 받고 여섯 군데의 센터 모두에 푹신한 놀이터를 만들어 주려고 해요.

관리자: 스펀지 바닥, 공 풀장, 공기주입식 고무 성 같은 거 말인가요?

학생: 맞아요.

관리자: 훌륭한 계획인 것 같아요. 행사가 성공하기를 바랍니다.

학생: 고맙습니다.

관리자: 뭘요. 그건 그렇고, 몇 장이나 붙일 계획인가요?

학생: 솔직히 말하면, 최대한 많이 붙이고 싶어요. 게다가 학생들이 쉽게 볼 수 있는 곳에 포스터를 붙이고 싶어요. 예를 들면 학생 학습관, 중앙 도서관, 학교 구내식당 같은 곳이요.

관리자: 대학 구내에는 학생이 지금 말한 곳을 포함해서, 총 14개의 게시판이 있어요. 그러니까 그 포스터를 우리에게 주면, 우리가 학생 대신 붙여 줄게요. 그런데 이렇게 큰 포스터는 교직원 건물이나 학과 건물의 게시판에 붙일 수 없어요. A5 형식만 허용되거든요.

학생: 크기 제한이 있는 것을 몰랐네요. 알려 주셔서 고맙습니다.

관리자: 천만에요. 그냥 분명히 해두고 싶어서 말씀드리는데, 게시판에 붙인 포스터는 2주가 지나면 제거될 겁니다. 자신들의 포스터 붙일 차례를 기다리는 사람들과 형평성을 맞춰야 하니까요.

학생이 교직원 건물 게시판에 포스터를 붙일 수 없는 이유는?

(A) 2주 동안 대기자 명단에 올라야 한다.
(B) 학생이 가져온 포스터의 크기가 너무 크다.
(C) 교직원 건물의 게시판은 교직원에 대한 공지문 전용이다.
(D) 학생은 학부로부터 허가를 받지 못했다.

해설 | 관리자는 이렇게 큰 포스터를 게시할 수 없다며, A5용지 크기의 포스터만 가능하다고 말한다.

어휘 | **bulletin board** 게시판 **fundraising event** 모금 행사 **early childhood** 유아(기) **host** 주최하다 **inflatable** (공기나 가스로) 부풀리게 되어 있는 **faculty** (대학의 한 학부의) 교수단, 학부

05

Listen to part of a discussion in a zoology class.

Professor (M): OK, everyone. You all remember what we discussed last time? We talked about how spotted hyenas are powerful, vicious hunters. What physical and behavioral features make them so deadly? Any idea? Yes, Jane?

Student 1 (F): Well, they have sharp eyesight and good hearing at night. And . . . they can run fast and for long distances. These features are all very helpful in hunting. What else . . . also, they have powerful upper bodies and jaws.

Professor: You're right, Jane. Despite what most people think, spotted hyenas don't just scavenge for what lions left behind. They hunt and kill in packs, 95 percent of what they eat coming from hunting.

Student 2 (M): Yeah, they hunt just about any animal they can find, including small hippos. I even heard that they can eat a whole zebra leaving almost no leftovers.

Professor: Very good. They can dissolve almost anything in their stomachs. Now, today we'll be looking at the female of the species. There are a few interesting things about the female spotted hyena. First, she is the more muscular and aggressive of the two sexes. Second, she has a unique anatomy which makes it impossible for males to mate with her without her consent. So essentially, she gets to select her mates, which is unusual among mammals. For all these reasons, spotted hyena societies are matriarchal, meaning the females have all the power in their societies. Even baby girl cubs dominate the boys. This status is especially important when rearing young, since the dominant females can take as much food as they want.

다음 중 점박이 하이에나에 대해 옳은 것은?

3개의 답을 고르시오.

(A) 암컷은 수컷보다 몸집이 더 작다.
(B) 수컷은 암컷보다 사회적 권력이 더 작다.
(C) 약하고 병든 동물들만 사냥한다.
(D) 강한 위산을 갖고 있다.
(E) 암컷이 번식을 위한 짝을 고른다.

해설 | 점박이 하이에나는 거의 모든 먹이를 위에서 분해할 수 있다고 했으므로 위산이 강력하다는 점을 추론할 수 있으며, 또한 독특한 신체 구조를 갖는 암컷이 짝을 고르게 되는데, 이러한 이유로 암컷이 하이에나 사회의 모든 권력을 갖고 있다고 설명하고 있다.

어휘 | **vicious** 잔인한, 포악한　**deadly** 치명적인, 생명을 앗아가는　**scavenge for** ~을 찾아다니다　**leftover** (식사 후에) 남은 음식　**dissolve** 분해하다, 녹이다　**muscular** 근육이 발달한　**aggressive** 호전적인　**anatomy** 해부학적 구조　**consent** 동의, 허락　**matriarchal** 모계 중심의　**cub** (곰·사자·여우 등의) 새끼　**dominate** 지배[군림]하다　**dominant** 우세한

06

Listen to part of a lecture in an art history class.

Professor (F): Over the past few sessions, we've been talking a lot about the works of the very influential Spanish painter Pablo Picasso. We've covered the surreal imagery of many of his early paintings and how this all led to Cubism, a new style of painting that redefined twentieth-century art. Well . . . Jim, can you explain

미술사 강의 중 일부를 들으시오.

교수 (여): 우리는 지난 몇 번의 수업에 걸쳐, 매우 영향력 있는 스페인 화가인 Pablo Picasso의 작품에 대해 많은 것을 알아보았습니다. 그의 초기 그림의 초현실주의적인 이미지와 이것이 어떻게 20세기 예술을 재정의한 새로운 그림 양식인 입체파로 이어졌는지도 다루었죠. 음… Jim, 입체파에 대해 간단히 설명해 보겠어요?

briefly about Cubism for class?

Student (M): Yes. Um . . . as we all can see from Picasso's works, in Cubist artwork, the artists analyze, break up, and reassemble objects in an abstracted form.

Professor: Thank you, Jim. Let's move on to some of Picasso's later works. In particular, we will be looking at the famous painting entitled *Guernica*. Now, *Guernica* is in Picasso's signature style – in particular, it has a bizarre appearance, trying to show all the angles of different subjects at once. However, this painting is very different in that the images are very disturbing. We see people screaming, dying, and holding dead bodies – much grimmer than his other work. This is because *Guernica* was painted as a protest against the bombing of the Spanish town Guernica. Um, for those who may not know, here's the whole story. In the 1930s, Spain was in the middle of a horrible civil war between republican forces and fascists. In fact, this conflict was something of a warning of World War II. In 1937, Spain's fascist forces bombed the town Guernica in one of the war's most brutal episodes. Disgusted by this, Picasso decided to depict the horror as only he could, hoping that it would rouse support against the fascists in Spain.

학생 (남): 네. 음… Picasso의 작품들을 보면 모두 알 수 있듯이, 입체주의 미술 작품에서 미술가는 대상을 추상적인 형태로 분석하고, 분해하고, 재조립합니다.

교수: 고마워요, Jim. 그러면 오늘은 Picasso의 후기 작품으로 넘어가 보도록 할게요. 특히, 〈게르니카〉라는 제목의 유명한 그림에 대해 알아볼 거예요. 자, 〈게르니카〉는 Picasso의 대표적 양식으로 그려졌습니다. 특히 한 번에 여러 가지 주제를 모든 각도로 보여주려 하는 기이한 형태를 하고 있다는 데서 그렇죠. 그러나 이 그림은 이미지가 매우 충격적이란 점에서 다른 작품들과 매우 다릅니다. 사람들이 비명을 지르고 죽어가고 시체를 안고 있는 모습이 등장하며, 그의 다른 작품보다 훨씬 섬뜩하죠. 이것은 〈게르니카〉가 게르니카라는 스페인 마을에 대한 폭격에 항의하는 의미로 그려졌기 때문입니다. 음, 모르는 사람을 위해서 이야기의 전말을 소개하죠. 1930년대에 스페인은 공화당 세력과 파시스트 간에 벌어진 끔찍한 내전 한가운데에 있었습니다. 사실, 이 전쟁은 제2차 세계 대전의 전초전과도 같은 것이었어요. 1937년 이 전쟁의 가장 잔인한 사건 중 하나로 스페인의 파시스트 세력은 게르니카 마을을 폭격했습니다. 이에 환멸을 느낀 Picasso는 스페인 파시스트에 반대하는 여론을 일으키기를 바라며, 그만의 방법으로 그 공포를 그리기로 했습니다.

Picasso가 〈게르니카〉를 그린 이유는?

(A) 스페인 마을의 파괴를 비난하기 위해
(B) 입체파를 가장 잘 반영한 미술작품을 창작하기 위해
(C) 제2차 세계 대전에 반대하는 시위를 벌이기 위해
(D) 스페인의 군사력을 기념하기 위해

해설 | 교수는 강의 후반부에서 스페인 파시스트가 게르니카 마을에 폭탄을 투여했던 사실을 언급하며, Picasso가 그러한 스페인 파시스트에 반대 여론을 불러 일으키기 위해 이 그림을 그렸다고 설명하고 있다.

어휘 | **surreal** 초현실주의의   **cubism** 입체파, 큐비즘   **bizarre** 기이한, 별난   **disturbing** 충격적인, 불온한   **grim** 섬뜩한, 불길한   **republican** 공화당(국)의   **fascist** 파시스트, 국수주의자   **brutal** 잔인한   **depict** 그리다, 묘사하다

Listening Practice

01 (D)   **02** (C)   **03** (B), (C)

Listen to a conversation between a student and a professor.

Student (F): Hey, Professor Clark.

Professor (M): Good morning, Jessica. What's up?

Student: Well, I was looking through the syllabus for our Modern British literature class, and I saw that there were four required texts on there.

Professor: Correct.

Student: Um, but at the bookstore, the total cost for all these books is over two hundred dollars. And there aren't any used copies of them left, so all I would be able to get would be the new ones, which are way more expensive. Q01 So I was thinking about saving some money by not buying some.

Professor: *[Apprehensive]* I see. How exactly would you do this?

Student: Well, I have an older version of the short story anthology that you have listed here. So I can just use that, right? I mean,

학생과 교수의 대화를 들으시오.

학생 (여): 안녕하세요, Clark 교수님.

교수 (남): 안녕, Jessica. 무슨 일이지?

학생: 그게, 현대 영국 문학 강의 계획서를 훑어봤는데 필요한 교재가 네 권이 있는 걸 봤어요.

교수: 맞아.

학생: 어, 그런데 서점에서 이 모든 교재의 총 가격이 200달러가 넘더라고요. 게다가 중고 서적은 남아 있는 게 없어서 새것을 살 수밖에 없는데, 가격이 훨씬 더 비싸요. 몇 권을 사지 않으면 돈을 아낄 수 있지 않을까 생각하고 있어요.

교수: *[염려하며]* 그렇구나. 정확히 어떻게 할 생각이지?

학생: 그게, 여기 목록에 나와 있는 단편 소설 작품집의 옛날 버전이 저한테 있거든요. 그것을 그냥 사용해도 되지 않나요? 제 말은 같은 소설에 많은 돈을 쓸

why spend a lot of money just for the same stories?

Professor: Q02 Because the anthology I have listed on there has some new analyses that aren't included in the older versions. And believe me, we will be going over a lot of these analyses throughout the semester.

Student: OK, I understand. But what about the book of critical essays? These should be pretty easy to find online, or even in the library.

Professor: I don't believe so. Q03(C) The essays in that book are new, and they were actually written specifically for that book. That means they won't appear in any literary journals or anywhere else. Q03(B) And besides, you won't be able to find it in the school library.

Student: Really? Why not?

Professor: Because the library does not circulate classroom textbooks. Makes sense, really. After all, the school makes money by selling these books, so why make them accessible for free?

Student: I see, and I guess I'll also have to buy the history book and James Joyce novel you have listed on the syllabus.

Professor: Actually, the Joyce novel will probably be available in the library, since it is not technically a textbook. Or if you prefer, you'll probably be able to find it easily in any public library. Also, I can recommend a bookstore off campus that usually carries these materials. They're a little bit cheaper than the campus bookstore, too.

Student: Well, that'll help a little, I suppose.

필요는 없잖아요?

교수: 내가 목록에 올려놓은 작품집에는 옛날 버전에 없는 분석 자료가 새로 실려 있기 때문이야. 그리고 내 말을 믿어도 좋아. 이번 학기 내내 그 분석 자료들을 많이 다루게 될 거야.

학생: 네, 알겠습니다. 하지만 평론책은 어떤가요? 이런 평론문들은 인터넷이나 도서관에서도 찾기 쉽잖아요.

교수: 그렇지 않아. 그 책에 나와 있는 평론문들은 새로운 글인데다, 특별히 그 책을 위해서 쓰였단다. 어떤 문학 학술지나 다른 곳에서는 찾을 수 없을 거라는 의미란다. 게다가 그 책은 학교 도서관에서도 찾을 수 없을 거야.

학생: 정말이요? 왜죠?

교수: 왜냐하면 도서관에서 수업 교재는 대출을 해주지 않거든. 그도 그럴 것이, 학교가 이 책들을 판매해서 돈을 버는데 왜 무료로 사용할 수 있게 하겠니?

학생: 알겠어요, 그리고 강의 계획서 목록에 교수님이 올려놓으신 역사책하고 James Joyce의 소설도 사야 할 것 같은데요.

교수: 사실 Joyce의 그 소설은 엄밀히 말해서 교과서라고 할 수 없기 때문에 도서관에서 빌릴 수 있을 거야. 혹은 네가 원한다면, 어느 공립 도서관에서나 쉽게 찾을 수 있을 거야. 또는 이 교재들을 팔 만한 교외의 서점을 소개해줄 수도 있단다. 교내 서점보다는 좀 더 저렴하기도 할 거야.

학생: 글쎄요, 조금은 도움이 되겠네요.

01 학생이 교수를 찾아간 이유는?
(A) 지역 도서관에 대한 정보를 얻기 위해
(B) 수강 과목의 강의 계획서에 대해 물어보기 위해
(C) 다른 버전의 교재에 대해 논의하기 위해
(D) 수업에 들어가는 돈을 절약하는 방법을 의논하기 위해

해설 | Main Idea 학생은 수업에 필요한 책의 값이 비싸다며 교수에게 돈을 절약하기 위해 사지 않아도 되는 책이 있는지 문의하고 있다.

02 교수에 따르면, 학생이 새 버전의 단편 소설 작품집이 필요한 이유는?
(A) 새로운 연습 문제가 들어가 있다.
(B) 책의 구성이 바뀌었다.
(C) 새로운 분석 자료가 들어가 있다.
(D) 영국 역사를 논하고 있다.

해설 | Detail 학생이 왜 똑같은 소설인데 많은 돈을 들여 새 책을 사야 하는지 묻자, 교수는 새 버전의 작품집에는 기존 책에는 없는 분석 자료들이 새로이 수록되었기 때문이라고 설명하고 있다.

03 다음 중 교수가 평론책에 대해 말한 것은?
2개의 답을 고르시오.
(A) 인터넷에서 무료로 제공된다.
(B) 학교 도서관에서는 구할 수 없다.
(C) 평론문들은 새로이 쓰였다.
(D) 학생은 그 책의 새로운 버전을 살 필요가 없다.

해설 | Detail 교수는 평론문들이 이 책을 위해 특별히 쓰였으며, 이 평론문들은 교과서이기 때문에 학교 도서관에서 대출해 주지 않을 것이라고 말하고 있다.

어휘 | anthology 작품집, 명시선   critical essay 평론문   accessible 사용할 수 있는   technically 엄밀히 말해서

Chapter 03 Function

Sample Question

p.37

Listen to a conversation between a student and a professor.

Student (F): Professor Johnson, I'd like to ask some quick questions about the presentation on the local public art project.

Professor (M): Sure, come on in.

Student: Basically, you asked us to find local public arts that contain instrumental value rather than intrinsic value. I understand that I should look beyond mere aesthetic value, but isn't it too broad? I'm not really sure where to focus.

Professor: Good question. 🎧 When looking for instrumental value, it doesn't mean simply looking for functions and other aspects completely detached from the aesthetic perspective. But rather, through the artwork, there should be something educative, something that could create convenience, boost local and tourist attendance, and provide employment . . . Do you follow me?

Student: Yes, I get it. So there should be benefits resulting from the artwork, but they can manifest in a variety of ways, either from its artistic meaning or its function.

Professor: Exactly. So what was your topic for the presentation?

Student: I was going to talk about the big traffic light tree in Canary Wharf, but now that I think of it, I need to find a better example.

학생과 교수의 대화를 들으시오.

학생 (여): Johnson 교수님, 지역 공공 미술 프로젝트에 대한 프레젠테이션에 관해 급히 여쭤볼 것이 있습니다.

교수 (남): 그래, 들어오렴.

학생: 기본적으로 교수님은 우리에게 본질적 가치보다 도구적 가치가 있는 지역의 공공 미술품을 찾아보라고 하셨잖아요. 저는 단순한 미학적 가치 이상의 것을 찾아야 한다고 생각하는데요, 너무 범위가 넓지 않나요? 어디에 초점을 맞춰야 할지 잘 모르겠어요.

교수: 좋은 질문이야. 도구적 가치를 찾을 때는 단지 미학적 관점에서 완전히 동떨어진 기능들과 기타 측면들을 찾는 것은 아니란다. 하지만 오히려 그 미술품 안에 뭔가 교육적이고, 뭔가 편의를 창조하고, 현지인이나 관광객들의 참여를 유도할 수 있고 고용을 창출할 수 있는 것이 있을 거야… 내 말 알아듣겠니?

학생: 네, 알겠어요. 그러니까 미술품들이 주는 이점들이 있지만, 그것들은 다양한 방식으로 나타날 수 있다는 말씀이죠. 그것의 예술적 의미 아니면 기능을 통해서요.

교수: 맞아. 그런데 네 프레젠테이션의 주제는 뭐니?

학생: 카나리 워프에 있는 커다란 신호등 나무에 대해 이야기하려고 했는데요, 생각해보니 더 좋은 예를 찾아야 할 것 같아요.

대화의 일부를 다시 듣고 질문에 답하시오.
교수가 다음과 같이 말하는 이유는?
"Do you follow me?"
(A) 학생에게 논의를 계속하기 위해 나중에 오라고 요청하기 위해
(B) 학생에게 설명해줄 것이 많이 남아 있지 않은 것을 나타내기 위해
(C) 정중한 방법으로 학생과의 대화를 중단하기 위해
(D) 학생이 그의 말을 이해하고 있는지 확인하기 위해

어휘 | **instrumental** 도구적인   **intrinsic** 본질적인   **aesthetic** 미학적인   **manifest** 나타나다

Basic Drill

p.38

| 01 (A) | 02 (C) | 03 (B) | 04 (C) | 05 (C) | 06 (A) |

01

Listen to a conversation between a student and a clerk at the Student Health Center.

Clerk (F): *[Greeting]* Hello. What can I do for you today?

Student (M): Hi, I just started attending the university this week, and I needed to speak with a doctor. I, uh, have asthma and some allergy problems, so I might have to get lots of treatment here in the future.

학생과 학생 건강 센터 직원의 대화를 들으시오.

직원 (여): *[환영하며]* 안녕하세요. 오늘은 무엇을 도와드릴까요?

학생 (남): 안녕하세요, 저는 이번 주부터 대학에 다니기 시작했고 의사에게 진료를 받아야 해서요. 저는, 어, 천식하고 약간의 알레르기가 있어요. 그래서 앞으로 여기서 치료를 많이 받아야 할지도 모르겠어요.

Clerk: OK, that's not a problem. Um, may I see your student ID, please?

Student: Uh, sure. Here.

Clerk: Thanks. *[Pause]* OK, John Bailey, right?

Student: Right.

Clerk: Great. 🎧 Well, according to your record, you have been assigned to Group 5, which is headed by Dr. McCarthy. I can schedule an appointment with him sometime tomorrow, if you'd like.

Student: Uh, sure. But I don't get the whole "Group 5" deal.

Clerk: Ah, pardon me. Because this is such a big school, we've organized this Student Health Center into six miniature groups, and each group consists of a team of doctors, nurses, and other medical workers. Upon enrollment, each student is assigned to a specific group. This allows a single group to get familiar with your medical history and needs, making it easier and more efficient for everyone.

Student: OK, that makes sense. But tell me, can I change my group if I want to later on?

Clerk: Oh, yes, absolutely.

Student: That sounds great.

직원: 네, 괜찮습니다. 음, 학생증을 보여 주시겠어요?

학생: 네, 물론이죠. 여기요.

직원: 고마워요. *[잠시 후]* 좋아요, John Bailey, 맞죠?

학생: 맞아요.

직원: 좋아요. 음, 기록에 따르면 McCarthy 박사님께서 담당이신 5번 그룹에 배정되어 있네요. 원한다면, 내일 그 선생님하고 예약해 줄 수 있어요.

학생: 어, 네. 그런데 '5번 그룹'이 무엇인지 이해가 안 되네요.

직원: 아, 미안해요. 우리 학교는 규모가 크기 때문에 학생 건강 센터를 6개의 소그룹으로 묶고, 각 그룹은 한 팀의 의사와 간호사, 그리고 다른 의료 직원들로 구성되거든요. 등록하는 즉시, 각 학생은 특정 그룹에 배정을 받아요. 그러면 한 그룹에서 학생의 병력과 필요 사항들을 좀 더 잘 알 수 있고, 그럼으로써 모두에게 더 편하고 더 효율적이죠.

학생: 네, 이해가 가네요. 하지만 나중에 제가 원한다면 그룹을 바꿀 수도 있나요?

직원: 오, 네. 당연하죠.

학생: 좋네요.

대화의 일부를 다시 듣고 질문에 답하시오.
학생이 다음과 같이 말하는 이유는?
"Uh, sure. But I don't get the whole "Group 5" deal."

(A) 직원에게 더 자세한 설명을 해줄 것을 요청하기 위해
(B) 직원에게 자신의 그룹을 바꿔달라고 하기 위해
(C) 배정에 대한 불쾌감을 나타내기 위해
(D) 직원에게 자신의 의료 필요 사항들을 상기시키기 위해

해설 | 학생은 직원에게 이해가 잘 안 된다고 말함으로써 직원에게 더 자세한 설명을 이끌어내고 있다.

어휘 | **asthma** 천식   **assign** 배정하다   **medical history** 병력

02

Listen to part of a discussion in an entomology class.

Professor (M): Alright, let's continue our discussion of how certain species coexist with each other by looking at the phenomenon known as symbiosis. Symbiosis is a relationship between two species in which they mutually benefit each other. In other words, they help each other out. Now, I'd like to stress the concept of a mutual benefit, since some forms of symbiosis can be parasitic, where only one species benefits. 🎧 OK, does anyone know of any examples of symbiosis?

Student (F): Um, wouldn't bees and flowers have this kind of mutual relationship, in the sense that bees spread pollen from flowers, while the flowers in return provide nourishment for the bees?

곤충학 수업 중 토론의 일부를 들으시오.

교수 (남): 좋습니다. 공생이라고 알려진 현상을 살펴봄으로써, 특정 종들이 서로 어떻게 공존하는지에 대한 논의를 계속하겠습니다. 공생은 두 개의 종이 서로에게 이익을 주는 관계를 말합니다. 다른 말로 하면, 서로를 돕는다는 것이죠. 자, 저는 여기서 상호 이익이라는 개념을 강조하고 싶어요. 어떤 공생의 형태는 한쪽만이 이익을 취하는 기생 관계가 될 수 있기 때문이죠. 자, 공생의 사례를 아는 사람 있나요?

학생 (여): 음, 벌들은 꽃의 꽃가루를 퍼뜨려 주고, 꽃들은 보답으로 벌들에게 양분을 제공한다는 의미에서 벌과 꽃이 이런 종류의 상호 관계를 맺고 있지 않나요?

Professor: Right. You're definitely on the right track! Today, I'd like to look at the specific symbiotic relationship between the Bullhorn Acacia tree and the ants that live around the tree. The relationship of these trees and ants is a little different from that of bees and flowers. You see, the Bullhorn Acacia tree lacks any kind of substances that can be used in defense against insects and animals that might feed on it. So the Bullhorn ants, which live in the hollowed-out thorns, provide the tree with protection by attacking anything harmful that might come in contact with it. The tree not only provides the ants with a place to live, but the ants also feed on protein-rich substances the tree produces, called Beltian bodies, which are essential for their survival.

교수: 맞아요. 학생은 정말 올바르게 알고 있군요! 오늘, 저는 불혼아카시아와 이 나무의 주변에 사는 개미들 간의 독특한 공생 관계를 설명하고 싶어요. 이 나무와 개미의 관계는 벌과 꽃의 관계와는 조금 다릅니다. 불혼아카시아는 이 나무를 먹고 사는 곤충과 동물을 방어하는 데 쓸 수 있는 어떤 물질도 갖고 있질 않아요. 그래서 이 나무의 움푹 파인 가시 속에 사는 불혼개미는 이 나무와 접촉할 수 있는 해로운 것은 무엇이든지 공격함으로써 나무에 보호를 제공합니다. 나무는 개미에게 살 장소를 제공할 뿐 아니라, 개미는 그 나무가 만들어내는 단백질이 풍부한 물질을 먹고 살아요. 이 물질은 벨트체(Beltian body)라고 불리는데 개미의 생존에 필수적입니다.

강의의 일부를 다시 듣고 질문에 답하시오.
교수가 다음과 같이 말할 때 의미하는 것은?
"You're definitely on the right track!"

(A) 학생에게 공생에 대해 더 자세히 설명하도록 촉구한다.
(B) 학생은 공생의 개념을 이해하지 못하고 있다.
(C) 학생이 적절한 사례를 든 것을 칭찬한다.
(D) 학생이 말한 공생의 사례는 부정확하다.

해설 | 교수는 공생의 사례를 들어 달라고 요청했고, 꽃과 벌의 사례를 제시한 학생에게 올바르게 알고 있다고 하니, 그 학생의 적절한 설명에 칭찬한 것이라고 볼 수 있다.

어휘 | entomology 곤충학   coexist with ~와 공존하다   symbiosis (서로 다른 생물체 간의) 공생(共生)   mutually 서로, 상호간에   parasitic 기생하는   in the sense that ~하는 의미에서   pollen 꽃가루, 화분   in return (~에 대한) 보답[답례]으로   be on the right track 올바른 방향으로 나아가다   feed on ~을 먹고 살다   thorn 가시   come in contact with ~와 접촉하다

03

Listen to part of a lecture in a political science class.

Professor (F): When discussing American politics in the late twentieth century, we must take a close look at the Watergate scandal, which destroyed the presidency and political career of Richard Nixon. The problem began when burglars, hired by people in President Nixon's administration, were caught stealing important documents from the Watergate Hotel offices of Nixon's political opponents.

At first, no one knew the burglars were acting on the orders of the president. Then the burglars and political officials began to provide information and names to congressional investigators. As things got worse, Nixon fired as well as demanded the resignation of many officials. This was in order to cover up his administration's guilt. In a particularly disturbing example, he even had his officials fire the federal prosecutor investigating the burglary and cover-up.

Nixon himself didn't cooperate with investigators either. When they requested that he submit a personal tape recording as evidence, Nixon provided a copy in which much dialogue was suspiciously edited out. You can just imagine how all of this looked to the country. Nixon's popularity plummeted, and he finally resigned on August 9, 1974 to avoid being impeached as a political official.

His successor, Gerald Ford, who had not been elected to either the vice presidency or presidency, pardoned Nixon, saving the disgraced president from any criminal charges. Thus, it seemed to many that the president had broken the law and would get away with it. For Americans, this created a severe and long-lasting mistrust of the federal government.

정치학 강의 중 일부를 들으시오.

교수 (여): 20세기 후반 미국의 정치에 대해 이야기할 때 우리는 워터게이트 사건을 자세히 살펴봐야 하는데, 이것은 Richard Nixon의 대통령직과 정치 경력의 파멸을 가져온 사건이에요. 이 문제는 Nixon 대통령 행정부의 사람들이 고용한 도둑들이 Nixon의 정치적 반대자들이 있던 워터게이트 호텔의 사무실에서 중요한 문서를 훔치다가 잡힘으로써 시작되었어요.

처음에는 아무도 그 도둑들이 대통령의 명령을 받고 행동했다는 사실을 몰랐어요. 그후 그 도둑들과 정치 관료들은 의회 조사관들에게 정보를 내놓고 이름을 대기 시작했죠. 상황이 악화되면서 Nixon은 많은 관료를 해고하거나 사임을 요구했어요. 이는 행정부의 죄를 은폐하기 위해서였죠. 특히 충격적인 예로, 그는 부하 직원을 시켜 이 절도 및 은폐 사건을 조사하던 연방 검찰관마저 해고했어요.

Nixon 자신도 조사관들에게 협조하지 않았어요. 조사관들이 그에게 개인 기록 테이프를 증거로 제출하라고 요청했을 때, Nixon은 대화의 많은 부분이 수상쩍게 삭제된 복사본을 제공하였어요. 여러분은 이 모든 사태가 전 국민에게 어떻게 비쳤을지 상상할 수 있겠죠. Nixon의 인기는 급락했고 그는 결국 1974년 8월 9일, 정치 관료로서의 탄핵을 피하고자 사임하였어요.

부통령직이나 대통령직에 당선되지 않은 채 후임자가 된 Gerald Ford는 Nixon을 사면하여, 이 망신 당한 대통령이 어떤 형사 고발도 받지 않도록 해 주었어요. 그래서 많은 사람에게 대통령이 법을 어기고도 처벌을 모면한 것으로 보였어요. 이 사건은 미국인들에게 연방 정부에 대한 심각하고 오래 지속된 불신을 자아냈죠.

강의의 일부를 다시 듣고 질문에 답하시오.
교수가 다음과 같이 말할 때 의미하는 것은?
"You can just imagine how all of this looked to the country."
(A) 교수는 당시 국민들의 감정을 정확히 설명할 수 없다.
(B) Nixon의 행동은 미국인들 사이에서 매우 부정적인 여론을 낳았다.
(C) Nixon의 행동에 대해 대다수 미국인들은 다른 의견들을 가졌다.
(D) 학생들은 결코 미국인들의 심경을 알지 못할 것이다.

해설 | 교수는 Nixon의 인기가 급락했고 결국 사임했다고 설명하고 있다. 즉, 앞서 언급한 Nixon의 행동이 국민들에게 부정적으로 비춰졌음을 말하려고 한 것이다.

어휘 | **scandal** (부정·횡령 등의) 사건, 추문 **presidency** 대통령직 **opponent** 반대자 **congressional** 국회의, 의회의 **investigator** 조사관 **resignation** 사임 **federal** 연방의, 연방 정부의 **prosecutor** 검찰관, 검사 **cover-up** 은폐 **submit** 제출하다 **suspiciously** 수상쩍게, 의심스럽게 **plummet** 급락하다, 폭락하다 **impeach** 탄핵하다 **successor** 후임자 **criminal charge** 형사 고발 **get away with** (벌·비난 등을) 모면하다

04

Listen to a conversation between a student and a professor.

Professor (M): Ah, Melissa, how are you these days?

Student (F): 🎧 Hi, Professor Smith. I'm doing OK. Do you have a moment to talk?

Professor: Sure, what about?

Student: It's about our test, specifically about my grade.

Professor: The test? Melissa, your class took that two days ago. I promise I'll return them in a timely manner, but I don't work that fast.

Student: That's not a problem. Actually, I don't need to get my test back to know that I did poorly on it. That's why I wanted to talk to you.

Professor: Well, what makes you so sure that you didn't do well?

Student: For starters, I only finished half the test before our time ran out. I guess I spent so much time writing the first two essays that I didn't leave myself time to finish the rest of the test.

Professor: I see. Well, I'm sorry to say it, Melissa, but effective time management is an essential academic skill, and you're going to have to learn it in order to be successful in college.

Student: [Resigned] I know. I just wanted to ask if there's enough time left in the semester for me to rebound from this test.

Professor: Well, I haven't seen your test yet, so I don't know exactly how bad the damage is, but we have almost a third of the semester remaining, and your class grades are pretty good, so I think you can probably rest easy.

Student: I'm relieved to hear that. Thank you, Professor.

학생과 교수의 대화를 들으시오.

교수 (남): 아, Melissa. 요즘 어떻게 지내니?

학생 (여): 안녕하세요, Smith 교수님. 잘 지내고 있어요. 잠깐 이야기 좀 할 수 있을까요?

교수: 물론이지, 무슨 일이니?

학생: 시험에 관한 거예요. 특히 제 점수에 관해서요.

교수: 시험? Melissa, 너희 반은 이틀 전에 시험을 봤잖니. 때가 되면 늦지 않게 돌려주겠다고 약속하마. 하지만 그렇게 빨리는 못한단다.

학생: 그건 문제가 아니에요. 사실 제 시험지를 받고 제가 못했다는 것을 확인하고 싶지는 않아요. 그래서 교수님과 이야기하고 싶었던 거예요.

교수: 글쎄, 왜 그렇게 네가 못했다고 확신하니?

학생: 우선요, 시험 시간이 다 되었는데 제가 시험지를 절반밖에 끝내지 못했거든요. 처음 두 개의 에세이를 작성하는 데 너무 많은 시간을 써버려서 나머지 시험 문제들을 끝낼 시간이 남지 않았어요.

교수: 그렇구나. 글쎄, 이렇게 말해서 미안하지만, Melissa, 효율적인 시간 관리는 중요한 학업 능력이고, 성공적인 대학 생활을 위해서는 그걸 배워야 할 거야.

학생: [체념하며] 알고 있어요. 다만 제가 이번 학기에 이 시험을 만회할 시간이 충분히 남았는지 여쭤보고 싶었어요.

교수: 글쎄, 아직 네 시험지를 보지 않아서 얼마나 나쁜지는 정확히 모르겠다만, 학기의 거의 3분의 1이 남아 있고 네 수업 성적도 꽤 좋으니까 안심해도 될 것 같구나.

학생: 그 말씀을 들으니 안심이 돼요. 고맙습니다, 교수님.

대화의 일부를 다시 듣고 질문에 답하시오.
교수가 다음과 같이 말하는 이유는?
"Melissa, your class took that two days ago."

(A) 학생에게 이미 시험을 놓쳤다는 사실을 암시하기 위해
(B) 자신과 학생이 똑같은 시험에 대해 이야기하고 있는지 명확히 확인하기 위해
(C) 아직은 시험을 채점할 수 없었음을 시사하기 위해
(D) 학생과 시험에 대해 이야기하는 것을 꺼리고 있음을 나타내기 위해

해설 | "… but I don't work that fast"라는 교수의 말을 통해, 교수는 학생에게 시험 날짜를 상기시킴으로써 시험 결과가 나오기는 아직 이르다는 것을 나타내려 했음을 알 수 있다.

어휘 | **run out** (시간·돈 등이) 다 되다   **rebound** 만회하다, 제자리로 돌아오다   **rest easy** 안심하다

05

Listen to part of a lecture in an environmental science class.

Professor (F): We've been talking about water pollution this week. As we discussed last time, pollution of our lakes, rivers, and oceans has become a serious problem, as garbage and waste products are accumulating at an alarming rate. But there is another type of pollution in water that is having a harmful effect on marine life, which is not often talked about. I'm referring to noise pollution in water.

Now, noise pollution in water is not as easily apparent as other pollutants from oil spills or waste products floating around in the water. However, the increase of human activity in water, especially with commercial shipping boats, oil and mineral extraction sites, and even motorboats, has drastically increased the amount of sound travelling underwater. 🎧 I'd like to point out that sound travels extremely fast in water, about four times faster than in air. That, however, is not the only issue. Not only does it travel faster than in air, but it covers more distance and is louder due to the high density of water. Now, you can imagine how bad the repercussions would be, right?

These human-made sounds are interfering with several species of marine life, such as whales and dolphins, which use sounds to communicate with each other over long distances. Many species of marine life also rely on underwater communication when mating, as well as warning others of oncoming predators. As you can imagine, if species of marine life cannot communicate effectively to mate or defend themselves, there is a great possibility their numbers will decrease.

환경과학 강의 중 일부를 들으시오.

교수 (여): 우리는 이번 주에 수질 오염에 대해 이야기해 왔습니다. 지난 시간에 논의했듯이, 쓰레기와 산업폐기물이 급속도로 늘어나면서 우리의 호수, 강, 바다의 오염은 심각한 문제가 되었어요. 하지만 현재 해양 생물에 나쁜 영향을 끼치고 있는 또 다른 수질 오염이 있는데, 이것은 많이 이야기되고 있지 않아요. 물속의 소음 공해에 대해 말하는 거예요.

자, 물속의 소음 공해는 물에 떠다니는 기름 유출이나 산업폐기물 같은 다른 오염원만큼 쉽게 드러나진 않아요. 하지만 특히 상업용 화물선, 석유 및 광물 채굴지, 심지어 모터보트와 더불어 물속에서의 인간 활동이 증가함에 따라 물속을 지나다니는 소리의 양도 급격하게 증가했습니다. 저는 음향의 전달 속도가 물속에서 매우 빠르며, 공기에서보다 4배 정도 빠르다는 점을 시사하고 싶어요. 그런데, 그것만이 문제가 아닙니다. 물속에서 소리는 공기에서보다 더 빠르게 전달될 뿐 아니라, 물의 높은 밀도 때문에 더 먼 거리까지 더 크게 전달됩니다. 이제는 여러분들도 이것이 얼마나 안 좋은 영향을 끼칠지 상상이 될 겁니다. 그렇죠?

인간이 만든 이러한 소리는 고래와 돌고래 같은 몇몇 해양 동물 종들의 활동을 방해합니다. 이 동물들은 소리를 이용해서 먼 거리에 있는 동료들과 서로 의사소통을 하죠. 많은 해양 생물 종들은 또 짝짓기할 때 뿐 아니라, 동료들에게 다가오는 포식자를 경고할 때에도 이같은 수중 교신에 의존합니다. 여러분들도 상상할 수 있듯이, 해양 생물 종들이 짝짓기를 하거나 자신들을 방어하기 위해 효과적으로 의사소통하지 못한다면, 이들의 개체수가 감소할 가능성이 매우 커집니다.

강의의 일부를 다시 듣고 질문에 답하시오.
교수가 다음과 같이 말할 때 의미하는 것은?
"That, however, is not the only issue."

(A) 소리는 실제로 예상보다 훨씬 더 빨리 그리고 더 멀리 전달된다.
(B) 소리가 물속에서 전달되는 속도는 가장 중요한 요소이다.
(C) 소리의 범위와 크기도 그 문제의 원인이 된다.
(D) 소리가 물속에서 매우 빠르게 전달된다는 사실은 중요하지 않다.

해설 | 교수는 그것만이 문제가 아니라고 말한 뒤, 물의 높은 밀도 때문에 소리가 더 멀리, 더 크게 전달된다고 지적하고 있다.

어휘 | **waste product** 산업폐기물   **accumulate** 늘다, 쌓이다   **at an alarming rate** 급속도로   **refer to** ~를 말하다, 나타내다
pollutant 오염물질, 오염원   **oil spill** (해상의) 기름 유출   **float** (물 위나 공중에서) 떠[흘러]가다[떠돌다]   **extraction** 채굴, 추출
due to ~ 때문에   **high density** 높은 [고]밀도   **repercussion** (어떤 사건이 초래한, 보통 좋지 못한, 간접적인) 영향
interfere with ~을 방해하다   **oncoming** 다가오는

06

Listen to part of a discussion in a literature class.

Professor (M): Now, the seventeenth century saw many wars, political upheavals, and natural disasters that forever changed England. However, this century also saw some amazing English literature composed, particularly John Milton's 1667 epic poem *Paradise Lost*. 🎧 Before we get into a detailed discussion, let's go over the plot quickly.

Student 1 (F): Why bother? Isn't the story just about the Garden of Eden from the Bible?

Professor: Yes, but not everyone here is familiar with the Bible. The poem describes how the Devil, the main villain in Christianity, starts out as an angel in heaven who rebels against God. God then sends him to Hell. In retaliation, the Devil tempts Adam and Eve, the first man and woman created by God, to sin. In turn, God exiles humans from the Garden of Eden, or earthly paradise. So that's the basic plotline. But one of the real remarkable qualities of this poem is how Milton portrays the Devil as a sympathetic figure.

Student 2 (M): OK, so how do you make the most evil character in the world sympathetic? And why?

Professor: Well, Milton's Devil is an ambitious character who can't settle for being second best; plus, he's very clever, articulate, charming, and, one could argue, brave. But Milton is only using the Devil to address the objections people usually make about God's actions. Milton brings such questions up in order to answer them and explain why they are wrong. So what Milton really meant is that while the Devil is tempting, he is ultimately wrong and doomed to fail.

문학 수업 중 토론의 일부를 들으시오.

교수 (남): 자, 17세기에는 영국을 영원히 바꿔놓은 전쟁과 정치적 격변, 자연재해가 많이 있었습니다. 하지만 이 세기에는 뛰어난 영국의 문학 작품들도 쓰였는데요, 특히 1667년 John Milton의 서사시 『실낙원』이 대표작이죠. 자세한 논의로 들어가기 전에 줄거리를 간략히 알아보도록 하죠.

학생 1 (여): 그럴 필요가 있나요? 그냥 성경에 나오는 에덴동산 이야기 아닌가요?

교수: 그래요, 하지만 여기 모두가 성경을 잘 알고 있지는 않잖아요. 이 시는 기독교의 대표적인 악역인 사탄이 천사에서 시작해 어떻게 신에게 반란을 일으키는지를 그리고 있습니다. 신은 사탄을 지옥으로 보내죠. 그에 대한 보복으로, 사탄은 신이 창조한 최초의 남자와 여자인 Adam과 Eve를 유혹해 죄를 짓게 합니다. 결국, 신은 인간을 지상 낙원인 에덴 동산에서 추방하죠. 자, 이것이 기본적인 줄거리입니다. 하지만 이 시의 정말 주목할 만한 특징 중 하나는 Milton이 사탄을 어떻게 공감을 자아내는 대상으로 그려냈는지에 있습니다.

학생 2 (남): 그런데요, 세상에서 가장 사악한 인물을 어떻게 공감되게 만들 수 있죠? 그리고 왜요?

교수: 글쎄요, Milton이 그린 사탄은 2인자가 되는 것에 만족하지 못하는 야망이 큰 인물이에요. 게다가, 매우 영리하고, 명확하고, 매력적이며, 반대할지도 모르겠지만 용감하기도 하죠. 하지만 Milton은 단지 사람들이 신의 행동에 대해 주로 제기하는 이의들에 답하기 위해 사탄을 사용한 것입니다. Milton은 그것들에 답하고 왜 틀렸는지를 설명해주기 위해 그러한 쟁점들을 제기한 것이에요. 즉, Milton이 정말로 말하고자 했던 것은 사탄이 유혹적이기는 하지만, 궁극적으로 나쁘고, 결국 실패할 운명에 처해 있다는 것이죠.

강의의 일부를 다시 듣고 질문에 답하시오.
교수가 다음과 같이 말하는 이유는?
"Yes, but not everyone here is familiar with the Bible."

(A) 정보를 좀더 줄 것임을 나타내기 위해
(B) 학생이 전적으로 옳지는 않다는 것을 시사하기 위해
(C) 모두가 이 주제를 알고 있지 않다는 것에 대해 불만을 표현하기 위해
(D) 성서 이야기에 대해 더 가르치지 않은 것을 사과하기 위해

해설 | 학생이 굳이 줄거리를 말할 필요가 있냐고 묻자, 교수는 성경에 대해 모르는 학생들이 있다며 줄거리에 대한 정보를 제공하고 있다.

어휘 | **retaliation** 보복　**tempt** 유혹하다　**exile** 추방하다　**sympathetic** 공감을 자아내는, (독자에게) 호소하는　**articulate** 명확한, 조리 있는　**doomed to** ~할 운명에 처한

Listening Practice

p.40

01 (B)　**02** (B)　**03** (C)

Listen to part of a discussion in an American history class.

Professor (F): Today we're going to continue our look at the American Revolution. Most of you should be well aware of this political upheaval, known as the first modern revolution, which occurred between 1765 and 1783.

미국 역사학 수업 중 토론의 일부를 들으시오.

교수 (여): 오늘은 미국 독립 혁명에 대한 이야기를 이어서 할 거예요. 여러분들도 최초의 근대적 혁명으로 알려져 있고, 1765년에서 1783년에 일어난 이 정치적 격변에 대해 잘 알고 있을 겁니다.

Due to this revolution, American colonists in the thirteen American colonies overturned the authority of Great Britain and established the United States of America. OK, well . . . before we start an in-depth discussion about the revolution, I'd like to talk about some events that took place before the actual fighting of the revolution began. **Q01** There were many events that helped the independence movement, which convinced many Americans to unite against the British. One such incident was the so-called Boston Massacre on March 5, 1770.

This incident occurred as tensions were building up between colonists and the British, who were increasing taxes on the American colonies. On this day, a mob of townspeople in Boston were getting kind of unruly. Before too long, the British troops opened fire and killed five male civilians and injured six others in the crowd.

Student 1 (M): **Q02** And, from what I understand, the soldiers weren't really punished for this, right?

Professor: Um, that's basically true, Alex. Only two of the soldiers were given reduced sentences.

Student 1: So to the colonists, it looked like British soldiers could just come to their towns and shoot at them without penalty. [Sarcastically] Huh, I see why Americans ended up rebelling against Britain.

Student 2 (F): But it's not as simple as you think. It was actually the crowd who started it. Even one of the people who was shot by the troops admitted, before he died, that the crowd started getting violent first. Some of them even had weapons like swords and guns, and provoked the troops by throwing objects and yelling. And despite all this, the troops followed their orders not to fire until someone fired the first shot. But no one knows who fired it.

Professor: **Q03** You're right, Selene. These are well-established facts. Alex, though, does bring up a very important point everyone should understand about the colonists' feelings. See, this incident was a valuable propaganda tool for those who hated British rule. As I previously mentioned, the British were already unpopular. Once newspapers with political agendas got hold of the story, they made it look like the soldiers were bloodthirsty brutes, and the British were tyrants. You've got to admit that this was pretty smart on their part.

---

01 토론의 주된 내용은?
(A) 미국 독립 혁명의 전투
(B) 전쟁의 도화선이 된 보스턴 학살 사건
(C) 영국 군대의 잔학 행위
(D) 정치적 의제를 효과적으로 이용하는 방법

02 강의의 일부를 다시 듣고 질문에 답하시오.
학생이 다음과 같이 말할 때 의미하는 것은?
"Huh, I see why Americans ended up rebelling against Britain."
(A) 영국 군대는 잔인성 때문에 비난 받을 만하다.
(B) 미국인들이 반란을 일으킨 이유는 분명하다.
(C) 그는 당시 식민지 주민들의 관점을 이해할 수 있기를 바란다.
(D) 반란의 원인에 대해서 더 많은 토론이 있어야 한다.

03 강의의 일부를 다시 듣고 질문에 답하시오.
교수가 다음과 같이 말하는 이유는?
"Alex, though, does bring up a very important point everyone should understand about the colonists' feelings."

(A) 주제에 관해 학생들이 자신의 의견을 표현하도록 권유하기 위해
(B) 학생들에게 이 사건의 전말을 아는 사람이 아무도 없다는 점을 상기시키기 위해
(C) 식민지 주민들이 이 사건을 어떻게 보았는지로 수업의 초점을 돌리기 위해
(D) Alex가 주제를 정확히 이해하고 있는 것을 칭찬하기 위해

해설 | Function 교수는 남학생이 식민지 주민들의 감정을 이해하는 데 중요한 사항을 제기했다고 언급하며, 식민지 주민들의 시각에서 바라본 사건에 초점을 두어 논의를 이어나가고 있다.

어휘 | **unite** 단결하다　**mob** 폭도, 군중　**unruly** 제어할 수 없는, 난폭한　**troop** 군대　**penalty** 처벌　**sword** 칼, 검　**propaganda** 선전　**agenda** 의제　**bloodthirsty** 피에 굶주린　**brute** 짐승　**tyrant** 폭군, 전제 군주

Chapter 04 Attitude

Sample Question

p.43

Listen to part of a discussion in a marine biology class.

Professor (M): We are going to take a look today at the diet of one of the marine food chain's lowest species, zooplankton. Zooplankton are extremely small organisms found in bodies of water, usually at the surface.

Student (F): I guess their small size doesn't allow them to escape easily from predators.

Professor: Well, not exactly. While it is true that they normally drift along with water currents, marine biologists have noticed that zooplankton do migrate to lower depths of water to avoid predators during the day and then go up closer to the surface of the water at night to feed on phytoplankton.

Student: So are phytoplankton their main source of food?

Professor: Umm, phytoplankton make up a large portion of their diet, but they also feed on other organic material that flows into the water from the surrounding environment. The problem is greater amounts of pollution in the environment mean that zooplankton are digesting high levels of toxins. *[Resolutely]* We urgently need more measures in place to minimize the pollutants ingested by zooplankton, as they form the base structure of marine food chain and ecosystem. The pollution has a detrimental impact on the entire food chain that will only get worse if we do nothing about it.

해양 생물학 수업 중 토론의 일부를 들으시오.

교수 (남): 오늘은 해양 먹이사슬에서 가장 아래에 있는 종의 하나인 동물성 플랑크톤의 먹이에 대해 알아보겠습니다. 동물성 플랑크톤은 물에서, 일반적으로 물의 표면에서 볼 수 있는 극도로 작은 생물체입니다.

학생 (여): 저는 그것들의 크기가 작아 포식 동물들로부터 쉽게 도망칠 수 없을 것 같은데요.

교수: 음, 꼭 그렇지는 않아요. 일반적으로 해류를 따라 떠돌아다닌다는 것은 사실이지만, 해양 생물학자들은 동물성 플랑크톤이 낮에는 포식 동물들을 피해 물에서 더 깊은 곳으로 이동했다가 밤에는 식물성 플랑크톤을 잡아먹기 위해 수면 가까이 올라온다는 사실을 발견했죠.

학생: 그러면 식물성 플랑크톤이 그들의 주요 먹잇감인가요?

교수: 음, 식물성 플랑크톤이 먹이에서 큰 비중을 차지하고 있지만, 이것들은 주변 환경에서 물로 흘러들어오는 다른 유기물들도 먹고 살아요. 문제는 바로, 늘어나는 환경 오염물질은 동물성 플랑크톤이 고도의 유독성 물질을 먹고 있다는 것을 의미한다는 거죠. *[단호한 어조로]* 동물성 플랑크톤은 해양 먹이사슬과 생태계의 하부 구조를 형성하고 있기 때문에, 우리는 동물성 플랑크톤이 먹는 오염물질을 최소화하기 위해 추가 조치가 긴급히 필요해요. 오염물질은 전체 먹이사슬에 해로운 영향을 미치는데, 이에 대해 우리가 아무것도 하지 않으면 더 악화될 거예요.

동물성 플랑크톤에 대한 교수의 태도는?
(A) 그들에 미치는 오염의 영향이 그리 크지 않다고 생각한다.
(B) 해양 먹이사슬에서의 그들의 역할에 더 많은 주의를 기울여야 한다고 주장한다.
(C) 그들에 대한 더 많은 연구가 필요하다고 주장한다.
(D) 그들의 증가하는 수는 해양 먹이사슬에 영향을 미친다고 생각한다.

어휘 | **food chain** 먹이사슬　**zooplankton** 동물성 플랑크톤　**phytoplankton** 식물성 플랑크톤　**urgently** 긴급히　**pollutant** 오염물질　**ecosystem** 생태계　**detrimental** 해로운

Basic Drill

p.44

01 (A)　**02** (B)　**03** (C)　**04** (B)　**05** (D)　**06** (D)

01

Listen to a conversation between a student and a professor.

Student (M): *[Reluctantly]* Um, Dr. Gordon, can I come in for a minute? I really need to talk to you about something.

Professor (F): Of course, Aaron. You sound so serious. What's up?

학생과 교수의 대화를 들으시오.

학생 (남): *[망설이며]* 음, Gordon 박사님, 잠깐 들어가도 될까요? 꼭 말씀드려야 할 것이 있는데요.

교수 (여): 물론이지, Aaron. 무척 심각한 것 같은데, 무슨 일이니?

Student: Well, this is kind of difficult to say, but I think I'm going to have to drop your special biology seminar.

Professor: *[Disappointed]* Oh, I see.

Student: It's nothing against you, and I really enjoy the course, but I've been looking around for a part-time job in order to save up some money. I found a waiter position that's only in the evening, and I'd have to drop your class because it's at the same time. I'm really sorry about this.

Professor: Well, Aaron, you know your priorities better than anyone else, but consider this: The seminar I'm teaching could be very helpful for your career in biology, right? And you can always find other jobs just to save some money, and you can find some that will provide better experience than being a waiter. But as for the seminar, well, who knows when you'll get the chance to study this material again?

Student: Yeah, that's a good point. But I'm still going to have to think about this some more.

Professor: OK, I understand.

학생: 음, 말씀드리기 좀 어렵지만, 제가 교수님의 특별 생물학 세미나를 그만두어야 할 것 같아요.

교수: *[실망하여]* 오, 그렇구나.

학생: 교수님에게 나쁜 감정이 있는 것은 아니고요, 저도 그 과정을 정말 잘 듣고 있어요. 하지만 제가 돈을 좀 모으기 위해서 시간제 일자리를 찾고 있었거든요. 저녁에만 일하는 식당 종업원 자리를 하나 찾았는데, 시간이 겹쳐서 수업을 그만두어야 할 것 같아요. 정말 죄송해요.

교수: 글쎄, Aaron. 너에게 무엇이 우선 사항인지는 누구보다도 네가 더 잘 알겠지. 하지만 이렇게 생각해보렴. 내가 가르치고 있는 세미나는 네 생물학 경력에 매우 큰 도움이 될 거란다, 그렇지? 그리고 돈을 모으기 위해서라면 다른 일자리도 항상 찾을 수 있고, 식당 종업원이 되는 것보다 더 좋은 경험을 할 수 있는 다른 자리를 찾을 수도 있을 거야. 하지만 세미나에 관해선, 글쎄다, 이런 내용을 공부할 기회를 언제 다시 얻을 수 있을지 누가 알겠니?

학생: 네, 좋은 지적을 해주셨어요. 하지만 전 그래도 이 문제에 대해 좀 더 생각해 보아야 할 것 같아요.

교수: 그래, 이해한단다.

학생이 일자리를 얻는 것에 대한 교수의 의견은?

(A) 자신의 수업을 듣는 것만큼 학생에게 꼭 필요한 것은 아니다.
(B) 지금함으로써 학생이 책임감 있는 사람이라는 것을 보여 준다.
(C) 다른 수업에 방해가 될 것이다.
(D) 학생에게 유용한 경력을 제공해줄 것이다.

해설 | 교수는 생물학 수업의 필요성과 함께 일자리는 언제든지 구할 수 있다고 말하면서, 일자리보다는 수업에 더 중요성을 두며 학생을 설득하고 있다.

어휘 | **drop** (하던 일·논의를) 그만두다[중단하다]   **look around for** ~을 찾아 돌아다니다   **priority** 우선 사항

02

Listen to part of a lecture in an anthropology class.

Professor (M): OK, everyone, let's take a look at the culture of the Maori, the native people of New Zealand. Like many tribal peoples, the Maori went through great hardships and cultural transformations when Europeans colonized their homeland. However, many of their traditions have survived to this day, even if the Maori spread out into urban cultures. I tell you, it's especially nice to see how these traditions are still popular among Maori youth.

Now, some practices are not done for the same reasons as they originally were, but they have been adapted into contemporary styles. For instance, many young Maori men get the distinct facial tattoos that tribesmen wore in pre-colonial days, but without going through the same rituals. Also, ritualistic war dances have been taken up by Maori male soccer players, who perform their dances to get ready for a game. Other customs have always been widely practiced. One is the *hongi*, or a unique greeting in which two people press their noses together. The Maori still hold large gatherings called *hangis*, or large feasts with steamed fish and vegetables, which are like popular barbecues. Also, large funeral wakes called *tangihangas* are still often held and attended by Maori from all over the island, as most Maori have close relationships with their extended families.

인류학 강의 중 일부를 들으시오.

교수 (남): 좋아요, 여러분, 뉴질랜드 원주민인 마오리족 문화에 대해서 살펴보도록 하죠. 많은 부족들처럼, 마오리족 역시 유럽인들이 자신들의 고향을 식민지화했을 때 큰 어려움과 문화적 변화를 겪었습니다. 하지만 마오리족 사람들이 퍼져 도시 문화권으로 유입되었음에도, 전통의 많은 부분이 오늘날까지도 살아 남았습니다. 사실, 이러한 전통이 마오리족 젊은이들 사이에서 아직도 많은 인기를 누리는 것을 보는 것은 특히나 기쁜 일입니다.

현재 몇몇 관습들은 원래의 취지대로 행해지지는 않지만, 현대 스타일에 맞추어졌습니다. 예를 들어, 많은 젊은 마오리족 남자들은 식민지 시대 이전에 부족민들이 하던 독특한 얼굴 문신을 하지만, 예전과 같은 의식을 거치지 않습니다. 또한, 마오리족 남자 축구 선수들은 의식으로 행하던 전쟁 춤을 시합에 대비하기 위해서 춥니다. 다른 풍습들도 항상 널리 행해져 왔습니다. 하나는 홍이(hongi)로 두 명이 서로의 코를 맞대는 독특한 인사법입니다. 마오리족은 아직도 항이스(hangis)라고 하는 연회를 열어 찐 생선과 야채로 성대한 연회를 엽니다. 그것은 인기있는 바베큐 파티와 같습니다. 또한, 섬 전체의 마오리족이 참석한 가운데 탕이항아스(tangihangas)라는 큰 규모의 장례식 경야가 종종 열리기도 하는데, 이는 대부분 마오리족이 그들의 대가족들과 밀접한 관계를 맺고 있기 때문입니다.

마오리족 젊은이들에 대한 교수의 태도는?

(A) 그들이 시골 고향을 떠나지 않았으면 하고 바란다.
(B) 그들이 전통 문화를 받아들인 것을 높이 평가한다.
(C) 너무 많은 이들이 자신의 전통을 잊어버려 안타깝다.
(D) 그들이 도시 문화를 좀 더 받아들였으면 하고 바란다.

해설 | "I tell you, it's especially nice to see how these traditions are still popular among Maori youth"라는 교수의 말을 통해, 마오리족 젊은이들 사이에 전통 문화가 인기를 누리는 것에 대해 기쁘게 생각하고 있음을 알 수 있다.

어휘 | **adapt** (새로운 용도·상황에) 맞추다[조정하다]   **contemporary** 현대의, 동시대의   **tribesman** 부족민   **ritual** 의식   **feast** 연회   **wake** (초상집에서의) 경야(經夜)

03

Listen to part of a discussion in a music history class.

Professor (F): Alright, everybody. As we've been discussing some of the amazing classical music and composers of the nineteenth century, we should take a quick look at one unique musician. I'm talking about the Hungarian pianist Franz Liszt. Would anyone happen to know anything about him?

Student 1 (M): Um, I've heard a little bit about him before. All I remember is that he was a really fast player.

Professor: Uh-huh, that's right. In fact, Liszt was the fastest and most impressive piano player of his day, and perhaps of all time. However, I'm speaking from a technical standpoint here. As a player, he mastered many techniques and could play with blinding speed. This gave his compositions a distinct style that is easy to recognize. Most of them, though, um, seem to be rather mechanical to me. While technically brilliant, they lack the emotion and thoughtfulness found in works by his contemporaries, particularly those of Frédéric Chopin.

Student 2 (F): So I guess that he wasn't as famous as Chopin or other composers, huh?

Professor: Oh, quite the contrary. He attracted wide, excited audiences with his incredible playing. In fact, his fame was comparable to that of modern day rock or pop stars.

음악사 수업 중 토론의 일부를 들으시오.

교수 (여): 좋아요, 여러분. 19세기의 뛰어난 고전 음악과 작곡가들에 대해 논의하는 가운데, 독창적인 음악가 한 명에 대해 간단히 살펴보아야 할 것 같네요. 제가 말하고 있는 사람은 바로 헝가리의 피아니스트인 Franz Liszt입니다. 그에 대해서 조금이라도 알고 있는 사람 있나요?

학생 1 (남): 음, 전에 그에 대한 이야기를 조금 들어본 적 있어요. 제가 기억하는 것은 그가 피아노를 정말 빨리 쳤다는 것밖에 없지만요.

교수: 네, 맞아요. 실제로 Liszt는 그가 살던 당시에, 그리고 아마도 전 시대를 통틀어, 피아노를 가장 빠르고 인상적으로 연주하는 연주가였습니다. 그러나 이것은 기술적인 면에서 그렇다는 것입니다. 연주가로서 그는 많은 기술을 연마했고 눈부신 속도로 연주할 수 있었죠. 이것이 그가 작곡한 곡에 독특한 스타일을 입혀 그의 곡인지 알아보기 쉽게 해줍니다. 하지만, 음, 대부분의 곡이 저에게는 기계적인 느낌이 들어요. 기술적인 면에서는 뛰어났지만, 동시대에 나온 다른 작품들, 특히 Frédéric Chopin의 작품에서 발견되는 정서적인 면이나 깊이 면에서는 부족하죠.

학생 2 (여): 그렇다면 그는 Chopin이나 다른 작곡가들만큼 유명하지는 않았겠네요?

교수: 오, 오히려 그 반대였어요. 그는 놀라운 연주 실력으로 많은 열혈 팬을 매혹시켰어요. 사실, 그의 명성은 오늘날의 록스타나 팝스타와 맞먹었답니다.

Franz Liszt의 작품에 대한 교수의 의견은?

(A) Frédéric Chopin의 작품보다 뛰어나다고 생각한다.
(B) 대부분의 19세기 작품들과 비슷하게 들린다고 생각한다.
(C) 뛰어난 연주 실력을 과시하지만, 별로 감동을 주지는 않는다고 생각한다.
(D) 감상자들 사이에서 더 유명해져야 한다고 생각한다.

해설 | 교수는 Franz Liszt가 기술적인 면에서는 뛰어났지만, 그의 작품들이 정서적으로 깊은 감동을 주지는 않는다고 생각하고 있다.

어휘 | **technical** 기술적인, 전문적인   **blinding** 눈을 부시게 하는, 현혹시키는   **mechanical** 기계적인   **comparable to** ~에 맞먹는

04

Listen to a conversation between a student and a clerk at the Student Service Center.

Clerk (M): Good morning. What can I help you with today?

학생과 학생 서비스 센터 직원의 대화를 들으시오.

직원 (남): 안녕하세요. 오늘은 무엇을 도와드릴까요?

Student (F): Hi, um, I came here to ask about the special outreach program run by the college's business school.

Clerk: *[Slightly puzzled]* Uh, well, there are a couple of them. Which one do you have in mind?

Student: I mean the one where students working for a business degree visit local high schools and give workshops for high school students who are interested in pursuing a business degree. You know, just giving the kids an idea of what it takes to make it through business school.

Clerk: Oh, OK. I know the program you're talking about – the HELP program. I have some information pamphlets about the program, and you can talk with people who are participating in the program for more information, too.

Student: Great.

Clerk: Now, I should mention that you have to be working on your Master of Business Administration Degree before you can participate in the program. Are you currently enrolled in that?

Student: Um, no, not yet. Does that mean I can't join the program?

Clerk: *[Apologetically]* Oh, I'm afraid not. Sorry.

Student: Well, that's understandable. It only makes sense that it should be MBA students working with the kids – they have the most experience. I can wait a little longer before I sign up for the program.

Clerk: OK. In the meantime, there are some other outreach programs in the business school I can tell you about, if you're interested.

Student: Sure. I'd appreciate it.

학생 (여): 안녕하세요, 어, 경영대학원에서 운영하는 특별 봉사 활동에 대해 문의하러 왔어요.

직원: *[약간 난처해하며]* 어, 글쎄요. 두 가지가 있는데요. 어떤 것을 생각하고 있나요?

학생: 경영학을 공부하는 학생들이 지역 고등학교에 가서 경영학 학위를 취득하는 데에 관심이 있는 고등학생들에게 워크숍을 해주는 프로그램이에요. 아이들한테 경영대학원을 다니려면 무엇을 갖춰야 하는지에 관한 정보를 주는 것 있잖아요.

직원: 오, 그래요. 무슨 프로그램을 말하는지 알겠군요. 바로 HELP 프로그램이네요. 프로그램과 관련된 정보가 담긴 팸플릿이 몇 장 있는데, 학생이 더 많은 것을 알고 싶다면 그 프로그램에 참여하고 있는 다른 사람들과 이야기해 볼 수도 있어요.

학생: 잘됐네요.

직원: 그런데, 그 프로그램에 참여하기 전에 학생이 반드시 경영학 석사 과정을 밟는 중이어야 한다는 것을 말해줘야 하겠군요. 지금 석사 과정 중인가요?

학생: 어, 아뇨, 아직 아닌데요. 그러면 제가 프로그램에 참여할 수 없다는 말씀이신가요?

직원: *[미안해하며]* 오, 미안하지만, 그래요.

학생: 음, 그럴 만도 해요. 아이들을 상대로 하려면 MBA 학생이어야 한다는 게 말이 되겠죠. 아무래도 경험이 제일 많으니까요. 그 프로그램에 들어가려면 저는 좀 더 기다려야겠네요.

직원: 그래요. 그러는 동안 혹시 관심이 있다면, 경영대학원에서 운영하는 다른 봉사 활동에 대해서 말해 줄 수 있어요.

학생: 좋아요. 감사합니다.

경영대학원에서 운영하는 특별 봉사 활동에 대한 학생의 생각은?
(A) 더 많은 신입생들에게 경영학 학위를 취득하도록 장려하는 데 도움이 된다.
(B) 자격 있는 학생들만이 참여해야 한다는 것이 타당하다.
(C) 더 많은 학생들이 참여할 수 있게 한다면 더 효과적일 것이다.
(D) 호기심 있는 고등학교 학생들을 더 많이 도울 수 있다면 더 좋을 것이다.

해설 | 경영학 석사 과정을 하고 있어야만 참여할 수 있다는 직원의 말에, 학생은 "Well, that's understandable"이라고 답하며 경험이 많은 MBA 학생이 참여하는 것이 타당하다고 말하고 있다.

어휘 | **outreach program** (정부나 사회단체에서 도움이 필요한 사람들과 연결해주는) 봉사(복지) 활동 **Master** 석사 학위 (소지자)

05

Listen to part of a lecture in a geology class.

Professor (F): As you all know very well, volcanic eruptions pose a serious threat to human life and surrounding areas. As a result, scientists who study volcanoes have developed several ways of predicting when an eruption might occur in an active volcano to avoid the potential for devastating consequences. Actually, the methods which volcanologists have come up with to determine whether an eruption will take place are quite sophisticated.

지질학 강의 중 일부를 들으시오.

교수 (여): 여러분들 모두 잘 아시겠지만, 화산 폭발은 인간의 생명과 주변 지역에 심각한 위험을 줍니다. 그 결과, 화산을 연구하는 과학자들은 대단히 파괴적인 결과를 초래할 잠재적 위험을 피하고자, 활화산에서 폭발이 일어날 수 있는 시기를 예측하는 몇 가지 방법을 개발했죠. 사실, 화산학자들이 폭발이 일어날지 여부를 판단하기 위해 생각해낸 방법들은 상당히 복잡합니다.

One of the primary methods of predicting volcanic eruptions is by measuring the seismic activity emanating from the volcano. In other words, there are more earthquakes and tremors caused by the volcano as magma flows up to the surface and creates a buildup of pressure in the tunnels beneath the volcano. This pressure buildup also causes the volcano to swell in size, which is another determining factor, referred to as volcanic deformation. A rise in the level and speed of gas emission is also a further indication of an awakening volcano, because volcanoes emit a lot of gases, especially sulphur dioxide.

Lastly, and this one seems to be the most promising, scientists are working on developing new methods of satellite imagery to track volcanic activity and make more accurate predictions of eruptions. It is important to remember that each volcano displays different patterns of activity, so a combination of methods is ideal. OK, let's take a look now at one of the most dramatic volcanic explosions in recent history, Mount St. Helens, and look at how volcanologists were able to detect early warning of eruption.

화산 폭발을 예측하는 주요 방법 중 하나는 화산에서 나오는 지진 활동을 측정하는 거예요. 다시 말해, 마그마가 지표면으로 올라와 화산 밑에 있는 터널에 압력이 증가하면 화산에 의한 지진과 미진(微震)이 더 많아지게 됩니다. 이런 압력의 증가는 또 화산을 크게 만드는데, 이것을 화산 변형이라고 하며 또 하나의 판단 요소가 되죠. 가스 방출의 수준과 속도가 높아지면 이것 역시 화산 활동의 개시를 알리는 추가적 징조인데, 화산은 많은 가스, 특히 아황산가스를 방출하기 때문입니다.

마지막으로, 그리고 이것이 가장 유망한 방법 같은데요, 과학자들은 위성 사진으로 화산 활동을 추적하고 화산 폭발을 더욱 정확하게 예측하는 새로운 방법을 개발하기 위해 연구 중입니다. 각각의 화산은 서로 다른 활동 패턴을 보이므로, 여러 방법의 조합이 이상적이라는 사실을 명심하는 것이 중요합니다. 자, 이제 현대 역사에서 가장 극적인 화산 폭발 중 하나가 일어났던 세인트헬렌스 산의 폭발을 살펴보고, 화산학자들이 어떻게 폭발의 조기 징후를 탐지할 수 있었는지를 알아봅시다.

화산 폭발을 예측하는 학문에 대한 교수의 태도는?
(A) 화산 폭발을 예측하는 것은 거의 생명을 구할 수 없을 것으로 생각한다.
(B) 폭발을 예측하는 더 안전한 방법이 필요하다고 생각한다.
(C) 폭발을 예측하는 방법들이 더 발전할 필요는 없다고 생각한다.
(D) 위성 사진이 폭발에 대한 더 많은 예측을 가능하게 해줄 것이라고 생각한다.

해설 | 교수는 위성 사진을 이용하여 폭발을 예측하는 방법을 가장 유망한 방법으로 소개하면서 이것을 이용하면 화산 활동의 추적과 폭발에 대한 더 정확한 예측이 가능해질 것이라고 말한다.

어휘 | pose a threat 위험이 되다   active volcano 활화산   devastating 대단히 파괴적인
come up with (해방, 방안 등을) 생각해내다, 제시[제안]하다   seismic activity 지진 활동   emanate from ~에서 나오다
tremor 미진(微震)   buildup 증가, 고조   swell 증가[팽창]하다, 부풀다   indication 징조, 조짐   combination 조합[결합](물)

06

Listen to part of a discussion in a history class.

Professor (M): Now we are going to look at the Seven Years' War, which lasted from 1756 to 1763, and was Europe's last major war before the French Revolution. It basically started as a dispute over some territory between Austria and Prussia, um, a German state that no longer exists. Does anyone here know anything of this conflict?

Student (F): Well, I know that Prussia essentially won under the leadership of Frederick the Great. And while his political reforms and rule were controversial, I just can't believe his skills as a strategist. I mean, he even rivals, and I'd say surpasses, the great Napoleon Bonaparte.

Professor: OK, that's good. We'll get to Frederick in a minute and discuss how impressive his leadership was, especially against an enemy coalition that included Austria, France, Russia, Spain, and several German states. But Prussia had a very valuable ally in Britain. Now, Britain's involvement was crucial in this war and its outcome. Does anyone know why?

Student: Um, didn't Britain help Prussia by fighting French colonies overseas?

역사학 수업 중 토론의 일부를 들으시오.

교수 (남): 자, 1756년부터 1763년까지 지속되었고, 프랑스 대혁명 전에 유럽에서 마지막으로 일어난 중요한 전쟁이었던 7년 전쟁에 대해 살펴보도록 하겠습니다. 원래 그 전쟁은 오스트리아와 현재는 없어진 독일의 주였던 프로이센 간의 영토 분쟁으로 시작되었습니다. 이 전쟁에 대해 조금이라도 아는 사람이 있나요?

학생 (여): 글쎄요, 제가 아는 건 프로이센이 Frederick 대왕의 지도로 전쟁에서 이겼다는 것이에요. 그리고 그의 정치 개혁과 통치는 논란의 여지가 있었지만, 전략가로서의 그의 능력은 믿기 힘들 정도예요. 제 말은, 그가 그 위대한 Napoleon Bonaparte에 대적하거나, 능가한다고도 할 수 있을 것 같아요.

교수: 그래요, 좋아요. 잠시 후에 우리는 Frederick을 살펴보고, 그의 지도력, 특히 오스트리아, 프랑스, 러시아, 스페인 및 다른 독일 국가들을 포함한 적국의 연합에 맞선 그의 지도력이 얼마나 인상적이었는지에 대해서 이야기할 거예요. 하지만 프로이센에게는 매우 귀중한 동맹국인 영국이 있었어요. 자, 영국의 개입은 이 전쟁과 그 결과에 결정적이었어요. 그 이유를 아는 사람 있나요?

학생: 음, 영국이 해외에서 프랑스 식민지들과 싸워서 프로이센을 돕지 않았나요?

Professor: Right, very good. And this is one reason why the war was so important. By dragging in the colonial territories of France and Britain, the war actually covered large parts of the globe – Asia, North Africa, and North America. It was especially important in North America because the defeat of France's side forced France to give up most of its North American territories to Britain. This put the British in control of most of North America, shaping the culture and political future of that region.

교수: 맞아요, 잘 말했어요. 그리고 바로 이것이 그 전쟁이 그토록 중요했던 이유 중 하나에요. 프랑스와 영국의 식민지들을 끌어들임으로써 그 전쟁은 실제로 아시아, 북아프리카, 북아메리카 등 지구의 많은 지역에서 일어났습니다. 이 점은 북아메리카의 경우 특히 중요한데, 프랑스 측의 패배로 프랑스가 대부분의 북아메리카 영토를 영국에 내주어야 했기 때문이에요. 그럼으로써 영국이 북아메리카 대부분을 지배하게 되었고, 그 지역의 문화와 정치적 미래를 형성하게 되었어요.

Frederick 대왕에 대한 학생의 의견은?
(A) 그는 뛰어난 정치적 지도자가 아니었다.
(B) Napoleon이 그보다 더 뛰어난 군사 전략가였다.
(C) 그의 정치적 개혁 시도는 매우 존경할 만하다.
(D) 군사 지도자로서의 그의 능력은 감탄할 만하다.

해설 | 학생은 프로이센이 Frederick 대왕의 지도로 전쟁에서 이겼음을 지적하며 전략가로서의 그의 능력은 Napoleon을 능가한다고 말하고 있다.

어휘 | **dispute** 분쟁, 논쟁 **Prussia** 프로이센 (독일 북부의 주) **reform** 개혁 **strategist** 전략가 **surpass** 능가하다 **coalition** 연합, 제휴 **ally** 동맹국 **outcome** 결과 **drag in** (사건·사고 등에) 끌어들이다 **defeat** 패배

Listening Practice p.46

01 (C) **02** (D) **03** (A)

Listen to a conversation between a student and a university administrator.

Admin. (F): What can I do for you, Jacob?

Student (M): It's about an urgent matter. I feel like it is of the utmost importance that an information center be set up on campus.

Admin.: An information center? What kind of information center?

Student: I mean a one-stop information center for incoming freshmen.

Admin.: Well, we already have department buildings where students can drop by at any time for information on each major. Plus, the student center has valuable information for students, too.

Student: Q01 Yes, that's true, but based on the three years that I've spent here at our university, I feel like there were times when I, as well as other students, did not know how to deal with certain matters or was confused about the step-by-step process for various issues. On top of that, students need some place where they can gather more information on not only educational matters, but also everyday matters such as housing, student safety, extracurricular activities, and so on.

Admin.: You feel like our current facilities are not sufficient enough?

Student: Exactly.

학생과 대학교 관리자의 대화를 들으시오.

관리자 (여): 어떻게 도와 드릴까요, Jacob?

학생 (남): 긴급한 일 때문에 왔어요. 저는 교내에 정보센터를 설립하는 것이 매우 중요하다고 생각합니다.

관리자: 정보센터? 어떤 정보센터요?

학생: 새로 들어오는 신입생들을 위한 원스톱 정보센터를 말하는 거예요.

관리자: 음, 우리 학교에는 학생들이 언제라도 들러서 전공에 대한 정보를 얻을 수 있는 학부 건물들이 이미 있잖아요. 게다가 학생센터에도 귀중한 정보가 있고요.

학생: 네, 맞아요. 하지만 제가 우리 학교에서 보낸 3년의 경험을 바탕으로 생각해보면, 저도 다른 학생들처럼 특정 문제들을 어떻게 처리해야 할지 모르거나 다양한 사안들을 처리하는 단계적 절차에 대해 혼동한 적이 있었던 것 같아요. 게다가 학생들한테는 교육적 문제뿐 아니라, 주거, 학생 안전, 과외 활동 같은 일상적인 문제들에 대해 더 많은 정보를 얻을 수 있는 장소가 필요해요.

관리자: 학생은 현재의 우리 시설들이 충분하지 않다고 생각하는군요?

학생: 맞습니다.

Admin.: Well . . . I'll take your suggestion into consideration and possibly bring it up at the next university board meeting. But as you may already know, we are not overflowing with funds, and a new facility will put a significant strain on our resources. Maybe you can search for alternative avenues to fulfill this need. How about something like an online center where there wouldn't be a need to physically build a new facility and where we wouldn't have to exhaust upkeep expenditures?

Student: I've actually already thought that idea through, but I really feel like a physical center is necessary. Some students have trouble surfing the web, and a lot of times we can't find the answers to specific questions on an online forum. Q02 As far as the financial implications of a one-stop center, I've already come up with some ideas to cut costs. For instance, we wouldn't have to build a whole new facility . . . it could be set up in an unused space on campus or even share the same space as the student center. Also, we could use student volunteers or even community volunteers.

Admin.: Q03 You do raise some valid points. I'll tell you what, if you can come up with a rigid proposal and detailed budget, I will present it at our next meeting.

관리자: 음… 학생의 제안을 검토해 보고, 가능하다면 다음 대학 이사회 때 안건으로 올려 볼게요. 하지만 학생도 이미 잘 알고 있겠지만, 우리는 자금이 넘쳐나지 않아요. 새로운 시설을 짓는 것은 우리의 재원에 큰 부담을 줄 겁니다. 아마도 학생이 이런 필요성을 충족시켜 줄 대체 방안을 찾아볼 수도 있지 않을까요? 실제로 새로운 시설을 지을 필요가 없고, 유지비를 다 써 버릴 필요도 없는 온라인 센터 같은 것은 어떤가요?

학생: 사실 그 생각도 이미 해봤는데요, 저는 실제 센터가 필요하다고 생각해요. 어떤 학생들은 인터넷 검색을 하는 데 문제를 겪고 있고요, 온라인 포럼에서 특정 문제에 대한 답을 찾을 수 없는 경우가 아주 많아요. 원스톱 센터의 금전적 영향에 대해서는, 이미 비용을 줄일 아이디어를 몇 가지 생각해 놓았어요. 예를 들어, 우리는 완전히 새로운 시설을 지을 필요는 없어요… 교내의 사용하지 않는 공간에 세워도 되고요, 학생센터가 있는 공간을 같이 써도 됩니다. 또한 우리는 학생 자원봉사자나 지역사회의 자원봉사자들도 활용할 수 있어요.

관리자: 타당한 의견을 제시해 줬어요. 있잖아요, 학생이 확실한 제안과 상세한 예산을 짜오면 내가 다음 회의 때 제시할게요.

01 현재의 학생 정보 지원 시스템에 대한 학생의 의견은?
(A) 1학년 학생들에게는 충분히 만족스럽다.
(B) 기본적인 수준에 전혀 미치지 못한다.
(C) 학생들에게 충분한 서비스를 제공하지 않는다.
(D) 약간의 수정을 거치면 완벽해질 수 있다.

해설 | Attitude   학생은 자신의 3년간의 경험을 토대로 하여, 학생들이 교육적 문제뿐 아니라 다양한 문제를 해결하는 데 충분한 정보와 지도를 받고 있지 못하다고 불평하고 있다.

02 원스톱 정보센터 건설을 실현하는 데 있어 비용을 절감하는 방법으로 학생이 제시한 예는?
(A) 임시 센터를 세우는 것
(B) 모금 행사를 벌이는 것
(C) 온라인 정보센터를 만드는 것
(D) 자원봉사자를 고용하는 것

해설 | Detail   학생은 비용 절감 방안 중 하나로 학생이나 지역사회 주민 중에서 자원봉사자를 모집할 수 있다고 말하고 있다.

03 대화 끝에서 학생의 제안에 대한 관리자의 태도는?
(A) 고려할 가치가 있다고 생각한다.
(B) 실행 가능한 방안으로 고려하지 않는다.
(C) 정보를 제공하는 최선의 방법이라고 생각한다.
(D) 엄청난 돈의 낭비라고 생각한다.

해설 | Attitude   관리자는 대화 끝에서 학생이 제안을 구체화해서 예산 계획과 함께 가져오면 회의 때 제시하겠다고 했으므로 고려할 가치가 있는 아이디어라고 보고 있는 것이다.

어휘 | **urgent** 긴급한, 시급한   **incoming** 들어오는, 도착하는   **on top of that** 게다가, 그 위에   **extracurricular** 과외의, 정식 학과 이외의   **bring up** (화제를) 꺼내다   **overflow with** ~이 넘치다[넘쳐흐르다]   **put a strain on** ~에 부담을 주다   **exhaust** 다 써 버리다, 고갈시키다   **upkeep** 유지[비]   **forum** 포럼, (토론의) 장   **implication** 영향, 결과   **come up with** ~을 생각해내다

Chapter 05 Organization

Sample Question

p.49

Listen to part of a lecture in a literature class.

Professor (F): Today we're going to discuss one of my favorite authors of all time: Victor Hugo, a great nineteenth-century French novelist. Many of you are probably familiar with some of his famous works, even if you don't realize it. A lot of them have been made into successful movies or plays you've most likely seen. For example, here's a very good one for you: *Notre-Dame de Paris*, more famously known in English as *The Hunchback of Notre Dame*. I'm pretty sure all of you have heard of this title. This novel tells the tragic story of a deformed but kind man who tries to save the woman he loves from an unruly mob in Renaissance France. The novel is an excellent examination of religious hypocrisy and social justice. My personal favorite, though, is probably *Les Misérables*, or *The Miserables*, which is now also a famous musical. This is an epic story of love and war set right before the French Revolution. In it, Hugo offers some of his most powerful criticism of Paris's social conditions and the problems of its poorer residents.

문학 강의 중 일부를 들으시오.

교수 (여): 오늘은 제가 시대를 통틀어 가장 좋아하는 작가 중 한 명인 19세기 프랑스 소설가 Victor Hugo에 대해 논의해보도록 하겠어요. 미처 깨닫지 못하고 있을 수도 있지만, 여러분 중 상당수는 아마도 그의 유명한 작품 중 일부를 알고 있을 거예요. 많은 작품이 여러분들이 보았을 법한 성공적인 영화나 연극으로 만들어졌거든요. 예를 들어, 여러분에게 매우 좋은 작품이 하나 있어요. 그것은 『노트르담 드 파리』인데, 영어로는 『노트르담의 꼽추』로 더 유명하게 알려져 있죠. 여러분 모두 이 제목을 들어봤을 겁니다. 이 소설은 프랑스 르네상스 시대에 불구의 몸이지만 착한 한 남자가 광포한 폭도들로부터 사랑하는 여자를 구하려는 비극적인 이야기입니다. 이 소설은 종교적 위선과 사회 정의를 탁월하게 그려낸 작품이죠. 하지만 개인적으로 제가 가장 좋아하는 작품은 『레미제라블』, 혹은 『비천한 사람들』이라고 할 수 있는데요, 지금은 유명한 뮤지컬도 만들어졌죠. 이것은 프랑스 혁명 직전을 무대로 한 사랑과 전쟁의 서사시입니다. 이 책에서 Hugo는 파리의 사회 환경 및 가난한 주민들이 처한 문제점에 대해 가장 강력한 비판을 합니다.

교수가 Victor Hugo를 설명하는 방식은?
(A) 그가 쓴 소설의 예를 제공함으로써
(B) 그의 영향력에 대해 설명함으로써
(C) 그를 다른 프랑스 작가들과 비교함으로써
(D) 그의 일대기를 간략하게 제공함으로써

어휘 | **hunchback** 꼽추　**tragic** 비극적인　**deformed** 불구의　**hypocrisy** 위선

Basic Drill

p.50

| 01 (B) | 02 (D) | 03 (A) | 04 (B) | 05 (C) | 06 (B) |

01

Listen to a conversation between a student and a professor.

Student (F): Professor Camden, I'm still struggling with the concept of birdsong as music, rather than just a simple signal. How can we tell that it's music? As far as I know, music is accompanied by harmony, certain rhythms, emotion, and patterns.

Professor (M): Then that is too narrow a definition for music. Think about John Cage's modern music. It is full of disharmony and irregular rhythms.

Student: Oh, that's right.

Professor: But birdsong is a lot easier to locate a harmony. Have you read the research paper that I recommended in the last class?

Student: No, I haven't yet.

학생과 교수의 대화를 들으시오.

학생 (여): Camden 교수님, 저는 새소리가 단순한 신호가 아니라 음악이라는 개념과 아직도 씨름하고 있어요. 그것이 음악이라는 것을 우리가 어떻게 알죠? 제가 알기로는, 음악은 화음, 일정한 리듬, 감정, 그리고 패턴이 수반되는데요.

교수 (남): 그렇다면 그것은 음악에 대한 정의치고는 너무 좁지. John Cage의 현대 음악에 대해 생각해 보자. 그것은 불협화음과 불규칙한 리듬으로 가득 차 있잖니.

학생: 아, 맞아요.

교수: 하지만 새소리는 화음을 찾기가 훨씬 더 쉽지. 지난 강의 시간에 내가 추천했던 연구 논문을 읽어 봤니?

학생: 아뇨, 아직이요.

Professor: Oh, I think you should. It would help you a lot. According to the paper, some experts analyzed over 110 song types from male hermit thrushes, and found that the notes in their songs fit into a harmonic series. A harmonic series is a sequence of notes based on multiples of a baseline pitch.

Student: Oh, I heard it's a principal part of human music, as it determines what aesthetically pleasing combinations are possible.

Professor: Yes, you're right.

Student: That's amazing. So birds have their own music scales.

Professor: Yes, but it's quite hasty to compare human music with birdsong. You'd better read the paper if you want a deeper understanding about the topic.

Student: OK, professor. Thank you for your time.

교수가 John Cage의 음악에 대해 이야기하는 이유는?
(A) 조화로운 현대 음악을 보여주는 사례를 들기 위해
(B) 학생의 음악에 대한 정의가 너무 제한적이라는 것을 나타내기 위해
(C) 인간의 음악을 통해 학생이 새소리를 이해하도록 돕기 위해
(D) 음악을 화음의 진행이라는 관점에서 새소리와 비교하기 위해

어휘 | birdsong 새소리, 새의 지저귐   be accompanied by ~을 수반[동반]하다   disharmony 불협화음   locate ~의 정확한 위치를 찾아내다
fit into ~에 꼭 들어맞다, 적합[적응]하다   sequence (일련의) 연속, 순서   baseline 기초, (비교의) 기준치[점]   hasty 성급한

02

Listen to part of a lecture in an archaeology class.

Professor (F): Now, today we are going to talk about Angkor Wat, one of the most impressive ancient temples found in Southeast Asia. This structure was built in twelfth-century Cambodia, then known as *Khmer*, to honor the Hindu god *Vishnu*, and it acted as a kind of burial site for the king at the time.

Now, Angkor Wat is more than just a remarkable historical find. It also has some of the most exquisite sculptural designs of any ancient building. On its extensive walls are numerous statues that represent creatures and characters from Hindu mythology. Some of these sculptures portray beautiful female goddesses and angels as well as depictions of heaven and hell from Hinduism. However, perhaps most impressive are the carvings that show episodes from two major Hindu epic poems, the *Ramayana* and the *Mahabharata*. These carvings are especially remarkable for the great detail put into showing the battles from these poems.

What is equally remarkable is how Angkor Wat has survived this long, despite all the cultural changes in the region. First off, it remained intact as Buddhism gradually replaced Hinduism over the next few hundred years. Buddhist monks actually used Angkor Wat as a monastery, and it eventually became an important destination for pilgrims. Later, when the French took over Cambodia in the nineteenth century, Angkor Wat became the subject of archaeological interest. This led to efforts to preserve it for study.

교수가 힌두교 서사시에 대해 논의하는 이유는?
(A) 앙코르와트가 지어진 본래의 이유를 설명하기 위해
(B) 크메르의 종교 예술과 시가 어떻게 변화했는지 보여주기 위해
(C) 앙코르와트에 대한 신화를 설명하기 위해
(D) 앙코르와트 조각의 주제를 묘사하기 위해

해설 | 교수는 앙코르와트 사원에 새겨진 조각들의 아름다움을 설명하면서, 그 조각들이 묘사하고 있는 것으로 힌두교 신화와 두 개의 힌두 서사시를 언급하고 있다.

어휘 | **burial site** 매장지　**exquisite** 매우 아름다운, 정교한　**intact** 온전한, 손상되지 않은　**monk** 수도승, 수도사　**monastery** 수도원　**pilgrim** 순례자　**preserve** 보존하다

03

Listen to part of a discussion in a physics class.

Professor (M): All right, the concept I'd like to look at today is how Sir Isaac Newton's third law, the principle of action and reaction, is applied to rocket science. Before doing so, let's take an example of his third law and apply it to a daily activity. When you walk, as your foot touches or "acts" on the ground, it pushes the ground backward. In turn, the ground reacts to your foot and pushes you forward. In this way, two opposing forces end up exerting themselves against each other.

Student (F): I understand that example well, but how does it apply to rockets?

Professor: OK, the key point is opposing forces working against each other. You see, the fuel inside the rocket ignites and combines with oxygen. As the fuel burns inside the engine, huge amounts of gases are discharged at the base of the rocket at an extremely high speed. These discharged gas molecules accelerate away from the rocket, creating a force which thrusts the rocket forward. Now, some scientists were skeptical that these forces would work in space, since space is a vacuum and no force would be present to act against the rocket. This is not true, however, since the opposing force is created by the exhaust discharged by the rocket, thus accelerating it forward. In other words, the rocket overcomes all other forces by using its own fuel to push against itself.

물리학 수업 중 토론의 일부를 들으시오.

교수 (남): 좋습니다. 오늘 내가 다루고 싶은 개념은 Isaac Newton 경의 제3법칙, 즉 작용과 반작용의 법칙이 로켓 과학에 어떻게 적용되는가 하는 것입니다. 그렇게 하기 전에, 그의 제3법칙을 예로 들어, 그것을 일상적인 활동에 적용해 봅시다. 여러분이 걸어갈 때 여러분의 발은 땅에 닿거나 '작용을 하고', 이때 발은 땅을 뒤로 밀어내죠. 결국, 땅은 여러분의 발에 반작용해서 여러분을 앞으로 밉니다. 이런 식으로 두 개의 반대되는 힘이 결과적으로 상대방에게 힘을 행사하는 셈입니다.

학생 (여): 그 예는 잘 이해가 되는데요, 그것이 로켓에는 어떻게 적용되나요?

교수: 자, 핵심은 대립하는 두 힘이 상대방에게 작용한다는 점입니다. 그러니까, 로켓 내부에 실린 연료는 점화되어 산소와 결합합니다. 엔진 안에서 연료가 연소될 때, 로켓의 바닥에서 엄청난 양의 가스가 초고속으로 분출되죠. 이 분출된 가스의 분자들이 로켓으로부터 고속으로 날아가면서 로켓을 앞으로 밀어 올리는 힘이 생성됩니다. 자, 일부 과학자들은 이런 힘이 우주에서도 작용할지에 대해 회의적이었습니다. 우주는 진공 상태이고 로켓에 반작용을 일으킬 힘이 존재하지 않을 것이기 때문이죠. 하지만 이것은 사실이 아닙니다. 반발력은 로켓에서 분출된 배기가스에 의해 발생하고, 따라서 이것이 로켓을 앞으로 가속화시키기 때문이죠. 다른 말로 하면, 로켓은 자체의 연료를 사용하여 몸체를 스스로 밀어 올림으로써 다른 모든 물리적 힘을 극복합니다.

교수가 Newton의 물리학과 로켓의 개념을 소개하는 방식은?
(A) 제3법칙이 일상생활에서 어떻게 발생하는지를 설명함으로써
(B) 한 학생에게 뉴턴의 제3법칙의 예를 들어보라고 요청함으로써
(C) 로켓에서 상대방에 작용하는 힘들을 자세히 설명함으로써
(D) 운동의 3가지 법칙을 하나하나 설명함으로써

해설 | 교수는 Newton의 제3법칙이 로켓 과학에 적용되는 원리를 설명하기 전에 제3법칙이 실생활에서 어떻게 적용되는지를 알아보기 위해 인간이 땅 위를 걷는 동작을 예로 삼아 설명하고 있다.

어휘 | **apply** 적용하다　**in turn** 결국[결과적으로]　**end up -ing** 결국 ~하게 되다　**ignite** 점화되다　**discharge** (기체·에너지 등을) 방출하다　**thrust** (거칠게) 밀다, 밀치다　**exhaust** (자동차 등의) 배기가스　**overcome** 극복하다, (남을) 이기다

04

Listen to a conversation between a student and a registrar.

Registrar (F): Good morning, sir. You must be Jeff, right?

학생과 학적과 직원의 대화를 들으시오.

직원 (여): 안녕하세요. Jeff 씨군요, 맞죠?

Student (M): Yes, that's me. I came by just to get some specifics about applying for graduation.

Registrar: Oh, sure. So are you going to graduate this year?

Student: I am, and I just need to know what's needed.

Registrar: Hmm, I can tell you the general requirements. First, you need to have the minimum number of credit hours.

Student: I think I'm fine on that. I'll have 120 hours completed by the end of this semester.

Registrar: Well, that is usually the minimum, but just to be safe, you should check with the department of your major. Sometimes more classes are needed, or there will be some extra stipulations. For example, some departments require special sessions in the computer lab, regardless of how many credit hours you already have. Only your department can tell you for sure, though. Oh, have you fulfilled a language requirement yet? I saw a student last semester who couldn't even apply for graduation because she hadn't met this requirement.

Student: Yes, I did it before the beginning of my third year. So . . . how do I register for graduation?

Registrar: Well, that can all be done online at the university's registration site. Here, I'll give you the address. Also, you must clear all fines on your student account before you graduate.

Student: Ah, yes, I think I have some small fines on there. I'll take care of those now. Thanks.

학생 (남): 네, 맞아요. 졸업 신청을 하는 데 필요한 세부 사항을 좀 알아보려고 들렀어요.

직원: 오, 그렇군요. 그럼, 올해 졸업하시는 건가요?

학생: 네, 그래서 필요한 게 무엇인지 알아야 해요.

직원: 음, 일반적인 요건을 알려드릴 수 있어요. 우선, 최소 이수 학점 시간을 충족시켜야 해요.

학생: 그 점에 대해선 문제가 없는 것 같아요. 이번 학기 말까지 120학점 시간을 모두 끝낼 거라서요.

직원: 어, 대개는 그게 최소죠. 하지만 혹시 모르니, 전공 학과에 확인을 해보셔야 해요. 때때로 더 많은 수업이 요구되기도 하고, 또는 다른 추가 규정이 있을 수도 있거든요. 예를 들면, 어떤 학과에서는 학점 시간을 이미 얼마나 취득했느냐에 상관없이 컴퓨터실에서 하는 특별 수업을 요구하기도 해요. 학생의 학과에서만 확실히 말해줄 수 있겠지만요. 참, 언어 필요조건을 충족시키셨나요? 지난 학기에 이 조건을 충족시키지 못해서 졸업을 신청조차 하지 못한 학생을 봤어요.

학생: 네, 3학년이 시작되기 전에 했어요. 그러면… 졸업 신청은 어떻게 할 수 있나요?

직원: 그게요, 대학교 등록 사이트를 통해 온라인으로 전부 다 하게 되어 있어요. 여기 제가 주소를 알려줄게요. 그리고 졸업하기 전에 학생 계좌에 남아 있는 모든 벌금을 내야 해요.

학생: 아, 그렇군요. 벌금이 약간 남아 있는 것 같아요. 바로 해결하도록 하죠. 감사합니다.

학적과 직원이 컴퓨터실을 언급하는 이유는?
(A) 학생에게 졸업에 필요한 강좌 중 누락된 것을 상기시켜주기 위해
(B) 추가 졸업 요건에 대한 예를 들어주기 위해
(C) 졸업 신청 절차를 설명하기 위해
(D) 다른 학과의 학업 내용과 비교하기 위해

해설 | 직원은 졸업 요건에 대해 학과에 따라 추가 규정(extra stipulations)이 있을 수 있다면서, 그 예로 컴퓨터실에서 진행되는 수업을 들었다.

어휘 | credit (이수) 학점   stipulation 규정   register for ~에 등록하다   fine 벌금

05

Listen to part of a lecture in a zoology class.

Professor (M): OK, guys, today we'll be discussing a subject I'm sure you'll all like: poisonous snakes. There are so many in the world, but for now we're just going to look at some of the most well-known.

Now, first, I'm sure all of you have heard of the king cobra. One reason why it's so famous is because, of all venomous snakes, it's the greatest in size. It grows to an average of about 12 feet, though some reach up to 18 feet in length. It covers a wide range of territory throughout Southeast Asia, and it is a very fearsome hunter that preys on other snakes.

동물학 강의 중 일부를 들으시오.

교수 (남): 자, 여러분, 오늘은 여러분들이 전부 좋아할 만한 주제에 대해 이야기하겠어요. 바로 독사랍니다. 세계에는 정말 많은 독사가 있지만, 이번 시간에는 가장 유명한 것 몇 가지만 살펴보도록 할게요.

자, 우선, 여러분 모두 킹코브라에 대해서 들어보았을 거로 생각해요. 이 뱀이 그토록 유명한 한 가지 이유는 모든 독사 중에서 크기가 가장 크기 때문입니다. 평균 약 12피트 정도까지 자라며, 어떤 것들은 길이가 18피트에 이르기도 해요. 이 뱀은 동남아시아 전역에 서식하며, 다른 뱀들을 잡아먹는 무시무시한 사냥꾼이죠.

Also famous is the black mamba, which is very large too, growing to around an average of 7 to 8 feet. It is the most dangerous venomous snake in Africa and also a fearsome hunter because of its powerful venom, its aggressive behavior, and its remarkable speed. In fact, it is the world's fastest land snake, capable of reaching speeds up to 12 miles per hour, making it especially deadly to the smaller mammals and birds it hunts.

Another famous snake is the highly venomous coral snake, which is usually less than half the size of the black mamba. This species is found throughout tropical climates in the Americas, Asia, and Africa, and it primarily preys on other snakes, as the king cobra does. In America, this snake is often confused with similar-looking but non-venomous snakes, particularly the kingsnake.

다른 유명한 뱀으로는 블랙맘바를 들 수 있어요. 이것 역시 매우 크고, 평균 7에서 8피트 정도로 자랍니다. 이것은 아프리카에서 가장 위험한 독사이며, 또 매우 강력한 독과 공격적인 습성, 놀라운 속도 때문에 아주 무서운 사냥꾼이기도 하죠. 사실, 이 뱀은 지상에서 가장 빠른 뱀으로 시속 12마일까지 속도를 낼 수 있어서, 이 뱀의 사냥감인 작은 포유류나 조류에게는 특히 치명적입니다.

또 다른 유명한 뱀으로는 독성이 매우 강한 산호 뱀이 있는데, 이것의 크기는 보통 블랙맘바의 절반도 안 돼요. 이 종은 아메리카, 아시아, 아프리카 대륙의 열대 기후 전역에서 발견되며, 킹코브라처럼 다른 뱀들을 주요 먹이로 삼습니다. 아메리카 지역에서 이 뱀은 비슷하게 생겼지만 독이 없는 다른 뱀들, 특히 왕뱀과 자주 혼동됩니다.

교수가 킹코브라를 설명하는 방식은?
(A) 다른 두 종의 독사들과 비교함으로써
(B) 독이 먹이에 얼마나 치명적인지를 보여 줌으로써
(C) 뚜렷한 특징들과 특성들을 설명함으로써
(D) 종들을 서식지의 위치에 따라 분류함으로써

해설 | 교수는 뱀 중에서 가장 유명한 킹코브라를 설명하겠다고 한 뒤, 그것의 크기와 포악한 성질 등, 킹코브라의 특징들을 소개하고 있다.

어휘 | **poisonous** 독성의 **venomous** 독이 있는 **fearsome** 무시무시한 **prey on** ~을 잡아먹다 **aggressive** 공격적인 **coral snake** 산호 뱀

06

Listen to part of a discussion in a psychology class.

Professor (F): In our discussions of the human mind, we have learned some interesting things. Well, today we are going to look at what many psychoanalysts call defense mechanisms. I'm sure at least one of you knows what these are. Yes, Terry?

Student 1 (M): I believe that they are mental behaviors that protect people from unpleasant thoughts or feelings.

Professor: Well, that's part of it. The concept was first proposed by the famous Sigmund Freud in 1894. Freud determined that some emotions are so painful that they threaten a person's mental well-being. If a person can't resolve these feelings, he will set up unconscious defense mechanisms.

Uh, here, say a man is in love with a woman who is married to his best friend. He feels extreme guilt or shame, but he cannot change his love for her. Well, according to Freud, the man's mind will set up defense mechanisms. These may cause him to ignore his love or recognize it as a different emotion that doesn't cause him guilt.

Student 2 (F): *[Hesitant]* Hmm . . . I might understand this better if I knew exactly how these mechanisms work.

Professor: Um, they actually work in many different ways. In repression, for instance, a person simply pushes a painful memory, emotion, or idea deep into their own subconscious. Research shows that this mostly happens with memories of child abuse, where a helpless child will push memories of the experience out of

심리학 수업 중 토론의 일부를 들으시오.

교수 (여): 우리는 인간의 마음에 대한 토론에서 몇 가지 흥미로운 사실들에 대해 배웠습니다. 자, 오늘은 많은 정신분석학자들이 방어 기제라고 부르는 것에 대해서 살펴볼 것입니다. 이것이 무엇인지 여러분 중 적어도 한 명은 알고 있을 거로 생각하는데요. 네, Terry?

학생 1 (남): 사람들을 불쾌한 생각이나 감정으로부터 보호하는 정신적 행동이라고 알고 있는데요.

교수: 음, 어느 정도는 맞는 말이에요. 이 개념은 1894년에 그 유명한 Sigmund Freud가 처음으로 제안했어요. Freud는 어떤 감정은 너무나 고통스러워서 사람의 정신 건강을 위협할 정도라고 규정했어요. 이런 감정을 해결하지 못하면, 무의식적으로 방어 기제를 세우게 되는 거죠.

어, 그러니까, 어떤 남자가 자신의 가장 친한 친구와 결혼한 여자와 사랑에 빠졌다고 해봅시다. 그는 극도의 죄책감과 수치심을 느끼지만, 그 여자를 향한 사랑을 바꿀 수가 없어요. 글쎄요, Freud에 따르면, 이 남자의 마음은 방어 기제를 만들 것입니다. 그로 인해 그는 자신의 사랑을 무시하거나, 혹은 그것을 자신에게 죄책감을 일으키지 않을 만한 다른 감정으로 인식하게 되죠.

학생 2 (여): [주저하며] 음, 이 방어 기제가 정확히 어떻게 작용하는지 알 수 있다면 이해가 더 쉬울 것 같아요.

교수: 음, 이것은 여러 다른 방식으로 작용합니다. 예를 들어, 억압의 경우에는 고통스러운 기억이나 감정, 생각을 잠재의식 깊은 곳에 그냥 밀어 넣습니다. 연구에 따르면, 이는 주로 아동 학대 기억이 있을 때 발생하는데, 이 경우 의지할 곳 없는 아이는 의식적인 기억으로부터 그 경험에 대한 기억을 밀어낸다고 합니다. 다른 방식으로는 감정을 무시하는 것에서 생산적인 활동으로 돌리는 것까지

conscious memory. Other methods involve everything from ignoring feelings to channeling them into productive activities. Now, let's go over some of them.

다양합니다. 자, 그중 몇 가지를 살펴보죠.

교수가 억압에 대해 논의하는 이유는?
(A) 여러 방어 기제 방법들을 대조하기 위해
(B) 방어 기제가 어떻게 작용하는지 더 명확히 설명하기 위해
(C) 방어 기제가 무엇인지 정의를 내리기 위해
(D) 방어 기제가 얼마나 심한 정신적 피해를 일으키는지 강조하기 위해

해설 | 한 학생이 방어 기제가 어떻게 작용하는지를 묻자 교수는 억압을 예로 들어 설명하고 있다.

어휘 | **psychoanalyst** 정신분석학자　**defense mechanism** [심리] 방어 기제　**resolve** 해결하다　**unconscious** 무의식의　**guilt** 죄책감　**shame** 수치심　**repression** 억압　**subconscious** 잠재의식　**child abuse** 아동 학대　**channel into** (정보·관심·노력 등을) ~으로 돌리다

Listening Practice

p.52

01 (B), (C)　　**02** (B)　　**03** (A)

Listen to a conversation between a student and a professor.

Student (F): Professor Watkins, I just wanted to double-check the content that'll be included on the midterm next week.

Professor (M): Yes, Kate, I was just drafting an e-mail to send out to the class regarding a change I made. Q01(B) I know I originally said during the lecture that it was going to be on chapters 23 and 24, but I decided yesterday to add chapter 25 also.

Student: Oh no! That's going to be a lot of info to study and review! Is there a reason you're adding chapter 25, which covers the New Deal?

Professor: Q02 Well, as you know, the Roaring Twenties and the Great Depression go hand in hand. You must talk about one if you're going to talk about the other. However, the New Deal is also just as important and closely related to the situation during that period in U.S. history.

Student: Q03 Will you be having a review session before the midterm? I think it would help a lot if you went over some of the key points you'll be covering.

Professor: [Laughing] You're one step ahead of me with everything today, Kate. I was going to add that to the e-mail as well. Q01(C) I'll be holding two review sessions. One will be tomorrow, and the second will be the day before the exam. I'm choosing to hold two so that everyone would be able to make it to at least one of them. But if you can attend both, that's also great since I will be going over different material. It'll most definitely be beneficial for you.

Student: Just in case I'm not able to make it to any of the sessions, can you tell me what will be on the test with regard to the New Deal? How much detail will we have to know about the different programs?

학생과 교수의 대화를 들으시오.

학생 (여): Watkins 교수님, 다음 주에 있을 중간고사에 포함될 내용을 한 번 더 확인하고 싶어서요.

교수 (남): 그래, Kate, 내가 바꾼 부분에 대하여 학생들에게 보낼 이메일의 초안을 작성하고 있었단다. 원래 강의 시간에는 23장과 24장이 범위라고 말한 것은 알지만, 어제 25장도 포함하기로 결정했단다.

학생: 아, 안 돼요! 그러면 공부하고 복습할 게 너무 많아져요! 25장을 추가하신 이유가 있나요? 그것은 뉴딜 정책을 다루고 있는데요.

교수: 음, 너도 알다시피, 광란의 20년대와 대공황 시기는 서로 관련돼 있단다. 한쪽을 이야기하려면 다른 한쪽도 반드시 이야기해야 하지. 그런데 뉴딜 정책도 마찬가지로 중요하고, 미국 역사에서 그 시대의 상황과 밀접하게 연관되어 있지.

학생: 중간고사 전에 복습하는 시간을 가질 예정이세요? 교수님이 포함할 핵심들을 조금 복습하면 많이 도움이 될 것 같아서요.

교수: [웃으며] 오늘 모든 면에서 나보다 한발 앞서가는구나, Kate. 그것 역시 이메일에 추가하려 했는데. 두 번의 복습 시간을 가질 생각이다. 하나는 내일이고, 두 번째 시간은 시험 전날에 있을 거야. 나는 모든 학생이 둘 중 적어도 하나의 시간에 참석할 수 있도록 두 시간을 하려고 해. 하지만 두 시간 다 참석할 수 있다면 그것도 좋지. 나는 다른 내용을 복습할 거니까. 이것은 틀림없이 너에게 이로울 거야.

학생: 혹시 제가 두 시간 다 참석하지 못할 경우가 있을까 봐 여쭤보는데요, 뉴딜 정책과 관련하여 시험에는 어떤 내용이 나올지 알려주실 수 있나요? 여러 프로그램에 대해 얼마나 자세히 알아야 하나요?

Professor: Let's see . . . You should already be well aware that the New Deal was installed under President Franklin Delano Roosevelt, and that it was in response to the severely depressed economy. Regarding the specific programs established under the New Deal, you will have to explain at least a few of them briefly. Please try to make it out to at least one of the review sessions.

교수: 글쎄… 뉴딜 정책이 Franklin Delano Roosevelt 대통령 재임 시에 도입되었고, 심각한 경제 불황에 대한 대책이었다는 것은 너도 잘 알겠지. 뉴딜 정책 하에서 수립된 특정 프로그램에 관하여는, 적어도 그중 몇 가지는 간략히 설명해야 할 거야. 복습 시간 중 적어도 한 번은 참석할 수 있도록 노력하렴.

01 대화의 주된 내용은?
2개의 답을 고르시오.

(A) 미국 역사 과목에서 학기 내내 논의할 주제들
(B) 곧 있을 중간고사에 포함될 내용
(C) 복습을 위한 추가 수업에 대한 정보
(D) 대공황과 Franklin Delano Roosevelt 대통령의 역할

해설 | Main Idea 교수와 학생은 곧 있을 중간고사의 범위와 교수가 특별히 제공할 추가 수업 시간에 대해 이야기하고 있다.

02 교수가 광란의 20년대와 대공황에 대해 이야기하는 이유는?

(A) 중요한 시대의 예를 들기 위해
(B) 자신이 뉴딜 정책을 중간고사에 포함시킨 이유를 설명하기 위해
(C) 각 복습 시간에 한 주제씩 다룰 것임을 학생에게 알려 주기 위해
(D) 학생에게 시험 준비를 얼마나 많이 해야 하는지를 경고하기 위해

해설 | Organization 교수는 광란의 20년대와 대공황 시대는 서로 관련돼 있고, 뉴딜 정책도 그 시대의 상황에 밀접하게 연관되어 있기 때문에 뉴딜 정책 부분도 중간고사에 포함시켰다고 설명하고 있다.

03 대화의 일부를 다시 듣고 질문에 답하시오.
교수가 다음과 같이 말할 때 의미하는 것은?
"You're one step ahead of me with everything today, Kate."

(A) 학생은 이미 계획되어 있는 복습 시간을 제의했다.
(B) 학생은 교수가 자기 사무실에 도착하기 직전에 그곳에 도착했다.
(C) 학생은 곧 있을 중간고사 범위에 들어가는 장들에 대한 복습을 이미 끝냈다.
(D) 학생은 중간고사에 한 장이 추가될 것임을 정확히 추측했다.

해설 | Function 교수가 시험에 대비하여 특별 복습 시간을 가지려고 마음먹고 있는데, 학생이 마침 그런 시간을 제의했다.

어휘 | double-check 다시 한 번 확인하다, 재확인하다   **midterm** 중간고사   **draft** 초안[원고]을 작성하다
New Deal 뉴딜 정책(Franklin D. Roosevelt 미국 대통령이 1933년에 도입한 경제 부흥과 사회 보장의 증진 정책)
Roaring Twenties 광란의 20년대(사람들이 활기와 자신감에 넘치던 1920~29년 사이의 시기를 말함)   **Great Depression** 대공황
go hand in hand 관련되다, 함께 가다   **make it** (모임 등에) 참석하다, 성공하다   **in response to** ~에 응하여, 대응하여

Chapter 06 Connecting Content

Sample Question   p.55

Listen to part of a lecture in a chemistry class.

Professor (M): Mercury is a chemical element that has several unique properties. Today though, we're only going to focus on two of its properties, its temperature and its ability to alloy with other metals. **(C) OK, mercury is the only common metal that has a liquid form at ordinary room temperature.** This is actually the main reason mercury is used in devices such as thermometers, since the liquid will expand or contract based on changes in temperature. This is because it has quite a low boiling point for a metal.

(D) The second property I'd like to look at is mercury's ability to combine fairly easily with almost all metals, except for iron, platinum, and tungsten. These metal alloys are referred to as amalgams. One of the most common amalgams is the silver-mercury amalgam, which is generally used in dentistry to fill cavities. Another common amalgam is the gold-mercury amalgam, which is used in the extraction of gold from ore. The gold particles from the ore dissolve into the mercury part of the alloy, facilitating the collection of very small particles of gold.

화학 강의 중 일부를 들으시오.

교수 (남): 수은은 여러 독특한 성질을 띤 화학 원소입니다. 하지만 오늘 우리는 그중 두 가지, 즉 수은의 온도와 수은이 다른 금속과 합금하는 능력을 집중적으로 살펴보겠습니다. 자, 수은은 보통의 상온에서 액체 상태를 띠는 유일한 보통 금속입니다. 이것은 실제로 수은이 온도계 같은 기구에 사용되는 주된 이유입니다. 이 액체는 온도의 변화에 따라 팽창하거나 수축하기 때문이죠. 이것은 수은이 금속치고는 비등점이 낮기 때문입니다.

제가 살펴보고 싶은 두 번째 성질은 철, 백금, 텅스텐을 제외하고 거의 모든 금속과 상당히 쉽게 결합하는 수은의 능력입니다. 이런 금속 합금을 아말감이라고 합니다. 가장 흔한 형태의 아말감 중 하나는 은-수은의 아말감인데, 이것은 일반적으로 치과 의술에서 치아의 구멍을 메꾸는 데 사용되지요. 흔히 쓰이는 또 다른 아말감은 금-수은 아말감인데, 이것은 광석에서 금을 추출하는 과정에서 사용됩니다. 광석에 함유된 금 입자들은 이 합금의 수은 부분으로 용해되어, 매우 작은 금 입자들을 채집하는 것이 용이해집니다.

강의에서 교수는 수은의 몇 가지 성질을 설명한다. 다음 각 사항이 포함되는지 표시하시오.
각 사항에 대해 알맞은 항목에 표시하시오.

	포함	미포함
(A) 산에 잘 반응한다.		✔
(B) 빙점이 가장 낮다.		✔
(C) 표준 상온에서 액체 형태를 띤다.	✔	
(D) 금속과 쉽게 결합한다.	✔	

어휘 | **chemical element** (화학) 원소(元素)   **property** 성질   **alloy** 합금하다   **common metal** 보통 금속   **room temperature** 상온   **boiling point** 비등점, 끓는점   **combine with** ~와 결합하다   **amalgam** 아말감(흔히 치과에서 쓰는 수은과 다른 금속의 합금), 혼합[결합]물   **dentistry** 치과 의술, 치과 의학   **cavity** (치아에 생긴) 구멍, 와동   **extraction** 추출, 뽑아냄[얻어냄]   **ore** 광석   **facilitate** 용이하게[가능하게] 하다

Basic Drill   p.56

01 [Yes – (A), (B)], [No – (C), (D)]   02 [Leonardo – (B), (D)], [Michelangelo – (A), (C)]
03 [Upper-class Areas – (B)], [Middle-class Areas – (A)], [Lower-class Areas – (C), (D)]   04 (B) – (D) – (C) – (A)
05 [Dermal – (C)], [Vascular – (B)], [Ground – (A), (D)]   06 (B) – (A) – (D) – (C)

01

Listen to a conversation between a student and a professor.

Professor (F): Well, hello, Steven. I haven't seen you in a while. Are you feeling any better?

Student (M): Yeah, a little. Thanks for asking, Dr. Watkins. I'm sorry that I missed your class for the past week, but I could barely even get out of bed. Anyway, I needed to come by and ask about what I missed from class. I heard that there was a lot of work to make up.

학생과 교수의 대화를 들으시오.

교수 (여): 그래, 안녕, Steven. 못 본 지 꽤 되었구나. 몸은 좀 나아졌니?

학생 (남): 네, 조금요. 물어봐 주셔서 감사해요, Watkins 박사님. 지난주에 수업을 빠진 건 죄송해요. 하지만 침대 밖으로 나오는 것도 겨우 할 수 있었어요. 어쨌든 놓친 수업 내용에 대해 여쭤보려고 들렀는데요. 만회할 내용이 많다고 들었어요.

Professor: Well, just a few things. **(A)** First off, we had a test on chapters five through eight from the textbook, and you'll have to make that up by the end of the week.

Student: **(D)** OK. What about the oral presentations for our special readings?

Professor: Oh, don't worry about that. I decided to save those for the end of the term. Everyone needs more time on them, and, uh, honestly, I'm too busy to grade those right now. **(C)** However, I need you to finish that short essay on the apartheid era in South Africa.

Student: Oh, don't worry. I've already finished that. In fact, I brought it with me. Here you go.

Professor: Ah, great. **(B)** Then the only other thing that's left is the outline for your research paper. I'll need that by the end of the week, too.

Student: Oh! I completely forgot about that. Yeah, I'll get started on that right away.

교수: 글쎄, 그냥 몇 개 정도란다. 우선, 교과서 5장에서 8장까지 시험을 봤는데, 이번 주말까지는 그것을 만회해야 할 것 같구나.

학생: 알겠어요. 특별 읽기 과제에 대한 구두 발표는 어떻게 되나요?

교수: 오, 그것은 걱정하지 않아도 된단다. 학기 말로 미루기로 했거든. 모두 시간이 좀 더 필요하고, 어, 솔직히 말하면 지금 당장은 내가 너무 바빠서 그것을 채점할 시간이 없구나. 하지만 남아프리카의 아파르트헤이트(인종 차별 정책) 시대에 대한 짧은 에세이는 써야 해.

학생: 오, 걱정하지 마세요. 그건 이미 다 썼어요. 사실은 여기 가져 왔답니다. 여기 있어요.

교수: 아, 잘됐구나. 그러면 마지막 남은 하나는 연구 논문에 대한 개요를 짜는 거야. 그것도 이번 주말까지 필요하단다.

학생: 오! 그걸 완전히 잊고 있었네요. 네, 바로 시작하도록 할게요.

대화에서 학생과 교수는 학생이 여전히 만회해야 할 과제에 대해 논의한다. 다음 각 사항이 과제인지 표시하시오.

각 사항에 대해 알맞은 항목에 표시하시오.

	예	아니오
(A) 교과서의 여러 장에 대한 시험	✔	
(B) 연구 논문에 대한 설명	✔	
(C) 남아프리카의 특정 시대에 대한 논술		✔
(D) 독후감에 대한 구두 발표		✔

해설 | 학생은 이번 주까지 시험과 연구 논문 개요를 끝내야 하며, 에세이는 이미 다 썼고, 구두 발표는 학기 말까지 기한이 연장되었으므로 만회할 필요가 없다.

어휘 | **make up** 만회하다　**apartheid** 아파르트헤이트(예전 남아프리카공화국의 인종 차별 정책)

02

Listen to part of a discussion in an art history class.

Professor (M): OK, everyone. Today's discussion is about the two most important artists of the Renaissance — Michelangelo and Leonardo. Before discussing their works, we're going to look at their lives. Who knows about Leonardo's origins?

Student 1 (F): Well, I know he was born in Florence in, um, 1452.

Professor: OK, that's a start. He also excelled in numerous arts and other pursuits at an early age. **(D)** As a young man, he was employed by the Duke of Milan and produced a few works there, but political turmoil forced him to leave in 1499. Over the course of the next 12 or so years, he returned to Florence and then back to Milan, producing some of his most famous works. **(B)** In 1516, he relocated to France, where he died three years later. Now, around the same time, Michelangelo was also creating some of the greatest works of art in the world. Born in 1475, he studied painting under a great teacher and also quickly excelled at arts. **(C)** As a young man, he spent about a year in Bologna doing some sculpting, and the rest of his life he jumped around between Florence and Rome, juggling numerous projects at once.

미술사 수업 중 토론의 일부를 들으시오.

교수 (남): 좋아요, 여러분. 오늘 토론은 르네상스 시대의 가장 중요한 두 명의 예술가인 Michelangelo와 Leonardo에 대한 것입니다. 그들의 작품에 대해 논의하기 전에 먼저 그들의 생애에 대해 살펴보도록 할게요. 누가 Leonardo의 출신에 대해 알고 있나요?

학생 1 (여): 음, 1452년에 피렌체에서 태어났다고 알고 있어요.

교수: 좋아요, 거기서 시작해보죠. 그는 또한 어린 나이에 많은 예술 및 다른 활동에 뛰어났어요. 그는 젊은 나이에 밀라노 공작에게 고용되어 밀라노에서 작품 몇 개를 창작했지만, 정치적 혼란으로 1499년에 그곳을 떠나야 했어요. 다음 12년 정도에 걸쳐 그는 피렌체에 돌아왔다가 다시 밀라노로 돌아갔는데, 이 시기에 그의 가장 유명한 몇몇 작품들을 만들죠. 1516년 그는 프랑스로 이주해 3년 후 그곳에서 사망했습니다. 자, 비슷한 시기에 Michelangelo 또한 세계에서 가장 위대한 예술 작품들을 만들고 있었답니다. 1475년 출생한 그는 훌륭한 스승 밑에서 회화를 배웠고, 역시 예술에 뛰어난 재능을 보였습니다. 그는 조각하면서 젊은 시절 볼로냐에서 1년 정도 살았고, 여생은 피렌체와 로마를 오가며 한 번에 많은 작품을 순조롭게 해냈습니다.

Student 2 (M): [A] Um, aren't you skipping over his work for the Medici family?

Professor: I was just getting to that. In fact, he was one of their most beloved artists, even sculpting tombs at the family's church. Let's go over some other projects he did for them.

강의에서 교수와 학생들은 Leonardo와 Michelangelo의 생애에 대해 논의한다. 다음 각 사항이 각 예술가의 삶과 관련 있는지 표시하시오.

각 사항에 대해 알맞은 항목에 표시하시오.

	Leonardo	Michelangelo
(A) Medici 가문의 무덤 작업을 했다.		✔
(B) 프랑스에서 말년을 보냈다.	✔	
(C) 볼로냐에서 조각하며 잠깐 살았다.		✔
(D) 밀라노 공작을 위해 일했다.	✔	

해설 | Leonardo는 젊을 때 밀라노 공작에 고용되어 있었고, 1516년에는 프랑스로 돌아와 여생을 보냈다. Michelangelo는 젊은 시절 약 1년간 조각하면서 볼로냐에 있었으며, Medici 가문의 사랑받는 화가로서 가족 교회 무덤 조각을 해주기도 하였다.

어휘 | **excel in** ~에 뛰어나다 **pursuit** 활동, 취미 **turmoil** 혼란 **relocate** 이주하다 **juggle** 순조롭게 해내다

03

Listen to part of a lecture in a sociology class.

Professor (F): In the 1940s, a new urbanization model became popular for planning the layout of a city, referred to as the multiple nuclei model. So . . . this model is characterized by the location of several concentrated areas of business that were spread out away from the downtown core. Well, due to the increase of car ownership, people had more access to move freely around the city from one section to the next, thereby removing the need to have to live near their respective workplaces.

In addition to the growth of various business centers, the emergence of residential neighborhoods also played an influential role in developing the new urban landscape. Residential areas were established based on, um, income, and the division between upper, middle, and lower class areas became more apparent. [B] Residents with higher income tended to move to the outskirts of the city or suburbs. These more affluent areas were characterized by, you know, large houses with huge expanses of property. [A] Residents with moderate incomes could also move away from the downtown core into areas still close to the center, but with greater security. Houses in these middle-class areas could afford the space for features like small swimming pools and gardens. [C] Lower-income areas tended to be closer to industrial areas with factories because, um, the residents may not have had cars to get them across the city to their workplace. [D] Houses were generally built very close together, with little-to-no space for yards or gardens.

사회학 강의 중 일부를 들으시오.

교수 (여): 1940년대에는 새로운 도시화 모델이 도시 공간 배치를 계획하는 데에 인기를 끌었는데, 이를 다핵심 모델이라고 합니다. 자… 이 모델의 특징은 도심에서 사방으로 퍼져 나가는 여러 개의 상업 중심 구역의 위치입니다. 음, 자동차의 소유가 증가했기 때문에, 사람들은 한 지역에서 다른 지역으로 자유롭게 도시 주변에서 이동할 수 있게 되었고, 따라서 자신들 각자의 직장 근처에 살 필요가 없어지게 되었죠.

여러 상업 중심 구역의 발전과 더불어, 주거 지역의 출현 또한 새로운 도시 경관이 발전하는 데에 영향력 있는 역할을 했습니다. 주거 지역은, 음, 소득을 바탕으로 형성되었고, 상류층, 중산층, 하류층 지역 간의 구분은 더욱 분명해졌습니다. 소득이 높은 주민들은 도시의 외곽, 즉 교외 지역으로 이주하는 경향이 있었죠. 이런 부촌들의 특징은 아시다시피, 엄청나게 넓은 부지에 지어진 큰 주택입니다. 중간 정도의 소득을 가진 주민들 역시 도심에서 벗어나서, 여전히 도심과는 가깝지만 훨씬 더 안전한 지역으로 이주할 수 있었습니다. 이런 중산층 지역에 있는 주택들은 작은 수영장과 정원 같은 특징들을 위한 공간을 갖출 수 있었습니다. 저소득 지역은 공장들이 들어서 있는 공업 지대에 더 가까운 경향이 있었습니다. 왜냐하면, 음, 그 주민들은 시내를 가로질러 직장까지 갈 수 있는 차를 소유하지 못했기 때문입니다. 주택들은 일반적으로 매우 조밀하게 지어져, 마당이나 정원이 들어설 공간이 거의 또는 전혀 없었습니다.

강의에서 교수는 다핵심 모델에서 소득을 근거로 형성된 지역들에 대해 논의한다. 다음 각 지역의 결정적인 특징으로 알맞은 것을 표시하시오.

각 사항에 대해 알맞은 항목에 표시하시오.

해설 | 교수는 세 가지 계층의 특징으로 상류층은 교외 지역에 주로 살고, 중산층은 도심에서는 조금 떨어져 있지만 생활이 안전한 곳에 살며, 차를 소유하지 못하는 하류층은 공업 지대 인근의 주택들이 조밀하게 지어진 지역에 산다는 점을 언급하고 있다.

	상류층 지역	중산층 지역	하류층 지역
(A) 더 수준 높은 안전을 제공한다.		✔	
(B) 교외 지역에 있다.	✔		
(C) 공장 지대에 근접하다.			✔
(D) 주택밀도가 높다.			✔

어휘 | **urbanization** 도시화 **layout** (책·정원·건물 등의) 공간 배치, 레이아웃 **multiple nuclei model** 다핵심 모델 **respective** 각각의 **emergence** 출현, 발생 **outskirt** 외곽, 교외 **moderate** 중간의, 보통의 **industrial area** 공업 지대, 산업 지역

04

Listen to a conversation between a student and an employee at the office of student affairs.

Student (F): Excuse me. This is the office of student affairs, right?

Employee (M): Yes. How can I help you?

Student: Well, I just started my first semester here, and I heard that there will be an orientation for freshmen next week.

Employee: Yes. It is a two-day program giving an overview of opportunities and resources available to you on campus. I highly recommend that you attend every event included in the program.

Student: Of course I will. Can you explain more about the events, please?

Employee: Sure. (B) The first event will be on Thursday morning. This is the welcoming assembly. Here you can pick up packets that have informational pamphlets, maps of the campus, and even some free school supplies. (D) Later that afternoon, there will be a special lunch with staff and members of our university, including the dean and the heads of some departments. This will give you a chance to get introduced and chat a little about what to expect from college life.

Student: OK, that's cool. (C) I also heard that there will be a campus fair on Friday afternoon. I was just wondering if it will cost money to get in.

Employee: Um, no, that will be free for all freshmen. (A) However, there will be a small charge for the film being shown later that night in the auditorium. For more detailed information about the orientation, please visit our university's website. You'll find out about plenty of other interesting events there.

Student: OK, thanks for the information.

학생과 학사과 직원의 대화를 들으시오.

학생 (여): 실례합니다. 여기가 학사과 사무실 맞나요?

직원 (남): 네. 어떻게 도와 드릴까요?

학생: 그게요, 제가 첫 학기를 막 시작했는데요, 다음 주에 신입생을 위한 오리엔테이션이 있다는 말을 들었어요

직원: 맞아요. 교내에서 학생들이 이용할 기회와 자원에 대해 개괄적으로 안내하는 이틀짜리 프로그램이에요. 이 프로그램에 포함된 모든 행사에 빠짐없이 참석하라고 권하고 싶어요.

학생: 물론 그렇게 해야죠. 이 행사들에 대해 더 자세히 설명해 주시겠어요?

직원: 네. 첫 번째 행사는 목요일 아침에 있을 거예요. 환영회죠. 여기에서 정보가 담긴 팸플릿 및 캠퍼스 지도, 게다가 무료 학용품까지 들어있는 꾸러미를 받을 수 있어요. 그날 오후에는 대학 학장님 및 학과장님들을 포함한 학교 직원들과 함께 하는 특별 오찬이 있을 겁니다. 여기에 참석하면 소개도 되고 대학 생활에서 기대할 수 있는 것들에 대한 이야기도 조금 나눌 수 있을 거예요.

학생: 좋군요. 금요일 오후에 학교 설명회가 열린다는 말도 들었어요. 참석하는데 참가비가 있나요?

직원: 음, 아니요. 신입생들에게는 무료랍니다. 하지만 그날 밤 강당에서 있을 영화 상영에는 약간의 요금이 있을 거예요. 오리엔테이션에 대한 자세한 정보가 필요하면 우리 대학교의 웹사이트에 들어가 보세요. 거기에 가면 많은 다른 재미있는 행사에 대해 알 수 있을 것입니다.

학생: 알겠습니다. 알려주셔서 감사합니다.

해설 | 목요일 아침에 환영회와 오후에 학교 직원들과의 특별 만찬이 열리며, 금요일에는 학교 설명회가 있다. 그리고 그날 밤에는 강당에서 영화 상영이 있다.

직원은 신입생들을 위해 열릴 몇 가지 특별 행사들을 설명한다. 이 행사들을 올바른 순서대로 나열하시오.

각 문장을 해당되는 곳으로 옮기시오.

1	(B) 유용한 여러 물품을 배포하는 환영회
2	(D) 학교 교직원들과 함께 하는 식사
3	(C) 무료로 열리는 학교 설명회
4	(A) 강당에서 영화 시청

어휘 | **overview** 개관, 개요　　**packet** (특정 목적용으로 제공되는 서류 등의) 꾸러미, 뭉치　　**charge** (상품·서비스에 대한) 요금

05

Listen to part of a discussion in a botany class.

Professor (F): All right, everybody, today we are going to look at how the tissues of angiosperms, or flowering plants, are structured. The tissues of a plant are organized to form three types of tissue systems. Who can name them for me?

Student (M): I can. They're the dermal tissue, the vascular tissue, and the ground tissue systems.

Professor: Excellent. Now, each of the tissue systems has distinct functions. First, the dermal tissue system is composed of two layers: the epidermis and the periderm. **(C)** The epidermis is a single layer of packed cells which covers and protects the plant. The periderm, or bark, also protects the plant from injury, prevents water loss, and insulates the plant.

Next is the vascular tissue system. This system consists of two important tissues called the xylem and phloem, which are responsible for transporting water, food, and other nutrients throughout the entire plant. Xylem is composed of two types of cells known as tracheids and vessel elements. They form tube-shaped structures that offer pathways for water and minerals to be transported from the roots to the leaves. **(B)** Phloem is made up of cells called sieve-tube cells and companion cells. These cells help transport sugar and nutrients produced during photosynthesis.

Finally, there is the ground tissue system. This is the largest tissue system of the plant, essentially the flesh of the plant. It mostly contains plant cells called parenchyma cells as well as some collenchymas and sclerenchyma cells. **(D)** Parenchyma cells synthesize and store organic products in a plant, and control photosynthesis. **(A)** Collenchyma cells and sclerenchyma cells have a support function in plants.

식물학 수업 중 토론의 일부를 들으시오.

교수 (여): 좋아요, 여러분, 오늘은 현화 식물이라고도 하는 속씨식물의 조직이 어떤 구조로 이루어져 있는지 알아보겠습니다. 식물의 조직은 세 종류의 조직 체계를 구성하게 되어 있습니다. 이것들의 이름을 댈 수 있는 사람 있나요?

학생 (남): 저요. 표피 조직계, 관다발 조직계, 기본 조직계입니다.

교수: 훌륭해요. 자, 각 조직계에는 고유한 기능들이 있어요. 우선, 표피 조직계는 두 개의 층으로 이루어져 있어요. 표피와 주피입니다. 표피는 식물을 감싸고 보호하는 세포들이 집합해 있는 단일 층이에요. 주피, 즉 껍질 역시 식물이 상처를 입지 않도록 보호해 주고, 수분의 유실을 막고, 그 식물을 보호해 주는 역할을 합니다.

다음은 관다발 조직계인데, 물관부와 체관부로 불리는 두 개의 중요 조직으로 이루어져 있으며, 이 조직들은 물과 양분 및 다른 영양분을 식물 전체에 운반하는 역할을 합니다. 물관부는 헛물관과 도관요소(導管要素)라는 두 종류의 세포로 이루어져 있어요. 이것들이 물과 미네랄이 뿌리에서 잎으로 전달되는 통로를 제공하는 튜브처럼 생긴 조직을 형성하고 있죠. 체관부는 체관 세포와 반(伴)세포라고 불리는 세포들로 구성되어 있습니다. 이 세포들은 광합성 과정에서 생성되는 당분과 영양분을 전달하는 데 기여합니다.

마지막으로 기본 조직계가 있습니다. 이것은 식물의 가장 큰 조직계로, 기본적으로 식물의 살이라고 할 수 있어요. 여기에는 주로 유세포(柔細胞)라는 식물 세포와 후각(厚角) 세포 및 후막(厚膜) 세포까지 포함돼 있어요. 유세포(柔細胞)는 유기물질을 합성하고 식물에 저장하며 광합성 과정을 조절합니다. 후각 세포와 후막 세포는 식물 내에서 지원하는 기능을 합니다.

교수는 식물의 세 가지 조직 체계에 대해 논의한다. 다음 설명이 어느 조직계에 해당하는지 표시하시오.

각 사항에 대해 알맞은 항목에 표시하시오.

	표피	관다발	기본
(A) 식물 내에서 지원 기능을 제공하는 식물 세포들로 구성되어 있다.			✓
(B) 물과 영양분의 수송에 도움을 주는 조직을 포함한다.		✓	
(C) 식물을 감싸고 보호하는 층들을 포함한다.	✓		
(D) 광합성을 담당하는 식물 세포들로 구성되어 있다.			✓

해설 | 표피 조직은 식물을 감싸고 보호하는 세포들의 집합체인 표피와 주피 조직을 포함하고, 관다발 조직은 물관부와 체관부로 이뤄져 물과 양분을 이동시켜 주며, 마지막으로 기본 조직은 광합성을 조절하는 유세포와 지원 기능을 담당하는 후각 세포 및 후막 세포를 포함한다.

어휘 | **tissue** 조직　**angiosperm** 속씨식물　**flowering plant** 현화 식물, 꽃식물　**dermal** 표피의, 피부의　**vascular** 관의, 혈관의　**epidermis** 표피　**periderm** 주피, 외피　**xylem** 물관부　**phloem** 체관부　**tracheid** 헛물관, 가도관　**vessel element** 도관요소(導管要素)　**sieve-tube cell** 체관 세포　**companion cell** 반(伴)세포　**photosynthesis** 광합성　**flesh** 살　**parenchyma cell** 유세포(柔細胞)　**collenchymas** 후각(厚角) 조직　**sclerenchyma cell** 후막(厚膜) 세포

06

Listen to part of a lecture in an American history class.

Professor (M): In our last lecture, we talked about the conflicts between northern and southern states, uh, particularly over the issue of slavery, which eventually led to the Civil War. Today, we are going to look at some of the attempts to resolve those conflicts and their effects.

(B) The first serious attempt to address the conflicts between the North and the South came with the Missouri Compromise of 1820. This bill basically split the nation into two areas: one in which slavery would not be allowed, and one in which it would be legal. States above the 36th parallel were to be free states, while those below would be slave states. This also applied to any new territories that became states later on. This was a delicate compromise, because the creation of new states would now automatically tip the balance of power towards the slave states or the free states. **(A)** For this reason, new states were generally admitted to the union in pairs, with one free state and one slave state entering at roughly the same time. This was the case with the admission of Missouri and Maine, and later on with Arkansas and Michigan.

(D) The Missouri Compromise held together until 1854, when it was effectively repealed by the Kansas-Nebraska Act, which gave new states the right to vote on whether they would become free or slave states. **(C)** Unfortunately, the Kansas-Nebraska Act unleashed a wave of violence, as supporters and opponents of slavery fought each other in the streets in advance of the voting. After the passage of the Kansas-Nebraska Act, the violence and hostility between the North and the South continued to build until it broke out in open war in 1861.

미국 역사학 강의 중 일부를 들으시오.

교수 (남): 지난 시간에 북부와 남부 주 간의 갈등, 어, 특히 결과적으로는 남북전쟁을 이끈 노예제 문제에 대해서 얘기해 보았습니다. 오늘은 이 갈등을 해소하려 했던 시도들과 그 영향들에 대해 살펴보겠어요.

남부와 북부 간의 갈등을 해소하려는 첫 번째 진지한 시도는 1820년의 미주리 협정과 함께 시작되었습니다. 기본적으로 이 법안은 미국을 두 지역, 즉 노예제가 허용되지 않는 지역과 노예제가 합법인 지역으로 나누었어요. 위도 36도선 위에 있는 주는 자유주가 되는 한편, 그 아래에 있는 주는 노예주가 되는 것이었죠. 또한 이 법안은 그 이후에 주(州)로 성립되는 새로운 영토에 모두 적용이 되었습니다. 이는 세심한 주의를 필요로 하는 협정이었는데, 왜냐하면 새로운 주의 탄생은 자동으로 세력 균형을 노예주나 자유주 쪽으로 기울게 할 것이기 때문이었어요. 이러한 이유로 새로운 주는 일반적으로 2개씩 연방에 가입이 되었는데, 즉 자유주 하나와 노예주 하나가 거의 비슷한 시기에 연방에 가입되는 것이었습니다. 미주리 주와 메인 주, 그리고 그 후 아칸소 주와 미시간 주의 가입이 이러한 사례에 해당합니다.

미주리 협정은 1854년까지 유지되다가, 새로운 주에게 자유주가 될지 노예주가 될지에 관한 투표권을 주었던 캔자스-네브래스카 법의 성립으로 폐지가 됩니다. 불행히도 캔자스-네브래스카 법은 폭력적 분위기를 부추겼고, 노예제 지지자들과 반대자들이 투표를 앞두고 서로 거리에서 싸우는 일이 일어났어요. 캔자스-네브래스카 법의 가결 이후, 북부와 남부 간의 이러한 폭력과 적개심은 점점 고조되어 1861년 전쟁의 발발로 이어졌습니다.

교수는 남북전쟁에 이르기까지의 사건들을 설명한다. 이 사건들을 올바른 순서대로 나열하시오.

각 문장을 해당되는 곳으로 옮기시오.

1	(B) 미주리 협정이 통과되었다.
2	(A) 나라가 자유주와 노예주로 나누어졌다.
3	(D) 캔자스-네브래스카 법이 제정되었다.
4	(C) 노예제 지지자와 반대자들이 서로 싸움을 벌였다.

해설 | 1820년 미국은 남북 간의 충돌을 막기 위해 노예제를 허용하는 주와 그렇지 않은 주로 분리시킨 미주리 협정을 통과시켰으며, 아칸소 주와 미시간 주가 이 협정에 따라 연방에 가입되었다. 그러나 이후 1854년, 노예제의 찬반을 해당 주의 결정에 위임하는 캔자스-네브래스카 법이 통과되었고, 이것은 노예제의 찬반 세력 간에 폭력 사태를 불러일으켰다.

어휘 | **bill** 법안   **parallel** 위도선   **delicate** 세심한 주의를 필요로 하는, 까다로운   **tip** 기울이다   **union** 연방   **repeal** 폐지하다, 무효로 하다   **unleash** 부추기다   **in advance of** ~에 앞서

Listening Practice

p.60

01 [Suggested – (B), (C)], [Not Suggested – (A), (D)]   02 (C)   03 (D)

Listen to a conversation between a student and a counselor at the university counseling center.

Counselor (F): Come on in, Jason.

학생과 대학 상담 센터 상담사의 대화를 들으시오.

상담사 (여): 어서 와요, Jason.

Student (M): Hello, counselor. Thank you for seeing me. I wanted to see you because I'm conflicted as to how many courses I should enroll in next semester. My enrollment date is tomorrow and I still have no clue what I should do! I feel like I'm behind everyone else, since I haven't yet been able to declare my major.

Counselor: Let's see here . . . Well, judging by the fact that you're already in the middle of your second year, I think it would serve you well to get all of your general education requirements out of the way first. I see here that you still have yet to fulfill your Reading and Composition requirement as well as the Philosophical and Linguistic Analysis requirement. The university also strongly urges students to declare their majors and start upper division courses by their third year, so you should take care of the three prerequisite political science courses you have left as well. Let's take a look . . . you still need Empirical Theory, International Relations, and Quantitative Methods.

Student: Wow, that's five classes! Don't students normally take three or four? I've never taken five courses in a semester before. I think it would be too difficult for me to keep up academically. I have extracurricular obligations that take up a lot of time, too.

Counselor: Q03 Yes, five courses would be quite a challenge, even though I've seen students excel with that type of course load. I've witnessed some students take six or even seven courses in one semester. Although I must admit, cases like that are extremely rare.

Student: I honestly don't think I would be able to survive the whole semester with that kind of schedule.

Counselor: Then I'll tell you what, there is another option we can explore. Q01(B) Finish up the two general education courses and two of the prerequisites. Q01(C) Q02-1 Then next year, I will make an exception for you to enroll in the remaining prerequisite course and upper division Political Science courses simultaneously.

Student: That sounds much more manageable. I think it'll still be a lot of work, though. I'm going to have to plan my schedule accordingly.

Counselor: Q02-2 Yes, no matter what, you'll still have to be diligent in your studies and activities.

Student: Thank you so much!

학생 (남): 안녕하세요, 상담사님. 만나주셔서 고맙습니다. 저는 다음 학기에 몇 과목을 수강해야 할지 갈등을 겪고 있어서 선생님을 뵙고 싶었어요. 등록일이 내일인데, 아직도 어떻게 해야 할지 전혀 모르겠어요! 아직 전공을 확실히 정하지 못해, 다른 사람들 모두에게 뒤처진 듯한 기분이에요.

상담사: 여기 보자… 음, 네가 이미 2학년의 중간에 와 있다는 사실로 판단하면, 우선 일반 교양 과목 요건들을 모두 해결하는 것이 너한테 좋을 것 같구나. 여기 보니 너는 아직도 읽기 및 작문 과목 외에 철학과 언어 분석 과목을 수강해야 해. 학교는 또 학생들에게 3학년까지는 전공을 정하고 고학년 과정을 시작하도록 촉구하고 있지. 그러니까 너는 남아 있는 세 개의 필수 정치학 과목을 들어야 하는구나. 어디 보자… 너는 아직 경험 이론, 국제 관계, 정량적 접근법을 들어야 하네.

학생: 와, 그러면 모두 다섯 과목이네요! 학생들은 보통 서너 과목을 듣지 않나요? 전에는 한 학기에 다섯 과목을 수강한 적이 없어요. 아무래도 저는 학업 면에서 따라가기가 너무 힘들 것 같아요. 또 많은 시간을 잡아먹는 교과 외의 의무 활동들이 있거든요.

상담사: 그래. 그 정도의 학업량에도 뛰어난 성적을 올린 학생들을 못 본 것은 아니지만, 다섯 과목은 상당한 부담이 될 거야. 나는 한 학기에 예닐곱 과목이나 수강한 학생들도 보았단다. 그런 경우는 매우 드물다는 점은 인정하지.

학생: 솔직히 말하면, 그런 학업 일정을 유지하면서 한 학기를 마칠 수 있을 것 같지 않아요.

상담사: 그렇다면 우리가 시도할 만한 다른 방법이 있단다. 일반 과목 두 개와 선수 과목 두 개를 끝내는 거지. 그리고 나서 내년에, 너한테만 예외적으로 남아 있는 선수 과목과 상급생 과정에 속하는 정치학 과목들을 동시에 수강할 수 있도록 해 줄게.

학생: 그게 훨씬 더 감당할 만하죠. 그래도 학업량이 많지만요. 제 일정을 거기에 맞춰 짜야 하겠군요.

상담사: 그래, 어쨌든 너는 공부와 활동을 부지런히 해야 할 거야.

학생: 대단히 고맙습니다!

---

01 대화에서 상담사와 학생은 학생의 내년 학업 일정에 대해 논의한다. 다음 각 사항이 상담사가 제안한 것인지 표시하시오.

각 사항에 대해 알맞은 항목에 표시하시오.

	제안함	제안하지 않음
(A) 남아 있는 선수 과목들을 먼저 마친다.		✔
(B) 총 네 과목에 등록한다.	✔	
(C) 선수 과목과 상급생 과정을 같이 수강한다.	✔	
(D) 일반 교육 과정 중 하나를 건너뛴다.		✔

해설 | Connecting Content 상담사는 올해에 일반 과목 두 개와 선수 과목 두 개를 끝내고 내년에 남아 있는 선수 과목 하나와 상급생 과정에 속하는 정치학 과목들을 들으라고 권하고 있다.

02 학생이 처한 상황에 대한 상담사의 태도는?
(A) 학생의 교과 외 활동에 대해 무관심하다.
(B) 학생이 더 많은 과목을 수강하도록 단호하게 권한다.
(C) 학생의 고생에 대해 동정적이다.
(D) 학생이 더 많은 학업량을 감당하기를 원하지 않는 것에 실망한다.

해설 | Attitude 상담사는 학생이 과도한 학업 일정에 난색을 보이자 학생에게만 예외적으로 나누어서 과목을 수강하라는 대안을 제시하고 계속 열심히 일과 학업을 병행하라고 격려하고 있다.

03 대화의 일부를 다시 듣고 질문에 답하시오.
상담사가 다음과 같이 말하는 이유는?
"I've witnessed some students take six or even seven courses in one semester."
(A) 학생이 더 많은 과목을 수강하도록 도전 의식을 북돋우기 위해
(B) 모든 학생은 학업 면에서 뛰어날 수 있다고 주장하기 위해
(C) 학생에게 또 다른 적절한 대안을 제시하기 위해
(D) 다섯 과목을 감당하는 것이 불가능하지 않다는 것을 보여 주기 위해

해설 | Function 상담사는 드물긴 하지만 한 학기에 예닐곱 과목을 수강하는 학생들도 봤다며 학생을 설득하고 있다.

어휘 | **conflicted** 갈등을 겪는 **as to** ~에 관해 **have no clue** 전혀 모르다 **declare** (대학에서 전공을) 결정하다 **judging by** (~이라는 사실)로 판단하건대 **requirement** 필요조건 **prerequisite** 선수 과목 **manageable** 감당[관리/처리]할 수 있는 **accordingly** 그에 맞춰, (상황에) 부응해서

Chapter 07 Inference

Sample Question
p.63

Listen to a conversation between a student and an employee at the university library.

Student (M): Hi, I'm looking for a part-time job at the library.

Employee (F): OK. Do you have a particular area you'd like to work in?

Student: I'm not sure. What kinds of jobs are available?

Employee: There are several positions available. One is a circulation assistant who checks out and renews books.

Student: Oh, so it's for sorting books, handing out, and accepting returned materials. How much is the hourly wage?

Employee: It's $7.50.

Student: That's not a lot of money. Hmm . . . is there any temporary full-time work for the summer semester?

Employee: Two positions are available at the moment. One is an inventory assistant. It pays $8.50 per hour. You need to monitor all the printers in the university libraries. Basically, your job will be refilling paper and toner supplies and picking up supplies from the business office.

Student: That doesn't sound too hard. What about the other one?

Employee: The other one is a teaching assistant at the library.

Student: Um, I don't have any teaching experience, so I think the former position fits me better.

학생과 대학 도서관 직원의 대화를 들으시오.

학생 (남): 안녕하세요. 도서관에서의 시간제 일자리를 찾고 있는데요.

직원 (여): 좋아요. 혹시 일하고 싶은 특별한 분야가 있나요?

학생: 잘 모르겠어요. 어떤 일들이 가능한가요?

직원: 여러 자리가 나와 있어요. 하나는 대출 보조직인데 책을 대출하고 기한을 연장해주는 일을 합니다.

학생: 아, 그러면 책을 분류하고, 내보내고, 반납되는 자료를 접수하는 일이군요. 시급은 얼마인가요?

직원: 7달러 50센트예요.

학생: 많은 돈은 아니군요. 음… 임시직으로 여름 학기 동안 다닐 수 있는 전일제 자리는 없나요?

직원: 현재 두 자리가 나와 있어요. 하나는 물품 담당 보조직이에요. 이 일은 시간당 8달러 50센트를 줍니다. 대학 도서관들에 비치된 모든 프린터를 관리해야 해요. 기본적으로 할 일은 종이와 토너를 리필하고, 영업소에서 비품을 찾아오는 것이에요.

학생: 너무 힘든 일은 아닌 것 같네요. 다른 하나는 무슨 일인가요?

직원: 다른 하나는 도서관의 보조 교사직입니다.

학생: 음, 남을 가르쳐 본 경험은 없으니 이전에 말씀하신 자리가 제게 더 맞는 것 같아요.

학생에 대해 추론할 수 있는 것은?
(A) 여름방학 기간에 학점을 취득할 계획이다.
(B) 물품 담당 보조직을 다른 자리들보다 선호한다.
(C) 등록금을 충당하기 위해 돈을 벌어야 한다.
(D) 대출 보조직으로 근무한 경험이 있다.

어휘 | **check out** (도서관 등에서 책이나 자료를) 대출하다   **renew** 연장[갱신]하다   **temporary** 임시의, 일시적인

Basic Drill
p.64

| 01 (D) | 02 (A) | 03 (B) | 04 (C) | 05 (A) | 06 (C) |

01

Listen to a conversation between a student and a campus bookstore clerk.

Clerk (M): Good afternoon. How can I help you today?

Student (F): Oh, hey. I just purchased this computer software from here yesterday for a big project. But when I got home, I found out that it wasn't the right program.

Clerk: Oh, I'm sorry.

Student: That's OK. I actually found the software I did need. But, uh, I just wanted to return this for my money back.

Clerk: OK. Let's see. *[Pause]* Um, it looks like you already opened it.

Student: Yeah, I tried to use it and found out that it wasn't what I'd been looking for.

Clerk: *[Reluctantly]* Oh, I'm sorry. We don't accept returns on computer software once the package has already been opened.

Student: *[Really annoyed]* What? Are you serious?

Clerk: I'm afraid so. Sorry.

Student: OK. Can I at least sell it back to you and get some of my money back?

Clerk: I'm sorry. We only buy used books, not software.

Student: But I haven't even used it yet. So I guess I'm just stuck with it, huh?

Clerk: Well, not necessarily. On the campus's social networking website, there are lots of ads for students who are willing to buy or trade all kinds of programs.

Student: Hmm. It's better than nothing, I guess.

학생과 교내 서점 직원의 대화를 들으시오.

직원 (남): 안녕하세요. 오늘은 어떻게 도와 드릴까요?

학생 (여): 오, 안녕하세요. 제가 어제 여기에서 중요한 과제에 쓸 컴퓨터 소프트웨어를 구입했어요. 그런데 집에 가서 살펴보니까 알맞은 프로그램이 아니더라고요.

직원: 오, 죄송해요.

학생: 괜찮아요. 사실은 저한테 정말 필요한 소프트웨어가 뭔지 찾았거든요. 하지만, 어, 이건 반환하고 환불을 받았으면 해요.

직원: 그래요. 보죠. *[잠시 후]* 음, 학생이 이미 열어 본 것 같은데요.

학생: 네, 쓰려고 했다가 이것이 제가 찾던 것이 아니라는 것을 알게 되었거든요.

직원: *[마지못해]* 오, 죄송해요. 컴퓨터 소프트웨어는 일단 포장이 개봉되면 반품을 받지 않아요.

학생: *[정말 화가 나서]* 뭐라고요? 진심이세요?

직원: 네. 죄송해요.

학생: 알겠어요. 적어도 그럼 이것을 되팔고 제 돈의 일부라도 돌려받을 수 있나요?

직원: 미안해요. 중고책은 사지만 소프트웨어는 사지 않아요.

학생: 하지만 저는 이걸 아직 사용하지도 않았단 말이에요. 그러면 전 그냥 어쩔 수 없는 건가요?

직원: 글쎄요, 꼭 그렇지만은 않아요. 교내 소셜 네트워킹 웹사이트에 보면 학생들이 온갖 종류의 프로그램을 사거나 교환하려고 내놓은 광고가 많거든요.

학생: 음. 아무것도 없는 것보다는 낫겠네요.

학생이 다음에 할 행동은?

(A) 소프트웨어가 작동되는 컴퓨터를 찾는다.
(B) 자신의 컴퓨터에 맞는 다른 프로그램을 산다.
(C) 서점에 소프트웨어를 되판다.
(D) 소프트웨어를 원하는 학생을 찾으려 한다.

해설 | 직원이 소프트웨어는 반품 또는 되팔기가 안 된다고 했으므로, 학생은 직원이 알려준 교내 소셜 네트워킹 웹사이트를 통해 소프트웨어를 원하는 학생을 찾으려고 할 것이다.

어휘 | reluctantly 마지못해, 꺼려하여

02

Listen to part of a discussion in a biology class.

Professor (M): In our discussions about keeping the body healthy, we have gone over a lot of vital nutrients. Today we're going to look at calcium, a crucial nutrient that people, unfortunately, often don't get enough of. So who knows why calcium is so important to us?

생물학 수업 중 토론의 일부를 들으시오.

교수 (남): 몸을 건강하게 유지하는 방법에 대한 논의에서 우리는 많은 필수 영양소에 대해 알아보았습니다. 오늘은 중요한 영양소이지만, 안타깝게도 사람들이 충분히 섭취하지 못하는 칼슘에 대해 살펴보겠어요. 자, 칼슘이 우리에게 왜 그토록 중요한지 누가 알고 있나요?

Student 1 (M): Well, I know that it's crucial to keeping bones and teeth strong and healthy.

Student 2 (F): It's also an important nutrient for your heart and nerves, too, right?

Professor: Yes, you're both correct. It provides support for bones and aids in numerous involuntary functions, like nerve transmission, blood-clotting, and muscle contractions, including those of the heart. Unfortunately, people don't get enough foods that contain lots of calcium, such as dairy products, leafy green vegetables, and some kinds of seafood.

Student 2: Then can't we just take pills with lots of calcium in them, like the multivitamin pills a lot of us take daily?

Professor: Well, that might help a little, but another problem is vitamin D consumption. See, vitamin D helps maintain certain hormones that regulate digestion and allow consumed calcium to enter the blood and bones. If these hormones aren't working properly, then they only allow so much calcium into the blood, no matter how much you consume.

학생 1 (남): 음, 칼슘이 뼈와 치아를 튼튼하고 건강하게 유지하는 데 중요하다고 아는데요.

학생 2 (여): 또한 심장과 신경에도 중요한 영양소이지 않나요?

교수: 네, 두 사람 다 맞아요. 칼슘은 뼈에 도움이 되고, 더불어 신경 전달, 혈액 응고, 그리고 심장을 포함한 근육의 수축과 같은 많은 불수의 기능을 도와줍니다. 안타깝게도 사람들은 유제품, 잎이 많은 녹색 채소, 일부 해산물 등 칼슘이 많이 함유된 식품을 충분히 섭취하지 않습니다.

학생 2: 그러면 그냥 칼슘이 많이 들어 있는 영양제를 먹으면 안 되나요? 많은 사람이 매일 복용하는 종합비타민제 같은 약 말이에요.

교수: 글쎄요. 조금은 도움이 되겠죠. 하지만 다른 문제점은 비타민 D 섭취에 있어요. 그러니까 비타민 D는 소화를 조절하고 섭취된 칼슘을 피와 뼈로 흡수되게 해주는 특정 호르몬을 유지하는 데 도움을 줍니다. 만약 이러한 호르몬이 제대로 작용하지 않는다면, 얼마나 많은 칼슘을 섭취했는지에 상관없이, 혈액으로 흡수되는 칼슘의 양은 한정되어 있는 거죠.

교수가 칼슘에 대해 암시하는 것은?
(A) 비타민 D를 충분히 섭취했을 때 가장 성공적으로 흡수된다.
(B) 많이 섭취해야 조금이라도 체내에 흡수될 수 있다.
(C) 식생활을 통해 비타민 D를 많이 섭취하면 칼슘을 먹을 필요가 없다.
(D) 심장을 건강하게 유지하는 데에 가장 중요한 영양소이다.

해설 | 칼슘의 흡수를 돕는 호르몬은 비타민 D를 통해 유지되므로, 비타민 D와 함께 섭취해야만 흡수가 제대로 이뤄진다는 것을 알 수 있다.

어휘 | vital 필수적인   nutrient 영양소   crucial 중요한   nerve 신경   involuntary 불수의, 본의 아닌   transmission 전달   blood-clotting 혈액 응고   contraction 수축   dairy product 유제품   leafy 잎이 많은   digestion 소화   properly 제대로, 적절히

03

Listen to part of a lecture in a history class.

Professor (F): We talked a good deal about England's historic defeat of the Spanish Armada in 1588, and the huge impact it had on the course of history . . . uh, not only in Europe, but in the New World as well.

As some of you pointed out, the defeat of the Spanish Armada really marked the beginning of the fall of Spanish sea power. After this point, the Spanish went into a long, slow decline as a colonial power, and the English rose to a position of dominance.

Anyway, because of its historical importance, the events that led to the defeat of the Spanish Armada have been . . . um, how should I put this . . . they have been, uh, dramatized in popular history. We have this image of a David and Goliath story, where the all-powerful Spanish Armada was defeated by the outnumbered and outgunned British fleet.

To some extent, that is accurate. This Spanish Armada certainly contained more ships than the British fleet. But the crews of the Spanish ships were young and inexperienced. Many of the Spanish ships had been built in haste and were of low quality.

역사학 강의 중 일부를 들으시오.

교수 (여): 우리는 지난 시간에 1588년 스페인의 무적함대를 격파한 영국의 역사적인 승리와 그것이 역사에 끼친… 그러니까, 유럽뿐 아니라 신세계의 역사에도 끼친 커다란 영향에 대해서 많이 이야기했습니다.

여러분 몇몇이 지적했듯이, 스페인 무적함대의 패배는 스페인 해군력 종말의 시작을 알렸습니다. 이 시점 이후로, 식민국으로서의 스페인은 장기간에 걸쳐 점차적인 쇠퇴에 접어들었으며, 영국은 지배적인 위치로 떠올랐어요.

어쨌든, 이러한 역사적인 중요성 때문에 스페인 무적함대의 격파를 초래한 사건들은… 음, 어떻게 말해야 할까요… 그러니까, 대중 역사에서 극화되어 왔습니다. 전적으로 강력한 스페인 무적함대가 수적으로나 군사력으로나 열세인 영국 함대에 의해 패배를 당했다는 점에서, 보통 다윗과 골리앗 이야기의 이미지를 떠올리곤 하죠.

어느 정도까지는 맞는 말이에요. 이 스페인 무적함대는 영국 함대보다 더 많은 선박을 갖추고 있었어요. 그러나 스페인 함대의 병사들은 어렸고 경험이 없었습니다. 많은 스페인 선박들은 급하게 건조되었고 품질도 낮았어요.

| The Spanish also lacked sufficient numbers of cannons and ammunition to fully arm their ships. So the numerical superiority of the Spanish is actually a little deceptive. | 게다가 스페인은 선박을 완전하게 무장시킬 만한 충분한 수의 대포나 탄약이 없었습니다. 그래서 스페인의 수적인 우세함은 사실 약간의 오해를 불러일으킵니다. |

교수가 영국 함대에 대해 암시하는 것은?
(A) 자국의 식민지 이익을 늘리기 위해 스페인과 싸우기를 열망했다.
(B) 실질적으로는 스페인 무적함대보다 많은 이점을 갖고 있었다.
(C) 스페인 무적함대를 무찌르기 한참 전부터 지배적인 해양 세력이었다.
(D) 수적인 우위 때문에 스페인의 무적함대를 격파할 수 있었다.

해설 | 스페인 함대는 영국 함대보다 수적으로 우세했지만, 급히 만들어졌고 숙련된 병사들과 충분한 대포와 탄약이 없었으므로, 사실상 이러한 점에서 영국 함대가 많은 유리한 조건을 갖고 있었음을 알 수 있다.

어휘 | **Armada** 스페인의 무적함대(1588년에 영국 해군에 의해 격파됨) **decline** 쇠퇴 **colonial** 식민지의 **outnumber** ~보다 수적으로 우세하다 **outgun** ~보다 군사력이 우세하다 **fleet** 함대 **to some extent** 어느 정도까지는 **in haste** 급하게 **sufficient** 충분한 **cannon** 대포 **ammunition** 탄약, 무기 **arm** 무장하다 **numerical** 수적인, 수의 **superiority** 우세함 **deceptive** 오해를 사는, 기만적인

04

| Listen to a conversation between a student and a professor.

Student (F): Dr. Carlson, hi, can I come in for a second? I wanted to ask you some questions about some of the assignments on our syllabus.

Professor (M): Sure, Julia. So what did you want to know?

Student: Well, I saw that we have a test coming up later this week about chapters eight and nine from the textbook. That seems to be a lot for one test.

Professor: Well, those two chapters both cover the topic of tropical rainforests, and they really need to be covered at the same time.

Student: 🎧 Hmm. It just seems like a lot to go over in such a short time. I mean, look at the chapters in here. I'm used to reading pages and pages at a time, but even I have my limits.

Professor: Well, sometimes being a university student means pushing your limits. But look, the material isn't that difficult. Most of the pages in those two chapters are just graphs and statistics that I don't expect you to memorize. Just make sure to get the basic ideas from them.

Student: [Relenting] Hmm, OK. Oh, the other thing I wanted to know was about our trip to the school library next week. Are we meeting in the classroom first or at the library?

Professor: Oh, we'll be meeting at the library, but I need to discuss the full details with everyone in our next session. | 학생과 교수의 대화를 들으시오.

학생 (여): Carlson 박사님, 안녕하세요. 잠시 들어가도 될까요? 강의 계획서에 나와 있는 과제들에 대해 질문을 좀 드리고 싶은데요.

교수 (남): 물론이지, Julia. 그래, 무엇을 알고 싶었니?

학생: 그게요. 이번 주 후반에 교과서 8장과 9장에 대한 시험이 있는 것을 봤는데요. 한 번에 시험 보기에는 양이 좀 많은 것 같아서요.

교수: 글쎄, 그 두 장은 모두 열대 우림이라는 주제를 다루고 있고, 꼭 동시에 다뤄져야 하는 내용이란다.

학생: 음, 이렇게 짧은 시간에 복습하기에는 많아 보여요. 제 말은, 여기 이 장들을 좀 보세요. 제가 아무리 한 번에 많은 페이지를 읽는 데 익숙해졌다고 해도, 저에게도 한계가 있다고요.

교수: 글쎄, 대학생이 된다는 것은 때로는 한계를 넓히는 것을 뜻하기도 해. 하지만 봐라, 내용이 그렇게 어렵지 않아. 이 두 장에 있는 페이지 대부분은 그래프와 통계들이어서 외울 필요가 없거든. 다만 이런 것으로부터 기본 개념은 꼭 알아두어야 한단다.

학생: [누그러진 듯이] 음, 알겠습니다. 아, 제가 알고 싶던 것이 하나 더 있는데요 다음 주에 갈 도서관 견학에 대한 거예요. 교실에서 먼저 모이는 건가요, 아니면 도서관에서 모이나요?

교수: 아, 도서관에서 모이게 될 것 같아. 하지만 다른 자세한 사항에 대해서는 다음 수업 때 모두가 모인 자리에서 이야기할게. |

대화의 일부를 다시 듣고 질문에 답하시오.
학생의 교과서에 대해 추론할 수 있는 것은?
(A) 짧은 시간에 끝낼 수 있다.
(B) 복잡한 자료를 다룬다.
(C) 장들의 내용이 매우 길다.
(D) 학생들에게 그렇게 유익한 정보를 주지 못한다.

해설 | 다시 듣기 부분에서 학생이 "It just seems like a lot to go over in such a short time"이라고 했으므로, 해당 장들은 분량 면에서 양이 많음을 알 수 있다.

어휘 | **go over** 복습하다 **push limit** 한계를 넓히다, 도전하다 **session** 수업

05

Listen to part of a discussion in an art class.

Professor (F): Good morning, class. Today we're going to look at the works of Louis Comfort Tiffany, one of the most prominent makers of modern stained-glass works. Has anyone seen any of his stained-glass pieces firsthand?

Student (M): I actually saw an exhibit of his lamps last year in a museum. They were incredible. Each lamp's glass was so clear, with so many colors. And it seemed so rich in texture as well. It was almost as if the light reflected through the lamp glass like a gemstone.

Professor: Great! I think you've just described the overall effect that Tiffany wanted to create with his stained-glass works. You see, Tiffany made several trips to Europe and was heavily influenced by the stained-glass windows he saw in medieval churches, which were meant to evoke a religious experience when looked at, rather than purely to let light into the building. As he developed his stained-glass technique, he focused on using opaque colors that would create a shimmering effect as the light passed through them.

Student: I remember that lighting effect was very impressive. I just wanted to admire the images of figures like dragonflies and butterflies that seemed to glow on his lamps.

Professor: Exactly. I'm glad you mentioned those pictures. He really brought depictions of insects and birds to life on his lamps. One of the ways he did so was by cooking his glass mixtures in a furnace over a low flame, which caused the glass to crack into small lines. These cracks would refract the light, making his pictures come alive.

예술 수업 중 토론의 일부를 들으시오.

교수 (여): 안녕하세요, 여러분. 오늘 우리는 가장 유명한 현대식 스테인드글라스 예술품 제작자 중 한 명인 Louis Comfort Tiffany의 작품에 대해 알아보려고 합니다. 그가 만든 스테인드글라스 작품을 직접 본 사람 있나요?

학생 (남): 저는 실제로 작년에 미술관에서 그가 만든 램프 전시회를 봤어요. 대단했어요. 각 램프의 유리가 너무 투명했고요, 색깔도 다양했습니다. 질감도 풍부했던 것 같아요. 마치 빛이 보석처럼 램프 유리 속으로 투과하는 것 같았어요.

교수: 좋아요! Tiffany가 스테인드글라스 작품을 통해 창조하고 싶어 했던 전체적인 효과를 잘 설명한 것 같군요. 그러니까 Tiffany는 유럽에 여러 번 갔었는데, 그곳 중세 교회에서 스테인드글라스로 만든 창을 보고 큰 영향을 받았어요. 그 창들은 단순히 빛을 건물 내부에 들이는 것이 아니라, 보았을 때 어떤 종교적인 경험을 마음속에서 일으키기 위한 것이었죠. 그는 자신만의 스테인드글라스 기법을 개발하면서, 빛이 그 작품을 투과할 때 아른거리는 효과를 낼 수 있도록 불투명한 색을 쓰는 데 주력했어요.

학생: 조명 효과가 매우 인상적이었던 것으로 기억합니다. 단지 저는 그 사람의 램프에서 빛이 나는 것처럼 보였던 잠자리와 나비 같은 이미지에 찬사를 보내고 싶었어요.

교수: 바로 그거에요. 그 그림들 이야기를 꺼내니 기쁘군요. 그는 정말 자기 램프 위에 묘사한 곤충과 새들의 그림에 생명을 불어넣었어요. 그가 그렇게 했던 방법 중 하나는 그가 유리 혼합물을 용광로 속에서 낮은 불에 구웠기 때문이죠. 이것 때문에 유리는 갈라지면서 작은 금들이 생겼어요. 이 금들이 빛을 굴절시켜, 그의 그림들이 살아있게 했던 거예요.

Louis Comfort Tiffany에 대해 추론할 수 있는 것은?
(A) 스테인드글라스 램프를 만들 때 빛의 효과에 엄청난 노력을 기울였다.
(B) 보석을 이용하여 자신의 스테인드글라스 작품의 조명 효과를 얻었다.
(C) 교회에서 자신의 램프로 종교적 경험을 자아내기 위해 노력했다.
(D) 자신의 스테인드글라스 램프로 기능적 목적을 달성하는 데 실패했다.

해설 | 교수는 강의에서 Tiffany가 특수한 조명 효과를 내기 위해 사용한 제작 기법을 자세하게 소개하는데, 이를 통해 Tiffany가 특수한 조명 효과를 위해 큰 노력을 기울였음을 추론할 수 있다.

어휘 | **prominent** 유명한, 중요한 **firsthand** 직접(으로), 바로 **rich in** ~이 풍부한[많은] **gemstone** 보석의 원석(原石), 준(準)보석 **overall** 전체의 **medieval** 중세의 **opaque** (유리·액체 등이) 불투명한 **shimmering** 아른거리는, 반짝이는 **crack** 금이 가다, (무엇이 갈라져 생긴) 금

06

Listen to part of a lecture in a zoology class.

Professor (M): There are a lot of factors that affect the evolution of animal populations. Today, though, we are only going to focus on one of these factors, a phenomenon known as allopatric speciation. Allopatric speciation is when the geographic location of an animal population plays a role in altering that population's gene flow.

동물학 강의 중 일부를 들으시오.

교수 (남): 동물 개체군 진화에 영향을 미치는 요인들은 많이 있습니다. 하지만 오늘 우리는 이 요인 중 하나에 집중할 텐데, 이는 이소적 종분화라고 알려진 현상이에요. 이소적 종분화는 동물 개체군의 지리적 위치가 그 개체군의 유전자 확산에 큰 역할을 하는 것입니다.

Generally what happens is that some sort of physical barrier, such as a mountain range or large body of water, isolates members of an animal species. Consequently, this physical barrier does not allow all the members of the species to regularly mate with each other, resulting in the species' genetic lineage to separate, creating two distinct gene flows. Even if the physical barrier is removed after a significantly long period of time and the two separated populations are reunited, the populations may remain distinct from each other genetically. The new species may also evolve its own unique traits, primarily as a result of adapting to its distinct environment.

An example of allopatric speciation is the emergence of two separate species of squirrels that line the north and south sides of the Grand Canyon. Although they were once part of a single population, the physical barrier of the Grand Canyon ended up splitting the squirrel species into two populations, which could no longer reproduce with each other. 🎧 However, it is interesting to note that although the gene flow of ground animals like the squirrel populations were affected by the Grand Canyon, bird populations were not affected by the formation of the Grand Canyon, since they could easily fly across it.

일반적으로 발생하는 것은 산맥이나 큰 수역과 같은 물리적 장벽이 동물 종의 구성원들을 고립시키는 거예요. 그 결과, 이 물리적 장벽은 그 종의 모든 구성원이 서로 규칙적인 짝짓기를 하지 못하도록 만들어서, 두 가지의 다른 유전자 확산을 일으키며 그 종의 유전적 계통을 분리시키게 되죠. 만약 상당히 오랜 시간 후에 그 물리적 장벽이 제거되고 두 개로 분리되었던 개체군이 재통합된다고 하더라도, 그 개체군들은 서로 유전적으로 다른 상태를 유지할 수도 있어요. 새로운 종은 주로 별개의 환경에 적응한 결과로써, 그들 고유의 특성을 진화시킬 수도 있죠.

이소적 종분화의 한 예는 그랜드캐니언의 북쪽과 남쪽에 있는 두 가지로 분리된 다람쥐 종의 출현이에요. 그들은 한때 하나의 개체군에 속했었지만, 그랜드캐니언이라는 물리적 장벽이 그 다람쥐 종들을 두 개의 개체군으로 나눠버렸고, 이들은 더이상 서로 번식할 수 없었어요. 하지만, 다람쥐 개체군과 같은 육상 동물들의 유전자 확산이 그랜드캐니언의 영향을 받았음에도 불구하고 조류 개체군들은 그랜드캐니언을 쉽게 날아다닐 수 있었기 때문에, 그랜드캐니언의 형성에 의해 영향을 받지 않았다는 점은 흥미롭죠.

강의의 일부를 다시 듣고 질문에 답하시오.
그랜드캐니언에 대해 추론할 수 있는 것은?

(A) 이 물리적 장벽은 주변 조류 개체군들의 유전자 확산을 변화시킬 수 있었다.
(B) 그랜드캐니언의 형성으로 인해 다양한 조류 종이 그곳에 서식한다.
(C) 조류 개체군들은 충분히 고립되지 않아서 이소적 종분화가 발생하지 않았다.
(D) 이 물리적 장벽은 다람쥐와 조류 개체군들의 유전자 확산에 영향을 주지 않았다.

해설 | 교수에 의하면 다람쥐 개체군과 같은 육상 동물과 달리 조류 개체군들은 쉽게 날아다닐 수 있었기 때문에 그랜드캐니언의 영향을 받지 않았다고 한다. 즉, 그랜드캐니언은 조류 개체군들을 충분히 고립시키지 못했기 때문에 이소적 종분화가 발생하지 않았다는 것을 추론할 수 있다.

어휘 | **allopatric speciation** 이소적 종분화　**gene flow** 유전자 확산(유동)　**lineage** 계통, 혈통

Listening Practice

p.66

01 (A), (D)　**02** (B)　**03** (C)

Listen to part of a lecture in an environmental science class.

Professor (F): Everyone, please take a seat and then we'll get started. So today we are going to continue our look at ecosystems throughout the United States, and today's focus will be on the Everglades. This immense region of wetlands on the Florida peninsula is more than 4,000 square miles wide, filled with tall grasses, trees, and other vegetation poking out through large pools.

Q01(D) Because it's located in the southeast continental United States, it is warm all year and receives large amounts of wind and rain from the Atlantic Ocean. The combination of these factors has created a unique marshland environment here, with many different varieties of plants and animals.

Essentially, the environment in the Florida Everglades is a mixture of tropical and temperate climates. The area has trees often found in temperate regions, such as oaks and maples, as well as trees found in tropical areas, such as mahogany trees.

환경과학 강의 중 일부를 들으시오.

교수 (여): 여러분, 모두 앉으세요. 그러면 시작할게요. 오늘은 계속해서 미국 전역의 생태계에 대해 알아보도록 하겠습니다. 오늘 이야기의 초점은 에버글레이즈 습지(濕地)입니다. 플로리다 반도에 있는 이 광활한 습지는 폭이 4천 제곱마일이 넘으며, 큰 풀, 나무, 그리고 큰 물 웅덩이에 솟아 있는 식물로 가득 차 있어요.

미대륙 남동쪽에 있기 때문에 1년 내내 따뜻하며, 대서양의 영향으로 바람이 많이 불고 비가 많이 내립니다. 이러한 요소들이 결합하여 다양한 동식물이 많이 사는 독특한 습지 환경이 만들어졌습니다.

기본적으로 플로리다 에버글레이즈 습지의 환경은 열대 기후와 온대 기후가 혼합된 것이라고 보면 됩니다. 이 지역에는 떡갈나무, 단풍나무와 같이 온대 지역에서 볼 수 있는 나무들은 물론, 마호가니 나무와 같이 열대 지역에서 볼 수 있는 나무들도 있습니다.

The nutrient-rich soil in this area also supports several other forms of plant life, though the ground itself is mostly a layer of oversaturated soil. Q01(A) Animal species of all kinds can be found in this ecosystem, too. Deer, foxes, numerous lizards and wading birds, and even manatees reside here. Oh, and of course, the famous alligators of the region, too.

Unfortunately, this beautiful environment is in danger. Q02 You see, development for more than a century or so has created many problems for the Everglades. A lot of canals were dug and dams were built in the Everglades to remove water from it. Draining large areas of the swamp in order to make it hospitable for humans has been extremely destructive. By trying to prevent, or at least reduce, the flooding that is so crucial to the area, we have actually disturbed the natural distribution of water there. As a result, many areas there have been blocked off to animals or completely flooded.

This deprives animals of their habitats. If more animal habitat is affected by human activity, we'll lose a lot of endangered animals, including wading birds and panthers. Furthermore, toxic algae and the rise in organic mercury threaten the animals that thrive on the Everglades water. Numerous species of animals here are already endangered, including the manatee. Q03 This has become such a problem that the region is now the focus of numerous conservation efforts, which are worth a quick look. The U.S. government is trying to restore the Everglades park by allocating funds, but improvement has been glacial.

영양분이 풍부하게 함유된 이 지역의 토양은 여러 다른 형태의 식물도 자라게 해주지만, 토양 자체는 주로 과포화토(過飽和土) 층으로 구성되어 있어요. 이곳 생태계에서는 온갖 종류의 동물들도 발견될 수 있습니다. 사슴, 여우, 수많은 도마뱀, 섭금류(涉禽類)의 새, 그리고 해우까지도 이곳에 서식하고 있죠. 아, 그리고 물론, 이 지역에서 유명한 악어도 있어요.

안타깝게도 이 아름다운 환경이 위험에 처해 있습니다. 한 세기가 넘도록 이어진 개발은 에버글레이즈 습지대에 많은 문제들을 일으켰어요. 물을 빼내기 위해 에버글레이즈 습지대에는 많은 수로와 댐이 건설되었어요. 인간에게 쾌적한 환경을 만들기 위해 넓은 늪지의 물을 빼내면서 극심한 파괴를 가져왔습니다. 범람이 이 지역에서 매우 중요하므로 범람을 막거나 적어도 줄이려고 노력함으로써, 사실 우리는 이 지역에서 이루어지는 자연적인 배수를 교란시킨 것입니다. 그 결과, 그곳의 많은 지역이 동물들이 살 수 없는 곳이 되거나 완전히 물에 잠기게 되었습니다.

이것은 동물들로부터 서식지를 빼앗았죠. 만약 인간의 활동 때문에 동물 서식지가 추가로 영향을 받는다면, 우리는 섭금류의 새와 검은 표범 같은 멸종 위기에 처해 있는 많은 동물을 잃게 될 것입니다. 더 나아가, 유독성 조류와 유기 수은의 증가는 에버글레이즈 습지대의 물에서 잘 살고 있는 동물들을 위협하고 있어요. 이미 해우를 포함한 수많은 동물 종들이 위험에 처해 있습니다. 이것은 큰 문제가 되어서 이제 이 지역에 수많은 보존 노력이 집중되고 있는데, 이에 대해 빨리 훑어보도록 하겠습니다. 미국 정부는 예산을 할당하여 에버글레이즈 습지대 공원을 복원하려고 하고 있지만, 진전의 속도는 더디기만 합니다.

01 교수에 따르면, 다음 중 에버글레이즈 습지대에 대해 옳은 것은?
2개의 답을 고르시오.

(A) 매우 다양한 야생 동물들이 있다.
(B) 강수량이 많지 않다.
(C) 미국 전역에 있다.
(D) 따뜻한 날씨가 지속된다.

해설 | Detail 교수는 이 지역이 1년 내내 따뜻하며, 사슴, 여우, 악어 등 온갖 종류의 동물들이 살고 있다고 설명하고 있다.

02 교수가 에버글레이즈 습지대 개발에 대해 논의하는 방식은?

(A) 그 지역 개발의 역사를 제시함으로써
(B) 개발의 해로운 영향을 설명함으로써
(C) 그곳을 개발하는 이유를 논의함으로써
(D) 그 지역에서 생산되는 제품의 예를 제시함으로써

해설 | Organization 강의 후반에서 교수는 "development for more than a century or so has created many problems for the Everglades"라고 언급하고, 개발이 그 지역 생태계에 끼친 악영향들에 대해 설명하고 있다.

03 교수에 따르면, 에버글레이즈 습지대에 대해 결론 내릴 수 있는 것은?

(A) 그 지역의 환경은 사람들이 살기에는 그다지 좋지 않다.
(B) 그 지역을 보존하려는 미국 정부의 노력은 매우 효과적이다.
(C) 그 지역에 대한 위협을 제거하기 위해 더 효율적인 조치들을 마련할 필요가 있다.
(D) 수로와 댐이 그 지역을 동물들이 살기에 더 쾌적하게 만들었다.

해설 | Inference 교수는 미국 정부가 예산을 투입하여 이 습지대의 공원을 복원하려고 하지만 진전이 더디다고 말했으므로 더 효율적인 조치가 필요하다고 생각하고 있음을 알 수 있다.

어휘 | **Everglades** 에버글레이즈 습지대(미국 플로리다 주의 소택지) **peninsula** 반도 **vegetation** 식물, 초목 **poke out** 솟아 있다, 쑥 내다 **continental** 대륙의 **marshland** 습지, 소택지 **temperate** 온대의 **oak** 떡갈나무, 오크(나무) **maple** 단풍나무 **mahogany** 마호가니(적갈색이 나는 열대산 나무의 목재) **plant life** 식물 **oversaturated** 과포화(過飽和) 상태의 **lizard** 도마뱀 **wading bird** 섭금류의 새(두루미·백로·황새 따위) **manatee** 해우 **in danger** 위험에 처한 **swamp** 늪, 습지 **hospitable** (환경 등이) 쾌적한, 적절한 **distribution** 분배 **deprive A of B** A에게서 B를 빼앗다 **habitat** 서식지 **alga** 조류, 해조 (pl. algae) **organic mercury** 유기 수은 **thrive** 번성하다 **endangered** (멸종) 위험에 처한 **conservation** 보존, 보호

PART B | Approaching Themes

Chapter 08 Office Hours

Intensive Drill 1
p.72

01 (B)   **02** (C)   **03** (D)   **04** (A)

Listen to a conversation between a student and a professor.

Student (F): Hey, Dr. Ted.

Professor (M): Oh, hi, Liz. What's up?

Student: Um, I heard that next semester you are giving a famous course on microcredit in Third World nations.

Professor: [Chuckles] Well, I wouldn't exactly call it famous, but, yes, I am holding it next semester. Are you interested?

Student: Yeah, since I've started studying economics. **Q02** But the problem is that I've already registered for all my courses for next semester, and I already have the maximum amount of classes allowed. And I really need to take all of those classes. Since I'll already have plenty on my plate, **Q01** I was wondering if I could audit your course, so I could learn the material without doing the work.

Professor: **Q04** 🎧 Hmm. If it were solely up to me, then yeah, I'd be happy to have you sit in, but there might be one problem. See, the Economics Department only allows audits for classes that haven't been completely filled. However . . . I suppose that because of your outstanding reputation in the department, they would make an exception for you with a little persuasion from me, of course.

Student: I appreciate it. Wow, just think, taking a great course and for free!

Professor: Oh, hold on. There's still the standard fee for registering for an audited course, although it will be a little bit cheaper than for a formal course.

Student: [Surprised] Are you serious? Even though I'm not getting a grade or any credit for it? I hadn't even thought of paying for auditing a class.

Professor: Yep. **Q03** It's only fair. After all, students who audit courses still benefit from a professor's services. They shouldn't get a free ride just because they're not getting a grade. Don't you agree?

Student: That's true, but it's a little annoying. What's the point of paying for a class if you aren't going to get any credit for it?

Professor: That's a good point, and I can sympathize with you. Money is no small matter, but it seems like you really want to take the course, Liz. And I don't teach it every year, so this could be your last chance.

학생과 교수의 대화를 들으시오.

학생 (여): 안녕하세요, Ted 박사님.

교수 (남): 어, 안녕, Liz. 무슨 일이니?

학생: 음, 교수님이 다음 학기에 제3세계 국가들의 소액 신용대출에 관한 유명한 수업을 하실 거라고 들었어요.

교수: [웃으며] 글쎄, 꼭 유명하다고 말하지는 않겠지만, 맞아, 다음 학기에 할 거란다. 관심 있니?

학생: 네, 제가 경제학 공부를 시작했기 때문이에요. 하지만 저는 이미 다음 학기에 들을 모든 과목을 등록했다는 것이 문제에요. 그리고 이미 허용된 수업의 최대치를 신청했거든요. 그리고 그 수업들은 정말 전부 들어야 하는 거예요. 제가 할 일이 이미 너무 많아서 그런데요, 제가 교수님 수업을 청강하면 안 될까 궁금해서요. 그러면 과제를 하지 않고도 그 내용을 배울 수 있을 테니까요.

교수: 음, 그게 전적으로 나에게 달린 문제라면, 그래, 기꺼이 네가 청강할 수 있도록 해줄 거야. 그런데 한 가지 문제가 생길 수 있어. 그게 말이지, 경제학과에서는 정원이 차지 않은 수업에 한해서만 청강을 허락하거든. 하지만… 학과 내에서의 너의 뛰어난 명성을 고려하면 아마도 예외로 해주지 않을까 하고 생각한다. 물론 나도 설득을 좀 해야겠지만.

학생: 정말 감사해요. 와, 생각해 보세요, 대단한 수업을 듣게 되다니, 그것도 무료로!

교수: 어, 잠시만. 청강 과목으로 등록해도 기본 수업료는 있단다. 정규 과목보다는 약간 더 싸겠지만.

학생: [놀라서] 정말이에요? 그 과목에 점수나 학점을 받지 않는데도요? 청강과목에 돈을 지급한다는 생각은 해 본 적이 없어요.

교수: 그렇단다. 그래야 공평하지. 어쨌든 청강하는 학생들도 결국 교수의 서비스로부터 혜택을 받는 것이잖니. 점수를 받지 않는다고 해서 무임승차를 할 수는 없지. 그렇게 생각하지 않니?

학생: 맞는 말이기는 하지만, 조금 화가 나네요. 학점을 인정받지 않는데 돈을 지급할 이유가 무엇이죠?

교수: 좋은 지적이구나. 그리고 네 말에 공감해. 돈은 작은 문제가 아니니까. 하지만 Liz, 너 이 수업을 정말 듣고 싶어 하는 것 같은데. 내가 이 수업을 매년 맡는 것이 아니라서 말이야, 이번이 너의 마지막 기회일지도 모른단다.

Student: Yeah, I really do. I still need all my other classes, though, so maybe I'll just sign up to audit and then see what happens. Thanks, Dr. Ted.

Professor: Sure, anytime.

학생: 네, 정말 듣고 싶어요. 하지만 다른 수업들도 모두 들어야 하니까, 아마도 청강 신청을 한 뒤 두고 봐야겠네요. 감사합니다, Ted 박사님.

교수: 천만에, 언제든지.

01 학생이 교수를 찾아간 이유는?
(A) 다음 학기에 교수의 수업을 듣는다는 것을 알려주기 위해
(B) 학점 취득 없이 다음 학기에 교수의 수업을 듣는 것에 대해 논의하기 위해
(C) 교수가 자신의 가장 인기 있는 수업 중 하나를 언제 가르칠지 묻기 위해
(D) 다음 학기에 어떤 과목을 들어야 할지 문의하기 위해

해설 | Main Idea 학생이 교수의 한 수업을 언급하며 "I was wondering if I could audit your course"라고 말했으므로 그 수업을 청강할 수 있는지 문의하러 온 것임을 알 수 있다.

02 학생이 해당 수업을 수강하고 학점을 받는 대신 청강하기를 원하는 이유는?
(A) 지급할 만한 충분한 돈이 없다.
(B) 그 수업에서 잘하지 못할까 봐 걱정된다.
(C) 이미 너무 많은 수업을 신청했다.
(D) 졸업 논문을 쓰기 위한 정보가 필요하다.

해설 | Detail 학생은 이미 다음 학기 등록을 마쳤고 허용된 수업의 최대치를 신청했다고 말하면서 교수에게 청강 가능 여부를 묻고 있다.

03 학생들이 청강 과목에 대해 돈을 지급하는 것에 대한 교수의 의견은?
(A) 돈이 많지 않은 학생들에게 가혹하다고 생각한다.
(B) 학점 인정 없이 수업료를 부과하는 것에 대해 대학 측에 화가 난다.
(C) 오로지 학교 정책이라는 이유로 받아들여야 한다고 생각한다.
(D) 교수들이 서비스를 제공하므로 그것이 필요하다고 생각한다.

해설 | Attitude 수업을 청강할 때에도 수업료가 있다는 것에 대해 학생이 놀라자, 교수는 "It's only fair"라고 답하고 그 이유로 청강생들 역시 교수의 서비스로부터 혜택을 받기 때문이라고 설명하고 있다.

04 대화의 일부를 다시 듣고 질문에 답하시오.
교수가 암시하는 것은?
(A) 그 수업은 최대 정원에 달했다.
(B) 학생은 경제학을 잘하지 못한다.
(C) 학생이 받아들여질 것으로 생각하지 않는다.
(D) 학생과 교수는 별로 친하지 않다.

해설 | Inference 교수는 정원 미달 수업에 한해서만 청강할 수 있다면서 학생의 청강이 쉽지 않을 것을 나타내고 있으므로, 자신의 수업은 이미 최대 정원에 달했음을 암시하고 있다.

어휘 | **microcredit** 소액 신용대출　**have plenty on one's plate** 할 일이 많다　**audit** 청강하다　**outstanding** 뛰어난　**get a free ride** 무임승차하다, 공짜로 즐기다　**sign up** 신청하다, 가입하다

Intensive Drill 2　　　　　　　　　　　　　　　　　　　　　　　　　　p.74

01 (C)　**02** (C), (D), (E)　**03** (C)　**04** (C)

Listen to a conversation between a student and a professor.

Professor (F): Hey, Jack. Q01 I'm sorry to tell you this, but the chance of raising your essay score even if we reassess it is slim to none.

Student (M): Is it because I couldn't meet the minimum word limit? I know I should've written up to 5,000 words, but I only made it up to around 4,700 words.

학생과 교수의 대화를 들으시오.

교수 (여): 안녕, Jack. 이런 말 해서 미안하지만, 우리가 재평가해도 네 에세이 점수를 높일 가능성은 아주 희박하단다.

학생 (남): 제가 최소 글자 수를 채우지 못했기 때문인가요? 저도 알아요. 5,000단어까지 썼어야 했는데, 겨우 4,700단어 정도만 썼죠.

Professor: Well, that wasn't a critical issue, as we accept word differences around 250 words.

Student: Oh, was it because of the number of references I used, then? I remember you emphasized that we should refer to at least 10 to 15 books or journals, but I used exactly 10 books for my reference.

Professor: Well, reference was one of the issues, even though it wasn't about how many books you cited. Q02(C) Some of your references were seriously outdated.

Student: In my defense, I wanted to include some classic ideas in my essay.

Professor: Q02(D) I understand what you mean. It's good to include some of the journals about early stages of theories, but you should be careful when the ideas were later proven to be wrong.

Student: What do you mean?

Professor: Let me show you an example. Here, you cited a 1980s' theory about the difference in brain activity and process when conscious and unconscious.

Student: Yes, the theory said that brain activity and process are more complex when we are conscious.

Professor: Q04 But the theory was proven wrong when researchers at the University of Michigan conducted an experiment to show that even when we are unconscious, brain activity and processes are as complex as when we are conscious.

Student: I should have researched more thoroughly.

Professor: Q02(E) Besides, you ignored the reference style. You should not regard such guidelines lightly. They are as important as your essay contents.

Student: I don't know what to tell you. I should have been more careful.

Professor: Well, have you ever taken any seminars dealing with how to write an academic essay? There are many good sessions taught by graduate tutors at our university, and they would definitely include how to cite references and use reference styles.

Student: Hmm, I think I really need one.

Professor: Good. Another thing is, this essay represents 60 percent of your overall grade, but you only achieved around 40 percent. I'm sure you're aware of the fact that the final exam takes up 40 percent.

Student: Does it mean that I already failed this course?

Professor: Q03 You can still pass it if you get a nearly perfect score on the final exam.

Student: OK, I understand what you're saying. Thank you for the advice.

교수: 음, 그것은 중요한 문제가 아니야. 250단어 정도의 차이는 봐주니까.

학생: 아, 그러면 제가 사용한 참고 문헌의 수 때문인가요? 우리는 적어도 10개에서 15개의 책이나 학술지를 봐야 한다고 교수님께서 강조하셨던 것이 생각나요. 하지만 저는 정확하게 10권의 책을 참고 문헌으로 사용했어요.

교수: 글쎄, 얼마나 많은 책을 인용했는지에 대한 것은 아니었지만, 참고 문헌도 문제 중 하나였지. 네 참고 문헌 중 일부는 심할 정도로 구식이었어.

학생: 변명하자면, 저는 제 에세이에 약간 고전적인 개념들을 포함하고 싶었어요.

교수: 네 의도는 알겠어. 이론들의 초기 단계에 관한 일부 학술지를 포함한 것은 좋지만, 그 개념들이 나중에 잘못된 것으로 판명된 경우에는 신중해야 한단다.

학생: 무슨 말씀이신가요?

교수: 예를 하나 들어볼게. 여기, 너는 인간이 의식적일 때와 무의식적일 때, 두뇌 활동과 처리 과정의 차이점에 관하여 80년대의 한 이론을 인용했더구나.

학생: 네, 그 이론에 의하면 우리가 의식적일 때 두뇌 활동과 처리 과정이 더 복잡합니다.

교수: 하지만 그 이론은 미시간 대학의 학자들이 실험을 해서 우리가 무의식적일 때에도 두뇌 활동과 처리 과정이 우리가 의식적일 때만큼 복잡하다는 사실을 밝혀냈을 때 잘못된 것으로 드러났지.

학생: 제가 더 철저하게 조사를 했었어야 했군요.

교수: 게다가 너는 참고 문헌 표기법도 무시했더구나. 그런 가이드라인을 가볍게 여기면 안 된단다. 그것들은 에세이 내용만큼 중요하니까.

학생: 무슨 말씀을 드려야 할지 모르겠습니다. 제가 더 주의를 기울였어야 했어요.

교수: 음, 혹시 학문적 에세이 작성법을 다룬 세미나에 참석한 적이 있니? 우리 대학교에는 졸업생 개인 교사들이 가르치는 훌륭한 강좌들이 많이 있는데, 그런 강좌들에는 참고 문헌 인용법과 참고 표시법이 틀림없이 포함될 거야.

학생: 음, 저한테는 그런 강좌가 정말 필요한 것 같아요.

교수: 좋아. 또 하나는, 이 에세이가 네 전체 성적 비중에서 60%에 해당한다는 거야. 그런데 너는 40% 정도밖에 얻지 못했어. 기말고사가 40%를 차지한다는 사실은 너도 잘 알고 있으리라 생각하는데.

학생: 제가 이미 이 과목에서 낙제했다는 말씀인가요?

교수: 네가 기말고사에서 거의 만점을 받으면 아직 통과할 가능성은 있어.

학생: 알겠습니다. 무슨 말씀인지 잘 알겠어요. 조언해 주셔서 고맙습니다.

01 학생의 문제는?
(A) 자기가 쓴 에세이의 내용을 완전히 이해하지 못하고 있다.
(B) 늦게 제출해서 에세이 점수가 깎였다.
(C) 에세이 점수를 낮게 받을 가능성이 높다.
(D) 에세이와 기말고사에서 모두 낙제했기 때문에 과목을 통과할 수 없다.

해설 | Main Idea 교수는 학생의 에세이 점수를 높일 가능성은 아주 희박하다고 말한다.

02 교수에 따르면, 학생이 제출한 에세이의 문제점은?
3개의 답을 고르시오.
(A) 글자 수 제한 규정을 충족시키지 못한 것
(B) 참고 문헌을 충분히 이용하지 않은 것
(C) 시대에 뒤진 참고 문헌을 이용한 것
(D) 오류로 드러난 개념을 인용한 것
(E) 참고 문헌 표기법을 지키지 못한 것

해설 | Detail 교수는 학생이 심할 정도로 구식인 참고 문헌을 에세이에 이용했고, 나중에 오류로 판명된 이론을 인용하였으며, 참고 문헌 표기법도 지키지 않았다고 차례로 지적하고 있다.

03 교수가 기말고사를 언급하는 이유는?
(A) 학생이 그 시험을 볼 자격이 없음을 알려주기 위해
(B) 학생에게 기말고사 일정을 상기시켜 주기 위해
(C) 학생에게 이 과목을 통과하려면 그 시험을 잘 봐야 한다는 사실을 경고하기 위해
(D) 시험에서 만점을 받기는 매우 어려울 것이라고 말하기 위해

해설 | Organization 교수는 학생의 에세이 점수가 낮기 때문에 기말고사 성적을 잘 받아야 과목을 통과할 수 있다고 말한다.

04 대화의 일부를 다시 듣고 질문에 답하시오.
학생이 다음과 같이 말할 때 의미하는 것은?
"I don't know what to tell you."
(A) 자기가 무슨 말을 하려고 했는지 생각나지 않는다.
(B) 교수가 자신의 문제점을 지적한 것에 불쾌함을 느낀다.
(C) 에세이를 잘 못 쓴 것에 창피함을 느낀다.
(D) 내용과 참고 문헌 중 어느 것이 더 중요한지 모른다.

해설 | Function 교수가 학생이 쓴 에세이의 문제점을 지적한 뒤에 나온 말이므로 학생은 부끄러움을 느낀 것이다.

어휘 | reassess 재평가하다　be slim to none (가능성이) 아주 희박하다　reference 참고[인용] 문헌, 참고
refer to (정보를 알아내기 위해) ~을 보다, ~을 나타내다　outdated (더 이상 쓸모가 없게) 구식인　in my defense 변명을 하자면
reference style 참고 문헌 표기법　academic 학문의　represent (~에) 해당[상당]하다　final exam 기말고사

Intensive Drill 3　　　　　　　　　　　　　　　　　　　　　　　　　　　　　　　　　　　p.76

01 (C), (D)　　02 (A)　　03 (C) – (D) – (B) – (A)　　04 (C)

Listen to a conversation between a student and a professor.

Student (F): Good afternoon, Professor Elkin. I'm sorry to bother you, but can I get a waiver form for the field trip next week?

Professor (M): It could be a good chance to discover a future career, though. Q01(C) Why don't you want to go?

Student: Well, honestly, I participated in last year's field trip, and I was a bit disappointed.

Professor: Can I ask why you were disappointed?

Student: The trip was just a visit to many local companies. I hoped to see some larger international businesses.

학생과 교수의 대화를 들으시오.

학생 (여): 안녕하세요, Elkin 교수님. 귀찮게 해드려 죄송하지만, 다음 주에 있을 현장 학습의 참석 면제 서류를 얻을 수 있을까요?

교수 (남): 하지만 그것은 미래의 직업을 발견할 훌륭한 기회가 될 수 있을 텐데. 왜 안 가려고 하는 거지?

학생: 그게요, 솔직히 말씀드리면, 작년에 있었던 현장 학습에 참여했었는데, 좀 실망스러웠거든요.

교수: 왜 실망했는지 물어도 될까?

학생: 그 현장 학습은 그냥 지역의 많은 회사들을 방문하는 것이었어요. 더 큰 국제적 기업을 가보고 싶었거든요.

Professor: The purpose of the last trip was to show our students how businesses are run and what specific skills are necessary to join local companies. I'm sorry that it wasn't that helpful to you.

Student: Also, I think there should've been a limit on the number of participants. It was so crowded wherever we went that I could barely listen to what the staff said about their respective companies.

Professor: Yes, I can't deny there were too many participants last year. Q02 I'm planning to set a limit this year. In addition, during this field trip . . . get this . . . there will be many alumni coming from many different business areas to share their experiences. I think this would be a very useful experience.

Student: That sounds great. Q01(D) Can you give me more information about the field trip?

Professor: Sure. Q03(C) Firstly, all the participants will be divided into several groups according to their interests, such as business management, accounting, finance, or marketing. Then each group will have a Q&A session with the seniors who are currently working in their field of interest.

Student: That's exactly the kind of thing I wanted!

Professor: Q03(D) And it's going to be even more informative because on the second day, you will get to visit the workplaces of your alumni and see how they work. Q03(B) After that, you will have another Q&A session with them to ask more questions in depth. Q03(A) And on the last day, we will have a résumé workshop where participants can go over their résumés with our graduate tutors and professors.

Student: Sounds good. Q04 One thing I'd like to ask is, I'm interested in sports business management . . . will this field trip be still helpful to me?

Professor: Oh, what a coincidence. For business management, one of the alumni is a chief executive of the English Premier League and will take those who are interested in sports business management to the City Football Club to talk with senior staff at the club.

Student: Please ignore my initial request for a waiver for this field trip. Thank you, professor.

교수: 지난번 현장 학습의 목적은 학생들에게 기업이 어떻게 운영되고 지역의 회사들에 들어가려면 어떤 특정한 기술이 필요한지를 보여 주는 것이었단다. 너에게는 그렇게 큰 도움이 되지 않았다니 유감이구나.

학생: 또 저는 참가자의 수에도 제한이 있어야 했다고 생각해요. 가는 곳마다 너무 사람이 많아 각 회사의 직원들이 자기 회사에 대해 뭐라고 말하는지 거의 들을 수가 없었어요.

교수: 그래, 작년에 참가자가 너무 많았다는 점은 부인할 수 없지. 올해에는 제한을 둘 계획이야. 게다가 이번 현장 학습 기간에는… 있잖니… 여러 사업 분야에서 일하는 졸업생들이 와서 자신의 경험담을 들려줄 거란다. 이것은 매우 유용한 경험이 될 것 같아.

학생: 좋은 것 같아요. 이번 현장 학습에 대해 정보를 더 주실 수 있나요?

교수: 물론이지. 우선 모든 참가자는 기업 경영, 회계, 재무, 마케팅 등 자신의 관심 분야에 따라 몇 개의 그룹으로 나뉠 거야. 그런 다음, 각 그룹은 현재 자신의 관심 분야에서 일하고 있는 선배들과 질의 · 응답 시간을 가질 예정이란다.

학생: 그게 바로 제가 원했던 종류의 활동이에요!

교수: 이번 현장 학습은 훨씬 더 유익할 거야. 왜냐하면, 둘째 날에 너희들은 졸업생들의 직장을 방문하여 그들이 어떻게 일하고 있는지를 보게 될 테니까. 그 일이 끝나면, 그들과 또 한 차례 질의 · 응답 시간을 갖고 더욱 깊이 있는 질문을 할 수 있단다. 그리고 마지막 날에는 이력서 작성 연수회가 열리는데, 여기서 참가자들은 우리의 졸업생 개인 교사들, 그리고 교수들과 함께 자신의 이력서를 검토할 수 있단다.

학생: 좋네요. 한 가지 묻고 싶은 게 있는데요, 저는 스포츠 비즈니스 경영에 관심이 있는데요… 이번 현장 학습이 여전히 저에게 도움이 될까요?

교수: 이런 우연의 일치가 있나. 비즈니스 경영에 관해서 말인데, 우리 졸업생 중 하나가 영국 프리미어 리그의 최고 책임자인데 그 사람이 스포츠 비즈니스 경영에 관심이 있는 사람들을 도시 축구 클럽에 데리고 가서 그 클럽의 고위 직원들과 이야기를 나눌 거야.

학생: 아까 제가 이번 현장 학습 참석 면제 서류를 달라고 했던 것은 없던 일로 해 주세요. 감사합니다, 교수님.

01 대화의 주된 내용은?
  2개의 답을 고르시오.
  (A) 학생들을 위해 실용적인 현장 학습을 계획하는 방법
  (B) 현장 학습에 참여하는 졸업생들에 대한 정보
  (C) 학생이 현장 학습에 가고 싶어 하지 않는 이유
  (D) 현장 학습에 대한 자세한 정보

해설 | Main Idea 교수는 학생이 현장 학습에 참석하지 않기 위해 면제 서류를 얻으려고 오자, 가고 싶어 하지 않는 이유를 묻고, 이번 현장 학습의 내용과 특징을 자세히 설명해 주고 있다.

02 교수가 다음 주 현장 학습에 대해 암시하는 것은?
  (A) 학생들에게 더욱 유용한 방식으로 개선되었다.
  (B) 가능한 한 많은 학생들을 만족시키기 위해 개선이 필요하다.
  (C) 비즈니스 경영 분야에 중점을 두고 있다.
  (D) 작년 현장 학습보다 더 많은 참가자를 허용할 것이다.

해설 | Inference 학생이 작년 현장 학습에 실망하여 이번엔 안 가려고 하자, 이번 현장 학습에 포함된 많은 유용한 프로그램들을 소개하면서 많이 개선되었다는 사실을 은연중에 나타내고 있다.

03 교수는 현장 학습의 활동들을 설명한다. 이 활동들을 올바른 순서대로 나열하시오.

각 문장을 해당되는 곳으로 옮기시오.

1	(C) 학생들은 자신의 직업적 관심 분야에 따라 몇 개의 그룹으로 나뉠 것이다.
2	(D) 학생들은 일터의 직접적인 경험을 위해 졸업생들이 일하는 직장을 방문할 것이다.
3	(B) 졸업생들과 그들이 일하는 직장에서 질의·응답 시간을 가질 것이다.
4	(A) 이력서와 직업 계획을 준비하기 위한 연수회가 열릴 예정이다.

해설 | Connecting Content 교수는 이번 현장 학습의 일정을 소개하면서, 첫째, 참가자들을 관심 분야별로 나누고, 졸업생들의 직장을 직접 방문하며 그들과 질의·응답 시간을 갖고, 마지막 날에는 이력서 작성을 위한 연수회를 하게 된다고 설명한다.

04 대화의 일부를 다시 듣고 질문에 답하시오.
교수가 다음과 같이 말하는 이유는?
"Oh, what a coincidence."

(A) 학생이 너무 많이 질문하고 있다는 사실을 보여 주기 위해
(B) 학생의 질문이 답하기 너무 어렵다는 뜻을 넌지시 알리기 위해
(C) 학생에게 매우 유익할 정보를 자세히 알려 주기 위해
(D) 학생의 제안을 현장 학습에 반영하기 위해

해설 | Function 교수는 학생이 관심을 두고 있는 스포츠 비즈니스 경영과 관련하여 이번 현장 학습에 그 분야에서 일하는 졸업생을 초빙하여 스포츠 비즈니스 경영에 대한 특별한 학습 활동이 계획되어 있다는 점을 알려주려고 한다.

어휘 | **waiver** 면제[포기] 서류 **field trip** 현장 학습, 견학 여행 **respective** 각자의, 각각의 **alumni** 졸업생들 **in depth** 깊이[심도 있게] **go over** ~을 검토[점검]하다 **coincidence** 우연의 일치 **chief executive** (회사나 조직의) 최고 책임자[최고위자]

Mini Test 1
p.78

01 (C)   **02** (D)   **03** (A), (C)   **04** (B)

Listen to a conversation between a student and a professor.

Student (M): Dr. Robinson, can I come in?

Professor (F): Of course, David. So, what can I help you with today?

Student: It's about the upcoming research paper in our Japanese history class. I really want to get a good grade on it, especially considering some of my recent grades.

Professor: Well, your quiz grade last week caught my attention, but I wouldn't stress about that too much. There's plenty of time left in the semester to get back on track. Still, I'm glad to see that you're thinking about the paper. It is a considerable chunk of your final grade. So, do you have questions about the format?

Student: Oh, not at all. I'm pretty solid on all that from my notes. Q01-1 No, actually, what I'm really struggling with is a topic. I know none of us can write on the same thing, and everyone else has already picked out what they're going to do.

Professor: [A little surprised] Oh? I thought you'd have been among the first.

학생과 교수의 대화를 들으시오.

학생 (남): Robinson 박사님, 들어가도 될까요?

교수 (여): 물론이지, David. 그래, 오늘 뭘 도와줄까?

학생: 일본 역사 수업에서 곧 써야 할 연구 보고서 때문인데요. 저는 그 보고서에서 정말 좋은 점수를 받고 싶거든요. 특히 저의 최근 성적을 생각하면요.

교수: 음, 지난주에 봤던 네 퀴즈 성적이 걸리기는 하더구나. 하지만 나라면 그것에 대해 너무 걱정하지는 않을 거야. 아직 이번 학기에 정상으로 돌아올 시간이 충분히 남아 있잖니. 어쨌든, 네가 보고서에 관해 생각하고 있다는 사실을 알게 되어 기쁘구나. 그 보고서가 최종 성적에서 상당한 부분을 차지하니까. 그래, 형식에 대해 질문이 있는 거니?

학생: 아, 아니에요. 그것에 대해서는 노트에 적어놔서 잘 알고 있어요. 그게 아니라, 사실 제가 정말 고심하고 있는 것은 주제에요. 아무도 같은 주제에 대해 쓰면 안 되는 것으로 알고 있는데, 다른 사람들 모두 이미 자신이 쓸 주제를 골라버렸거든요.

교수: [조금 놀라며] 그래? 나는 네가 가장 먼저 고른 사람 중 하나라고 생각했는데.

Student: Q02 Uh, to tell the truth, I was weighing the options between two pretty solid topics, but I just couldn't decide on which to do. Then in our last class, I found out that two other people already settled on them, so now I'm kind of in a bind. Q01-2 I was wondering if I could get some help choosing a topic.

Professor: Hmm . . . well, if I remember correctly, nobody has chosen to write about religious persecution during the Edo period, but that's just a suggestion.

Student: Q04 Ah, that's as good as anything I can come up with.

Professor: Just remember that I need a proposal by the end of this week.

Student: I've been wondering about that. I have two months to get all my research and organizing done. So why is there such a rush for us to get our proposals in to you?

Professor: You know, there are a lot of stages to writing this paper. Q03(A) I'll need to see at least two rough drafts before the final so I can be sure it's coming along well. You'd be surprised at how many students completely change their topics midway through a research paper . . . it never turns out well in the end. Q03(C) Also, I want to prevent plagiarism. If two students write on the similar topic, they may present the similar specific facts and analyses. How am I to know that one didn't copy the other?

Student: Yeah, you're right. Thanks. I appreciate your advice.

Professor: You're welcome.

학생: 어, 사실은요, 거의 확실한 주제 두 개 중 무엇을 선택할지 심사숙고하고 있었는데, 어느 것을 할지 확실히 결정할 수가 없었어요. 그런데 지난 수업 시간에 다른 두 사람이 이미 그 두 주제를 결정했다는 걸 알았죠. 그래서 지금 좀 난처하게 되었어요. 주제를 정하는 데 도움을 좀 받을 수 있을까 해서요.

교수: 음… 글쎄, 내가 정확히 기억하고 있다면, 에도 시대의 종교 박해에 대해서는 아무도 고르지 않았다고 알고 있어. 이건 하나의 제안일 뿐이지만.

학생: 어, 지금 제가 떠올릴 수 있는 어떤 것만큼 좋은데요.

교수: 이번 주말까지 계획안을 내야 한다는 점을 기억하렴.

학생: 그 점이 궁금했었는데요. 자료를 조사하고 구성하는 시간이 총 두 달이라고 알고 있는데, 교수님께 왜 그렇게 급하게 계획안을 내야 하나요?

교수: 너도 알겠지만, 이 보고서를 쓰는 데에는 여러 단계를 거쳐야 해. 최종본을 완성하기 전까지 잘 진행되고 있는지 확실히 하기 위해서는 적어도 두 번의 초고를 봐야 한단다. 얼마나 많은 학생이 보고서 중도에 주제를 완전히 바꾸는지 알면 놀랄 거다… 그러면 결국 결코 잘 되는 법이 없지. 또 하나, 나는 표절을 방지하고 싶단다. 만약 두 명의 학생이 비슷한 주제에 대해서 쓴다면, 그 두 학생이 비슷한 구체적 사실과 분석을 낼 수도 있거든. 한 명이 다른 한 명의 것을 베끼지 않았다고 어떻게 알 수 있겠니?

학생: 네, 교수님 말씀이 맞네요. 조언해 주셔서 감사합니다.

교수: 천만에.

---

01 학생이 교수를 찾아간 이유는?
(A) 연구 보고서의 형식에 관해 물어보기 위해
(B) 일본 에도 시대에 관한 정보를 얻기 위해
(C) 연구 보고서 주제에 대해 문의하기 위해
(D) 연구 보고서 계획안을 제출하기 위해

해설 | Main Idea 대화 초반 "No, actually, what I'm really struggling with is a topic"이라는 학생의 말을 통해 연구 보고서 주제에 대해 문의하러 온 것임을 알 수 있다.

02 연구 보고서에 대해 학생이 겪고 있는 문제점은?
(A) 주제에 대해 알고 있는 것이 거의 없다.
(B) 교수가 마감일을 연장해줘야 한다.
(C) 그 주제에 대해 충분한 정보를 얻을 수 없다.
(D) 보고서 주제를 찾을 수 없다.

해설 | Detail 자신이 생각한 주제를 다른 사람들이 이미 선택했다고 했으므로, 주제를 찾지 못했음을 알 수 있다.

03 교수가 학생들이 연구 보고서 주제에 대해 사전 승인을 받아야 한다고 주장하는 이유는?
2개의 답을 고르시오.
(A) 장기 과제의 진행 상황을 점검하기 위해
(B) 학생들이 너무 광범위한 주제를 택하지 않도록 확인하기 위해
(C) 한 학생이 다른 학생의 보고서를 베낄 가능성을 줄이기 위해
(D) 학생들이 보고서 형식을 제대로 따르고 있는지 확실히 하기 위해

해설 | Detail 교수는 학생들의 진행 상황 확인과 표절 방지를 사전 승인의 이유로 설명하고 있다.

04 학생이 다음에 할 행동은?
(A) 주제를 조사한 뒤 교수에게 다시 이야기하러 온다.
(B) 교수가 제안한 주제를 바탕으로 보고서 계획안을 작성한다.
(C) 다른 사람이 그의 주제에 대해 쓰고 있지 않은지 학급의 학생들과 확인한다.
(D) 교수가 제안한 주제의 초점을 좁혀 보려 노력한다.

해설 | Inference 교수가 아직 아무도 선택하지 않은 주제를 제안하자 학생이 "Ah, that's as good as anything I can come up with"라고 답했으며, 이번 주까지 계획안을 제출해야 하므로 학생은 교수가 제안한 주제를 바탕으로 보고서 계획안을 작성할 것임을 추측할 수 있다.

어휘 | **get back on track** 정상으로 돌아오다　**considerable** 상당한　**weigh** 심사숙고하다　**settle on** 결정하다　**be in a bind** 난처하게 되다
persecution 박해　**come up with** 떠올리다, 제안하다　**draft** 초고　**midway** 중도에　**plagiarism** 표절

Mini Test 2

p.80

01 (D)　**02** (B)　**03** [Pintia – (B), (D)], [Pollentia – (A), (C)]　**04** (A)

Listen to a conversation between a student and a professor.

Student (F): Hey, Professor Maxwell. You wanted me to drop by?

Professor (M): Yes, Janet! I think we may have to talk for a while.

Student: Uh oh . . . did I do something wrong?

Professor: No, not at all. I just had a few things I was wondering about in regards to your research paper.

Student: Oh! Did you have a chance to look over my archaeological excavation site proposal? Isn't it exciting?

Professor: Yes, very much so. Seems like you'll be travelling all the way to Spain for your project. Spain is such a beautiful country and I enjoy it thoroughly every time I go. Do you speak any Spanish?

Student: Yes, I do speak some, although I'm not fluent. I can't wait! **Q01** I've loved the Spanish language and culture since I first learned the language as a freshman in high school, but I have yet to be able to visit.

Professor: I'm so happy for you, oh, but before we get too off topic . . . I just had a few questions about your excavation site.

Student: Well, it's Las Ruedas, just outside of Pintia.

Professor: Well, why did you decide on Pintia? I know you mentioned you were drawn to it because it would give you a chance to study people who have not been researched extensively . . . but as far as location and site, I feel like there are so many better options.

Student: Is it because the site is too small? I was actually looking at the Pollentia site in Alcudia, but I felt like it would be better to research a topic that other students probably wouldn't pursue. **Q03(A)** The Pollentia site would be dealing with Roman culture, and I felt like too many of the others would write about it as well.

Professor: That's very true, but it's not just because of the size of the site. There's also the location. **Q03(B)** Pintia is in the central part of Spain, **Q03(C)** whereas Alcudia is a coastal area. Not only will it be more enjoyable for you because of the ocean, but there also will be stark differences in the types of artifacts that you'll uncover based on where the sites are.

Student: Well, I thought I'd gone through all the pros and cons meticulously. Are there any other factors that I should have considered?

학생과 교수의 대화를 들으시오.

학생 (여): 안녕하세요, Maxwell 교수님. 제가 잠깐 들르길 원하셨다고요?

교수 (남): 응, Janet! 우리 얘기를 좀 해야 할 것 같구나.

학생: 어, 이런… 제가 뭘 잘못했나요?

교수: 아니, 전혀. 그저 네 연구 보고서와 관련해서 궁금한게 몇 가지 있어서.

학생: 오! 제 고고학 발굴 장소 제안서를 보신 건가요? 흥미롭지 않나요?

교수: 그래, 매우 그렇더구나. 네 프로젝트를 위해 스페인까지 갈 계획인 것 같던데. 스페인은 정말 아름다운 나라라서 갈 때마다 충분히 즐긴단다. 스페인어는 좀 하니?

학생: 네, 유창하진 않지만, 조금 해요. 너무 기대돼요! 고등학교 1학년 때 처음 스페인 언어를 배웠을 때부터 스페인의 언어와 문화를 좋아했어요. 하지만 아직 방문하지는 못했죠.

교수: 네가 그렇다니 정말 기쁘구나, 어, 하지만 주제에서 너무 벗어나기 전에… 네 발굴 장소에 대해 몇 가지 질문이 있단다.

학생: 음, 라스 루에다스라는 곳이고요, 삔띠아 바로 외곽에 있어요.

교수: 음, 왜 삔띠아를 택했니? 대대적으로 조사되지 않았던 사람들을 연구할 기회를 가질 수 있어서 네가 거기에 매료된 거라고 얘기했던 것으로 아는데… 하지만 위치와 장소로 보면 더 나은 선택사항들이 많을 것 같구나.

학생: 그 유적지가 너무 작아서요? 사실 알쿠디아에 있는 폴렌시아를 보려고 했는데요, 다른 학생들이 추구하지 않을 만한 주제를 연구하는 게 더 나을 거로 생각했어요. 폴렌시아 유적지는 로마 문화에 대해 다룰 텐데, 너무 많은 다른 학생들이 그것에 관해 쓸 것으로 생각했거든요.

교수: 그건 사실이지만, 단지 그 유적지의 규모 때문만은 아니란다. 위치에 대한 것도 있지. 삔띠아는 스페인의 중심부에 있고, 알쿠디아는 해안 지역이거든. 바다로 인해 네가 더 즐길 수 있을 뿐만 아니라, 유적지에 따라 네가 발견할 수 있는 인공 유물의 종류에도 극명한 차이가 있을 거야.

학생: 음, 저는 제가 꼼꼼하게 모든 장단점을 살펴봤다고 생각했어요. 제가 고려했어야 하는 또 다른 요인들이 있나요?

Professor: Yes, actually. Q02 Pollentia was uncovered way back in the seventeenth century, so there has been extensive research on the discoveries from the site since the 1930s. That means there is a plenty of information and analysis you can investigate. Q03(D) On the other hand, it's been less than 15 years since comprehensive studies have taken place on the gravesites in Pintia.

Student: Q04 Professor Maxwell, is it OK if I reconsider my proposal and get back to you by tomorrow?

Professor: Sure, Janet. No problem.

교수: 사실 그렇단다. 폴렌시아는 오래전인 17세기에 발견되어, 1930년대 이후로 그 유적지에서 발견된 것에 대해 광범위한 연구가 이뤄졌지. 그건 네가 조사할 수 있는 풍부한 정보와 분석 자료가 있다는 것을 의미하지. 반대로, 삔띠아의 묘지들에 대한 포괄적인 연구가 시작된 것은 15년도 채 되지 않았단다.

학생: Maxwell 교수님, 제 제안서에 대해 재고해보고 내일 다시 찾아와도 괜찮을까요?

교수: 물론이지, Janet. 괜찮단다.

---

01 학생이 말한 스페인에 가는 것에 대해 들뜬 이유는?
(A) 경치를 좋아한다.
(B) 스페인어를 매우 잘한다.
(C) 이전에 가 본 적이 있고 그곳에서의 시간을 즐겼다.
(D) 스페인의 문화에 매료되었다.

해설 | Detail 학생이 "I've loved the Spanish language and culture since I first learned the language"라고 말한 것으로 보아 스페인 문화에 매료되었음을 알 수 있다.

02 교수가 삔띠아 유적지가 광범위하게 연구된 연수를 언급하는 이유는?
(A) 폴렌시아 문명이 삔띠아의 문명보다 훨씬 더 오래 지속되었다는 것을 보여주기 위해
(B) 삔띠아에 대한 연구 자료가 많지 않을지도 모른다는 것을 언급하기 위해
(C) 발굴지가 연구 프로젝트를 위한 시간 요건을 만족하게 하는지에 대해 나타내기 위해
(D) 이곳이 충분히 오랫동안 연구되고 분석되었다는 것을 강조하기 위해

해설 | Organization 교수는 폴렌시아는 연구가 시작된 지 오래되어 정보와 분석 자료가 풍부하다고 말한다. 이와 반대로, 삔띠아는 연구 연수가 오래되지 않아 연구 자료가 많지 않을 것을 지적한다.

03 대화에서 학생과 교수는 두 가지 고고학 유적지의 차이점에 대해 논의한다. 다음 각 사항이 삔띠아나 폴렌시아와 관련 있는지 표시하시오.
각 사항에 대해 알맞은 항목에 표시하시오.

	삔띠아	폴렌시아
(A) 로마 문화		✔
(B) 내륙 위치	✔	
(C) 해안 지역		✔
(D) 매장지	✔	

해설 | Connecting Content 대화에 따르면, 삔띠아는 스페인의 중심부인 내륙에 있고 폴렌시아는 해안 지역이므로, (B)는 삔띠아와 관련되고 (C)는 폴렌시아와 관련된다. 또한 학생이 "The Pollentia site would be dealing with Roman culture"라고 말한 것으로 보아 (A)는 폴렌시아와 관련이 있다. 마지막으로 교수가 "since comprehensive studies have taken place on the gravesites in Pintia"라고 말한 것으로 보아 (D)는 삔띠아와 관련된 것으로 볼 수 있다.

04 연구할 유적지와 관련된 교수의 제안에 대한 학생의 태도는?
(A) 신중히 고려해 볼 가치가 있다고 생각한다.
(B) 제안을 받아들여 그녀의 선택을 바꿀 준비가 되어 있다.
(C) 그녀의 상황에 적절하지 않다고 생각한다.
(D) 그녀의 처음 선택보다 더 낫지 않다고 확신한다.

해설 | Attitude 학생은 자신이 제출한 제안서에 대해 재고해보고 다시 찾아와도 괜찮을지 묻는다. 교수의 제안이 신중히 고려해 볼 가치가 있으므로 이렇게 말했음을 알 수 있다.

어휘 | research paper 연구 논문 **archaeological** 고고학의 **excavation** 발굴(지) **extensively** 대대적으로, 광범위하게 **stark** 극명한 **artifact** 인공 유물, 공예품

---

iBT Practice p.82

01 (D) **02** (D) **03** (C) **04** (A), (D) **05** (B)

Listen to a conversation between a student and a professor.

Student (M): Hey, Dr. Gray, you got a minute?

Professor (F): Sure, Andrew. What can I do for you?

Student: Well, first off, I wanted to tell you that you're an excellent science teacher. I think I'm finally grasping biology, thanks to you, and I've actually developed kind of an interest in the subject.

Professor: Thank you. I'm flattered, but you didn't come just to tell me that, am I right?

Student: [Laughing] No. I was also wondering if I could ask you something. See, this is my senior year, and I have one more semester to go. Now, I'm wrapping up a degree in physical therapy.

Professor: Good. That's an interesting field, and a growing industry, too.

Student: Well, you're right about the second part. I don't know . . . Q02 I guess over the years I've just grown a little disenchanted. I'm not really sure I want to spend my life doing this.

Professor: Well, I suppose it's better that you've realized this now than a couple of years down the road.

Student: Yeah, that's kind of the way I see it. Anyway, I'm still going to get my degree in physical therapy. I mean, I only have a couple of more courses to go, so I might as well. Q01-1 But I also think I'm going to start working on a degree in microbiology.

Professor: A double major?

Student: Uh-huh. I've already looked into it. Since I've completed all my core courses anyway, I figure it'll add about three semesters to my graduation date. I can live with that. Q01-2 Of course, I need an academic advisor from the Biology Department so I can sign up, and . . .

Professor: [Interrupting] And that's where I come in.

Student: You've got it.

Professor: I get where you're coming from, Andrew. But I think it would be beneficial if we talked this through a bit. Q03 Well, you said that you think you could get all the extra course work done within three semesters. That sounds overly optimistic to me.

Student: Well, granted, I'll have to take a pretty heavy course load in each of those semesters, and I'll have to take courses this summer and next, but I really think it's doable.

Professor: Q05🎧 OK, but what about money? An extra three semesters of tuition adds up, especially if you're planning on taking classes over the summer too. Also, there's the level of the coursework. A few students in the biology program do get really high grades, but they're not the norm. In fact, of all the departments in the university, we have the highest number of students who drop out or end up switching majors.

Student: But Dr. Gray, you know how hard of a worker I am, and don't worry about money. I'm very certain that I'll get one of the scholarships I've applied for. Besides, I've been saving up for a long time, and I have other resources.

Professor: Well, you make a good point, and you have proven that you're a diligent worker. Q04(A) Tell you what, since you don't have to decide anything until next semester anyway, why don't you finish up your work now and speak with me at the end of this semester? Q04(D) In fact, talk to some of the other professors and students in the Biology Department and see what it's like. I believe your commitment, but getting their input can also give you an idea of which courses to take, and stuff like that. OK?

Student: Yes, that sounds reasonable. Thanks.

학생: 하지만 Gray 박사님, 제가 얼마나 열심히 하는지 아시잖아요. 그리고 돈은 걱정 안 하셔도 돼요. 제가 신청해둔 장학금 중 하나는 받을 수 있을 거라 확신하거든요. 게다가 오랫동안 저축을 해오기도 했고, 다른 수단들도 있어요.

교수: 음, 맞는 말이구나. 그리고 네가 성실한 학생이라는 사실도 이미 증명해 보였지. 그럼 이렇게 하자. 어차피 다음 학기까지는 아무것도 결정하지 않아도 되니까, 지금은 공부를 마치고 이번 학기 말에 나하고 다시 이야기하는 것이 어떻겠니? 사실, 생물학과에 있는 다른 교수들과 다른 학생들과도 이야기를 해보고 어떤지 알아보거라. 네 결심이 확고하다는 것은 알지만, 그 사람들의 생각을 들어본다면 네가 어떤 과목을 듣고 싶은지 등에 대한 정보를 얻을 수도 있을 거야. 그렇지?

학생: 네, 맞는 말씀인 것 같네요. 감사합니다.

01 학생이 교수를 방문한 이유는?
(A) 생물학 학위를 받도록 도와준 것에 대해 감사하기 위해
(B) 생물학을 전공하는 데 필요한 공부에 대해 문의하기 위해
(C) 현재 전공을 그만두는 것에 대한 조언을 구하기 위해
(D) 생물학 전공을 시작하는 데 있어 도움을 요청하기 위해

해설 | Main Idea 미생물학 전공을 고려 중임을 설명하며 "I need an academic advisor from the Biology Department so I can sign up"이라고 말하므로 생물학 전공을 등록하는 데 교수의 도움이 필요해서 왔음을 알 수 있다.

02 학생이 생물학 학위를 받고 싶어 하는 이유는?
(A) 과학에 흥미가 매우 많다.
(B) 다른 공부에서는 낙제했다.
(C) 교수의 조언을 따르고 있다.
(D) 직업 목표에 대해 다시 생각하고 있다.

해설 | Detail "I guess over the years I've just grown a little disenchanted. I'm not really sure I want to spend my life doing this" 라는 학생의 말을 통해 자신의 전공인 물리치료를 직업으로 삼는 것에 대해 재고 중임을 알 수 있다.

03 복수 전공을 하는 것에 대한 교수의 의견은?
(A) 직업을 위한 귀중한 경험을 제공한다.
(B) 쓸데없는 시간과 돈의 낭비이다.
(C) 일반적으로 학생들에게는 너무 많은 학업량이다.
(D) 두 개가 비슷한 과정일 때만 해야 한다.

해설 | Attitude 학생이 세 학기 안에 필요한 과목들을 다 끝낼 수 있을 거라고 말하자, 교수는 "That sounds overly optimistic to me"라고 말했다. 이것은 학생의 생각과는 달리 학업량이 많다고 생각했기 때문이다.

04 학생이 처한 상황과 관련하여 교수가 제안하는 것은?
2개의 답을 고르시오.
(A) 이번 학기에는 현재의 학업에만 집중하기
(B) 이번 학기가 끝나기 전에 결정하기
(C) 여유 시간에 생물학에 대한 기본 지식을 얻기
(D) 생물학 전공자와 교수들에게 조언을 구하기

해설 | Detail 교수는 대화 끝에서 이번 학기가 끝나고 다시 얘기하자고 말한 뒤, 그동안 생물학을 전공하는 학생들과 교수들을 만나 정보를 더 얻으라고 조언하고 있다.

05 대화의 일부를 다시 듣고 질문에 답하시오.
생물학 과정에 대해 추론할 수 있는 것은?
(A) 학생의 현재 전공만큼 인기가 높지 않다.
(B) 많은 학생이 어려워한다.
(C) 다른 과정보다 돈과 시간이 더 많이 들어간다.
(D) 과학 관련 전공 중에서 가장 명망이 높다.

해설 | Inference 자퇴하거나 전공을 바꾸는 학생이 가장 많다는 것은 그만큼 생물학 전공이 매우 어렵다는 것을 암시해 준다.

어휘 | **flattered** 기쁜, 우쭐해지는 **wrap up** 마무리하다, 마치다 **physical therapy** 물리치료 **disenchanted** 흥미가 없는 **down the road** 장래에 **microbiology** 미생물학 **core** 핵심의 **doable** 할 수 있는 **drop out** 자퇴하다 **input** 정보

Chapter 09 Service Encounters

Intensive Drill 1
p.86

01 (C) 02 (A) 03 (D) 04 (B)

Listen to a conversation between a student and a clerk at the registrar's office.

Student (F): Hi. I had some trouble registering for classes online. Could you help me out with that?

Clerk (M): Sure. May I see your student ID? *[Pause]* Thanks. OK . . . Ms. Davis, so what exactly was the problem?

Student: Well, I was checking to make sure that there was space available in some courses, but when I tried to register for them, an error message popped up.

Clerk: What did it say?

Student: Uh, I'm not sure.

Clerk: No problem. Let's pull your classes up. Do you, uh, have a list of the classes?

Student: Uh, yeah. Here it is.

Clerk: OK . . . let's see. Ah, here's the problem. You're trying to register for 18 credit hours.

Student: Uh-huh . . .

Clerk: Well, taking 18 or more credit hours requires special permission from your academic department.

Student: What? I've never heard that before.

Clerk: It's pretty common at most colleges. Q02 It's so students don't take on more than they can handle. Um, can I ask why you want to take so many?

Student: I just want to finish all my courses sooner, so I can graduate sooner. If I take at least six a semester, I can graduate a semester early. Is that right?

Clerk: Q01 That's up to your department head. If your grades are good, then they probably won't object. Otherwise, they'll likely suggest a lighter course-load. Q04 Anyway, set up an appointment with your department and talk to them. If they agree, they'll give you a waiver. Bring that back here, and we'll get you straightened out. But, uh, if you don't mind some advice, I'd sign up for some of your courses right now.

Student: If I just have to come back here anyway . . .

Clerk: But this guarantees you a spot in those courses. You can register for five without department permission, so you might as well do it now.

Student: *[Pause]* Makes sense. But I have to leave out one for the time being, huh? Tough choice. I want them all.

Clerk: Then consider this. Q03 Four of the courses on your list – Chemistry 154, Biology 202, History 233, and Math 217 – are only offered in the fall semester, so you should definitely sign up for those right now. The other two are offered in both spring and fall, so you can take them later.

Student: Good point. OK, sign me up for those four. I guess the English and psychology courses will have to wait until I talk with my department head.

직원: 그럼 이렇게 해보세요. 학생의 목록에 있는 과목 중 화학 154, 생물학 202, 역사 233, 수학 217, 이 네 개는 가을 학기에만 열리니까, 학생이 지금 꼭 등록하는 것이 좋겠군요. 나머지 두 개는 봄 학기에도 열리고 가을 학기에도 열리니까 다음에 수강해도 되죠.

학생: 좋은 생각이네요. 좋아요, 그 네 과목을 등록해 주세요. 영어와 심리학 과목은 학과장님과 의논을 할 때까지 기다려야겠네요.

01 18학점을 수강하려는 학생의 계획에 대한 직원의 생각은?
 (A) 매우 의욕에 찬 학생이라는 것을 보여준다.
 (B) 그렇게 많은 과목을 들으면 어려움을 겪을 것이다.
 (C) 학생의 성적이 좋으면 허락을 받을 것이다.
 (D) 더 일찍 자신에게 이야기했어야 했다.

해설 | Attitude 학생의 성적에 따라 학과장의 승인이 있을 것이라고 했으므로 성적이 좋으면 허락받을 것으로 생각하고 있음을 알 수 있다.

02 대학이 18학점 이상을 들으려는 학생들에게 허가를 받도록 하는 이유는?
 (A) 비현실적인 수업량을 방지하기 위해
 (B) 학생들이 전공과 관련된 수업만을 수강하도록 하기 위해
 (C) 다른 학생들에게도 충분한 수업 자리를 보장해주기 위해
 (D) 학생들이 반드시 4년을 채워 수업을 듣고 학비를 내도록 하기 위해

해설 | Detail "It's so students don't take on more than they can handle"이라는 직원의 말을 통해 학생들이 감당할 수 있는 수준의 수업량으로 이수 학점을 제한하고 있음을 알 수 있다.

03 직원이 학생에게 즉시 등록하라고 권유하는 과목은?
 (A) 전공과 가장 관련이 있는 과목들
 (B) 가장 빨리 정원이 마감되는 과목들
 (C) 자신이 가장 잘 할 것 같은 과목들
 (D) 1년에 한 번만 개설되는 과목들

해설 | Detail 직원은 가을 학기에만 열리는 수업을 먼저 등록하라고 조언하고 있다.

04 대화의 일부를 다시 듣고 질문에 답하시오.
 학생이 다음과 같이 말할 때 의미하는 것은?
 "If I just have to come back here anyway . . ."
 (A) 지금은 수업을 등록할 시간이 없다.
 (B) 직원이 왜 그런 제안을 하는지 이유를 모르겠다.
 (C) 어떤 수업을 등록할지 생각할 시간이 더 필요하다.
 (D) 수업에 등록하기 전에 학과장과 의논해야 한다.

해설 | Function 수업 중 일부는 지금 등록하라는 직원의 조언에 어차피 다시 와야 하는데 그럴 필요가 있냐고 의문을 제기하고 있으므로, 학생은 직원이 왜 그런 제안을 하는지 이해하지 못했음을 알 수 있다.

어휘 | **object** 반대하다 **waiver** 면제[포기] 서류 **straighten out** 해결하다, 정리하다 **leave out** 빼다 **for the time being** 지금, 당분간

Intensive Drill 2   p.88

01 (D)   **02** (A)   **03** (C)   **04** (A)

Listen to a conversation between a student and a librarian.

Student (M): Excuse me. Q01 Can you help me out with finding some books? I need them for my geology assignment due this Friday, but I can't find them here. I'm kind of getting frustrated.

학생과 사서의 대화를 들으시오.

학생 (남): 실례합니다. 책 찾는 것 좀 도와주시겠어요? 이번 주 금요일까지 제출해야 하는 지질학 과제 때문에 필요한데, 여기에서 찾을 수가 없네요. 좌절감을 갖게 되려 해요.

Librarian (F): No worries. I'll help you out. I'm sure you've tried searching for them through the library catalog, right?

Student: Yes, I have. The web catalog says those books are in the library, so I've checked the sections where those books should be, but I couldn't find them.

Librarian: Q04 I don't mean to offend you, but did you get the right reference numbers? Sometimes, those long numbers are really confusing.

Student: Yes, I made sure that I got the right numbers. I even double-checked them.

Librarian: OK, I will check our system for you. Can you give me the titles of the books?

Student: OK. The first one is *Intraplate Volcanism*.

Librarian: *Intraplate Volcanism* by R. W. Johnson. Yes, it's in the library. On our library staff system, it is in the 'just returned' section. I think it hasn't been placed in the 900s section yet.

Student: So should I just go look for the book there?

Librarian: Yes, that would be the fastest way to get it. Do you know where the 'just returned' section is?

Student: Yes, I do. Thank you. Oh, I need to find another book. It's called *Volcanic New Zealand* by E. Taylor.

Librarian: Alright. *Volcanic New Zealand*, let's see . . . OK, I know why you couldn't find it. Do you see this 'A' here?

Student: You mean the red one? Yes, what is it?

Librarian: It means that the book is in the library archive. Not many people know that, but it's all explained in the library guide. Q02 This little 'A' means 'Archive' and if you see an 'O,' that means 'Off-campus'. I'm letting you know just for your information.

Student: Thank you, it's very useful. Should I also go to the archive to pick up this book?

Librarian: Oh, no. Only library staff can access the archive. I'll get it for you. It will take about five minutes. Q03 In the meantime, you can go and collect the book you're looking for from the 'just returned' section.

Student: That's a good idea. Thank you so much for your help.

Librarian: You're welcome. See you when you come back.

사서 (여): 걱정하지 마세요. 제가 도와 드릴게요. 물론 도서관 카탈로그에서 그 책들을 찾아봤겠죠?

학생: 네, 찾아봤어요. 인터넷 카탈로그에는 도서관에 그 책들이 있다고 되어 있어요. 그래서 그 책들이 있을 구역들을 확인해봤는데 찾을 수가 없었어요.

사서: 기분 상하게 할 생각은 없는데요, 혹시 참조 번호들은 정확했나요? 가끔 그 번호들은 너무 길어서 정말 헷갈리거든요.

학생: 네, 번호들이 정확한지 확인했어요. 한 번 더 확인하기도 했어요.

사서: 좋습니다. 제가 우리 컴퓨터로 확인을 해보죠. 책 제목을 알려 주시겠어요?

학생: 첫 번째 책은 『Intraplate Volcanism』이에요.

사서: R.W. Johnson이 쓴 『Intraplate Volcanism』이군요. 네, 도서관이 있어요. 우리 직원용 컴퓨터를 보니까, '방금 반납된 책들' 섹션에 있군요. 900번대 섹션에는 아직 갖다 놓지 않은 것 같아요.

학생: 그러면 제가 그냥 거기 가서 찾아야 하나요?

사서: 네, 그게 가장 빠른 방법일 거예요. '방금 반납된 책들' 섹션이 어디에 있는지 아세요?

학생: 네, 알아요. 감사합니다. 아, 책 한 권을 더 찾아야 해요. E. Taylor가 쓴 『Volcanic New Zealand』라는 책인데요.

사서: 알았어요. 『Volcanic New Zealand』라, 봅시다… 네, 학생이 못 찾는 이유를 알겠네요. 여기 'A'자 보이죠?

학생: 빨간색으로 쓴 글자 말씀이세요? 네, 그게 뭐죠?

사서: 이것은 그 책이 도서관 기록보관소에 있다는 뜻이에요. 모르는 사람들이 많은데요, 도서관 가이드에 보면 다 설명이 되어 있어요. 이 작은 'A'는 '기록보관소(Archive)'를 뜻하고요, 'O'가 보이면 그것은 '캠퍼스 외에 나가 있음(Off-campus)'이라는 뜻이에요. 그냥 참고로 하는 말입니다.

학생: 고맙습니다. 아주 많이 도움이 되었어요. 이 책도 기록보관소에 가서 가져와야 하나요?

사서: 오, 아니에요. 기록보관소는 도서관 직원들만 출입할 수 있습니다. 내가 가져다 줄게요. 5분 정도 걸릴 겁니다. 내가 갔다 오는 동안, 학생은 '방금 반납된 책들' 섹션에 가서 찾고 있던 책을 가져오면 되겠군요.

학생: 좋은 생각이네요. 도와주셔서 정말 고맙습니다.

사서: 뭘요. 갔다 와서 봅시다.

---

01 대화의 주제는?

(A) 참조 번호 읽기
(B) 도서관 웹사이트를 통해 카탈로그 검색하기
(C) 책들을 학교 도서관에 반납하기
(D) 과제에 필요한 책들을 찾기

해설 | Main Idea 학생은 금요일까지 제출해야 하는 지질학 과제 때문에 필요한 책을 찾을 수 없다고 말하며 사서에게 도움을 청하고 있다.

02 사서가 'O'자를 언급하는 이유는?

(A) 나중에 유용할지도 모르는 정보를 제공하기 위해
(B) 'A'자와 'O'자의 중요한 차이를 알려주기 위해
(C) 학생이 책 몇 권을 못 찾는 이유를 설명하기 위해
(D) 학생이 과제에 필요한 책들을 찾을 수 있는 곳을 알려주기 위해

해설 | Organization 사서는 학생에게 참고로 알아두라면서 'O'자의 의미를 설명해준다.

03 학생이 다음에 할 행동은?

(A) 도서관 기록보관소에서 자신이 필요로 하는 책을 찾는다.
(B) 사서가 기록보관소에서 책을 갖고 올 때까지 기다린다.
(C) '방금 반납된 책들' 섹션에 가서 자신이 필요로 하는 책을 갖고 온다.
(D) 900번대 섹션에 가서 자신에게 필요한 책을 찾아본다.

해설 | Inference 사서가 자신이 기록보관소에 갔다 오는 동안, 학생에게 '방금 반납된 책들' 섹션에 가서 찾고 있던 책을 가져오라고 제의하자 학생이 '좋은 생각'이라고 수긍한다.

04 대화의 일부를 다시 듣고 질문에 답하시오.
사서가 다음과 같이 말할 때 의미하는 것은?
"*Intraplate Volcanism* by R. W. Johnson."

(A) 자기가 올바른 책을 찾는지 확인하고자 한다.
(B) 학생이 책 제목을 잘못 말했음을 알려 준다.
(C) 학생이 그 책을 원하는 이유를 이해하지 못한다.
(D) 학생이 책의 저자 이름을 말하지 않은 것을 나무란다.

해설 | Function 사서는 자기 컴퓨터로 학생이 원하는 책을 검색하기 위해 책 제목을 재차 확인하고 있다.

어휘 | offend 기분 상하게 하다   **reference number** 참조 번호   **archive** 기록보관소, 공문서

Intensive Drill 3   p.90

01 (A), (D)   **02** (B)   **03** [Included – (A), (C)], [Not Included – (B), (D)]   **04** (B)

Listen to a conversation between a student and an employee at the Student Career Center.

Student (F): Hello. Q01(A) I'd like to apply for a workshop for job interview preparation.

Employee (M): OK. Do you mean the Academic Job Interview Workshop led by Professor Williams?

Student: Yes, the one during the second week of July. Q02 Last time I attended the Résumé Workshop also led by Professor Williams, and it was really helpful. Thanks to the program, I got an interview offer from one of the top international IT companies.

Employee: That's great. Congratulations.

Student: Thank you. Anyway, Professor Williams also recommended this program, so I'd like to enroll.

Employee: OK. The first program of this workshop is already fully booked, so I can help you register for the second round. Is that alright, though?

Student: When does the second one start?

Employee: It will start on the 29th of July.

학생과 진로 상담 센터 직원의 대화를 들으시오.

학생 (여): 안녕하세요. 취업 면접 준비를 위한 워크숍 참가를 신청하러 왔습니다.

직원 (남): 네. Williams 교수님이 지도하는 학구적인 취업 면접 워크숍을 말하는 거죠?

학생: 네, 7월 둘째 주에 열리는 워크숍이요. 지난번에도 Williams 교수님이 지도하는 이력서 워크숍에 참가했는데, 매우 많은 도움이 되었어요. 저는 그 프로그램 덕분에, 한 정상급 국제 IT 회사에서 면접 제의를 받았어요.

직원: 잘됐네요. 축하합니다.

학생: 고맙습니다. 어쨌든 Williams 교수님이 이 프로그램도 추천해 주셨어요. 그래서 등록하고 싶어요.

직원: 알았어요. 이 워크숍의 첫 번째 프로그램은 이미 정원이 다 찼으니까 두 번째 프로그램에 등록할 수 있게 도와 드릴게요. 괜찮죠?

학생: 두 번째 프로그램은 언제 시작하나요?

직원: 7월 29일에 시작될 거예요.

Student: Oh, no. My job interview is on the 22nd, a week before the second program. I won't need the workshop by the time it starts. Can I just join the first one? I think it wouldn't be too much to ask you to add just one more seat.

Employee: I wish I could. The limit of placement is 40 people, but due to so many requests, we extended it to 50 and it's already fully booked.

Student: But I really have to prepare the interview. I don't want to miss the workshop.

Employee: I'm sorry. If you really want to prepare for your interview through a course, there is one thing you can do.

Student: I'm all ears. Please tell me.

Employee: Q01(D) There will be a short interview course at the beginning of this summer session, starting from . . . let me check . . . yes, starting from next Tuesday, and it ends on the 18th of July.

Student: That's perfect! How is the course organized?

Employee: It's twice a week, every Tuesday and Thursday. It's going to be one and a half hours per session.

Student: Does the course include mock interviews?

Employee: Certainly. The course also provides group discussions where your course mates give you practical advice. There will also be sessions to prepare for tough interview questions.

Student: That's great. Will the mock interviews be digitally recorded?

Employee: No, I'm afraid not. Q03(A) It's just a simple oral interview. There will be at least 60 students taking this class, so it would be very difficult for us to have all mock interviews recorded.

Student: Q03(C) I understand, but will I at least get feedback from the course professors?

Employee: Of course.

Student: Q04 Well, I think this is it. I'll take this course.

---

01 대화의 주된 내용은?
2개의 답을 고르시오.

(A) 학생이 인터뷰 워크숍에 등록할 수 있는지 알아보기
(B) 면접 워크숍과 면접 준비 강좌 비교하기
(C) 면접 워크숍을 개선하기 위한 의견 제시하기
(D) 면접 준비 강좌에 대한 정보 얻기

02 학생이 면접 제의를 받은 것을 언급하는 이유는?

(A) 자신이 기회를 얻었다는 사실을 자랑하기 위해
(B) Williams 교수의 워크숍이 얼마나 효과적이었는지를 언급하기 위해
(C) 면접을 잘 보는 법에 대한 조언을 구하기 위해
(D) 자신이 Williams 교수의 워크숍을 수강해야 하는 이유를 설명하기 위해

학생: 아, 안돼요. 취업 면접이 두 번째 프로그램 일주일 전인 22일에 있어요. 그 프로그램이 시작될 때에는 저는 이미 워크숍이 필요 없죠. 첫 번째 워크숍에 참가할 수 없을까요? 딱 한 자리만 추가해 달라는 건데 그렇게 무리한 부탁은 아닌 것 같은데요.

직원: 저도 그렇게 해드릴 수 있으면 좋지요. 정원은 40명이에요. 그런데 요청이 너무 많아서 정원을 50명으로 늘렸는데, 그것도 이미 다 예약이 되었어요.

학생: 하지만 정말 이번 면접을 잘 준비해야 해요. 이번 워크숍을 놓치고 싶지 않아요.

직원: 미안합니다. 강좌를 통해 면접을 준비하고 싶으면 학생이 할 수 있는 일이 한 가지 있어요.

학생: 열심히 듣고 있어요. 어서 말해 주세요.

직원: 이번 여름 학기 초에 단기 면접 강좌가 있을 거예요. 시작하는 날이… 확인해 볼게요… 네, 다음 주 화요일에 시작해서 7월 18일에 끝나는군요.

학생: 완벽해요! 그 강좌는 어떻게 구성되어 있죠?

직원: 일주일에 두 번, 화요일과 목요일에 열려요. 한 번에 한 시간 반 걸릴 겁니다.

학생: 이 강좌에는 모의 면접 시간도 포함되어 있나요?

직원: 물론이죠. 이 강좌는 또 참가자의 강좌 파트너들이 실질적인 조언을 주는 그룹 토의 시간도 제공합니다. 여기에는 또 어려운 면접 질문에 대비하는 시간도 있을 거예요.

학생: 좋군요. 모의 면접은 디지털 기기로 녹화되나요?

직원: 아뇨, 유감스럽지만 그렇지는 않아요. 이것은 단순한 구두 면접이에요. 이 강좌를 적어도 60명이 수강할 것이라서, 우리가 그 모든 모의 면접을 녹화하기는 정말 힘들 겁니다.

학생: 이해가 됩니다. 하지만 적어도 강좌를 맡은 교수님의 평가는 받을 수 있겠죠?

직원: 물론이죠.

학생: 음, 이것인 것 같아요. 이 강좌를 수강하겠어요.

해설 | Main Idea 인터뷰 워크숍에 등록하러 온 학생에게 직원은 정원이 다 찬 이번 워크숍 대신 여름 학기에 열리는 다른 워크숍 등록을 권하고, 학생은 그것에 대한 정보를 얻고 있다.

해설 | Organization 학생은 Williams 교수의 이력서 워크숍을 들은 후 면접 제의까지 받았다고 하므로, 그 교수의 워크숍이 매우 효과적이었음을 강조하고 있다는 것을 알 수 있다.

03 대화에서 직원은 여름 학기의 면접 준비 강좌에 대해 설명한다. 다음 각 사항이 포함되는지 표시하시오.

각 사항에 대해 알맞은 항목에 표시하시오.

	포함	미포함
(A) 단순한 구두 면접을 제공한다.	✔	
(B) 모의 면접을 디지털 기기로 녹화한다.		✔
(C) 모의 면접에 대한 교수의 평가가 제공된다.	✔	
(D) Williams 교수가 지도한다.		✔

해설 | Connecting Content 직원은 여름에 열리는 단기 면접 강좌에 대한 학생의 질문에 이번 강좌는 디지털 기기로 녹화되지 않는 구두 면접 실습이 제공되고, 담당 교수의 평가가 제공된다고 설명한다.

04 면접 준비 강좌에 대해 추론할 수 있는 것은?
 (A) 직원은 Williams 교수가 지도하는 면접 워크숍보다 이 강좌를 더 선호한다.
 (B) 면접 워크숍에 대한 최선의 대안적 해결책이다.
 (C) 여기에는 면접 워크숍만큼 많은 프로그램이 포함되어 있지 않다.
 (D) 이 강좌는 취업 지원자들 사이에서 평판이 좋다.

해설 | Inference 직원은 여름 학기 때 열리는 단기 취업 준비 강좌를 대안으로 권유하고 있다. 강좌 관련 설명을 들은 학생은 "Well, I think this is it. I'll take this course"라고 말하며 강좌를 듣기로 결정한다.

어휘 | résumé 이력서   **be all ears** 열심히 듣다   **mock** 모의의, 거짓된

Mini Test 1
p.92

01 (B)   **02** (B), (D)   **03** (A)   **04** (C)

Listen to a conversation between a student and a clerk at the Campus Security Department.

Student (M): *[Frustrated]* Excuse me, could I possibly get some help?

Clerk (F): Sure. What do you need?

Student: Q01-1 Well, last night I left my car parked across the street in another dorm's parking lot. This morning I went there and found these two tickets on my windshield. *[Annoyed]* What's the deal?

Clerk: Let's see. *[Pause]* The first ticket's actually a warning from the Campus Security Department, telling you to move your vehicle. The second one is a ticket, though. Apparently, you didn't move your car in time. The fine is $50.

Student: *[Annoyed]* Q01-2 That's so unfair. I never saw the warning, and besides, I had no choice but to park there.

Clerk: Why's that?

Student: Q04 🎧 Well, there's never any parking space at my own dorm. It's close to the library, so visitors park in our parking lot all the time. Plus, the university is doing construction and has a big section of our parking lot blocked off. Because of those two things, it's practically impossible to find a space. When I got back around ten last night, all the spaces were already taken, so I parked in front of Hoffman Hall. The next morning I had these tickets. I had to park my car somewhere, didn't I?

학생과 교내 경비 사무실 직원의 대화를 들으시오.

학생 (남): *[낙담해서]* 죄송합니다만, 제가 도움을 좀 받을 수 있을까요?

직원 (여): 물론이죠. 무엇을 도와드릴까요?

학생: 있잖아요, 제가 어젯밤에 길 건너편에 있는 다른 기숙사의 주차장에 차를 주차했거든요. 오늘 아침에 갔더니 앞유리에 이 딱지 두 장이 붙어 있는 거예요. *[화가 나서]* 어떻게 된 건가요?

직원: 어디 봐요. *[잠시 후]* 사실 첫 번째 딱지는 교내 경비 사무실에서 차를 옮기라고 남긴 경고장이에요. 하지만 두 번째 것은 딱지네요. 제시간에 차를 치우지 않은 것 같군요. 벌금이 50달러에요.

학생: *[화가 나서]* 그건 매우 불공평해요. 전 경고장을 본 적도 없고, 게다가 그곳에 주차하는 것 말고는 다른 방법이 없었다고요.

직원: 그건 왜죠?

학생: 그러니까요. 제가 사는 기숙사에는 주차할 공간이 전혀 없어요. 도서관에서 가깝기 때문에 방문객들이 항상 우리 주차장에 주차하거든요. 게다가, 학교 측에서 공사를 하느라 주차장에서 상당 부분을 막아 놓았잖아요. 그 두 가지 때문에 주차 공간을 찾는 게 실질적으로 불가능해요. 제가 어젯밤 열 시쯤에 돌아왔을 때 모든 자리는 이미 다 차 있어서 호프만 홀 앞에 주차한 거라고요. 그다음 날 이 딱지들을 받았고요. 저도 어딘가에는 차를 세워야 하지 않겠습니까?

Clerk: I understand, but my hands are tied. Q02(B) Whenever you have trouble finding a parking space in your parking lot, then try parking up at the basketball stadium.

Student: OK, that'll help. But it's not right that I got a fine when there weren't many options.

Clerk: Well, then contact the head of Parking Services. Here's his e-mail address. Explain your situation and he might even cancel the fine, but I can't promise anything.

Student: All right, but what about visitors who violate parking rules? They're not students, so they can't be punished, right?

Clerk: Actually, we deal with them, too. We leave them warnings if they park in spaces reserved for students and faculty. If the visitors do it a second time, they get fines from the city itself, and then they get their vehicles towed away after a third violation.

Student: Q03 Well, it's not working. This morning there were at least four visiting cars in our dorm's lot.

Clerk: Q02(D) Hmm . . . All I can say is that if you spot an unauthorized vehicle in your dorm's lot, call Parking Services directly.

Student: What good will that do?

Clerk: If you report a violation, then we'll send an officer out to ticket and possibly tow the car right then.

Student: OK. It's better than nothing.

직원: 이해는 되지만, 저도 어쩔 수가 없군요. 그곳에서 주차 공간을 찾기가 힘들면, 농구 경기장에 주차를 해봐요.

학생: 알겠어요, 도움이 되겠군요. 하지만 제가 선택권이 별로 없었는데도 벌금을 내야 하는 것은 옳지 않아요.

직원: 글쎄요, 그러면 주차과 책임자에게 연락해 보세요. 여기 이메일 주소가 있어요. 학생의 상황을 설명하면 벌금을 취소해 줄지도 몰라요. 제가 보장해 줄 수는 없지만요.

학생: 좋아요. 하지만 주차 규칙을 위반한 방문객들은 어떤가요? 그 사람들은 학생이 아니니까, 처벌받지 않나요?

직원: 사실 그 사람들도 우리가 처리합니다. 우리는 방문객들이 학생과 교직원에게 지정된 자리에 주차하면 경고장을 남겨요. 만약 두 번째 위반하면 시에서 부과하는 벌금을 내야 하고요. 그리고 세 번째 위반하면 그들 차량을 견인한답니다.

학생: 글쎄요. 효과가 없는 것 같군요. 오늘 아침에 우리 기숙사 주차장에 방문객 차가 최소 네 대는 있었다고요.

직원: 음… 저로서는 학생이 학생 기숙사 자리에서 허가되지 않은 차량을 보면 바로 주차과에 신고하라는 말밖에 해줄 수가 없군요.

학생: 그게 무슨 소용이죠?

직원: 위반 사실을 신고하면, 우리가 사람을 보내서 딱지를 끊고, 바로 그 차를 견인하도록 할 거예요.

학생: 알았어요. 그나마 낫군요.

---

01 학생이 교내 경비 사무실을 찾아간 이유는?
(A) 그가 받은 주차 위반 딱지의 벌금을 내기 위해
(B) 주차 위반 딱지를 받은 것에 대해 항의하기 위해
(C) 방문객에게 주차 위반 딱지를 발부할 것을 요청하기 위해
(D) 엄격한 주차 규정에 대해 불평하기 위해

02 직원이 학생에게 제안하는 것은?
2개의 답을 고르시오.
(A) 다른 기숙사에서는 주차 규정 준수하기
(B) 농구 경기장에 주차하기
(C) 자신의 상사가 딱지를 검토할 때까지 벌금 무시하기
(D) 주차 위반 사례가 있으면 신고하기

03 자신이 주차할 곳에 주차한 방문객들에게 딱지를 끊는 것에 대한 학생의 생각은?
(A) 이 정책은 지금까지 별로 효과가 없었다.
(B) 대학 측은 이 문제를 즉시 해결해야 한다.
(C) 벌금 액수를 늘려야 한다.
(D) 대학 측은 딱지를 끊기 전 경고를 더 많이 주어야 한다.

해설 | Main Idea 대화 초반에 학생이 주차 위반 딱지를 보여주며 "What's the deal?"이라고 묻고 있으며, 이후 "That's so unfair"라고 억울함을 호소하는 것으로 보아 발급 받은 딱지에 대해 항의하러 간 것임을 알 수 있다.

해설 | Detail 학생이 부족한 주차 공간에 대해 항의하자 직원은 주차 공간이 없을 시 농구장에 주차할 것과 불법으로 주차된 방문객 차량을 주차과에 신고하라고 제안하고 있다.

해설 | Attitude 직원이 불법 주차를 한 방문객들에게 취하는 조치에 대해 설명하자 학생은 "Well, it's not working"이라고 말하고 있다.

04 대화의 일부를 다시 듣고 질문에 답하시오.
학생이 다음과 같이 말하는 이유는?
"I had to park my car somewhere, didn't I?"

(A) 어디에 주차하든 상관없다는 점을 나타내기 위해
(B) 자신이 정확히 어디에 주차했는지 설명하기 위해
(C) 그 문제에 대해 선택의 여지가 없었음을 강조하기 위해
(D) 딱지를 받은 것에 대한 놀라움을 표현하기 위해

해설 | Function 어딘가에는 차를 세워야 하지 않았겠냐는 말은 지정된 장소에는 그만한 공간이 없었음을 나타내고자 한 말이다.

어휘 | **windshield** (자동차의) 앞유리 **fine** 벌금 **one's hands are tied** 어쩔 수 없다 **violate** 위반하다 **reserved** 지정된 **vehicle** 차량 **tow** 견인하다 **unauthorized** 허가되지 않은

Mini Test 2
p.94

01 (A), (D) **02** (A) **03** (C) **04** (B), (D)

Listen to a conversation between a student and a housing coordinator.

Student (F): Hi, I'm looking for Mr. Wilkes.

Coordinator (M): That's me.

Student: Hi, I'm Tiffany Parker. We have a three o'clock appointment.

Coordinator: Ah, come in. Have a seat. So, what was it that you wanted to see me about?

Student: Well, I'm considering taking classes over the summer. My parents don't live close enough for me to commute, and I heard that my dorm's going to close for renovations. So, uh, what are my options?

Coordinator: Hmm . . . Well, first, do you know how many courses you'll be taking?

Student: Not yet. Does that make a difference?

Coordinator: Yes, mostly in terms of costs, though. **Q01(A)** Full-time students pay lower housing costs than students enrolled only part-time. **Q01(D)** Also, full-time students get first pick for their rooms. To be honest, though, in the summer that's usually not a factor.

Student: OK. Uh, for right now, let's assume I'll be a full-time student.

Coordinator: All right. In that case, housing's no different than for the fall or spring terms. You can have a room in one of the two dormitories open during the summer, which are Linser and Hamilton Halls. Also, if there are any vacancies, you can even get a suite.

Student: What's the difference?

Coordinator: A suite is basically set up like an apartment, except that it's on campus. Each suite is shared by three students. There's a common living room, but each student has their own separate bedroom.

학생과 기숙사 담당 직원의 대화를 들으시오.

학생 (여): 안녕하세요. Wilkes 씨를 찾아왔는데요.

직원 (남): 바로 전데요.

학생: 안녕하세요, 저는 Tiffany Parker예요. 세 시에 약속을 잡았거든요.

직원: 아, 들어오세요. 앉으세요. 그래, 무슨 일로 저를 보자고 했죠?

학생: 음, 제가 여름 동안 수업을 들을까 생각 중인데요. 저희 부모님이 제가 통학할 만한 거리에 살지 않으세요. 그런데 기숙사가 보수 공사로 닫힐 거라는 말을 들었거든요. 그래서 말인데요, 무슨 방법이 없을까요?

직원: 음… 글쎄요, 우선 과목을 몇 개나 들을 건지 알고 있나요?

학생: 아직 몰라요. 무슨 차이가 있나요?

직원: 네. 주로 비용 때문이죠. 정규 학생들은 시간제 학생들에 비해 기숙사비가 더 싸거든요. 또 정규 학생이면 먼저 방을 고를 수가 있어요. 하지만 솔직히 말하자면, 여름에는 별문제 아니에요.

학생: 그렇군요. 어, 우선 제가 정규 학생이라고 가정해보죠.

직원: 좋아요. 그렇다면 가을이나 봄 학기와 차이가 없어요. 여름 동안 개방해두는 기숙사로 린저와 해밀턴 홀 두 개가 있는데, 거기 방을 쓰면 되고요. 그리고 빈방이 있으면 스위트를 얻을 수도 있을 거예요.

학생: 차이점이 뭔가요?

직원: 스위트는 교내에 있다는 걸 제외하면 기본적으로 아파트처럼 지어졌다고 보면 돼요. 각 스위트는 학생 세 명이 함께 쓰게 되어 있어요. 거실은 공동으로 쓰지만, 학생 각자가 침실은 따로 쓰죠.

Student: Q02 You mean you don't have to share a room with anyone? Why didn't I know about this last semester?

Coordinator: Q03 Well, suites are generally reserved for upperclassmen. But during the summer term, occupancy rate is so low that we waive that requirement.

Student: What about the dining halls? Are any of them open during the summer?

Coordinator: No. Q04(B) The cafeterias in the academic buildings are open, and the restaurants in the student center are, too, but the dining halls themselves are closed. Also, there isn't a student meal plan during the summer term.

Student: Really? Then how am I supposed to eat?

Coordinator: Q04(D) Well, again, there are still cafeterias and plenty of local restaurants. But yeah, you do have to kind of fend for yourself.

Student: Fair enough, I guess. So how do I register for a room?

Coordinator: Register for classes first. Then just bring your schedule back here. Once we've verified that you're enrolled full-time, we'll get you fixed up.

학생: 그러니까 다른 사람과 방을 같이 안 써도 된다는 말씀이죠? 왜 지난 학기에는 이걸 몰랐을까요?

직원: 음, 스위트는 일반적으로 상급생들에게 배정되거든요. 하지만 여름 계절 학기 동안에는 사용률이 워낙 낮아서 그런 조건을 적용하지 않는 거죠.

학생: 대식당은 어떤가요? 여름 동안 문 여는 곳이 있나요?

직원: 아니요. 대학 건물들 안에 있는 구내식당들과 학생 센터의 식당들은 여는데, 대식당은 닫아요. 그리고 여름 계절 학기 동안에는 학생 식단이 없답니다.

학생: 정말이요? 그러면 식사는 어떻게 해결하죠?

직원: 글쎄요, 다시 말하지만, 구내식당도 있고 이 지역 식당들도 많으니까요. 하지만 맞아요, 학생 혼자 힘으로 꾸려나가야 하죠.

학생: 괜찮은 것 같네요. 그런데 방은 어떻게 신청하나요?

직원: 우선 수업을 등록하세요. 그런 다음에 다시 여기로 시간표를 가져오기만 하면 돼요. 학생이 정규로 등록한 것을 확인만 하면 신청해 줄게요.

---

01 정규 학생들을 위한 여름 기숙사에 대해 옳은 것은?
2개의 답을 고르시오.

(A) 시간제 학생들보다 기숙사비가 더 싸다.
(B) 정규 학생들은 룸메이트가 있지만, 시간제 학생들은 없다.
(C) 정규 학생들만이 여름 동안 스위트에 살 수 있다.
(D) 정규 학생들은 기숙사 배정에 있어 우대를 받는다.

해설 | Detail 정규 학생들은 시간제로 등록한 학생들보다 기숙사비가 싸고, 방을 먼저 고를 수 있다.

02 스위트에 대한 학생의 의견은?

(A) 기숙사보다 더 나은 생활 환경을 제공한다.
(B) 상급생만 이용할 수 있는 것은 불공평하다.
(C) 기숙사들과 크게 다르지 않다.
(D) 모든 기숙사가 스위트로 개조되어야 한다.

해설 | Attitude 침실을 따로 쓴다는 직원의 말에 놀라워하며 "Why didn't I know about this last semester?"라고 말하고 있으므로 학생은 스위트를 쓸 의향이 있으며 기숙사보다 더 좋게 느끼고 있음을 알 수 있다.

03 직원이 여름 교내 기숙사에 대해 암시하는 것은?

(A) 가을과 봄 학기 동안보다 더 비싸다.
(B) 학생들의 기숙사 선택권이 더 많다.
(C) 교내에 사는 학생들이 더 적기 때문에 숙박 규정이 느슨하다.
(D) 일반적으로 여름에는 상급생만이 교내에 살 수 있다.

해설 | Inference 여름에는 낮은 사용률 때문에 원래 상급생에게만 배정되는 스위트를 모두에게 허용하고 있다.

04 다음 중 여름 학기 동안 선택이 가능한 식사 방법은?
2개의 답을 고르시오.

(A) 교내 대식당
(B) 학생 센터 내의 식당
(C) 학생 식단
(D) 교외의 현지 식당

해설 | Detail 직원은 대식당 대신 학생 센터 내의 식당과 교외의 현지 식당들을 이용할 수 있다고 설명하고 있다.

어휘 | **commute** 통학(통근)하다 **vacancy** 빈 방 **suite** 스위트, 붙은 방 **occupancy** (건물·방·토지 등의) 사용 **waive** (규칙 등을) 적용하지 않다 **fend for oneself** 혼자 힘으로 꾸려나가다 **verify** 확인하다

iBT Practice

01 (A) **02** (B) **03** (B), (C) **04** (B) – (A) – (D) – (C) **05** (D)

Listen to a conversation between a student and a clerk at the Student Union Office.

Student (M): Hello, uh, I'm looking for the Student Union Office. Am I in the right place?

Clerk (F): [Cheerfully] Yes, sir, you certainly are. How may I be of service to you?

Student: Q01 Well, I wanted to start a special club for students and faculty members here. I know a lot of people who are interested, and we all decided that it would be best to use campus facilities for our meetings. I heard that this is the place to go to fill out the forms and get started.

Clerk: Right, but it's a little bit more complicated than that. It would help me to know what kind of club you're starting up.

Student: We'd like to set up a film club. We'd probably meet about once a month to view different movies, particularly films that a lot of us are studying for classes. That's OK, right?

Clerk: Uh, yeah, that sounds fine. The main reason I asked is because I needed to know how to classify the organization. It sounds like this is a typical activity club, which is OK.

Student: Just out of curiosity, why does the club need to be classified?

Clerk: Q02 Oh, it's mostly for funding purposes. Basically, activity clubs can't receive funding from the Student Government Association. Other groups that aren't activity clubs, like the school band, fraternities, and such are funded because they perform important functions for the school. You, uh, didn't need any such funding, did you?

Student: I hadn't planned on it, no.

Clerk: Great, then. I'll go over the basics with you quickly. Q03(C) The first thing you need to do is make up a roster of your potential membership. There are no specific rules about how many people you should have, but I can tell you that the more people you have, the better your chances are of getting approval. Generally, any club with less than ten official members doesn't get serious consideration.

Student: OK, got it. I'll get the roster and application papers over to the Director of Student Living.

Clerk: Q03(B) Remember to include a constitution, too.

Student: [Surprised] Are you serious? A constitution? We're just going to watch movies. Why do we need to write up a constitution?

Clerk: Well, it's just a formality to clearly establish your goals, activities, and guidelines. For your group, it doesn't have to be anything long and formal. Here, you can find an example of the format on our website.

학생과 학생회 사무실 직원의 대화를 들으시오.

학생 (남): 안녕하세요. 어, 학생회 사무실을 찾고 있는데요. 제가 잘 찾아 왔나요?

직원 (여): [기쁘게] 네, 아주 잘 찾아왔어요. 어떻게 도와주면 될까요?

학생: 어, 우리 학교 학생들과 교직원을 위해 특별한 클럽을 하나 만들고 싶어서요. 관심 있는 사람을 많이 알고 있는데, 우리 모두 모임 장소로 학교 시설을 사용하는 것이 좋겠다고 결정했거든요. 여기가 신청서를 작성하고 활동을 시작할 수 있는 장소라고 들었어요.

직원: 맞아요, 그렇지만 그보다는 좀 더 복잡하답니다. 어떤 종류의 클럽을 만들려고 하는 것인지 알면 좋겠는데요.

학생: 영화 클럽을 만들려고요. 한 달에 한 번 정도 모여서 여러 종류의 영화, 특히 우리 다수가 수업에서 공부하고 있는 영화를 보려고 해요. 괜찮지요?

직원: 어, 네, 괜찮을 것 같군요. 제가 물어본 가장 큰 이유는 그 조직을 어떻게 구분해야 하는지 알아야 하기 때문이에요. 들어보니까 전형적인 취미 클럽 같은데, 그러면 괜찮아요.

학생: 그냥 궁금해서 여쭤보는데요, 왜 클럽이 분류되어야 하죠?

직원: 오, 주로 지원금 문제 때문이에요. 기본적으로 취미 클럽은 학생자치회 연합에서 지원금을 받을 수 없거든요. 취미 클럽이 아닌 학교 밴드나 남학생회 같은 단체는 학교를 위해 중요한 역할을 하기 때문에 지원금을 받을 수 있어요. 학생은, 어, 이런 지원금이 필요한 것은 아니죠?

학생: 네, 그럴 계획은 없었어요.

직원: 그렇다면 좋아요. 기본 사항에 대해 짧게 짚고 넘어가죠. 우선 학생이 해야 할 일은 가입 가능성이 있는 회원의 명단을 만드는 거예요. 얼마나 많은 회원이 있어야 하는지에 대한 특별한 규정은 없지만, 회원이 많을수록 승인받을 확률이 높아진다는 것은 말해줄 수 있어요. 일반적으로 공식 회원이 열 명 미만인 클럽은 진지한 검토 대상이 안돼요.

학생: 네, 알겠어요. 학생 생활 관리자에게 명단과 신청서를 내도록 할게요.

직원: 그리고 규약을 첨부하는 것도 잊지 말아요.

학생: [놀라며] 진심이세요? 규약이요? 우리는 그냥 영화만 볼 건데요. 왜 규약을 만들어야 하나요?

직원: 글쎄, 단지 클럽의 목표와 활동, 지침을 분명히 밝히기 위한 형식적인 절차라고 보면 돼요. 학생이 만들려는 모임의 경우엔 길지 않아도 되고 형식을 갖추지 않아도 돼요. 여기, 우리 웹사이트에서 형식에 대한 예를 찾을 수 있을 거예요.

Student: OK. How long will it take until we find out whether we've been approved or not?

Clerk: It's hard to say. Q04(B) The director has to send all paperwork to the Student Government Association for review. Q04(A) After he does this, you must also find a student senator to sponsor your club. Q04(D) This senator will propose an official bill in a session, and the Student Government then votes on approving your club.

Student: Wait a second, I didn't know that we had to go through the Student Government. What if they don't like the idea?

Clerk: Don't worry. They only reject clubs if the club has absolutely no academic relevance, or if it needs too much money. You shouldn't have a problem.

Student: Q04(C) Q05 Great. Now, what about getting a faculty or staff member for our adviser? I heard all school clubs need one.

Clerk: Well, that doesn't come until after you're approved. It's the paperwork that you need to be concerned with for now. Approval must be finalized before the end of the month.

Student: But that's only two weeks away! [Sighs] OK, I'll get right on it.

학생: 알겠어요. 우리가 승인되었는지 아닌지를 알려면 얼마나 걸리나요?

직원: 그건 말해주기 어려워요. 관리자가 검토를 위해 학생자치회 연합에 모든 서류를 보내야 하고요. 그가 그러고 나서, 학생은 학생의 클럽을 후원해줄 학생 위원을 찾아야 하죠. 그 위원은 회의 때 공식 법안으로 제안할 것이고, 그러면 학생회에서 학생의 클럽을 승인할지에 대해 투표를 할 거예요.

학생: 잠깐만요. 저는 이게 학생회를 거쳐야 하는 건지 몰랐어요. 만약 거기서 마음에 들어 하지 않으면 어떻게 되나요?

직원: 걱정 말아요. 학생회에서 승인하지 않는 클럽은 그 클럽이 학업적인 관련성이 전혀 없다든지, 돈이 너무 많이 든다든지 하는 경우뿐이에요. 학생에게는 문제가 없을 거예요.

학생: 좋아요. 그럼, 우리 고문으로 교수님이나 교직원을 구해야 한다는 것은 무슨 말인가요? 학교 클럽을 하려면 모두 필요하다고 들었는데요.

직원: 글쎄요. 그건 승인을 받은 후에 할 일이에요. 지금 신경 써야 할 것은 서류 작업이랍니다. 이번 달 안에 승인 절차가 모두 끝나야 해요.

학생: 그렇지만 두 주밖에 안 남았다고요! [한숨 쉬며] 알았어요. 바로 시작할게요.

---

01 학생이 학생회 사무실을 찾아간 이유는?
 (A) 클럽 창설을 위한 절차를 문의하기 위해
 (B) 취미 클럽 가입 신청서를 제출하기 위해
 (C) 자신의 클럽을 후원해줄 학생 위원을 구하기 위해
 (D) 취미 클럽 규약에 대한 예를 살펴보기 위해

해설 | Main Idea 대화 초반 "I heard that this is the place to go to fill out the forms and get started"라는 학생의 말을 통해 클럽을 창설하는 절차에 관해 문의하러 간 것임을 알 수 있다.

02 취미 클럽과 다른 단체들의 차이점은?
 (A) 취미 클럽은 학교에 비용을 지급해야 한다.
 (B) 취미 클럽은 학생자치회 연합의 자금을 쓸 수 없다.
 (C) 취미 클럽은 최소 10명의 회원이 있어야 한다.
 (D) 취미 클럽은 교내 시설을 전혀 사용할 수 없다.

해설 | Detail 직원은 취미 클럽의 경우 학교에 중요한 역할을 수행하는 다른 단체들과는 달리 학생자치회 연합으로부터 지원금을 받을 수 없다고 설명하고 있다.

03 클럽이 승인을 받기 전에 반드시 제출해야 하는 서류는?
 2개의 답을 고르시오.
 (A) 지원금 요청서
 (B) 지침 설명문
 (C) 회원 명부
 (D) 고문의 추천서

해설 | Detail 직원은 제출해야 할 기본 서류로 회원이 될 만한 사람들의 명부와 클럽의 목표, 활동, 지침 등이 포함된 규약을 언급했다.

04 대화에서 직원은 취미 클럽을 창설하는 단계에 대해 설명한다. 이 단계들을 올바른 순서대로 나열하시오.
 각 문장을 해당되는 곳으로 옮기시오.

1	(B) 모든 서류가 관리자에게 제출된다.
2	(A) 학생 위원이 그 클럽을 후원한다.
3	(D) 학생자치회 연합이 그 클럽에 대한 승인 여부를 결정한다.
4	(C) 클럽의 고문이 선출된다.

해설 | Connecting Content 우선 규약을 포함한 해당 서류들을 학생 생활 관리자에게 제출해야 하며, 관리자가 학생자치회 연합에 서류를 보내면 클럽을 지지해줄 학생 위원을 구해야 한다. 고문 선출은 승인을 받은 후에 할 일이므로 가장 마지막에 와야 한다.

05 대화의 일부를 다시 듣고 질문에 답하시오.
직원이 다음과 같이 말하는 이유는?
"It's the paperwork that you need to be concerned with for now."

(A) 학생이 복잡한 서류 작업을 주의해서 하도록 하기 위해
(B) 학생에게 모든 클럽이 서류를 작성해야 한다는 것을 상기시키기 위해
(C) 학생에게 학생회에서 서류를 거절할 수도 있다는 것을 경고하기 위해
(D) 학생이 서류를 가능한 한 빨리 제출하도록 촉구하기 위해

해설 | Function 학생이 고문 선정에 대해 묻자 그것은 나중에 할 일임을 알려주며 지금은 서류 작업에 신경 써야 한다고 말하고 있다. 즉, 현재 서류 제출을 가장 먼저 해야 한다는 것을 의미한다.

어휘 | **fraternity** 남학생회, 남학생 사교 클럽   **roster** 명단   **constitution** 규약   **formality** 형식적인[정식] 절차   **senator** 위원, 이사   **relevance** 관련성   **get right on** ~을 바로 시작하다

Chapter 10 Humanities

Intensive Drill 1
p.100

01 (D)　02 (A)　03 (B)　04 (C)　05 (B)

Listen to part of a lecture in an art history class.

Professor (M): Alright, I hope that everyone is wide awake this morning. We have a lot to cover. We're going to continue our look at sculpture in the ancient world. Q01-1 Today we're looking at the sculptures and statues of the ancient Romans. Now, to the average viewer, these works look very similar, perhaps even identical, to the classical statues found in ancient Greece. Well, uh, there is obviously a good reason for this. Like many other aspects of its culture, Rome owed much of its artistic style to the Greeks. The ancient Greeks developed numerous sculpting techniques that portrayed people naturally. Some techniques included sculpting statues with realistic proportions, while others gave the statues poses that made them appear dynamic and lively. The Romans naturally incorporated these conventions into their own sculptures.

It would be unfair, however, to say that the Romans simply aped Greek sculpture. Q01-2 Despite the influence of ancient Greek works on Roman sculpture, the two styles had many distinct differences. Q02-1 Part of this is due to the difference in their subject matter. See, Greek sculptures primarily portrayed mythological subjects, and their art was done mainly for its own beauty.

Q03 Roman sculptures, on the other hand, were generally sculptures of real-life people, and were essentially political or social advertisements. Julius Caesar, for example, commissioned numerous sculptures of himself to advertise and promote his reputation. Most other great Romans did the same.

Q02-2 Since Roman sculptors portrayed actual people, they were under greater limitations than Greek sculptors had been. Q04 If a Roman sculptor tried to idealize his subject, the image might be so changed that the public couldn't recognize the individual in the sculpture, which, of course, would totally miss the point of creating it in the first place. Q05 As a result, Roman sculptures tended to be much more realistic. People were portrayed as they appeared in real life. Many of Caesar's busts show that he was going bald. Those of Cicero do not portray him as being a particularly handsome man. That's not to say Roman sculptors didn't perform a little plastic surgery, but on the whole they tended to portray people as they were.

In contrast, since Greek art dealt with mythological figures and was meant primarily as an expression of beauty, Q02-3 it naturally lent itself to idealized images. A sculptor carving a statue of a goddess, for example, had total freedom to portray her however he wished. Also, Greek sculptures portrayed the human body as, uh, ideal, if not perfect. In other words, the bodies that appeared in Greek sculptures were the way humans should look — they were the perfect representation, even if they were an exaggeration of reality. Because they adhered to ideal beauty above all else, Greek sculptures tended to gloss over many of the unpleasant features found in Roman statues.

미술사 강의 중 일부를 들으시오.

교수 (남): 좋아요. 오늘 아침은 여러분 모두 잠에서 완전히 깬 상태이기를 바라요. 다루어야 할 것이 많거든요. 우리는 고대 세계의 조각품에 대해 계속 살펴보겠습니다. 오늘은 고대 로마인들의 조각품과 조각상에 대해 살펴보죠. 자, 보통 감상자들에게 이 작품들은 고대 그리스에서 발견되는 고전적인 조각상들과 매우 비슷하거나 같아 보입니다. 음, 여기에는 물론 그럴 만한 이유가 하나 있지요. 다른 많은 문화적 측면과 마찬가지로, 로마는 그리스인들에게서 많은 예술 양식을 빌려왔습니다. 고대 그리스인들은 사람을 자연스럽게 표현하는 수많은 조각 기술들을 발전시켰습니다. 그러한 기술들에는 조각상을 사실적인 비율로 조각하는 기술을 포함해서, 조각상이 역동적이고 살아있는 것처럼 보이게 하는 자세로 조각하는 기술 등이 있습니다. 로마인들은 자연스럽게 이러한 관행들을 자신들의 조각품에 포함했습니다.

그러나 로마인들이 단순히 그리스의 조각품을 흉내 내는 데 그쳤다고 하면 옳지 않을 것입니다. 고대 그리스 작품들이 로마의 조각에 끼친 영향이 크기는 하지만, 두 양식에는 뚜렷한 차이가 많이 있어요. 그것은 부분적으로 주제의 차이 때문입니다. 그러니까, 그리스 조각품은 주로 신화적인 대상들을 표현했고, 그들의 예술은 주로 그것의 아름다움을 표현하기 위해 행해진 것이었죠.

반면에, 로마의 조각품은 실재 인물의 조각품인 경우가 많았으며, 정치적 혹은 사회적으로 중요한 홍보 수단이었습니다. 예를 들어, Julius Caesar는 자신의 명성을 알리고 높이기 위해 수많은 자신의 조각품들을 주문했습니다. 다른 대부분의 로마 위인들 또한 그렇게 했고요.

로마 조각가들은 실재 인물들을 묘사했기 때문에 그리스 조각가들보다 훨씬 더 제약이 많았습니다. 만약 로마의 조각가가 대상을 이상화시키려 한다면, 그 이미지가 너무 바뀌어서 대중들은 조각된 사람이 누구인지 알아보지 못할 것이고, 그렇게 되면 당연히 애초에 그 조각상을 만든 이유가 사라질 것입니다. 그 결과, 로마 조각품은 훨씬 더 사실적인 경향이 있었습니다. 사람들은 실제 생활에서 보이는 모습 그대로 표현되었죠. 많은 Caesar의 흉상들은 그의 머리가 벗겨지고 있다는 것을 보여줍니다. Cicero의 흉상들은 그를 특별히 잘생긴 사람으로 표현하지 않았습니다. 그렇다고 해서 로마 조각가들이 성형 수술을 전혀 가하지 않았다는 것은 아니지만, 대체로 그들은 사람을 있는 그대로 표현하는 경향이 있었습니다.

대조적으로, 그리스 예술은 신화적 인물을 다루었고 아름다움의 표현을 주요 목적으로 삼았기 때문에, 자연스럽게 이상화된 이미지를 추구했습니다. 예를 들어, 여신상을 조각한 조각가에게는 자신이 원하는 대로 여신을 표현할 완전한 자유가 있었습니다. 또한, 그리스 조각품은 인체를, 완벽하지는 않더라도 이상적으로 표현했습니다. 다시 말하면, 그리스 조각품에 나타나는 신체는 인간이 보여야 할 이상적인 모습으로, 현실적으로는 과장일지라도 완벽한 표현이었던 것이죠. 그리스 조각품들은 다른 무엇보다도 이상적인 미를 신봉했기 때문에, 로마 조각상에서 발견되는 많은 인체의 보기 좋지 않은 특징들을 숨기는 경향이 있었습니다.

Chapter 10 Humanities　A79

01 강의의 주제는?
(A) 로마 조각의 목적
(B) 그리스 조각과 로마 조각의 대표적인 조각상들
(C) 그리스 기술이 로마 조각에 끼친 영향
(D) 그리스 조각과 로마 조각의 차이점

해설 | Main Idea 강의 서두에서 교수는 "Today we're looking at the sculptures and statues of the ancient Romans"라고 강의 주제를 밝히고, 이어서 그리스와 로마 조각상의 차이점에 대해 중점적으로 설명하고 있다.

02 교수가 주제에 대해 논의하는 방식은?
(A) 조각품의 대상과 그 대상의 표현 방식을 비교함으로써
(B) 그리스인의 조각 기술과 로마인의 조각 기술을 설명함으로써
(C) 로마 조각품의 기원을 설명하고 그 예들을 보여줌으로써
(D) 그리스 신화와 그것이 조각상에 어떻게 표현되었는지를 설명함으로써

해설 | Organization 교수는 그리스와 로마 조각품이 각각 신화적인 대상과 현실의 인물을 조각했으므로 로마 조각품은 사실적인 경향을, 그리스 조각품은 이상화된 이미지를 추구하는 경향이 있다고 설명하고 있다.

03 대다수 로마 조각품의 목적은?
(A) 로마 신화를 이야기하기 위해
(B) 권력자들을 찬미하기 위해
(C) 인체의 아름다움을 표현하기 위해
(D) 건물의 외관을 장식하기 위해

해설 | Detail 로마 조각품은 중요한 정치적, 사회적 홍보 수단으로, 주로 권력자들이 자신의 명성을 알리고 높이기 위해 사용했다.

04 많은 로마 조각품이 덜 매력적인 특징들을 갖는 이유는?
(A) 예술가들이 그리스의 영향력을 반대했다.
(B) 예술가들이 특정 이상들을 표현하기 위해 과장법을 사용했다.
(C) 조각상들은 조각 대상을 사실적으로 반영했다.
(D) 후원자들이 미숙한 조각가들을 고용했다.

해설 | Detail 로마 조각상들은 권력자들의 명성을 높이는 데 이용되었으므로 대중들이 그 조각상이 누구를 나타내는지 알아볼 수 있도록 사실적으로 표현하는 경향이 있었다.

05 강의의 일부를 다시 듣고 질문에 답하시오.
교수가 다음과 같이 말할 때 의미하는 것은?
"That's not to say Roman sculptors didn't perform a little plastic surgery"
(A) 로마 조각가들은 때때로 자신의 이전 실수를 고치기 위해 다시 작업했다.
(B) 로마 조각가들도 조각 대상의 외모를 향상시키려는 시도를 약간 했었다.
(C) 로마 조각가들은 많은 조각 대상의 외모에 만족하지 못했다.
(D) 로마 조각가들은 매력적인 조각 대상만을 고르려고 신경을 썼다.

해설 | Function 교수가 로마 조각상의 사실적인 경향을 설명하며 "That's not to say Roman sculptors didn't perform a little plastic surgery"라고 말한 것은 로마 조각가들 역시 어느 정도 때에 따라 외모에 수정을 가했다는 것을 나타낸다.

어휘 | **identical** 같은, 동일한 **proportion** 비율 **incorporate** 포함하다 **ape** 흉내 내다 **commission** 주문하다, 의뢰하다 **bust** 흉상, 반신상 **plastic surgery** 성형 수술 **exaggeration** 과장 **adhere** (신념·주의 등을) 신봉하다 **gloss over** 숨기다, 덮어버리다

Intensive Drill 2
p.102

01 (B) **02** (B) **03** (A) **04** (B) **05** (B) – (A) – (D) – (C)

Listen to part of a discussion in a history class.

Professor (F): OK, let's quickly look at a scientific term related to today's topic. Does anyone know what biomimicry is?

Student 1 (M): Isn't it imitating nature in developing new products?

역사 수업 중 토론의 일부를 들으시오.

교수 (여): 좋아요, 오늘 주제와 관련된 과학 용어를 잠시 살펴봅시다. 자연모방이 무엇인지 아는 사람 있나요?

학생 1 (남): 새로운 제품을 개발하는 데에서 자연을 모방하는 것 아닌가요?

Professor: That's right. Nature has inspired humans throughout history in their technological innovations. Biomimicry is an approach to innovation in which humans imitate nature's designs to create human solutions. For example, barbed wire, which was invented back in the nineteenth century, was modeled after the thorny orange tree. Q01 Today, we'll look at one of the most extensive endeavors of biomimicry in history, that is, the study of birds to enable human flight.

The history of human-powered flight has stretched over several thousand years since early human history. Q05(B) Hundreds of records and prints describe much earlier attempts by men such as Bladud, the King of Troja Nova, who bravely flapped the wings he built to fly like a bird . . . or perhaps an angel. Unfortunately, he became uh . . . how should I say, well, a genuine angel when he crashed. According to aviation historians, most of these early inventors focused only on the wing-flapping theory to develop bird-like wings despite repeated failures. Some suggest such rigorous efforts indeed had slowed the development of human-powered flight.

Now, you can probably guess the most legendary attempt to fly during the Renaissance . . . anyone?

Student 2 (F): Uh . . . Q02-1 Leonardo da Vinci's flying machines? But did he actually fly? I thought they were just sketches.

Professor: Correct. After keen observations of the anatomy and flight of birds and bats, Q05(A) Leonardo da Vinci created countless notes and sketches of flying machines, the most famous of which he called the "ornithopter." In his later designs, he tried to reflect the soaring, gliding, and landing of birds rather than their flapping. Now, to answer your question, well, Q02-2 there's no evidence that he actually built a working model. Nevertheless, his ideas should be regarded as the first true approach to human-powered flight.

Next, Giovanni Borelli, a professor of physiology and mathematics, comes into the picture. In 1680, Q03-1 he concluded that the power in human pectoral muscles is too small compared to that of birds and therefore not feasible for flight. I mean, Q05(D) he basically exploded the wind-flapping theory, suggesting that Q03-2 humans can't fly by simply flapping their imitation wings, no matter how well they are built. However, inventors somehow overlooked Borelli's studies. And Q04 it's a shame they did because they probably wasted at least two centuries of aviation technology by continuing to flap and fall.

Finally, in 1903, the Wright brothers succeeded in creating and flying the first airplane in human history. Actually, interestingly enough, they received no formal scientific education. They even claimed that their adventure simply began as a sport. In any case, just like their many predecessors, Q05(C) they turned to nature for inspiration by observing birds, specifically pigeons. But they also set aside all existing studies and made their own investigations. So in the end, their invention was the result of scrutinizing nature and science, not just haphazard trials or, as some might say, the "hard knock" approach of some of their predecessors.

교수: 맞아요. 역사를 통틀어 자연은 인간의 기술 혁신에 영감을 주어 왔어요. 자연모방은 인류가 자연의 디자인을 모방해서 새로운 해결책을 창조해내는, 혁신으로 가는 하나의 접근 방식이죠. 예를 들어, 가시철조망은 과거 19세기에 발명되었는데 가시가 있는 오렌지 나무를 본뜬 것이었어요. 오늘은 역사상 자연모방에서 가장 엄청난 노력을 기울인 것 중의 하나를 살펴볼 건데, 이것은 인간이 비행할 수 있도록 새를 연구한 것이에요.

인류 초기의 역사 이래로 사람의 힘으로 비행하는 것에 대한 역사는 수천 년이 넘게 이어져 왔어요. 수백 개의 기록과 인쇄물이 사람들에 의한 초기의 시도들을 설명하고 있는데 트로야노바(새로운 트로이)의 왕 Bladud와 같은 사람은 그가 제작한 날개를 용감하게 펼럭여서 새처럼… 또는 아마도 천사처럼 비행하려 했어요. 불행히도 그는 음… 어떻게 말해야 하지, 음, 바닥에 충돌했을 때 진짜 천사가 되고 말았어요. 항공사학자들에 의하면, 이들 초기 발명가들 대부분은 반복되는 실패에도 불구하고 새의 날개 같은 것을 개발하기 위해 날개를 퍼덕이는 이론에만 집중했다고 해요. 어떤 사학자들은 이런 식의 혹독한 노력이 인간의 힘으로 비행하는 것의 발전을 확실히 더디게 했을 거라고 말하죠.

자, 여러분은 아마도 르네상스 시대의 가장 전설적인 비행 시도를 짐작해볼 수 있을 건데요… 누구 아는 사람?

학생 2 (여): 어… Leonardo da Vinci의 비행 기계를 말씀하시는 건가요? 하지만 그가 정말로 비행했나요? 제 생각에는 그것들은 그냥 스케치였는데요.

교수: 맞아요. Leonardo da Vinci는 새와 박쥐의 해부학적 구조와 비행을 예리하게 관찰한 후에 비행 기계에 대한 많은 메모와 스케치를 남겼는데, 그중에서 가장 유명한 것이 그가 "날개 치기 비행기"라고 부른 것이에요. 그의 후기 설계에 보면 그는 새들의 날갯짓보다는 그들의 상승과 활공 그리고 착지를 반영하려 하고 있어요. 자, 여러분의 질문에 답해준다면, 그가 정말로 작동하는 모델을 만들어냈는지에 대한 증거는 그 어디에도 없어요. 그럼에도 불구하고 그의 아이디어는 인간의 힘으로 비행하는 것에 대한 최초의 진정한 접근이었던 것으로 여겨져야 해요.

다음으로는 생리학 및 수학과 교수였던 Giovanni Borelli를 살펴볼 거예요. 그는 1680년에 인류의 가슴 근육이 가지고 있는 힘이 새가 가지고 힘과 비교할 때 너무 약해 비행에는 적합하지 않다는 결론을 내렸어요. 내 얘기는 Borelli가 날개를 퍼덕여 비행하는 이론을 근본적으로 논파하고 인간이 날개를 흉내 낸 것을 아무리 잘 만들어내도 그저 퍼덕이는 것만으로는 날 수 없음을 말했다는 점이에요. 하지만 발명가들은 Borelli의 의견을 다소 경시했어요. 애석하게도, 그들이 계속해서 퍼덕이고 떨어지는 것을 계속하는 바람에 비행 기술을 발전시키는 데 적어도 200년은 허비한 셈이거든요.

마침내 1903년에 Wright 형제가 인류 역사상 최초의 비행기를 제작하고 비행하는 데에 성공했죠. 실제로 이들 형제가 제도권의 과학 교육을 전혀 받지 않았다는 것은 충분히 흥미로운 일이에요. 이들은 심지어 주장하기를, 그들의 모험이 그냥 스포츠로 시작되었다고 해요. 어쨌든 그들의 다른 선행자들과 마찬가지로 그들은 새를 관찰하는 것을 통해서 자연에서 영감을 얻고자 했었고 특히 비둘기를 관찰했어요. 하지만 그들은 또한 기존의 연구들을 제쳐놓고 그들 자신의 연구를 했죠. 그래서 결국 그들의 발명은 위험한 시도, 또는 일부 사람들이 말하는 것처럼 그들 선행자들의 "역경만 있는" 접근 방식이 아니라 자연과 과학을 세심히 살핀 결과였어요.

01 강의의 목적은?
(A) 자연모방을 이해하는 것에 관한 새로운 접근법을 소개하기 위해
(B) 인류 역사에서 자연모방의 한 예를 설명하기 위해
(C) 초기의 발명가들이 자연에 어떤 식으로 기대왔는지 입증하기 위해
(D) 초기 기술에서 자연모방의 중요성을 보여주기 위해

해설 | Main Idea 강의에서 교수는 인간이 자연모방을 통해 어떻게 비행에서 실패했고 또 그 실패에서 벗어나 어떤 식으로 자연모방에서 성공적인 영감을 얻게 되었는지를 설명한다. 즉, 교수는 강의를 통해서 인간이 조류의 비행을 관찰하고 이를 통해 인간의 비행으로 이어지게 된 자연모방의 한 예를 역사상의 과정들을 통해 설명하고 있다.

02 Leonardo da Vinci의 비행 기계들에 대해 추론할 수 있는 것은?
(A) 새나 박쥐에 대한 그의 예리한 관찰을 반드시 반영하고 있는 것은 아니었다.
(B) 아마도 개념화 단계에서만 남아 있었을 것이다.
(C) 비행에 대한 접근법인지는 논란거리이다.
(D) 많은 역사가들은 비행 기술에서의 진정한 혁신으로 여긴다.

해설 | Inference 수업을 듣던 학생 한 명이 Leonardo da Vinci의 비행 기계가 실제로 날았는지 물었고, 교수도 실제 작동하는 모형을 만들었는지에 대한 증거는 없다고 말하고 있으므로 개념화 단계 이상으로 나아가지 못했음을 유추할 수 있다.

03 다음 중 Borelli가 발견한 것에 대해 옳은 것은?
(A) 인간은 그들의 가슴 근육에서 비행할 수 있을 정도의 충분한 힘을 생성해낼 수 없다.
(B) 인간의 근육이 형성된 방식은 좀 더 복잡한 새와 같은 날개를 필요로 한다.
(C) 초기의 발명가들은 새의 가슴 근육에 대해 적절히 이해하지 못했다.
(D) Leonardo의 비행 기계들은 성공할 수도 있었는데, 왜냐하면 그가 인간의 근육에 대해 연구했기 때문이었다.

해설 | Detail Borelli 교수는 인간의 가슴 근육의 힘이 새의 가슴 근육의 힘에 비해서 너무 약해 날개를 아무리 잘 만들어도 날 수 없을 것이라는 결론을 내렸다. 인간은 날개를 활용해서 퍼덕이는 방식으로는 날 수 있을 정도로 충분한 힘을 생성해 낼 수 없다는 말과 같다.

04 초기 비행 발명가들 몇몇에 대한 교수의 의견은?
(A) 그들은 고집스러웠지만 성공적으로 비행할 수 있을 정도로 충분히 결단력을 갖지는 못했다.
(B) 결국에는 항공 기술의 발전을 지체시키게 되었다.
(C) 앞으로 더 연구하기 위해 그들의 작품들을 다시 방문하고 재평가해야 한다.
(D) 그들은 실패했지만, 이후에 그들을 계승하는 이들에게 영감이 되었다.

해설 | Attitude 교수는 Borelli에 의해 기존 방식으로는 인간이 비행할 수 없음이 밝혀졌지만, 초기 발명가들이 이를 간과하면서 최소 200년 동안 비행 기술이 발전하지 못하게 되었다고 애석해하고 있다. 즉, 기존 방식을 버리지 않고 이를 고수한 초기 비행 발명가들 때문에 비행 기술의 발전이 지체된 것이다.

05 교수는 역사상 인간 동력 비행기를 만들도록 이끈 사건들을 설명한다. 이 사건들을 올바른 순서대로 나열하시오.
각 문장을 해당되는 곳으로 옮기시오.

1	(B) 트로야노바의 Bladud는 날개를 모방한 것으로 날려고 시도한 후 바닥에 추락했다.
2	(A) Leonardo da Vinci는 비행 기계와 관련된 수많은 메모와 스케치를 남겼다.
3	(D) Borelli는 날개를 퍼덕여 나는 이론에 대한 그의 결론을 내렸다.
4	(C) Wright 형제는 새를 관찰함으로써 자연에서 영감을 얻고자 하였다.

해설 | Connecting Content 교수는 인류가 비행하는 방법을 발명하는 과정에서 겪은 시행착오들을 역사 순으로 설명하였다. 처음에 새의 날개 모양을 본뜬 것을 매달고 날갯짓 하다가 떨어져 죽은 Bladud에서부터 Leonardo da Vinci의 비행 기계 설계도, 그리고 날갯짓으로는 인간이 날 수 없다는 결론을 내린 Borelli와 Wright 형제가 이전까지의 이론들을 무시하고 자연만을 관찰하여 비행기 개발에 성공한 이야기까지 역사 순으로 설명한다.

어휘 | **biomimicry** 자연모방 **inspire** 영감을 주다 **barbed wire** 가시철조망 **thorny** 가시가 있는 **extensive** 엄청난 **endeavor** 노력 **genuine** 진짜의 **rigorous** 혹독한 **anatomy** 해부학적 구조 **physiology** 생리학 **pectoral** 가슴의 **feasible** 실현 가능한 **explode** 논파하다, 폭발하다 **predecessor** 선행자 **scrutinize** 세심히 살피다 **hard knock** 역경만 있는

Intensive Drill 3

01 (C)　　02 (C)　　03 (A), (B)　　04 (A)　　05 (B)

Listen to part of a discussion in an architecture class.

Professor (M): I'm going to start class today by showing you a picture that I'm sure all of you will be familiar with. What is this a picture of?

Student 1 (F): The Golden Gate Bridge.

Professor: Good, and the Golden Gate Bridge is what type of bridge?

Student 1: A suspension bridge.

Professor: Right, and these bridges are going to be the main focus of our discussion today. Q05 Let's just start off with a quick overview. What is the most prominent feature of a suspension bridge? Remember, the key word is suspension.

Student 2 (M): Well, they get their name from the fact that the main deck of the bridge is suspended by cables.

Professor: Excellent. In other types of bridges, the deck — or, uh, the road surface — is supported from underneath by a series of pylons. In a suspension bridge, however, the deck sort of hangs from a series of cables. Q01 Now, there are a number of benefits to building this sort of bridge. But as with anything else in engineering, almost any strength involves a trade-off with some sort of weaknesses. And this is primarily what we will be talking about today.

Q02 So, as we have already said, suspension bridges get most of their support from the cables that the deck hangs from. This means that there can be far fewer pylons to support the bridge from underneath, and far greater distance between those pylons. Why would that be helpful?

Student 1: It would be good for ships. Q03(B) If there are fewer pylons under the bridge, that would mean there would be more room for ships to pass under.

Professor: That's exactly right. In fact, the distance between the two main pylons of the Golden Gate Bridge is over 4,000 feet, which means there's plenty of room even for big container ships. In addition, it is better to build a suspension bridge because of its simpler construction. No access is needed from below the bridge while it's being constructed.

Q03(A) Uh, another advantage of having fewer pylons is that these supports take up most of the concrete used in a bridge project — and concrete is usually the biggest expense in building a bridge. So, in certain situations, a suspension bridge can be more economical.

OK, now on to disadvantages. Probably the biggest drawback to building a suspension bridge is that they are prone to something called aeroelastic flutter. That's, uh, basically just a fancy way of saying that these bridges swing in the wind, by the way.

건축학 수업 중 토론의 일부를 들으시오.

교수 (남): 오늘 수업은 여러분 모두가 잘 알고 있을 사진을 보여 주는 것으로 시작할게요. 이것이 무슨 사진인가요?

학생 1 (여): 금문교요.

교수: 좋아요. 그러면 금문교는 어떤 종류의 다리죠?

학생 1: 현수교입니다.

교수: 맞아요. 그리고 이런 다리들이 오늘 우리의 논의 주제가 될 거예요. 일단 간단한 개요로 시작해보죠. 현수교의 가장 두드러진 특징은 무엇인가요? 키워드는 '현수'라는 걸 기억하세요.

학생 2 (남): 음, 다리의 주 노면이 케이블에 매달려 있다는 사실에서 그 이름이 붙여졌어요.

교수: 맞아요. 다른 다리들은 다리의 노면, 즉 도로면이 노면 밑에 있는 여러 개의 기둥에 의해 지탱됩니다. 하지만 현수교에서는 노면이 여러 개의 케이블에 매달려 있어요. 자, 이러한 종류의 다리를 짓는 데에는 여러 장점이 있습니다. 하지만 공학에서 다른 모든 일이 그렇듯 장점이 있으면 그에 상응하는 단점도 있기 마련이죠. 그리고 이러한 점이 오늘 우리가 주로 살펴볼 내용이에요.

자, 우리가 이미 이야기했듯이 현수교는 노면을 매달고 있는 케이블에 의해 대부분 지탱됩니다. 즉, 이 말은 밑에서 다리를 받쳐주는 기둥 수가 훨씬 적어도 되고, 또 기둥 사이의 거리는 훨씬 멀어도 된다는 뜻이죠. 이것이 왜 유익할까요?

학생 1: 선박을 위해서 좋을 거예요. 다리 밑에 기둥이 더 적다면, 선박이 지나다닐 공간이 더 많을 테니까요.

교수: 정확히 맞아요. 사실, 금문교의 두 주요 기둥 사이의 거리는 4천 피트가 넘어서 큰 컨테이너 선박조차도 지나갈 수 있는 큰 공간이 있습니다. 게다가 건설하기가 더 간단하므로 현수교를 짓는 게 더 낫습니다. 건축하는 동안 사람이 다리 밑에서 접근할 필요가 없죠.

어, 기둥 수가 더 적은 것의 또 다른 이점은 다리 건설에 쓰이는 콘크리트 대부분이 이러한 지탱력을 확보하는 데 쓰이고, 콘크리트는 보통 다리 건설 비용에 가장 큰 부분을 차지한다는 것이죠. 그래서 특정 상황에서는 현수교가 더욱 경제적일 수 있지요.

좋아요, 이젠 단점에 대해 이야기해보죠. 현수교를 건설하는 데 가장 큰 약점은 아마도 공 탄성학적 흔들림을 받기 쉽다는 점일 것입니다. 그건 그렇고, 이 말은 기본적으로 다리가 바람에 의해 흔들리는 것을 전문적으로 말하는 거예요.

Student 2: They swing in the wind?

Professor: Oh, yeah. Q04 Actually, there was a bridge built just a few years before the Golden Gate Bridge called the Tacoma Narrows Bridge, which swung so much that it literally tore itself apart. So when designing a suspension bridge, wind resistance has to be a major design consideration.

학생 2: 바람에 흔들린다고요?

교수: 아, 네. 사실, 금문교가 건설되기 몇 년 전에 타코마 내로스교라는 다리가 건설되었는데, 너무 흔들리다 못해 말 그대로 부서져 버렸습니다. 그래서 현수교를 설계할 때 바람에 대한 저항력은 주요 설계 고려 사항이 되어야 합니다.

---

01 토론의 주된 내용은?
(A) 현수교 설계의 어려운 점
(B) 현수교를 건설하는 이유
(C) 현수교의 장점과 단점
(D) 현수교의 가장 잘 알려진 예

해설 | Main Idea 강의는 현수교의 장단점에 대해 논의하고 있다.

02 현수교가 다른 다리보다 기둥이 더 적게 필요한 이유는?
(A) 지탱할 노면이 더 가볍다.
(B) 설계상 콘크리트를 더 적게 사용한다.
(C) 노면을 지탱하기 위해 기둥에만 의존하지 않는다.
(D) 바람에 흔들리도록 설계되어 있다.

해설 | Detail 현수교는 노면이 케이블에 의해 먼저 지탱되고 있으므로, 다리를 받치는 기둥 수는 더 적게 요구된다.

03 현수교가 다른 다리보다 유리한 점은?
2개의 답을 고르시오.
(A) 때로는 적은 비용으로 건설할 수 있다.
(B) 해양 교통을 덜 방해한다.
(C) 더 넓은 해역을 가로지를 수 있다.
(D) 본질적으로 더 튼튼하다.

해설 | Detail 현수교는 다리를 지탱하는 기둥 수가 적어 다리 밑으로 선박이 지나다닐 공간이 더 넓으며, 기둥 건설에 쓰이는 콘크리트가 적게 들어 건설 비용을 절감할 수 있다.

04 교수가 타코마 내로스교를 언급하는 이유는?
(A) 현수교의 본질적인 설계상 약점을 예를 들어 설명하기 위해
(B) 현수교를 대체할 수 있는 설계법을 논의하기 위해
(C) 기술자들이 어떻게 금문교 설계법을 개선했는지 알려주기 위해
(D) 다음 논의 주제를 소개하기 위해

해설 | Organization 교수는 현수교의 단점인 공 탄성학적 흔들림에 대해 설명하면서, 그로 인해 무너졌던 타코마 내로스교를 예로 들었다.

05 강의의 일부를 다시 듣고 질문에 답하시오.
교수가 다음과 같이 말하는 이유는?
"Remember, the key word is suspension."
(A) 학생들에게 논의의 주제를 상기시키기 위해
(B) 그의 질문에 관해 학생들의 생각을 유도하기 위해
(C) 학생들이 이전 논의 내용에 초점을 두도록 하기 위해
(D) 오늘 논의에서 그 질문의 중요성을 강조하기 위해

해설 | Function 교수는 현수교의 특징에 대해 질문하고, 그 질문의 답에 대한 단서를 제공해줌으로써 학생들의 생각을 유도하고 있다.

어휘 | **suspension bridge** 현수교 **deck** (다리 구조 위에 있는) 노면 **pylon** (다리의) 기둥, 교각 **expense** 비용 **prone to** ~하기 쉬운, ~의 경향이 있는 **aeroelastic** 공 탄성학적 **flutter** 흔들림[떨림]

Mini Test 1
p.106

01 (B) 02 (C) 03 (A) 04 (D) 05 (C)

Listen to part of a lecture in a literature class.

Professor (F): OK, today we're looking at the famous Nicaraguan writer Rubén Darío. Most scholars credit Darío with almost single-handedly reviving Latin American poetry and literature around the beginning of the twentieth century. Indeed, his influential works would pave the way for many later Latin American writers. Q01 Now, as we begin to look at Darío's work, I should note that it does cover a wide range of subject matter and literary themes. This is due to some of the major influences on his prose and poetry.

Q02 We cannot discuss the beginning of Darío's poetry without first taking a look at French Parnassian poets. Active during the mid-nineteenth century, these poets were known for their commitment to objectivity, technical refinement, and description that tried to be as accurate as possible. These poets were also known for experimenting with rhythms, rhymes, and the overall format of French poetry. Also, in their later works, they began to focus on myths, epics, and sagas from other lands or time periods. For example, much of their subject matter came from the myths and legends of ancient Greece and India.

Many of these same characteristics are very prominent in Darío's early poetry and prose. Q03-1 In his first important book, *Azul*, he moved away from the conventional style of Spanish writing. For instance, instead of traditionally long, complex sentences, his are fairly simple and direct. Moreover, like Parnassian poetry, his language was objective, his word choice precise, and his subjects primarily focused on European and Asian tales. Q03-2 It was this book that essentially introduced a modern style of literature to Latin America.

Now, Darío's style would change in later years, as he began traveling around South America, Central America, and Europe. To better understand this, we must look at one of the most important developments in Darío's life: his stay in Europe, from 1898 to 1914. He traveled to Spain to serve as a foreign correspondent for a newspaper in Argentina. The principal reason for this was that Spain had lost a war with the United States in 1898. Consequently, it had surrendered some of its territories to the United States, and it had to relinquish its claim on Latin America.

For the next several years, as Darío reported on these developments and later worked as a diplomat, his views on life and art began to change. In particular, he was concerned about the future of Latin America once Spain was defeated. Q04 At this point, he became more concerned about the growing U.S. influence in the Western Hemisphere. Because of the cultural and economic differences between the United States and the Latin American nations, Darío understood that U.S. interests were bound to conflict with the interests of the smaller, weaker Latin American nations. Q05 Such concern caused him to write about these immediate political issues in his poetry, rather than write about imaginary subjects, as he had done earlier. Also, by expressing his hope for unity and a brighter future for Latin America, Darío would establish a trend for later Hispanic writers.

01 강의의 주제는?
  (A) Darío 시의 스타일
  (B) Darío의 작품을 형성한 요인들
  (C) Darío의 정치적 신념들
  (D) Darío가 스페인 문학에 영향을 끼친 방식

해설 | Main Idea 프랑스 고답파 시인들과 스페인의 패배 등, Darío의 작품에 영향을 끼쳤던 배경적 요인들에 대해 설명하고 있다.

02 교수가 프랑스 고답파 시인들을 언급하는 이유는?
  (A) 현대 문학의 기원을 설명하기 위해
  (B) 프랑스와 스페인 문학 형식을 비교하기 위해
  (C) Darío 초기 작품들의 특징을 설명하기 위해
  (D) 현대 문학과 Darío의 작품을 대조하기 위해

해설 | Organization 교수는 프랑스 고답파 시인들의 작품 특징을 살펴봄으로써 이것이 Darío 초기 작품들에서 어떻게 나타나고 있는지 설명하고 있다.

03 『청』이 Darío의 경력에 중요한 이유는?
  (A) Darío의 새로운 스페인 문체를 포함하고 있다.
  (B) Darío에게 영감을 준 시를 포함하고 있다.
  (C) Darío가 쓴 최초의 정치적 시를 포함하고 있다.
  (D) Darío의 유럽 시절에 대한 기록을 포함하고 있다.

해설 | Detail 교수는 『청』에서 보인 새로운 문체에 대해 설명하고 "It was this book that essentially introduced a modern style of literature to Latin America"라고 언급하고 있다.

04 미국에 대한 Darío의 감정에 대해 추론할 수 있는 것은?
  (A) 미국의 문화적 발전에 기뻐했다.
  (B) 미국이 스페인을 이긴 사실에 화가 나 있었다.
  (C) 미국이 라틴아메리카를 도울 거라고 안도했다.
  (D) 미국이 라틴아메리카를 지배할 것을 우려했다.

해설 | Inference 교수는 "he became more concerned about the growing U.S. influence in the Western Hemisphere"라고 말하며, Darío가 미국의 라틴아메리카에 대한 세력 증대에 대해 우려하고 있었음을 보여준다.

05 Darío의 후기작은 초기작과 어떻게 달랐는가?
  (A) 좀 더 복잡한 문장 구조를 사용했다.
  (B) 라틴아메리카에서 더 인기가 많았다.
  (C) 더 현실적인 주제를 다루었다.
  (D) 유럽 문학의 영향을 더 많이 받았다.

해설 | Detail 신화나 서사시, 무용담 등에 초점을 둔 고답파 시인들의 영향을 받은 초기 작품들과는 달리, 후기 작품에서는 스페인의 패배 및 미국의 영향력 증대와 관련한 라틴아메리카의 정치적 문제에 더 초점을 두었다.

어휘 | **credit A with B** B를 A의 공으로 믿다, 인정하다   **single-handedly** 혼자 힘으로   **indeed** 사실   **pave the way** ~의 길을 열다   **prose** 산문   **Parnassian (school)** 고답파(19세기 후반 프랑스의 예술 지상주의적인 시인의 한 파)   **commitment** 전념, 헌신   **objectivity** 객관성   **refinement** 세밀함   **rhyme** 운율   **saga** 무용담   **subject matter** (책·연설·그림 등의) 주제[소재]   **prominent** 두드러진, 눈에 띄는   **precise** 정확한   **correspondent** 특파원   **surrender** 넘겨주다   **territory** 영토   **relinquish** 포기[양도]하다, 손을 떼다   **diplomat** 외교관   **be bound to** 틀림없이 ~할 것이다

Mini Test 2
p.108

01 (B)   **02** (C)   **03** [Yes – (A), (D)], [No – (B), (C)]   **04** (A)   **05** (D)

Listen to part of a discussion in an art class.

Professor (M): OK, the video we just watched is a segment of a famous work titled *The Artist is Present* by Marina Abramovic, a renowned participatory artist. You've probably seen it already on the Internet, right?

Student 1 (F): Actually, when I was in London in 2014, I went to Abramovic's exhibition because I remembered her name from that video.

미술 수업 중 토론의 일부를 들으시오.

교수 (남): 좋아요, 이제 막 시청한 영상은 Marina Abramovic이라는 저명한 참여예술가의 유명한 작품 〈예술가가 여기에 있다(The Artist is Present)〉의 일부분이에요. 아마 여러분도 인터넷을 통해 이미 본 적 있을 거예요, 그렇죠?

학생 1 (여): 사실 제가 2014년에 런던에 있었을 때 Abramovic의 전시회에 간 적이 있었는데요, 바로 그 영상을 통해 그녀의 이름을 기억했기 때문이에요.

Professor: You did? You must've seen her *512 hours*. We'll talk about that shortly. *[Pause]* So, as you've seen in the video of *The Artist is Present*, she sits in a chair at a gallery and invites the visitors to sit opposite her to look into her eyes. The part where her former lover unexpectedly takes a seat and she cries as she reaches out her hands is quite . . . powerful, to say the least. Now, can anyone share their artistic insight on this?

Student 2 (M): Well, I see that the artwork, or should I say artist, invites the visitors to be not only physically engaged with her artistic presence but also become part of it. For example, along with other visitors, Abramovic's former lover made himself become a striking element of her artwork.

Professor: That's wonderful. Q01-1 What you said is precisely the idea behind participatory art, which is a growing trend now in contemporary art. Many artists try to create works in which visitors take an active role in the artistic content, instead of being passive observers of static objects. Q03(D) In effect, the artists want to add different social and cultural experiences that include people, rather than isolate them as in traditional art. Look at Paul Ramirez, who is one of the most influential participatory artists. He asks people to participate by contributing everyday things, like spare change or impromptu messages. Sometimes they leave a wish, or their own recollection of history. In return, Ramirez used them as performative pieces, or to make large-scale monuments. What could be the implication of these exchanges between Ramirez and the participants?

Student 2: Q02 Perhaps those exchanges manifest trust and social connections between the two parties. I mean, people contribute their things trusting that those things will become part of a meaningful artwork by the artist.

Professor: Yes, you're quite right, and that's how Ramirez connects himself with his participants. Q05🎧 Now, for many artists, Q03(A) participatory art serves as a critique of established art museums with exhibitions of stationary objects. Q01-2 In fact, many museums began to adopt participatory art as a wider trend to connect with increasingly indifferent visitors. They see it as a way to access not just art, but also an individual's creativity through art. And that, I believe, is fundamental in any genre of art.

Student 1: But when I saw Abramovic's work in London, Q01-3 Q04 I personally felt estranged rather than engaged. Most people, myself included, just followed the instructions for mundane activities like walking backward . . . staring at patches of color, kind of like, um, zombies. It just reminded me how people are sometimes afraid to question contemporary art even though they get nothing out of it.

Professor: Actually, some critics are concerned about that. With its growing popularity, Q01-4 participatory art can become another institutional framework that further alienates people who are, like you, intimidated or at least unfamiliar with it.

01 토론의 주된 목적은?
(A) 참여예술가들의 논쟁이 되는 작품들을 소개하기 위해
(B) 새로운 예술 경향의 개념과 효과를 토의하기 위해
(C) 기존 미술관의 현재 위상을 비판하기 위해
(D) 예술에 대한 사회적 접근의 중요성을 강조하기 위해

02 방문객들이 Paul Ramirez의 요청에 따라 작품에 기여하는 것에 대한 교수의 의견은?
(A) 사람들이 예술적 행위에서 어떻게 사회적 가치를 찾는지를 보여준다.
(B) 많은 미술관으로 하여금 전통적인 전시를 재평가하도록 하고 있다.
(C) 방문객과 예술가 간의 신뢰와 사회적인 연대를 보여준다.
(D) 개인의 창조성과 그들의 예술에 대한 기대의 전형적인 예시가 된다.

해설 | Attitude 교수가 직접 이 부분에 대해 설명하기보다는 학생의 의견을 구하고, 그러한 교환이 양쪽 사이의 신뢰와 사회적 연결을 드러내는 것 같다는 학생의 대답에 동의함으로써 교수 자신의 의견을 간접적으로 피력하고 있다.

03 교수는 참여예술의 발상과 예시들을 설명한다. 다음 각 사항이 참여예술의 일부로 언급되는지 표시하시오.
각 사항에 대해 알맞은 항목에 표시하시오.

	예	아니오
(A) 기존의 예술과 전통 방식의 전시에 도전한다.	✓	
(B) 참여예술의 많은 작품들이 인터넷에서 인기를 얻고 있다.		✓
(C) 방문객들은 어떠한 사전 이해 없이 작품에 참여할 것이 요구된다.		✓
(D) 참여예술의 예술가들은 사람들을 포함하는 사회적이고 문화적인 경험을 창조해내려고 한다.	✓	

해설 | Connecting Content 많은 예술가들에게 참여예술이 고정된 작품들만을 전시하는 기존의 미술관에 대한 비판으로 작용하고 있다고 하였으므로 기존 예술과 전시에 도전한다고 할 수 있다. 또한, 참여예술가들이 사람들과 작품 사이에 거리를 두는 게 아니라 사람들을 작품 안으로 끌어안는 사회적이고 문화적인 경험을 더하고 싶어한다고 하였으므로 이들이 사람들을 포함하는 사회적이고 문화적인 경험을 창조해내려고 한다고 할 수 있다.

04 런던에서 Abramovic의 작품을 관람한 학생은 무엇을 느꼈다고 말하는가?
(A) 그녀의 작품으로부터 거리감을 느꼈다.
(B) 방문객들과 좀 더 가까워짐을 느꼈다.
(C) 예술작품을 이해하도록 압박감을 느꼈다.
(D) 어려운 지시 사항에 혼란스러움을 느꼈다.

해설 | Detail "I personally felt estranged rather than engaged"라는 언급을 통해 학생이 작품에 몰입하지 못했고 작품과 감상자 사이에 간격이 있었음을 알 수 있다. 그러므로 학생은 Abramovic의 참여예술에 오히려 참여하지 못하고 거리감을 느꼈음을 알 수 있다.

05 강의의 일부를 다시 듣고 질문에 답하시오.
교수가 참여예술을 채택하는 기존 미술관들에 대해 암시하는 것은?
(A) 비판을 피하기 위해 참여예술에 더 개방적이다.
(B) 다양한 형태의 예술을 제공하기 위해 판단을 유보하려고 노력한다.
(C) 다양한 집단의 방문객들을 위해 예술에의 접근을 가능하게 하려고 한다.
(D) 예술의 기본 철학을 복원함으로써 사람들과 연결될 수 있기를 희망한다.

해설 | Inference 교수에 의하면 미술관들이 참여예술을 단순히 예술 그 자체로의 접근일 뿐만 아니라 예술을 통한 개개인의 창조력을 접할 수 있는 방법으로도 보고 있다고 말한다. 그리고 미술관들 스스로가 밝히고 있는 입장은 아니지만, 이러한 입장이 모든 예술 장르의 기본이라는 생각을 밝히고 있으므로 이를 통해 미술관이 참여예술을 채택하는 것에 대한 교수의 의견을 유추할 수 있다.

어휘 | **segment** 일부분, 부분 **participatory** 참여의 **opposite** 건너편에 **insight** 통찰력 **precisely** 정확하게, 꼭 **impromptu** 즉흥의 **performative** 수행적인 **manifest** (특히 감정·태도·특질을 분명히) 나타내다 **critique** 비평 **stationary** 정적인, 움직이지 않는 **fundamental** 기본적인, 근본적인 **estrange** 사이를 멀어지게 하다, 떼어 놓다 **institutional** 제도권의 **alienate** 멀어지게[소원하게] 만들다 **intimidate** 겁을 먹게 하다

iBT Practice

p.110

01 (A)   **02** (B)   **03** (C)   **04** (A)   **05** (A), (D)   **06** (D)

Listen to part of a discussion in an American history class.

Professor (F): Hey, everyone. I hope you guys had a relaxing weekend because we've got a lot of stuff to cover this week. As you know, we have been discussing the Progressive movement that sprang up in the nineteenth century, a time of great change for America. We discussed how this movement sought to improve a lot of social ills that were rampant at the time, or, uh, make social progress, as implied by the name. Who can tell me exactly how these Progressives tried to do that?

Student 1 (F): Well, they generally wanted more equality and more benefits for everyone in society. They wanted things like better public sanitation, health care, and more political rights for women, and for all Americans, really.

Professor: Yeah, that'll do for a quick review. **Q01** Now, two individuals that had an important but complicated impact on this movement were John D. Rockefeller and Andrew Carnegie. Just to review, Carnegie and Rockefeller were probably the two richest American industrialists of this time period. Can anyone tell me exactly how they figured into the Progressive movement?

Student 2 (M): Well, I know that Andrew Carnegie gave most of his fortune to various charities. He was about as famous for making donations as he was for being a steel tycoon.

Professor: **Q02-1** Um, yes, charity is part of it. Rockefeller was also very generous, as he was a devout Baptist and felt obligated to donate much to charity. Both men championed many progressive causes, particularly in education.

Carnegie, the more famous philanthropist, was especially interested in building libraries, and establishing schools such as the Carnegie Mellon University and the University of Birmingham in England. Rockefeller also established numerous schools, including the University of Chicago and Rockefeller University. **Q06** 🎧 Both men also established charitable foundations, supported education for African-Americans, which was very unusual at the time, and over time gave most of their fortunes to charitable causes. *[Pause]* Stacy, you look a little confused.

Student 1: Well, it's all new to me. I'd always heard some unflattering things about these two guys, like how they were ruthless businessmen that dominated their industries.

Professor: *[Pleased]* **Q02-2** Excellent, and this is why they were somewhat at odds with the Progressive movement, too. See, more so than any other industrialists at the time, **Q05(D)** these two practiced rather harsh methods: buying up all available resources, controlling the transportation of these resources, putting competitors out of business, and so forth.

This angered many Progressives, who saw such methods as the cause of widespread poverty and other evils they were trying to correct. Q03 Influential Progressives like Ida Tarbell and Washington Gladden targeted Rockefeller in particular and preached against his methods of obtaining massive wealth. They derided such ruthless tactics as immoral and the cause of much of the growing inequity and poverty in society.

Similarly, many in state and federal governments felt that these men wielded too much power. Politicians with progressive agendas, particularly Presidents Theodore Roosevelt, William Taft, and Woodrow Wilson, actively took on companies that had acquired vast wealth through ruthless and arguably immoral business practices, like Rockefeller's Standard Oil. Many of these companies, including Standard Oil, were broken up in the early twentieth century in order to create competition and a fairer playing field for other businesses. Despite their altruism, these industrialists were cutthroat businessmen first and philanthropists second.

Student 2: Isn't this a little unfair, at least to Carnegie? I mean, in addition to charity, he publicly supported the rights of labor unions, too.

Professor: Q04 Well, despite what he said publicly, his practices told a different story. In fact, both Carnegie and Rockefeller supported extreme measures to keep workers under control. It's interesting to note how involved they were in helping poor people out as a whole, yet they were rather removed from the poor that worked for them. Like most industrial laborers, their workers had overlong hours, unsafe conditions, and no real job security. And when workers tried to protest, they were silenced pretty brutally.

Q05(A)-1 One unfortunate example of this is the Homestead Strike in 1892. Here, management hired by Carnegie violently broke up a strike at his steel mill in Homestead, Pennsylvania. Innocent people were killed as a result, and Carnegie's reputation as a humanitarian was damaged.

Q05(A)-2 Rockefeller experienced a similar incident with the so-called Ludlow Massacre in 1914. Management at Rockefeller's Colorado Fuel and Iron in Ludlow, Colorado also violently broke up a strike and caused a fire, killing several workers and their families.

01 토론의 주제는?
(A) Rockefeller 및 Carnegie와 진보주의 운동과의 관계
(B) Rockefeller와 Carnegie가 엄청난 부자가 된 방법
(C) Carnegie와 Rockefeller의 경영진에 의해 야기된 노동 불안
(D) Carnegie와 Rockefeller가 돈을 기부한 많은 자선단체

해설 | Main Idea 강의는 19세기 미국 진보주의 운동에 긍정적이면서도 다른 한편으로는 무자비하고 부도덕한 경영 방식으로 영향을 끼쳤던 Rockefeller와 Carnegie에 대해 설명하고 있다.

02 교수가 토론을 구성하는 방식은?
(A) Carnegie의 권력 획득을 논의하고 Rockefeller의 권력 획득을 논의함으로써
(B) Carnegie와 Rockefeller의 자선 활동을 논의하고 이들에 대한 진보주의자들의 비판을 논의함으로써
(C) 진보주의 운동의 원인을 논의하고 그 효과를 논의함으로써
(D) 미국의 산업 사회로의 전환을 논의하고 Carnegie와 Rockefeller가 어떻게 이 변화를 가능하게 했는지 논의함으로써

해설 | Organization 교수는 먼저 그들이 진보주의 운동에 어떻게 연관되어 있었는지를 질문함으로써 그들의 자선 활동에 대해 논의하고, 이후 진보주의자들의 비판을 불러일으켰던 그들의 경영 방식에 대해 논의하고 있다.

03 진보주의자들이 Rockefeller와 Carnegie를 비판했던 이유는?
(A) 진보주의자들은 미국에서 산업의 확산을 반대했다.
(B) 진보주의자들은 이들이 대의를 위해 기부하지 않은 것에 분노했다.
(C) 진보주의자들은 이들의 사업 관행이 비도덕적이라고 생각했다.
(D) 진보주의자들은 이들이 정부의 권위를 침해한다고 생각했다.

해설 | Detail 진보주의자들은 이들의 무자비한 사업 방식이 사회의 빈곤과 불평등을 일으키는 원인이라고 보았으므로 매우 비도덕적이라고 생각했다.

04 Andrew Carnegie에 대한 교수의 의견은?
(A) 자선보다 사업에 더 많은 관심을 가졌다고 생각한다.
(B) 그의 사업 관행에 대해 너무 혹독한 비판을 받았다고 생각한다.
(C) Rockefeller만큼 자선을 많이 베풀지는 않았다고 생각한다.
(D) 자기 직원들에게 너무 친절했다고 생각한다.

해설 | Attitude 한 학생이 Carnegie를 옹호하는 질문을 하자, 교수는 "Well, despite what he said publicly, his practices told a different story"라고 답하고 Carnegie가 자신의 노동자들을 얼마나 탄압했는지 설명하고 있다. 이는 Carnegie가 대외적으로는 자선가였지만, 사실은 자신의 사업적 목적에 더 신경 쓰고 있었음을 나타낸다.

05 Carnegie와 Rockefeller가 무자비한 기업가였음을 보여 주는 예는?
2개의 답을 고르시오.
(A) 그들은 파업을 중지시키기 위해 폭력적인 조치를 했다.
(B) 그들은 사회적 이슈에 대해서는 전혀 관심이 없었으며, 자신들의 사업만 신경 썼다.
(C) 그들은 아무런 이유도 제시하지 않고 많은 노동자를 해고했다.
(D) 그들은 시장을 독점함으로써 빈곤과 불평등을 초래했다.

해설 | Detail 교수는 두 기업가가 무자비한 기업가임을 보여 주는 사례로 시장에 나와 있는 모든 원자재를 독점하여 경쟁 기업들을 도산시켰고, 노조의 파업을 무자비하게 진압하여 많은 사람의 희생을 초래했음을 지적한다.

06 강의의 일부를 다시 듣고 질문에 답하시오.
학생이 다음과 같이 말할 때 의미하는 것은?
"Well, it's all new to me."
(A) 학생은 Carnegie와 Rockefeller에 대한 이야기를 전혀 듣지 못했다.
(B) 학생은 교수가 제기한 주장을 믿지 않는다.
(C) 학생은 이 주제에 대한 교수의 강의를 이해하지 못한다.
(D) 학생은 Carnegie와 Rockefeller를 다른 관점에서 봤다.

해설 | Function 학생은 그동안 Carnegie와 Rockefeller에 대해 안 좋은 사실만 들어왔다고 했으므로, 두 사람이 자선과 교육에 힘써왔다는 사실과는 다른 관점에서 그들을 봤다는 것을 알 수 있다.

어휘 | **spring up** 일어나다, 생기다   **rampant** 만연한, 무성한   **devout** 독실한   **Baptist** 침례교인   **obligated** ~할 의무가 있는   **cause** 운동, 대의   **philanthropist** 박애주의자   **unflattering** 부정적인, 노골적인   **ruthless** 무자비한   **at odds with** ~와 대립하는   **preach** 설교하다   **deride** 조롱하다   **tactic** 술책, 책략   **inequity** 불평등   **wield** (권력 등을) 휘두르다   **take on** 공격하다   **acquire** 획득하다   **arguably** 이론의 여지는 있으나, 거의 틀림없이   **altruism** 이타주의   **cutthroat** 잔학한, (경쟁 등이) 과열된   **labor union** 노동 조합   **brutally** 무참히, 잔혹히

Chapter 11 Life Science

Intensive Drill 1

01 (C) 02 (D) 03 (A) 04 [New Approach – (B), (D)], [Old Approach – (A), (C)] 05 (D)

Listen to part of a discussion in a zoology class.

Professor (F): For many years, studies have revealed that chimpanzees have quite a few humanlike characteristics. For example, they can hunt using specific tools and . . . what else?

Student 1 (M): Is it true that chimpanzees mourn over the death of other chimpanzees?

Professor: Yes, there was a study on that, too. And more recently, another humanlike feature of chimpanzees has been confirmed after many years of debate among the experts.

Q01-1 Through many past experiments, scientists observed that chimpanzees were reluctant to share with others. This led to a conclusion that they were anti-social and self-regarding rather than pro-social and altruistic. But many fieldworkers were frustrated over such notions because they claimed to have observed spontaneously altruistic behavior in chimpanzees. Q03 And if you think about it, they were the people who spent substantially more hours with chimpanzees.

Student 1: Well, if the fieldworkers could observe chimpanzees' altruistic behavior, why couldn't the scientists?

Professor: Good question and, well, why don't I let some of you speculate on the answer to that?

Student 2 (F): Was it because of the environment? Maybe it was whether the chimpanzees were observed in the wild or in a lab. I mean, isn't it a well-known fact that most animals can behave differently when they're captured in a lab?

Professor: You have a point, but for this particular case, the fieldworkers raised the same claim over the lab chimpanzees they observed.

Student 2: Well, it could depend on how the scientists controlled their experiments. The fieldworkers might have interacted with chimpanzees in a different state of control.

Professor: In fact, they did. Q04(A) In earlier studies, chimps were given fairly complex tools so that they could use those tools to deliver food to themselves or others. But granting them such tools ended up testing their tool skills rather than their altruistic tendencies. Another problem with past experiments was that chimpanzees were placed far apart from each other. Q04(C) This prevented them from realizing the consequences of their behavior, how it could benefit others.

So, in this recent study, the researchers took a different approach. **Q04(D)** They used no complicated tools and placed the chimps next to each other so they could see their neighbor's reaction. **Q04(B)** During the experiment, the subject chimps were given 30 tokens in two different colors and were trained to understand that tokens can be exchanged for food. They also knew that one color represented getting banana slices to share with the other chimp nearby, while another color meant just getting their own food.

Almost 70 percent of the time, the subjects chose the tokens that granted food for them and food to share. **Q05** After seeing other additional evidence, **Q01-2** the researchers concluded that chimpanzees were indeed sensitive to the needs of others while fulfilling their own needs, and therefore they were pro-social and altruistic beings. This was quite the reverse from the earlier studies.

Student 1: It sounds like the past experiments themselves were the source of the failure in verifying the theory.

Professor: Yes, and such failure is not unique to this case. So keep in mind how such well-controlled experiments sometimes can change the evidence for your hypothesis.

따라서, 이 최근 연구에서는 연구원들이 다른 접근 방식을 취했어요. 그들은 복잡한 도구를 사용하지 않았고, 침팬지들이 다른 침팬지들의 반응을 볼 수 있도록 서로의 옆에 두었어요. 그 실험에서 실험 침팬지들은 두 가지 다른 색의 토큰을 30개씩 받았고, 그 토큰들이 음식과 교환될 수 있다는 것을 이해하도록 훈련 받았어요. 또한 한 가지 색은 근처에 있는 다른 침팬지와 나눠 먹을 수 있는 바나나 조각을 얻는다는 것을 나타내고, 다른 색은 자신의 음식만 얻는다는 것을 의미한 것도 알고 있었어요.

거의 70%의 시간 동안, 실험 침팬지들은 그들 자신의 음식과 나눠 먹을 수 있는 음식을 제공하는 토큰을 선택했어요. 다른 추가적인 증거를 본 후에, 연구원들은 침팬지들이 정말로 그들 자신의 욕구를 채우면서도 다른 이들의 욕구 또한 신경 쓰기 때문에 친사회적이고 이타적이라는 결론을 내렸어요. 이는 초기 연구들과는 상당히 반대되는 거였죠.

학생 1: 과거 실험들은 마치 그 이론을 입증하는 데 실패 요인이 되었던 것 같네요.

교수: 네, 그리고 그러한 실패가 이 경우에만 해당되는 것은 아니죠. 따라서 그런 잘 통제된 실험이 가끔 가설에 대한 증거를 어떻게 바꿀 수 있는지 명심하세요.

01 토론의 주된 목적은?
(A) 침팬지의 인간다운 특성에 대한 이론을 비판하기 위해
(B) 포획된 동물들을 관찰하는 최신 접근법에 대해 설명하기 위해
(C) 새로운 연구가 어떻게 상반되는 이론을 입증했는지 논의하기 위해
(D) 동물학에서 현장 연구자들의 중요한 역할을 강조하기 위해

해설 | Main Idea 강의에서 교수는 기존의 연구는 침팬지들이 반사회적이고 이기적이라고 주장했지만, 새로운 연구는 이와 반대로 침팬지들이 친사회적이고 이타적인 동물들이라는 결론을 냈다고 설명한다.

02 교수에 따르면, 침팬지 전문가들 사이에서 논란이 된 의견은?
(A) 침팬지들이 음식을 공유하기 위해 도구를 사용할 수 있는지
(B) 침팬지들이 관찰을 위해 포획되어야 하는지
(C) 침팬지들이 그들 집단에 속한 다른 침팬지들이 죽었을 때 애도하는지
(D) 침팬지들이 다른 침팬지들에 대한 배려를 보이는지

해설 | Detail 과거에는 침팬지들이 다른 이들과 공유하는 것을 꺼리고 반사회적이며 이기적이라고 생각되었지만, 최근에는 침팬지들이 자발적인 이타적 행동을 보여준다는 주장이 나왔다. 즉 침팬지들이 다른 침팬지들에 대한 배려를 보이는지에 대한 논란이 있었다.

03 현장 연구자들에 대한 교수의 태도는?
(A) 침팬지에 대한 그들의 주장이 인정받아 마땅하다고 생각한다.
(B) 그들이 종종 과장되고 비과학적인 주장을 늘어놓는다고 주장한다.
(C) 과학자들을 지원하는 데 있어 그들의 업무량이 많다고 생각한다.
(D) 그들이 침팬지들을 너무 심하게 관찰한다고 비판한다.

해설 | Attitude 교수는 현장 연구자들이야말로 침팬지들과 상당히 많은 시간을 보낸 사람들이라고 말하며, 이들의 연구 결과가 기존의 상반된 이론을 어떻게 반박하는지에 대해 설명한다.

04 토론에서 교수는 새로운 연구에 대한 접근법이 과거 실험들의 접근법과 어떻게 달랐는지 언급한다. 다음 각 사항이 새로운 접근법이나 기존의 접근법과 관련 있는지 표시하시오.
각 사항에 대해 알맞은 항목에 표시하시오.

	새로운 접근법	기존 접근법
(A) 침팬지들은 음식을 전달하기 위한 복잡한 도구를 받았다.		✔
(B) 침팬지들은 두 개의 선택사항 중 하나를 선택하도록 훈련받았다.	✔	
(C) 침팬지들은 그들 행동의 결과를 깨닫지 못했다.		✔
(D) 침팬지들은 서로의 옆에 있었다.	✔	

해설 | Connecting Content 강의에서 교수는 기존의 연구에서는 침팬지들이 복잡한 도구를 사용해야 했고, 서로에게서 너무 멀리 떨어져 있었으며, 그들 자신의 행동에 대한 결과를 깨달을 수 없었다고 설명한다. 반대로 새로운 연구에서는 복잡한 도구를 사용하지 않았고, 서로의 옆에 있었으며, 행동의 결과에 대해 인식할 수 있도록 하였다고 설명한다.

05 강의의 일부를 다시 듣고 질문에 답하시오.
교수가 침팬지들에 대한 과거 연구들에 대해 암시하는 것은?

(A) 그 연구들은 다소 독특한 침팬지의 본성을 고려하지 못했다.
(B) 연구원들은 증거를 통제하지 말았어야 한다.
(C) 결과물을 통제할 더 나은 방법이 있었을 것이다.
(D) 그 연구들에 많은 제약이 있었다는 사실은 실패로 이어졌다.

해설 | **Inference** 교수는 "So keep in mind how such well-controlled experiments sometimes can change the evidence for your hypothesis"라고 말하며, 침팬지들에 대한 과거 연구들이 실패한 원인은 너무 통제되었기 때문, 즉 너무 많은 제약이 있었기 때문임을 암시한다.

어휘 | **humanlike** 인간다운, 인간과 같은　**characteristic** 특성, 특질　**mourn** 애도하다　**confirm** 확인해 주다, 사실임을 보여주다　**anti-social** 반사회적인　**self-regarding** 이기적인, 자애의　**pro-social** 친사회적인　**altruistic** 이타적인　**fieldworker** 현장 연구자　**spontaneously** 자발적으로, 자연스럽게　**speculate** 추측하다, 짐작하다　**tendency** 성향, 기질　**subject** 연구[실험] 대상, 주제　**reverse** 반대　**verify** 입증하다, 확인하다　**well-controlled** 잘 통제[제어]된　**hypothesis** 가설, 추측

Intensive Drill 2　　　　　　　　　　　　　　　　　　　　　　　　　　　　p.116

01 (A), (C)　　**02** (B)　　**03** (A), (B), (E)　　**04** (A)　　**05** (B)

Listen to part of a lecture in a biology class.

Professor (M): If any of you have some knowledge in architecture, you're probably aware of the importance of a keystone. Q02 A keystone is placed at the top of an arch to secure the structure. Without the keystone, the whole arch and building around it will fall down. Q01(A)-1 In biology, there are keystone species that play a critical role in the ecosystems they live in. They can be plants or animals, carnivores or herbivores. Now, some of you might ask, "Don't all species rely on each other one way or the other?" Well, when you look at the big picture, yes, they do. Q01(A)-2 But the importance of a keystone species is how it creates or maintains the biodiversity of the ecological community even though it's not necessarily dominant in numbers. Q03(A) And just like a keystone in architecture, the absence of a keystone species can actually bring down the ecosystem altogether.

Then, what are these keystone species and how do they function in their habitats? Q01(C) There are several categories of keystone species. Let's start with the first one, the top predators. Top predators eat smaller animals at lower levels in the food chain and by doing so, they allow other species to thrive. One good example of keystone top predators is the sea otters of the Pacific Northwest. Q03(B) Now, sea otters may come across as far from being ferocious predators, but they are still carnivores that feed on sea urchins. And if they didn't, the sea urchins would crowd out and eat up the kelp in the ecosystem. Many aquatic species rely on seaweed like kelp as a major food source or as a hiding place from predators. So, without the sea otters, the sea urchins will take over and the biodiversity in the habitat will begin to decrease.

The next category of keystone species is the mutualists, which maintain a mutually beneficial relationship with a wide range of other species. Most fruit trees are keystone mutualists since they provide food and shelter to other animals like birds and monkeys. These animals, in return, disperse the seeds by depositing them in their droppings onto the ground, sometimes miles away from the tree.

생물학 강의 중 일부를 들으시오.

교수 (남): 여러분들이 건축에 대한 지식이 있다면, 아마도 쐐기돌의 중요성에 대해 알고 있을 거예요. 쐐기돌은 구조물을 안전하게 하려고 아치 꼭대기에 놓여져요. 그 쐐기돌이 없다면, 아치 전체와 그것을 둘러싼 건물은 무너질 거예요. 생물학에서는 자신들이 사는 생태계에서 중요한 역할을 하는 핵심종이 있어요. 식물이나 동물일 수도 있고, 육식 동물이거나 초식 동물일 수도 있죠. 자, "모든 종이 어느 쪽으로든 서로에게 의존하고 있는 것 아닌가요?"라고 물어볼 수도 있겠어요. 음, 큰 맥락에서 봤을 때, 네, 맞아요. 하지만 핵심종이 중요한 이유는 그 종이 꼭 수적으로 우세하지 않더라도, 생태 공동체에서 생물의 다양성을 만들어내거나 유지하는 방식 때문이에요. 그리고 건축에서의 쐐기돌처럼, 핵심종의 부재는 실제로 생태계 전부를 파멸시킬 수도 있어요.

그러면, 이 핵심종들은 무엇이며 그들의 서식지에서 어떤 기능을 할까요? 핵심종은 여러 범주로 나뉠 수 있어요. 첫 번째 범주, 상위 포식자부터 시작해보죠. 상위 포식자들은 먹이사슬의 하위 단계에 있는 작은 동물들을 잡아먹고, 그렇게 함으로써 다른 종들이 번창할 수 있도록 해줘요. 핵심종 상위 포식자의 좋은 예는 태평양 연안 북서부에 사는 해달이에요. 자, 해달은 흉포한 포식자가 아니라는 인상을 줄 수 있지만, 그들은 성게를 먹고 사는 육식 동물이에요. 그리고 만약 그들이 성게를 먹고 살지 않는다면, 성게는 생태계에서 다시마를 몰아내고 다 먹어 치울 거예요. 많은 수생종들이 다시마와 같은 해조류를 주요 식량 공급원이나 포식자로부터 숨을 수 있는 장소로 의존하죠. 따라서 해달이 없다면, 성게는 그 자리를 대체할 것이고, 서식지의 생물 다양성은 줄어들기 시작하겠죠.

핵심종의 다음 범주는 상리 공생 생물인데, 이들은 다양한 다른 종들과 함께 서로 유익한 관계를 유지하죠. 대부분의 과수는 상리 공생하는 핵심종인데, 새나 원숭이와 같은 다른 동물들에게 식량이나 쉼터를 제공하기 때문이죠. 그 보답으로 이 동물들은 배설물을 통해 땅에 씨앗을 퍼뜨리는데, 가끔 나무로부터 수 마일이나 멀리 갈 수도 있어요.

Q03(E) Then, there is also the category of ecosystem engineers which affect the habitats they live in by changing their physical environment. Let's look at the case of elephants in the African plains. Elephants knock over small trees like acacia for food, and this in effect controls the tree population. **Q04** Without elephants and their feeding behavior, the grasses would not be able to flourish in the plains and they would turn into woodlands. Consequently, grazing animals like zebras or antelopes would disappear from the ecosystem.

Q05 As an advocate of environmental preservation, I believe identifying keystone species is imperative for conservationists. They need to understand which species to target for conserving and promoting biodiversity in ecosystems. In many habitats, time is running out. So, clearly, isn't it much easier to protect just one species to sustain a whole ecosystem than trying to protect the entire range of life forms in a habitat?

그리고, 자신들이 사는 서식지의 물리적 환경을 변화시켜 영향을 끼치는 생태계 기사라고 하는 또 다른 범주도 있어요. 아프리카 평원의 코끼리의 경우를 보죠. 코끼리는 식량을 얻기 위해 아카시아와 같은 작은 나무를 쓰러뜨리는데, 이는 사실상 나무 개체 수를 조절해줘요. 코끼리와 그들의 섭식 행동이 없다면, 평원에서 풀이 번성하지 못할 것이고, 삼림지대로 바뀌어 버릴 거예요. 그 결과 얼룩말이나 영양 같은 방목 동물들은 생태계에서 없어지겠죠.

저는 환경 보존 옹호자로서, 핵심종을 확인하는 것은 환경보호 활동가들이 반드시 해야 하는 일이라고 생각해요. 그들은 생태계에서 생물의 다양성을 보존하고 조장하기 위해서 어떤 종을 목표로 삼아야 하는지 이해해야 하죠. 많은 서식지는 시간이 얼마 남지 않았어요. 따라서 서식지 한 곳의 전체 생물을 보호하려고 노력하는 것보다는 단 하나의 종을 보호해서 전체 생태계를 지속시키는 것이 분명히 더 쉽지 않나요?

01 강의의 주된 내용은?
2개의 답을 고르시오.

(A) 핵심종의 생태학적 중요성
(B) 핵심종으로부터 야기되는 이익과 피해
(C) 핵심종의 일반적인 분류
(D) 위기에 처한 핵심종을 보호하는 방법들

해설 | Main Idea 교수는 핵심종이 생태계에 미치는 중요성을 설명하며, 이와 함께 핵심종의 범주를 세 가지로 나누어 설명하고 있다.

02 교수가 건축에서의 쐐기돌을 언급하는 이유는?

(A) 두 학문 분야의 중요한 관련성을 강조하기 위해
(B) 쐐기돌의 역할과 생물학적 개념의 유사성을 비교하기 위해
(C) 생물학적인 핵심 개념을 새로운 관점에서 보기 위해
(D) 학제 간 연구의 중요성을 강조하기 위해

해설 | Organization 교수는 아치형 건물에서 쐐기돌(keystone)이 없으면 건물 전체가 무너질 수 있다고 하며, 생물학에서의 핵심종(keystone species)이 없으면 생태계가 파멸될 수도 있다고 말한다. 즉, 건축에서 쐐기돌(keystone)의 역할과 생물학적 개념에서 핵심종(keystone species)의 유사성을 비교하기 위해 쐐기돌을 언급하였다.

03 교수에 따르면, 다음 중 핵심종에 대해 옳은 것은?
3개의 답을 고르시오.

(A) 그들의 부재는 생태계의 파괴를 가져올 수 있다.
(B) 그들은 서식지에 있는 특정한 종을 몰아내는 것을 막을 수 있다.
(C) 다른 종들에 대한 영향은 그들의 적은 개체 수로 인해 제한된다.
(D) 일부를 제외하고 그들 대부분은 육식 동물이다.
(E) 그들은 서식지의 물리적 환경을 변화시키거나 유지시킬 수 있다.

해설 | Detail 교수는 핵심종의 부재는 생태계 전부를 파멸시킬 수도 있다고 하였다. 또한, 해달이 없다면 성게가 다시마를 다 먹어 치웠을 것이라고 말하며, 핵심종이 서식지에 있는 특정 종을 몰아내는 것을 막을 수 있다고 설명한다. 다음으로, 핵심종의 마지막 범주를 언급하며 이들은 자신들이 사는 서식지의 물리적 환경을 변화시켜 영향을 끼치는 존재라고 설명한다.

04 아프리카 평원에서 코끼리의 섭식 행동이 중요한 이유는?

(A) 다양한 방목 동물의 식량을 지원하는 초원을 유지시킨다.
(B) 작은 동물을 보호하는 나무의 확장을 조장한다.
(C) 다양한 씨앗을 퍼뜨리고 식물 다양성을 돕는다.
(D) 지배적인 포식자들의 개체 수를 점진적으로 감소시킨다.

해설 | Detail 교수는 코끼리와 그들의 섭식 행동이 없다면 평원이 삼림지대로 바뀌어서 방목 동물들의 생태계가 없어질 것이라고 말하였다.

05 핵심종을 목표로 삼아 환경을 보존하는 것에 대한 교수의 의견은?

(A) 환경에 대한 전체적인 영향은 여전히 불확실하다.
(B) 매우 중요하고 긴급한 것으로 여겨져야 한다.
(C) 너무 긴 절차 때문에 일부 경우에서는 효과가 없다.
(D) 다양한 종을 보호해야 할 필요성을 간과할 수 있다.

해설 | Attitude 교수는 강의 후반부에서 핵심종을 확인하는 것은 환경 보호 운동가들이 꼭 해야 하는 일이며, 많은 서식지는 시간이 얼마 남지 않았다고 말한다. 즉, 핵심종을 목표로 삼아 환경을 보존하는 것은 매우 중요하고 긴급한 것으로 여겨져야 한다는 의견을 내놓았다.

어휘 | **keystone** 쐐기돌　**secure** 안전하게 하다, 얻어 내다　**fall down** 쓰러지다　**keystone species** 핵심종　**ecosystem** 생태계　**carnivore** 육식 동물　**herbivore** 초식 동물　**biodiversity** 생물 다양성　**dominant** 우세한, 지배적인　**bring down** 파멸시키다, 붕괴시키다　**sea otter** 해달　**come across as** ~이라는 인상을 주다　**far from** 전혀 ~이 아닌　**ferocious** 흉포한, 맹렬한　**sea urchin** 성게　**crowd out** 몰아내다　**kelp** 다시마　**mutualist** 상리 공생 생물, 상호 부조론자　**shelter** 쉼터, 피난처　**in return** 보답으로, 대신에　**disperse** 퍼뜨리다, 확산시키다　**plain** 평원　**knock over** 쓰러뜨리다　**feeding behavior** 섭식 행동　**flourish** 번성하다, 번창하다　**woodland** 삼림지대　**consequently** 그 결과, 따라서　**grazing animal** 방목 동물　**antelope** 영양　**advocate** 옹호자, 지지자　**preservation** 보존, 보호　**identify** 확인하다, 알아보다　**imperative** 반드시 해야 하는, 긴요한　**conservationist** 환경보호 활동가　**conserve** 보존하다, 보호하다　**promote** 조장하다, 촉진시키다　**sustain** 지속시키다

Intensive Drill 3　　　　　　　　　　　　　　　　　　　　　　　　　　　p.118

01 (C)　**02** (B), (C)　**03** (D)　**04** (A)　**05** (D)

Listen to part of a lecture in a botany class.

Professor (M): Q05 OK, I know that you're all expecting your test grades back by today, but I was at a conference all weekend. But I won't keep you on edge. You should get everything back by Wednesday. Now it's time to get down to business. Q01-1 We are going to talk about a nasty little weed in American agriculture: the spotted knapweed, which is classified as an invasive species. Can anyone explain what an invasive species is, class?

Student (F): Well, isn't it a species that can cause harm to human, animal, or plant health? As a result, it adversely affects the environment and the economy.

Professor: Good job, Amy. Let's get to the spotted knapweed, then.

OK, after being introduced from Europe around a hundred years ago, this pest has caused a great deal of destruction by taking over millions of acres of farmland and pasture. This plant is especially prevalent in vast, rural areas with relatively unfriendly soil, such as Montana, Minnesota, North Dakota, and other areas in the northwest United States.

Q01-2 So, what makes this plant so threatening? Well, there are some natural advantages it has in competing for resources, and these allow it to spread easily and make it hard to kill. For example, the plant produces a toxin that kills off native grasses in its vicinity, allowing it to take over land from those grasses. It also has a stout, deep taproot that can consume deep water sources out of the reach of other plants, a big advantage in drier areas. Then there are its reproductive capabilities, which help the plant aggressively spread. The spotted knapweed reproduces by dispersing very light seeds into the air, which are carried off by the wind, on the undersides of cars, and in many other ways.

Now, its reproductive capabilities pose two problems for other plants. Q02(B) First, spotted knapweeds produce a large amount of seeds at any given time. A single plant can produce well over a thousand seeds every year. Q02(C) Second, the seeds can survive in the soil for over five years. This means that even if a farmer or rancher catches some spotted knapweed plants and kills them before an infestation, he still has to constantly check for new sprouts for a long time afterward.

식물학 강의 중 일부를 들으시오.

교수 (남): 자, 여러분이 오늘 시험 결과를 받을 것으로 기대하고 있다는 걸 아는데, 제가 주말 내내 회의에 참석했거든요. 하지만 계속 초조하게 하진 않을게요. 수요일까지는 모두 받을 수 있을 거예요. 자, 이제 본론으로 들어갈 시간이네요. 미국 농업에서 다루기 힘든 잡초인 반점뻐꾹채류에 대해서 이야기하도록 할 텐데, 이는 침입종으로 분류됩니다. 여러분, 침입종이 무엇인지 설명해 줄 수 있나요?

학생 (여): 음, 인간, 동물, 혹은 식물의 건강에 해를 입힐 수 있는 종이 아닌가요? 그 결과로, 환경이나 경제에 부정적인 영향을 미치기도 하고요.

교수: 잘했어요, Amy. 그러면 반점뻐꾹채류로 넘어가 보도록 하죠.

자, 약 백 년 전쯤에 유럽으로부터 유입된 후에, 이 해로운 식물은 수백만 에이커가 넘는 농경지와 목장을 뒤덮으며 대규모 파괴를 일으켜왔어요. 이 식물은 특히 몬태나, 미네소타, 노스다코타와 그 밖의 미국 북서부 지역처럼 토양이 비교적 척박한 광대한 시골 지역에 널리 퍼져 있습니다.

그러면 이 식물이 왜 그토록 위협적일까요? 이 식물은 영양분 경쟁에 있어 자연적으로 유리하기 때문에 쉽게 퍼질 수가 있으며 없애기가 어려워요. 예를 들어, 이 식물은 그 부근의 토종 풀을 죽이는 독성을 만들어 그 풀들을 죽이고 그 땅을 차지해 버리죠. 또한, 튼튼하고 깊게 뻗은 주근을 갖고 있기 때문에 다른 식물들이 닿을 수 없는 깊은 곳의 물을 다 써버릴 수가 있는데, 이는 건조한 지역에서 큰 이점이 되죠. 게다가 번식 능력이 뛰어나 공격적으로 퍼져나갈 수 있습니다. 반점뻐꾹채류는 공기 중에 매우 가벼운 씨를 퍼뜨림으로써 번식을 하는데, 바람에 실려 가거나 차 밑에 붙어 가는 등의 많은 방법으로 퍼져나갑니다.

자, 이러한 번식 능력은 다른 식물들에게 두 가지 문제를 일으킵니다. 첫째, 반점뻐꾹채류는 언제라도 씨를 대량으로 만들어 낼 수 있어요. 하나의 식물은 매년 천 개가 넘는 씨를 만들어낼 수 있지요. 둘째, 이 씨들은 5년이 넘도록 땅속에서 살아남을 수가 있습니다. 이 말은 만약 농부나 목장주가 반점뻐꾹채류를 발견하고 만연해지기 전에 죽인다고 해도, 그 후로도 오랫동안 새싹이 나지는 않을까 지속적인 확인을 해야 한다는 뜻입니다.

But that's another tricky part. **Q03** Killing them isn't so easy. The spotted knapweed has few natural enemies. There are a few insect species that eat it, and precious few other animals feed on the weed. In particular, cattle will not eat spotted knapweed unless there is absolutely nothing else. As you can see, this makes it dangerous not only to crop production, but also to livestock.

Q04 Of course, there are some herbicides that can kill the spotted knapweed. However, this would not really be my own first choice. You would have to use just the right amount, not too much or too little, and you have to know how to apply these chemicals. Otherwise, they can be just as harmful, if not more so, as the spotted knapweed they are meant to wipe out.

그런데, 바로 이것이 또 문제가 되는 부분입니다. 이것들을 죽이기가 그리 쉽지 않아요. 반점뻐꾹채류는 천적이 거의 없거든요, 이것을 먹는 곤충도 몇 종류밖에 없으며, 이 풀을 먹는 소중한 동물들도 몇 종류에 불과해요. 특히 소도 정말 다른 먹을 것이 없을 때가 아니면 반점뻐꾹채류를 먹지 않아요. 알겠지만, 이로 인해서 이 식물은 작물 생산뿐만 아니라 가축을 기르는 데도 위험한 존재가 될 수 있어요.

물론 반점뻐꾹채류를 죽일 수 있는 제초제가 몇 가지 있기는 해요. 하지만 저라면 이 방법을 첫 번째로 선택하지는 않겠어요. 제초제는 너무 많이도 너무 적게도 쓰면 안 되고, 딱 적정량만 사용해야 하며, 이 화학제품을 어떻게 쓰는지 잘 알아야 합니다. 그렇지 않으면 없애려고 한 반점뻐꾹채류만큼, 아니 어쩌면 더욱 해로울 수도 있어요.

01 강의의 주제는?
(A) 반점뻐꾹채류를 통제하는 방법
(B) 북아메리카에서 반점뻐꾹채류의 역사
(C) 반점뻐꾹채류가 위협적 존재인 이유
(D) 반점뻐꾹채류의 생활 주기

해설 | Main Idea 강의 초반에 교수는 반점뻐꾹채류에 대해 소개하고 "So, what makes this plant so threatening?"이라고 질문함으로써 그 식물이 왜 위협적인지에 대한 내용으로 강의를 이어나가고 있다.

02 다음 중 반점뻐꾹채류의 씨에 대해 옳은 것은?
2개의 답을 고르시오.
(A) 소나 양에 의해 먹힐 때가 많다.
(B) 한 번에 많은 수가 생성된다.
(C) 오랫동안 땅속에서 살아남을 수 있다.
(D) 매우 무거우며 두꺼운 껍질이 있다.

해설 | Detail 반점뻐꾹채류는 번식 능력이 매우 뛰어난 식물로서 언제라도 씨를 대량으로 만들어낼 수 있으며, 이 씨들은 5년이 넘도록 땅속에서 살아남을 수 있다.

03 반점뻐꾹채류를 없애기 어려운 한 가지 이유는?
(A) 빨리 자라도록 도와주는 특정 화학 물질을 함유하고 있다.
(B) 뿌리가 너무 깊어 땅속에서 파내기가 힘들다.
(C) 화학 제초제에 내성이 매우 강하다.
(D) 이 풀을 먹는 동물들이 많지 않다.

해설 | Detail 교수는 이 식물을 없애기가 쉽지 않은데 그 이유는 이것을 먹는 천적이 거의 없기 때문이라고 설명하고 있다.

04 화학 제초제 사용에 대한 교수의 생각은?
(A) 해초를 다루기에 위험 부담이 너무 크다.
(B) 해초를 없애는 데 가장 효과적인 방법이다.
(C) 다른 방법과 함께 사용되어야 한다.
(D) 대부분의 사람이 제대로 알고 있지 않다.

해설 | Attitude 마지막 부분에서 교수는 제초제를 제대로 사용하지 않으면 오히려 더 해로울 수 있다고 말하고 있다.

05 강의의 일부를 다시 듣고 질문에 답하시오.
교수가 다음과 같이 말하는 이유는?
"But I won't keep you on edge."
(A) 학생들에게 다음 과제에 대해 주의를 주기 위해
(B) 학생들에게 점수를 엄격히 매기지 않을 것을 약속하기 위해
(C) 학생들에게 강의가 막 시작할 것임을 의식하도록 하기 위해
(D) 학생들이 곧 점수를 받게 될 것임을 확인해 주기 위해

해설 | Function 아직 시험 결과가 나오지 않은 것에 대해 계속 초조하게 하지 않겠다는 것은 곧 시험 점수를 알려주겠다는 의미이다.

어휘 | on edge 초조하여　**nasty** 다루기 힘든　**pest** 해로운 동식물, 유해물　**prevalent** 널리 퍼진　**rural** 시골의　**stout** 튼튼한　**taproot** [식물] 주근, 곧은 뿌리　**infestation** 만연, 침략　**disperse** 퍼뜨리다　**sprout** 싹　**livestock** 가축　**herbicide** 제초제

Mini Test 1

01 (B) 02 (B) 03 (D) 04 (A), (D) 05 (A)

Listen to part of a discussion in a microbiology class.

Professor (F): Good afternoon, everybody. Let's get started. Q01-1 Today we're looking at organisms that human beings are immensely reliant upon. Can anyone guess what I'm talking about? [Pause] Yes, it's cyanobacteria we're going to discuss today. As you know, it is a form of bacteria that can be found in almost every terrestrial and aquatic habitat, such as oceans, fresh water, damp soil, and even temporarily moistened rocks in deserts.

Now, even though it is a phylum of bacteria, cyanobacteria, also called cyanophyta, are unusual in that they contain chlorophyll, like plants. Again, chlorophyll allows plants to capture sunlight to use in photosynthesis. Q04(D) Thus, cyanobacteria perform photosynthesis, which utilizes solar energy to break down soil and water into food. Who can tell me why this is important?

Student 1 (M): Well, a byproduct of photosynthesis is oxygen, right?

Professor: Very good. Yes, like plants, cyanobacteria release oxygen into the atmosphere. Q01-2 In fact, cyanobacteria were probably the first organisms to ever do this, and this process was primarily responsible for converting the early toxic atmosphere of the earth into something that modern animals could survive in.

As species of bacteria, cyanobacteria are one of the most basic forms of life on earth, evolving from the primordial ooze early on. So, about two billion years ago, cyanobacteria were found all throughout the oceans of the planet. Q03-1 In the absence of any plant life, cyanobacteria were the main sources of oxygen, a "waste" product of photosynthesis. Their production of oxygen ultimately set up an atmosphere that could sustain other forms of life that would arise.

But wait, it gets even more amazing. See, many scientists now believe that plant life evolved when its predecessors merged with cyanobacteria. Q02 Plant cells have bodies called chloroplasts, and these contain chlorophyll. Well, these chloroplasts were originally cyanobacteria that began living off early plant cells.

In time, the cells and the cyanobacteria became dependent on each other and formed a single organism. Q01-3 Q03-2 So, um, ultimately, plants became self-sustaining because of cyanobacteria. Also, consider this. We eat both plants and the animals that eat plants. Thus, you could say that cyanobacteria helped create the modern food chain that sustains us, too.

Q05 🎧 Now, cyanobacteria perform another crucial function for us. I don't suppose that anyone would know what that might be …?

Student 2 (F): Uh, well, since they are a kind of bacteria, I assume that they help fertilize soil by adding nitrogen to it.

미생물학 수업 중 토론의 일부를 들으시오.

교수 (여): 모두, 안녕하세요. 시작하도록 하죠. 오늘은 인간이 굉장히 의존하는 생물에 대해 알아보도록 하겠어요. 제가 뭘 이야기하려는지 아는 사람 있나요? [잠깐 멈춤] 네, 우리가 오늘 논의할 것은 시아노박테리아입니다. 알다시피, 이는 해양이나 담수, 습지, 심지어는 사막에서 일시적으로 젖은 바위와 같이, 거의 모든 육생 및 수생 서식지에서 발견될 수 있는 박테리아 종입니다.

자, 남조식물이라고도 불리는 시아노박테리아는 비록 박테리아 형태이긴 하지만, 식물처럼 엽록소를 갖고 있다는 데서 독특합니다. 다시 말하지만, 엽록소는 식물이 햇볕을 받아 광합성에 사용할 수 있게 해주죠. 그러므로 시아노박테리아는 태양에너지를 이용해 토양과 물을 음식으로 분해하는 광합성을 합니다. 이것이 왜 중요한지 누가 말해줄 수 있나요?

학생 1 (남): 글쎄요, 광합성의 부산물이 산소라서요?

교수: 매우 좋아요. 네, 식물처럼 시아노박테리아도 대기 중으로 산소를 방출합니다. 사실상 시아노박테리아가 이렇게 한 첫 번째 생물이었을 거예요. 그리고 그 과정은 초창기 지구의 유독한 대기를 오늘날의 동물들이 살 수 있는 대기로 전환하는 데 먼저 기여했습니다.

박테리아의 일종으로서 시아노박테리아는 지구상의 가장 기본적인 형태의 생물체이며, 초생의 습지에서 진화하였습니다. 약 20억 년 전, 시아노박테리아는 지구의 바다 전역에 걸쳐 서식하였어요. 당시에는 식물이 없었기 때문에, 시아노박테리아가 광합성의 '남은' 산물인 산소의 주요 공급원이었죠. 이들이 생산해낸 산소가 궁극적으로 다른 생명체를 생기게 하고 유지해준 대기를 구성했습니다.

그렇지만, 보세요. 이제 더 놀라워진답니다. 그러니까, 현재 많은 과학자들은 식물의 전신이었던 생물체가 이 시아노박테리아와 융합하면서 식물이 진화했다고 믿고 있어요. 식물 세포에는 엽록체라고 불리는 것이 있는데, 여기에 바로 엽록소가 있죠. 음, 이 엽록체가 원래 초기 식물 세포에 기생해 살던 시아노박테리아였답니다.

시간이 지나면서 그 세포와 시아노박테리아는 서로 종속적이 되고 단일 생물체를 형성하게 되었어요. 그래서, 음, 결국 식물은 시아노박테리아 덕분에 자립할 수 있게 된 것이죠. 또한, 이것을 생각해 보세요. 우리는 식물과 식물을 먹고 사는 동물을 모두 먹습니다. 그러니까 시아노박테리아가 우리를 유지해주는 현대의 먹이사슬 형성에도 도움을 주었다고 할 수 있죠.

자, 시아노박테리아는 우리에게 한 가지 더 매우 중요한 기능을 합니다. 그것이 무엇인지 아는 사람은 없을 것 같은데요…?

학생 2 (여): 어, 글쎄요, 이게 박테리아의 일종이니까, 토양에 질소를 보태서 비옥하게 해주는 것으로 짐작돼요.

Professor: Correct. In fact, cyanobacteria are one of the primary nitrogen fixers on earth. Q04(A) Essentially, they absorb nitrogen gas molecules from the atmosphere and transform them into various nitrogen compounds like nitrogen dioxide, ammonia, and so on. Q01-4 These compounds stay in the ground and provide important materials for plants. Particularly, plants use the compounds to create nucleic acids and proteins they need to grow. This is extremely important in agriculture, particularly in the rice paddies that produce most of the world's rice. The reason they are so fertile is because of all the cyanobacteria fixing nitrogen in these fields.

교수: 맞아요. 사실 시아노박테리아는 지구의 최초 질소 고정균 중 하나입니다. 근본적으로 시아노박테리아는 대기 중의 질소 기체 분자를 흡수해서, 이산화질소나 암모니아 등과 같은 다양한 질소 화합물로 변형시켜요. 이 화합물들은 땅속에 있으면서 식물에 필요한 중요 양분을 공급합니다. 특히 식물은 이 화합물을 사용해 성장에 필요한 핵산이나 단백질을 만들어내죠. 이 점은 농업, 특히 전 세계 벼의 대부분을 생산하는 논에서 굉장히 중요합니다. 논이 그렇게 비옥할 수 있는 이유는 논에 질소를 고정해주는 시아노박테리아 때문입니다.

---

01 논의되는 주제는?
(A) 시아노박테리아가 광합성을 하는 방법
(B) 다른 생물체가 시아노박테리아로부터 혜택을 받는 방법
(C) 식물의 진화에서 시아노박테리아의 역할
(D) 농업에 있어 시아노박테리아의 중요성

해설 | Main Idea 강의는 시아노박테리아와 그것이 지구 생물체에 어떻게 기여하는지에 대해 설명하고 있다.

02 교수가 식물 세포에 있는 엽록체에 대해 논의하는 이유는?
(A) 식물 세포의 복잡한 구조를 설명하기 위해
(B) 시아노박테리아가 식물 탄생에 어떻게 기여했는지 설명하기 위해
(C) 식물 세포와 시아노박테리아 세포를 비교하기 위해
(D) 광합성이 어떻게 작용하는지 보여주기 위해

해설 | Organization 교수는 본래 식물 세포의 엽록체가 바로 시아노박테리아였으며, 그것이 식물 세포와 합쳐지면서 식물의 자립이 가능해졌다고 설명하고 있다.

03 시아노박테리아에 대해 추론할 수 있는 것은?
(A) 지구 대기로부터 처음 영양을 공급받았다.
(B) 식물보다 더 많은 산소를 생산한다.
(C) 바다에서는 더는 발견되지 않는다.
(D) 동식물보다도 더 오래되었다.

해설 | Inference 시아노박테리아는 식물이 없을 당시에 최초의 산소 공급원이었으며, 이로 인해 식물과 그 식물을 먹고 사는 동물이 생겨났다고 했으므로, 그것이 동식물이 생겨나기 전부터 존재했었다는 것을 알 수 있다.

04 시아노박테리아가 할 수 있는 과정은?
2개의 답을 고르시오.
(A) 토양에 질소 화합물 생성하기
(B) 대기 중에 질소 방출하기
(C) 토양에 산소가 풍부한 화합물 방출하기
(D) 햇볕으로 스스로 양분 생성하기

해설 | Detail 시아노박테리아는 태양에너지를 이용해 토양과 물을 양분으로 분해하는 광합성을 하며, 대기 중의 질소로 질소 화합물을 만들어 토양에 양분을 공급한다.

05 강의의 일부를 다시 듣고 질문에 답하시오.
교수가 다음과 같이 말하는 이유는?
"I don't suppose that anyone would know what that might be . . . ?"
(A) 학생들을 토론에 참여시키기 위해
(B) 학생들이 충분히 공부하지 않은 것을 꾸짖기 위해
(C) 학생들에게 이 주제에 대해 더 많은 연구가 필요하다는 것을 나타내기 위해
(D) 계속 강의를 진행할 수 있도록 학생들의 질문을 막기 위해

해설 | Function 그것이 무엇인지 아는 사람이 없을 것 같다는 말은 아는 사람이 있으면 대답을 해보라는 의미로 학생들의 참여를 유도하기 위함이다.

어휘 | **organism** 생물, 유기체 **reliant** 의존하는 **cyanobacterium** 시아노박테리아 **utilize** 이용하다 **break down** 분해하다 **byproduct** 부산물 **primordial** 초생의, 원시의 **ooze** 습지 **ultimately** 궁극적으로 **sustain** 유지하다, 부양하다 **predecessor** 전신, 앞선 것 **merge** 융합하다, 합병하다 **live off** 기생하다 **fertilize** 비옥하게 하다 **nitrogen** 질소 **nitrogen fixer** 질소 고정균 **absorb** 흡수하다 **rice paddy** 논 **fertile** 비옥한

Mini Test 2

01 (D)   02 (A)   03 (B)   04 (C) – (E) – (A) – (D)   05 (A)

Listen to part of a lecture in a physiology class.

Professor (M): So . . . we discussed that animals can reach their maximum lifespans in protected environments. However, there are multiple factors that shorten our lifespans. **Q01** Now we will focus on the two most popular theories of aging: DNA damage theory and oxidative stress theory.

Alright, let's start with DNA damage theory first. This theory proposes that aging is a consequence of the accumulation of naturally occurring DNA damage that is not repaired. **Q02** Before we talk in depth about this theory, it is important that we recall the differences between DNA damage and DNA mutation. DNA damage is any physical abnormality in the DNA, such as when single and double strands break, while mutation is a change in the base sequence of the DNA. In other words, DNA damage can be recognized by enzymes and can be correctly repaired, whereas mutation can neither be recognized nor repaired by enzymes. Despite the differences, they are related in the way that DNA damage in frequently replicating cells can generate mutation. You won't be tested on the differences, but . . . um . . . you should know what causes the damage according to this theory. In the theory, this part is important . . . we will focus on DNA damage in slowly dividing or infrequently replicating cells, where unrepaired damage is likely to accumulate over time without becoming a mutation. Awhile back, I said that DNA damage includes single-strand break. This type of damage can block certain enzymes from doing their work on the strand. **Q03** For example, damage in the single strand of DNA can interfere with the critical process of forming proteins. Therefore, as we age, the accumulation of DNA damage will eventually reduce the number of proteins significantly. As a matter of fact, a reduced number of proteins is a sign of aging and thus the theory asserts that DNA damage contributes to aging.

Another major cause of aging is the accumulation of oxidative damage initiated by reactive oxygen species (ROS). **Q04(C)** **Q05** We know that in aerobic organisms, including humans, reactive oxygen species is an unavoidable by-product of mitochondrial respiration, a pathway for energy production. **Q04(E)** Due to their damaging effects, ROS are detoxified and broken down into benign molecules by enzymes, or anti-oxidant enzymes. However, this conversion is not 100% efficient. I mean ROS are left in our system. **Q04(A)** As a result, the residual ROS then accumulate in our cells and cause deleterious effects by reacting with proteins, lipids, and DNA. **Q04(D)** The oxidative stress done by accumulated ROS can contribute to senescence and promote degenerative diseases related to memory capability. Specifically, an experiment was demonstrated to show how oxidative damage can lead to cognitive dysfunction, in which rats performed better in cognitive tests after receiving metabolites that reduced the damage and improved brain function efficiency. As we can see from this experiment, by decreasing oxidation of cellular proteins, researchers were able to ameliorate the damaged condition.

생리학 강의 중 일부를 들으시오.

교수 (남): 자… 동물들은 보호된 환경에서 최대 수명에 도달할 수 있다는 것에 대해 얘기했었어요. 하지만 우리의 수명을 줄이는 많은 요인이 있죠. 이제 우리는 노화에 대해 가장 유명한 두 가지 이론에 초점을 둘 거예요. 바로 DNA 손상 이론과 산화성 스트레스 이론입니다.

그럼, DNA 손상 이론 먼저 시작해보죠. 이 이론은 노화가 자연적으로 발생하며 회복되지 않는 DNA 손상의 축적에 의한 결과라고 주장하죠. 이 이론에 대해 깊이 있게 얘기하기 전에, DNA 손상과 DNA 변이의 차이점을 생각해보는 것이 중요해요. DNA 손상은 단일 가닥이나 이중 가닥 DNA가 파괴되었을 때와 같이, DNA 상의 물리적인 이상을 의미하는 반면, 변이는 DNA의 염기 순서가 바뀐 것을 말합니다. 다시 말하면, DNA 손상은 효소에 의해 확인될 수 있고, 올바르게 회복될 수 있는 반면에, 변이는 효소에 의해 확인될 수도 없고 회복될 수도 없어요. 이런 차이점에도 불구하고, 계속 자가 복제하는 세포에서의 DNA 손상은 변이를 일으킬 수 있다는 점에서 그것들은 서로 관련이 있죠. 여러분들이 차이점에 대해 시험을 보지는 않겠지만, 음, 이 이론에 따라 그 손상을 일으키는 것이 무엇인지에 대해서는 알고 있어야 합니다. 이론에서 이 부분은 중요해요… 우리는 천천히 분할하거나 드물게 자가 복제하는 세포에서의 DNA 손상에 초점을 둘 건데, 여기서 회복되지 않는 손상은 시간이 지남에 따라 변이되지 않고 축적되기 쉽죠. 조금 전에 제가 DNA 손상이 단일 가닥 파괴를 포함한다고 말했죠. 이런 종류의 손상은 특정한 효소가 가닥에서 하는 역할을 막아버릴 수 있어요. 예를 들어, DNA의 단일 가닥에서의 손상은 단백질을 형성하는 중요한 과정을 방해할 수 있어요. 따라서 우리가 나이가 들면서 DNA 손상의 축적은 결국 단백질의 수를 현저하게 줄여버리는 거죠. 사실, 줄어든 단백질은 노화의 징후라고 할 수 있고, 그래서 이 이론은 DNA 손상이 노화의 원인이 된다고 주장하는 거예요.

노화의 또 다른 주요 원인은 활성 산소(ROS)에 의해 시작되는 산화적 손상의 축적이에요. 우리가 알기로 인간을 포함한 호기성 생물들에게 활성 산소는 에너지 생산을 위한 경로인 미토콘드리아 호흡으로부터의 피할 수 없는 부산물이죠. 그 손상 효과 때문에, 활성 산소는 효소 혹은 항산화 효소로 인해 해독되거나 양성 분자로 분해되죠. 하지만 이 전환은 100% 효과가 있는 것은 아니에요. 제 말은 활성 산소가 우리 인체에 남는다는 거예요. 그 결과로, 남아 있는 활성 산소는 우리 세포에 축적되고 단백질, 지질, DNA와 반응하면서 해로운 영향을 미치죠. 축적된 활성 산소로 인해 발생한 산화성 스트레스는 노화의 원인이 되고 기억력과 관련된 퇴행성 질환을 일으킬 수 있어요. 분명한 것은, 산화적 손상이 어떻게 인지적 기능 장애를 일으킬 수 있는지 보여주기 위한 연구가 입증됐는데, 손상을 줄여주고 뇌 기능을 효과적으로 향상시킨 대사 물질을 투여한 쥐들이 인지 검사에서 더 좋은 결과를 보여줬어요. 이 실험에서 볼 수 있듯이, 세포성 단백질의 산화를 줄임으로써 연구원들은 손상된 상태를 개선시킬 수 있었어요.

Now that we know the causes of aging, we can further discuss how we regulate lifespans according to these theories. Let's discuss in groups about several ways to increase lifespans, in other words, to inhibit the process of aging.

노화의 원인에 대해 알았으니까, 이 이론들에 따라 우리가 어떻게 수명을 조절할 수 있는지에 대해 더 얘기해볼 수 있겠죠. 그룹을 지어서 수명을 늘리는, 다시 말해 노화 작용을 억제할 수 있는 여러 가지 방법에 대해 논의해봅시다.

01 강의의 주된 목적은?
- (A) 세포에서의 산화적 손상 과정에 대해 설명하기 위해
- (B) DNA 손상과 변이를 구별하기 위해
- (C) 노화에 대한 이론들을 관련된 실험들을 통해 뒷받침하기 위해
- (D) 노화에 대한 현재의 유력한 이론들을 설명하기 위해

해설 | Main Idea 교수는 "Now we will focus on the two most popular theories of aging"이라고 말하며 노화에 대한 이론 두 가지, DNA 손상 이론과 산화성 스트레스 이론에 대해 설명한다.

02 교수가 DNA 손상 이론을 소개하는 방식은?
- (A) DNA 손상이 DNA 변이와 어떻게 다른지 명백하게 설명함으로써
- (B) 수명을 최대화시키는 방법에 대한 이전 토론을 복습함으로써
- (C) 몇몇 다른 유명한 이론들과 비교함으로써
- (D) 노화 이론에 대한 강의 개요를 말함으로써

해설 | Organization 교수는 DNA 손상 이론에 대해 깊이 있게 얘기하기 전에 DNA 손상과 DNA 변이의 차이점을 생각해 보는 것이 중요하다고 말하며 이 둘의 차이점에 대해 설명한다.

03 다음 중 DNA 손상 이론에 대해 옳은 것은?
- (A) 효소는 인체에 축적되고 DNA를 공격한다.
- (B) DNA 손상은 단백질 형성을 막는다.
- (C) 천천히 자가 복제하는 세포에서의 DNA 손상은 변이로 이어질 수 있다.
- (D) DNA 손상이 있는 세포는 인체에서 제거된다.

해설 | Detail 교수는 DNA 단일 가닥에서의 손상이 단백질을 형성하는 중요한 과정을 방해할 수 있다고 설명한다.

04 교수는 산화적 손상 과정의 단계들을 설명한다. 이 단계들을 올바른 순서대로 나열하시오.
각 문장을 해당되는 곳으로 옮기시오.
선택지 중 하나는 사용되지 않는다.

1	(C) 미토콘드리아 내에 활성 산소가 발생한다.
2	(E) 효소는 모든 ROS를 분해할 수는 없다.
3	(A) 활성 산소가 세포 내에 축적된다.
4	(D) 산화적 스트레스는 거대분자를 손상시키고 질병을 일으킨다.

(B) 호흡하는 동안 DNA 변이가 발생한다.

해설 | Connecting Content 교수는 산화적 손상 과정에 대해 설명하며, 미토콘드리아 호흡의 부산물로서 활성 산소가 발생하는데, 항산화 효소가 이 모든 활성 산소를 분해할 수는 없으므로 일부 활성 산소가 세포에 축적되고 결국 산화적 스트레스가 거대분자를 손상시키고 여러 질병을 일으킨다고 말한다.

05 강의의 일부를 다시 듣고 질문에 답하시오.
교수가 다음과 같이 말할 때 의미하는 것은?
"However, this conversion is not 100% efficient."
- (A) 항산화 효소는 모든 활성 산소를 양성 인자로 완전히 전환시키지 않는다.
- (B) 일부 활성 산소는 효소의 도움 없이도 무해해질 수 있다.
- (C) 미토콘드리아 호흡은 활성 산소가 우리 체내에 안전히 있을 수 있도록 해준다.
- (D) 단백질과 반응했을 때 모든 활성 산소가 위험한 영향을 끼치는 것은 아니다.

해설 | Function 강의에서 교수는 활성 산소가 효소 혹은 항산화 효소로 인해 해독되거나 양성 분자로 분해될 수 있는데, 이런 전환이 100% 효과가 있는 것은 아니라고 설명한다. 즉, 항산화 효소가 모든 활성 산소를 양성 인자로 완전히 전환시키는 것은 아님을 의미한다.

어휘 | **lifespan** 수명　**DNA damage theory** DNA 손상 이론　**oxidative stress theory** 산화적 스트레스 이론　**accumulation** 축적　**mutation** 변이　**abnormality** 이상, 기형　**strand** 가닥　**enzyme** 효소　**replicate** (자가) 복제하다　**protein** 단백질　**oxidative damage** 산화적 손상　**reactive oxygen species**(ROS) 활성 산소(종)　**aerobic** 호기성의, 유산소의　**by-product** 부산물, 부작용　**mitochondrial respiration** 미토콘드리아 호흡　**detoxify** 해독시키다　**benign** 양성의, 유순한　**molecule** 분자　**conversion** 전환　**deleterious** 해로운, 유해한　**lipid** 지질　**senescence** 노화, 노쇠　**degenerative** 퇴행성의　**cognitive dysfunction** 인지적 기능 장애　**metabolite** 대사 물질, 대사 산물　**ameliorate** 개선하다　**inhibit** 억제하다

iBT Practice

p.124

01 (C)   02 (C)   03 (B)   04 (A)   05 (D)   06 (B)

Listen to part of a discussion in a marine biology class.

Professor (F): Now, we're going to continue our discussion about the cognitive capabilities of different mammals, and today we are going to focus specifically on dolphins. Now, most of you have probably heard claims that dolphins are perhaps the most intelligent animals on the planet – right after humans, of course. Uh, who knows what evidence scientists have discovered that leads many to this conclusion? *[Pause]* Yes, Andy.

Student 1 (M): Don't dolphins have, like, really large brains, even larger than our brains?

Professor: Um, yes, that's true. The size of dolphins' brains, about 25 percent larger than human brains, is impressive, especially in relation to the size of their bodies. Q02 However, scientists believe that most of a dolphin's brain is related to detecting and processing its sonar waves and other sounds. As you all probably know, dolphins rely on sonar to navigate through the depths of the ocean, where it is too murky and deep to see. That's why most of their brain is apparently needed to operate this sort of second sight.

Student 2 (F): Q01 Well, I remember reading that dolphins have shown some capacity for problem-solving and abstract thinking, which has been seen in dozens of experiments.

Professor: Ah, this is what I was getting at. Yes, researchers who work with dolphins in captivity have observed all kinds of fascinating behavior that leads them to believe that dolphins are capable of many kinds of abstract thinking. Not only do they perform tricks, but they can also perform new kinds of previously unseen behavior on their own. Q05-1 One experiment showed that once trainers stopped rewarding dolphins for their usual tricks, the creatures eventually figured out that they were expected to perform new kinds of behavior. And they did, being rewarded for coming up with new acts.

Q05-2 Here's a famous example. Trainers at one facility would reward dolphins with fish whenever the dolphins brought trash from their pool. Well, the trainers discovered that one dolphin had been hoarding trash in a corner of her pool, bringing pieces of it to trainers frequently, like currency. Q03 Furthermore, the dolphin figured out she would get fish regardless of whether the trash was big or small, so she tore off small bits of garbage to get her treat. This showed that dolphins have a sense of how to manipulate consequences, as the dolphin had a system to maximize her rewards.

Student 2: Q06 I've heard that dolphins are so smart that they have their own language. Is this true?

Professor: Uh, that's a bit harder. Dolphins do communicate with a variety of sounds, such as clicks, grunts, whistles, and moans, but many scientists are reluctant to call this a full-blown language. There doesn't seem to be any evidence of structure or syntax in the sounds dolphins produce. Q04-1 So, officially, no, dolphins don't have a "language" as we would understand it. Nevertheless, there is ample evidence that they communicate with each other. Q05-3 Some experiments showed that dolphins that were expected to perform the same action managed to communicate effectively in order to coordinate the trick. For instance, when researchers wanted two dolphins to create a new behavior together, the two vanished underwater, talked it over, basically, and then jumped into the air and spat out water together.

Q04-2 Now, despite the debate over a dolphin language, there is proof that dolphins can understand complex language concepts, such as grammar and inverted sentence order. For example, dolphins are capable of not only recognizing different signs researchers give them, like "Frisbee," "jump," and "nudge," but recognizing these ideas in different sentences, like "nudge the Frisbee to the left box." Also, they could recognize the meaning of sentences even when the grammatical order was rearranged.

Student 1: I'm a little vague over how skills like hoarding trash help them in the wild.

Professor: Look at it this way. These examples show that dolphins have the mental capacity to creatively solve problems, so they can develop unique behaviors in order to adapt. Q05-4 For instance, dolphins have been observed using a number of unique methods to catch fish. These include clubbing fish with their tails, stunning them with sonar, encircling fish in strategic formations, maneuvering in and out of fishing nets to eat the catch, and so on. Dolphins also rely a lot on each other for learning different behaviors, and in order to understand this, we must look at the details of their social life.

교수: 어, 그것은 좀 더 어렵군요. 돌고래가 딸각하는 소리, 꿀꿀거리는 소리, 휘파람 소리, 신음 등 다양한 소리를 통해 의사소통을 하는 것은 사실입니다. 하지만 많은 과학자들은 이것을 완전한 언어라고 말하기를 꺼리고 있어요. 돌고래가 내는 소리에 구조나 통사적 체계가 있다는 증거는 없는 것으로 보입니다. 그래서 공식적으로는 아니요, 돌고래에게 우리가 아는 '언어'는 없습니다. 그런데도, 돌고래가 서로 의사소통을 한다는 증거는 상당히 많습니다. 몇몇 실험을 통해, 서로 같은 동작을 하기로 되어 있는 돌고래들이 묘기를 조화시키기 위해 효과적으로 의사소통을 하는 것을 볼 수가 있었습니다. 예를 들어, 연구자들은 돌고래 두 마리가 함께 새로운 동작을 만들어 내길 원했는데, 그 두 마리가 물속으로 사라져서 무엇보다도 서로 의견을 나누고, 공중으로 뛰어올라 동시에 물을 내뿜었답니다.

자, 돌고래 언어에 대한 논란에도 불구하고 돌고래가 문법이나 도치된 어순과 같은 복잡한 언어 개념을 이해한다는 증거가 있습니다. 예를 들어, 돌고래는 연구자들이 보내는 '프리스비'와 '점프' 그리고 '슬쩍 움직여'와 같은 다른 신호들을 알아듣는 것뿐만 아니라, 예를 들어 '프리스비를 왼쪽 상자 쪽으로 슬쩍 움직여'와 같이 다른 문장들 내의 이런 개념들도 알아들을 수 있답니다. 또한, 문법적으로 어순이 바뀌었을 때도 문장의 의미를 이해할 수 있었어요.

학생 1: 쓰레기를 모아두는 것과 같은 기술이 야생에서 어떻게 도움이 될지는 조금 모호해요.

교수: 이런 식으로 생각해 보세요. 이러한 예들이 보여주는 것은 돌고래에게 창의적으로 문제를 해결할 수 있는 정신적 능력이 있어서 환경에 적응하기 위해 특유의 행동을 할 수 있다는 것이죠. 예를 들어, 돌고래는 물고기를 잡기 위해 다수의 독특한 방법을 쓰는 것으로 관찰되어 왔습니다. 이러한 방법에는 물고기를 꼬리로 치거나, 수중 음파로 기절시키거나, 전략적 대형으로 물고기를 에워싸거나, 그물에 잡힌 물고기를 먹기 위해 그물 안팎으로 교묘히 움직인다든가 하는 등의 방법이 있습니다. 또한, 돌고래는 다른 행동을 배우기 위해서 서로 많이 의존하는데요. 이 점을 이해하기 위해서는 돌고래의 사회적 생활에 관해 자세히 알아봐야 해요.

---

01 화자들이 논의하는 주된 내용은?
(A) 돌고래가 서로 의사소통하는 방법
(B) 돌고래가 동작하도록 훈련시키는 실험
(C) 돌고래의 추상적, 창의적 사고 능력
(D) 돌고래가 보상을 받기 위해 개발하는 새로운 동작

해설 | Main Idea 한 학생이 돌고래의 문제 해결 능력과 추상적 사고 능력에 대해 언급하자 교수는 "Ah, this is what I was getting at"이라고 대답하며 그에 대한 논의를 이어가고 있다.

02 토론에 따르면, 돌고래가 뇌를 가장 많이 쓰는 곳은?
(A) 새로운 동작 개발하기
(B) 시각적 정보 처리하기
(C) 청각적 정보 파악하기
(D) 그들의 종과 소통하기

해설 | Detail 교수는 돌고래 뇌 대부분이 수중 음파와 다른 소리를 감지하고 처리하는 데 쓰인다고 설명하고 있다.

03 돌고래가 쓰레기를 조각조각 찢은 것이 중요한 의미는?
(A) 돌고래가 음식과 쓰레기를 구분할 수 있다.
(B) 돌고래가 결과와 미래 일에 대해 이해할 수 있다.
(C) 돌고래가 서로 생각을 전달할 수 있다.
(D) 돌고래가 문법이 바뀌어도 명령을 따를 수 있다.

해설 | Detail 실험에서 돌고래는 쓰레기를 가져올 때마다 생선을 보상받는 것을 인지하고 보상을 최대화하기 위해 쓰레기를 더 작게 찢어 결과를 조작하는 능력을 보여주었다.

04 교수가 돌고래와 인간 언어에 대해 암시하는 것은?
(A) 돌고래는 그들 자신만의 언어를 갖고 있지 않지만, 인간 언어의 개념은 이해한다.
(B) 돌고래는 서로 의사소통할 때 그들 자신만의 언어를 사용한다.
(C) 돌고래는 문장 구조를 분석함으로써 인간 언어를 이해한다.
(D) 돌고래가 그들 자신만의 언어를 가졌는지 아닌지는 종에 따라 다르다.

해설 | Inference 교수는 돌고래에게 우리가 아는 '언어'는 없지만, 문법이나 도치된 어순과 같은 복잡한 인간 언어의 개념을 이해한다는 증거가 있다고 설명하고 있다.

05 교수가 돌고래의 지능에 대해 논의하는 방식은?
(A) 돌고래 뇌의 독특한 구조를 설명함으로써
(B) 돌고래의 행동과 다른 포유류의 행동을 비교함으로써
(C) 돌고래가 육지 포유류로부터 진화한 것을 설명함으로써
(D) 실험과 관찰에서 가져온 예들을 제시함으로써

해설 | Organization 교수는 먹이 보상, 의사소통, 문제 해결 능력 등과 관련된 기존의 다양한 실험과 관찰의 예를 들어 돌고래의 지능에 대해 설명하고 있다.

06 강의의 일부를 다시 듣고 질문에 답하시오.
교수가 다음과 같이 말할 때 의미하는 것은?
"Uh, that's a bit harder."
(A) 답을 알지 못해 당황스럽다.
(B) 질문에 대한 답이 복잡하므로 조심스럽다.
(C) 돌고래가 매우 어려운 언어를 사용한다는 것을 인정한다.
(D) 질문을 이해하지 못해서 혼란스럽다.

해설 | Function 돌고래가 다양한 소리를 내긴 하지만 완전한 언어로 보기는 어려우므로 학생의 질문에 단정 지어 대답하기 조심스러웠음을 알 수 있다.

어휘 | cognitive 인지의 **sonar** 수중 음파 (탐지기) **murky** 어두운 **capacity** 능력 **abstract** 추상적인 **hoard** (몰래) 축적하다 **currency** 화폐, 지폐 **click** 딸각하는 소리 **grunt** 꿀꿀거리는 소리 **moan** 신음 **reluctant** 꺼리는, 내키지 않는 **full-blown** 완전한 **syntax** 통사론, 구문론 **ample** 상당한 **coordinate** 조화시키다 **spit out** 내뿜다 **inverted** 도치된 **Frisbee** 프리스비(플라스틱 원반) **nudge** 슬쩍 움직이다

Chapter 12 Physical Science

Intensive Drill 1

01 (B)   02 (C)   03 (A)   04 (B), (D)   05 [Yes – (A), (B), (D)], [No – (C)]

Listen to part of a discussion in an earth science class.

Professor (M): OK, has anyone read an article on "the coming of a mini ice age?" Some scientists predict that based on changing solar activity, our planet will experience a mini ice age starting around the 2030s. So, if they're on the right track, it will happen less than 15 years from now! So, I was wondering if you agree with this prediction.

Student 1 (F): Wait a minute. They're only looking at natural factors. Shouldn't they also count the increasing human causes that affect global warming? Wouldn't it offset the impact of natural cycles to a certain degree?

Professor: Q01-1 Of course, we can't ignore human impact. However, when you look at drastic periods of climate change such as ice ages, solar cycles and other natural factors like volcanic activity and ocean circulation play a principal role. Q02 In fact, the Sun has been cooling down over the last century. If this continues, the Earth will receive significantly less solar energy and quite possibly go into a mini ice age. But predicting the solar cycle is an extremely complicated process. So . . . well, let's not get into that just yet.

Now, this brings us to look at why and how ice ages have occurred on the Earth. Hopefully, you will gain insight into the possibility of mini ice age by the end of our discussion.

Q01-2 Alright, so paleoclimatologists have devised ingenious techniques to discover evidence of glacial cycles from the distant past. Their evidence came from the analysis of land deposits as well as sea floor sediment. Also, they simply drilled deep into ice. Q03 In the end, they discovered glacial cycles, in other words, ice ages occurred on the Earth over the last 3 million years with surprising regularity. Then, why did ice ages occur? I mentioned earlier that an ice age generally happens with the combination of . . . what?

Student 2 (M): Um . . . the solar cycle, for one, and . . . volcanic as well as oceanic activity, which are natural factors.

Professor: Perfect. What influences those last two particular factors?

Student 1: They are affected by continental positions. So, I guess, plate tectonics?

Professor: Ah ha! Q04(D) So, any considerable movement of continental plate boundaries brings profound changes to the pattern of oceanic and atmospheric circulation, followed by changes to the climate. These changes were critical in the development of ice ages.

지구과학 수업 중 토론의 일부를 들으시오.

교수 (남): 좋아요, '미니 빙하 시대의 도래'에 대한 기사를 읽은 사람 있나요? 변화하는 태양 활동에 기초하여 일부 과학자들은 우리 행성이 2030년대를 기점으로 하여 미니 빙하 시대를 경험하게 될 것이라고 예측하죠. 따라서 그들이 올바르게 예측했다면 지금으로부터 15년이 안되어 그 일이 발생할 거예요. 자, 여러분이 이 예측에 동의하는지 궁금하네요.

학생 1 (여): 잠시만요. 그들은 오직 자연적인 요인들만 보고 있어요. 지구 온난화에 미치는 사람들의 영향이 증가하고 있는 것도 고려해야 하는 거 아닌가요? 그게 어느 정도는 자연적 주기의 영향을 상쇄시켜주지 않을까요?

교수: 물론 인간의 영향을 무시할 수 없죠. 하지만 빙하기와 같은 극단적인 기후 변화를 보면, 태양 주기나 화산 활동, 해양 순환과 같은 자연적인 요인들이 주요 역할을 하죠. 사실 태양은 지난 세기 동안 차가워지고 있어요. 이게 계속된다면 지구는 태양에너지를 상당히 적게 받게 될 것이고 미니 빙하 시대에 들어갈 가능성이 꽤 크죠. 하지만 태양 주기를 예측하는 것은 매우 복잡한 과정이에요. 자… 음, 아직 그 얘기까지는 하지 말죠.

자, 이는 우리로 하여금 왜 그리고 어떻게 지구에 빙하기가 발생했는지를 보도록 해주죠. 오늘 토론의 후반부에는 여러분이 미니 빙하 시대의 가능성에 대해 통찰력을 갖기 바라요.

좋아요. 고기후학자들은 먼 과거의 빙하 주기에 대한 증거를 발견할 수 있는 기발한 기술을 고안해냈어요. 그 증거는 해저 침전물뿐만 아니라 육상 퇴적물 분석으로 발견됐어요. 또한, 단순히 빙하를 깊이 뚫기도 했어요. 결국, 빙하 주기를 발견해냈죠. 다시 말해 빙하 시대는 지난 3백만 년 동안 놀랍도록 규칙적으로 발생했어요. 그러면, 왜 빙하 시대가 발생했을까요? 제가 좀 전에 빙하 시대는 일반적으로 어떤 조합으로 이루어진다고 얘기했는데… 뭐죠?

학생 2 (남): 음… 하나는 태양 주기고, 그리고… 해양 활동뿐 아니라 화산 활동도 있었고요. 자연적 요인들이요.

교수: 완벽해요. 그 마지막 두 가지 특정 요인에는 어떤 것이 영향을 미치죠?

학생 1: 대륙적인 위치에 의해 영향을 받아요. 음, 판구조론인가요?

교수: 그렇죠! 자, 대륙판 경계의 상당한 이동은 해양 순환과 대기 순환 패턴에 엄청난 변화를 미치죠. 이는 기후 변화로 이어져요. 이 변화들은 빙하 시대 발달에 중대한 역할을 했죠.

Q04(B) Plate tectonics can also cause volcanic eruptions which discharge huge amounts of ash particles. These particles reduce the amount of solar radiation from reaching the Earth's surface and cause global cooling.

Student 2: Isn't there speculation that ice ages happened every 100,000 years? But those natural events arise more frequently.

Professor: True. **Q01-3** In fact, the 100,000-year cycle of glaciations is based on the Milankovich cycle. **Q05(B), (D)** It involves the shape of the Earth's orbit varying from elliptical to circular, and the slight tilt of its orbital axis around the Sun. These factors cause slow variations in the earth's orbital position which affect the amount of sunlight it receives. **Q05(A)** Based on these variations, Milankovitch predicted that ice ages would peak every 100,000 years. So, could we attempt to calculate the next possible one?

판구조론은 상당한 양의 화산재 입자를 방출하는 화산 폭발을 일으킬 수 있죠. 이 입자는 지구 표면에 도달하는 태양 복사량을 줄이고 지구 온난화를 일으켜요.

학생 2: 빙하 시대가 10만 년마다 발생했다는 추측이 있지 않나요? 하지만 그런 자연적인 현상들은 더 자주 일어나잖아요.

교수: 맞아요. 사실 빙하의 10만 년 주기는 Milankovich 주기에 기초한 거예요. 이는 타원형부터 원형까지 변화하는 지구 궤도의 모양과 태양 주변의 약간 기울어진 궤도 축과 관련 있죠. 이 요인들은 지구가 받는 햇빛의 양에 영향을 미치는 지구의 궤도 위치가 천천히 변화하도록 만들죠. 이 변화들에 기초하여, Milankovich는 빙하 시대가 10만 년마다 절정에 달한다고 예측했어요. 자, 다음 빙하 시대를 예측해 볼 수 있을까요?

---

01 강의의 주된 내용은?

(A) 다음 빙하 시대는 언제, 어떻게 발생할 것인지 예측하기
(B) 빙하 시대 연구에 관련된 단서들과 요인들
(C) 다양한 인간 활동이 빙하 주기에 끼치는 영향
(D) 마지막 빙하 시대의 원인과 발달 과정

해설 | Main Idea 교수는 태양 주기, 화산 활동, 해양 순환처럼 빙하기와 같은 기후 변화에 영향을 끼치는 자연적인 요인들, 고기후학자들이 고안해낸 빙하 주기의 증거를 발견할 수 있는 기술, 그리고 Milankovich 주기 등에 대해 설명하며 빙하 시대 연구에 관련된 단서들과 요인들에 대해 주로 얘기한다.

02 태양 주기에 기초한 미니 빙하 시대의 예측에 대한 교수의 의견은?

(A) 그것이 중요한 요인들을 간과하기 때문에 동의하지 않는다.
(B) 그것과 그것의 연구 과정에 동의한다.
(C) 매우 신중하게 이뤄져야 한다고 생각한다.
(D) 그런 예측은 필요하지 않다고 생각한다.

해설 | Attitude 교수는 태양 주기, 화산 활동, 해양 순환과 같은 자연적인 요인들이 빙하기와 같은 기후 변화에 영향을 미치는 주요 요인이긴 하지만 태양 주기를 예측하는 것은 매우 복잡한 과정이라고 말한다. 즉, 태양 주기에 기초한 빙하 시대의 예측은 매우 신중하게 이뤄져야 한다는 의견을 갖고 있음을 알 수 있다.

03 고기후학자들이 과거 빙하 주기의 증거를 알아낸 후에 발견한 것은?

(A) 지구의 빙하 시대는 규칙적인 패턴으로 발생하였다.
(B) 빙하 시대에 대한 기존 개념들은 놀랍도록 부정확하다.
(C) 인간 활동은 빙하 시대를 일으키는 데 주기적인 역할을 하지 않았다.
(D) 마지막 빙하 주기는 훨씬 더 최근에 발생했다.

해설 | Detail 강의에 의하면, 고기후학자들은 결국 빙하 주기를 발견해냈고, 지난 3백만 년 동안 놀랍도록 규칙적으로 발생했음을 알아냈다.

04 빙하 시대 발달로 이어질 수도 있는 대륙 이동의 결과들은?
2개의 답을 고르시오.

(A) 대륙 경계 모양의 변화
(B) 화산 폭발로 인한 화산재 입자 방출
(C) 화산 폭발 패턴의 형성
(D) 해양 순환과 대기 순환의 변화

해설 | Detail 교수에 의하면 대륙판 경계의 이동은 해양 순환과 대기 순환 패턴에 변화를 미치고, 판구조론은 상당한 양의 화산재 입자를 방출한다.

05 강의에서 교수는 빙하 시대를 예측하기 위해 Milankovich 주기와 관련된 요인들을 설명한다. 다음 각 사항이 예측과 관련 있는지 표시하시오.
각 사항에 대해 알맞은 항목에 표시하시오.

	예	아니오
(A) 10만 년마다 빙하 시대가 절정에 도달한다.	✓	
(B) 지구의 기울어진 궤도 축은 지구가 받는 햇빛의 양에 영향을 미친다.	✓	
(C) 지난 세기 동안 태양의 온도는 차가워지고 있다.		✓
(D) 지구 궤도 모양의 변화는 궤도 위치를 변화시킨다.	✓	

해설 | Connecting Content 교수는 강의의 후반부에서 Milankovich 주기에 대해 설명한다. 그에 따르면, 빙하 시대는 10만 년마다 절정에 달하고, 지구의 기울어진 궤도 축은 지구가 받는 햇빛의 양에 영향을 미치는 지구의 궤도 위치를 천천히 변화시킨다.

어휘 | **ice age** 빙하 시대, 빙하기　**solar** 태양의　**global warming** 지구 온난화　**offset** 상쇄하다, 벌충하다　**drastic** 극단적인, 급변하는　**volcanic** 화산의　**circulation** 순환　**paleoclimatologist** 고기후학자　**land deposit** 육상 퇴적물　**sea floor sediment** 해저 침전물　**plate tectonics** 판구조론　**eruption** 폭발, 분화　**discharge** 방출하다, 방출되다　**ash** 화산재, 재　**radiation** 복사　**orbit** 궤도　**elliptical** 타원형의　**peak** 절정[최고조]에 달하다

Intensive Drill 2　　　　　　　　　　　　　　　　　　　　　　　　　　　p.130

01 (C)　**02** (A)　**03** (D)　**04** (B)　**05** (B)

Listen to part of a lecture in a physics class.

Professor (F): In the last couple of classes, we've been talking about Einstein's theories of special and general relativity. Now as we've said already, he published the paper outlining special relativity in 1905 when he was just 25. And he followed that up with the more complete theory of general relativity just ten years later. So by the time he was 35, Einstein had already made his greatest contributions to the world of science. He worked for another 40 years, right up until his death in 1955, but after his theory of general relativity, none of his later work had the same kind of revolutionary impact.

Q01 Anyway, what we're going to focus on today is Einstein's approach to science: Not only how it contributed to his early success, but also how it was responsible for his lack of success later on.

Alright, so a lot of it has to do with how Einstein thought and worked. He was very intuitive in developing his theories. He followed his ideas about special and general relativity because they felt right to him. He just felt that this was the way the universe worked. He, uh, also had amazing confidence in his own intuition and was very independent. Well, he didn't really care what other people thought of his theories, because deep down he knew they were correct.

물리학 강의 중 일부를 들으시오.

교수 (여): 지난 두어 차례 강의를 통해, Einstein의 특수 상대성 이론과 일반 상대성 이론에 대해 이야기했었죠. 자, 이미 말했듯이, Einstein은 25살밖에 되지 않았던 1905년에 특수 상대성 이론을 개략적으로 설명하는 논문을 발표했어요. 그리고 겨우 10년 만에 더욱 완벽하게 정리된 일반 상대성 이론을 더했죠. 그래서 35살이 되었을 때, Einstein은 이미 과학계에 큰 기여를 하였습니다. 그는 1955년 사망할 때까지 약 40여 년간 연구를 계속하였지만, 상대성 이론 이후 이 이론과 같은 혁명적인 영향을 끼친 연구는 없었습니다.

어쨌든 오늘 우리가 알아볼 것은 과학에 대한 Einstein의 접근법이에요. 이것이 어떻게 그를 일찍이 성공으로 이끌었고, 어떻게 그 이후에는 성공하지 못하게 했는지에 대해 알아보겠어요.

좋아요, 이 문제의 많은 부분은 Einstein의 사고와 연구 방식과 관련이 있어요. 그는 이론을 발전시키는 데 있어서 굉장히 직관적이었죠. 그는 특수 상대성 이론과 일반 상대성 이론을 만들 때도 그것이 진실이라고 느꼈기 때문에 연구를 시작했습니다. 그는 단지 이것이 우주가 돌아가는 이치라고 느꼈죠. 또한, Einstein은, 자신의 직관에 굉장한 자신이 있었고 매우 독립적이었죠. 음, 그는 다른 사람들이 그의 이론에 대해 어떻게 생각하는지 별로 신경 쓰지 않았어요. 왜냐하면, 가슴 깊이 자신의 이론이 옳다는 것을 알고 있었기 때문입니다.

Q02 There's actually an interesting story about that. Right after he published his theory of special relativity, another group of scientists published the results of an experiment that seemed to disprove Einstein's theory. When Einstein was told about the experiment, he wasn't upset at all. He just said, "Well, their experiment is wrong." You see, he had total confidence in his theory because it felt right to him. In the end, of course, Einstein was proven to be correct. The other experiment was wrong, and later experiments proved that the theory of special relativity was correct. So in the case of special and general relativity, Einstein's intuitive way of thinking was a great asset. But later in his career it caused him major problems.

You see, the other major theory of that time period was quantum mechanics. Now, quantum mechanics is, to say the least, a strange theory. It makes some very, very unusual predictions about how the world works. Nevertheless, those predictions have been confirmed by countless numbers of experiments. **Q03** But to Einstein, the theory just felt wrong. He was sure that this couldn't be the way the universe really worked. No matter how much experimental evidence showed that quantum mechanics was correct, he just refused to believe it, and he spent much of his later career in fruitless attempts trying to disprove the theory. **Q04** Anyway, the moral of this story is while intuition is important to a scientist and can be a valuable tool, scientists must also be dispassionate. They have to be able to accept the conclusions drawn by the evidence available to them — even if they do not like those conclusions. **Q05** Einstein wasn't able to do this, and it cost him a great deal in his later career.

이것에 대해 재미있는 이야기가 하나 있어요. 특수 상대성 이론을 발표한 직후, 다른 과학자들이 Einstein의 이론을 반증하는 듯한 실험 결과를 발표했습니다. Einstein은 이 실험에 대한 이야기를 듣고도 전혀 화내지 않았어요. 그는 그저 '그들의 실험이 잘못되었다'라고 말할 뿐이었죠. 알다시피, 그는 자신의 이론이 옳다고 생각했기 때문에 그에 대한 확신이 있었습니다. 물론 결국엔 Einstein이 맞다는 것이 증명되었죠. 다른 실험이 틀렸던 것이었고, 그 이후의 실험은 특수 상대성 이론이 맞다는 것을 증명했어요. 그래서 특수·일반 상대성 이론 같은 경우엔 Einstein의 직관에 따른 사고방식이 아주 좋은 이점이 되었어요. 하지만 이것은 그의 연구 경력 후반에 큰 문제를 일으키기도 했습니다.

그 당시의 또 다른 주요 이론은 양자역학이었죠. 자, 양자역학은 조금도 과장하지 않고 이상한 논리입니다. 이 이론은 세계가 어떻게 돌아가는지를 설명하는 데 있어 매우 특이한 예측을 하죠. 그런데도 그 예측들은 수많은 연구를 통해 입증되어 왔습니다. 하지만 Einstein은 이 이론이 잘못되었다고 생각했어요. 그는 이 방법으로 우주가 돌아가는 것이 아니라고 확신했어요. 아무리 많은 실험 증거들이 양자역학이 옳다는 것을 보여줬어도, Einstein은 그것을 믿지 않았으며, 경력 후반 대부분을 이 이론을 반증하기 위한 헛된 시도에 다 써버렸습니다. 어쨌든, 이 이야기의 교훈은 직감이 과학자들에게 있어 중요하고 귀중한 도구가 될 수 있긴 하지만, 과학자들이 감정적이지 않을 필요도 있다는 사실이죠. 과학자들은 주어진 증거에서 나온 결과도 받아들일 줄 알아야 합니다. 그 결과가 마음에 들지 않더라도 말이죠. Einstein은 이렇게 하지 못했고, 그것은 그의 후반 경력에 많은 대가를 치르게 했습니다.

---

01 강의의 주제는?
(A) Einstein의 가장 큰 실패
(B) Einstein의 가장 영향력 있는 이론
(C) 과학에 대한 Einstein의 태도
(D) Einstein의 반증된 이론

해설 | Main Idea 강의는 Einstein의 성공과 실패에 영향을 끼쳤던 그의 과학에 대한 접근법(태도)에 대해 설명하고 있다.

02 교수가 Einstein의 과학에 대한 접근법을 설명하는 방식은?
(A) Einstein에 관한 두 가지 일화를 이야기함으로써
(B) 다른 위대한 과학자들의 접근법과 대조함으로써
(C) 그가 틀린 이론을 피하는 데 어떻게 도움을 주었는지 설명함으로써
(D) Einstein 접근법의 근원에 대해 논의함으로써

해설 | Organization 교수는 특수·일반 상대성 이론 및 양자역학 이론과 관련한 Einstein의 일화를 소개하면서 그의 직관에 의존하는 접근법에 대해 설명하고 있다.

03 Einstein이 양자역학을 판단한 방식은?
(A) 정확성을 입증하거나 부정하는 증거에 따라
(B) 자신의 이론에 얼마나 들어맞았는지에 따라
(C) 우주를 얼마나 완벽하게 설명했느냐에 따라
(D) 세상의 이치에 대한 자신의 본능적인 반응에 따라

해설 | Detail 교수는 Einstein이 이론을 발전시킬 때 매우 직관적이었으며 스스로 진실이라고 믿고 확신하는 것에 따라 연구를 해나갔다고 설명하고 있다. 따라서 양자역학을 판단할 때도 많은 연구들이 이 이론이 옳다는 것을 입증하였음에도 불구하고, 자신의 직관에 따라 잘못된 이론이라 믿었다.

04 교수가 과학자들에 대해 말한 내용은?
(A) Einstein의 본보기를 따르면 잘 될 것이다.
(B) 사적인 감정이 과학적 판단을 흐리게 해서는 안 된다.
(C) 확실한 증거가 없을 시에만 직관에 의존해야 한다.
(D) 이미 존재하는 이론을 반증하기보다 새로운 이론 개발에 집중해야 한다.

해설 | Detail 교수는 "Anyway, the moral of this story is while intuition is important to a scientist and can be a valuable tool, scientists must also be dispassionate"라고 하면서, 과학자들이 직관에만 의존해 감정적이 되지 말 것을 경고하고 있다.

05 양자역학을 반증하려 했던 Einstein의 시도에 대한 교수의 의견은?

(A) 다양한 발견으로 이어진 훌륭한 노력이었다.
(B) Einstein을 더 큰 성취로부터 멀게 한 무의미한 시도였다.
(C) 양자역학의 증거 부족을 생각하면 타당한 노력이었다.
(D) 그가 이번에는 직관에 의존하지 않았기 때문에 실패했다.

해설 | Attitude 교수는 과학자들이 단지 직관에만 의존하는 것이 아니라 감정적이지 않을 필요도 있다고 하면서, "Einstein wasn't able to do this, and it cost him a great deal in his later career"라고 말하고 있다.

어휘 | **follow something up** (방금 한 것에) ~을 더하다, 덧붙이다   **approach** 접근법   **disprove** 반증하다   **asset** 이점, 재산   **fruitless** 헛된
dispassionate 감정적이 아닌

Intensive Drill 3   p.132

01 (A)   02 (A), (D), (E)   03 [Pyrolysis – (A), (D)], [Gasification – (B), (C)]   04 (C)   05 (D)

Listen to part of a lecture in an environmental science class.

Professor (M): Last week, we looked at the implications of replacing fossil fuels with renewable energy sources such as solar and geothermal plants. Q01-1 Today, we'll examine another means of securing energy, namely, Waste-to-Energy, or WtE for short. WtE is the generation of energy in the form of heat or electricity from human waste. Waste from human activity has been increasing tremendously in both mass and diversity. This waste can cause harmful effects to the general environment as well as to human health. So, while the ongoing effort to reduce, reuse, and recycle waste is inevitable, the need for developing technologies to recover energy from waste is becoming critical.

Q01-2 The most common WtE implementation is incineration. It involves putting organic waste into incinerators for complete combustion at high temperatures, and the heat generated from it is used to create energy. Q02(A), (E) In spite of its popularity, incineration is a highly debated technology since it raises issues of safety and environmental impact. Q02(D) Even though more recently developed incineration plants claim to be vastly different from earlier types, they can't escape criticism for releasing harmful substances into the atmosphere, including heavy metals, dioxin, and acid gas. Q05🎧 Moreover, incineration leaves ash residues as high as 25 percent of its original volume, and these residues . . . well, they go nowhere but to landfills along with their undesirable byproducts. So, why is incineration still popular? Well, there are no alternatives cost-effective enough to compete with incineration yet.

And yes, there are other WtE emerging technologies that don't use direct combustion. For instance, pyrolysis and gasification are both thermal treatment methods regarded as more advanced alternatives to incineration. Q03(A) Pyrolysis uses mostly biomass and plastic waste as primary ingredients and heats them up without oxygen at very high temperatures. In the heat, the material first converts into complex molecules and gases. Then it goes into a combustion chamber to be reheated, but this time with oxygen. Q01-3 The final products generated from pyrolysis are liquid oil and gases which can be used as alternatives to fossil fuel. Q03(D) However, it also leaves charcoal as a byproduct that may create toxins and require landfilling, just like ash from incineration.

환경과학 강의 중 일부를 들으시오.

교수 (남): 지난주에 태양열 발전소와 지열 발전소와 같은 재생 가능한 에너지 자원으로 화석 연료를 대체하는 것의 영향에 대해 알아보았어요. 오늘은 약어로 WtE라고도 하는 이른바, 폐기물에너지라는 에너지를 확보하는 또 다른 방법에 대해 알아볼게요. 폐기물에너지는 인간의 쓰레기로부터 열에너지나 전기에너지의 형태로 에너지를 발생시키는 거에요. 인간 활동으로부터 생겨난 쓰레기는 그 양과 다양함에 있어서 엄청나게 증가하고 있어요. 이 쓰레기는 인간의 건강뿐만 아니라 일반 환경에도 해로운 영향을 미칠 수 있어요. 그래서 쓰레기를 줄이고 재활용하고 재생하기 위한 계속된 노력은 불가피하고, 쓰레기로부터 에너지를 재생시키기 위한 기술 발달의 필요성은 중요해지고 있어요.

폐기물에너지의 가장 일반적인 실행 방법은 소각이에요. 유기 폐기물을 높은 온도에서의 완전 연소를 위해 소각로에 넣고 이로부터 발생한 열은 에너지를 발생시키는 데 사용되죠. 인기에도 불구하고 소각은 안전성과 환경적 영향에 대한 문제를 일으키기 때문에 매우 논란이 되는 기술입니다. 좀 더 최근에 개발된 소각장은 이전 종류와 매우 다름에도 불구하고, 중금속, 다이옥신, 산성 가스를 포함한 해로운 물질을 대기에 배출한다는 비난을 피할 수 없어요. 게다가, 소각은 원래 용량의 25%만큼 많은 재 잔여물을 남기는데, 이 잔여물은... 음, 원치 않는 부산물과 함께 매립지에 쌓이게 되죠. 그런데 왜 소각이 여전히 인기가 있을까요? 음, 아직은 소각과 경쟁할 만큼 충분히 비용 효율이 높은 대안이 없기 때문이죠.

그리고 네, 직접적 연소 방법을 사용하지 않는 다른 폐기물에너지 신흥 기술들이 있어요. 예를 들면, 열분해나 가스화 모두 더 발달한 소각의 대안으로 여겨지는 열처리 방식이에요. 열분해는 주로 바이오매스와 플라스틱 폐기물을 주재료로 사용하고, 산소 없이 매우 높은 온도에서 그것들을 열처리해요. 열에서 그 물질은 먼저 복합 분자와 가스로 전환돼요. 그리고 나서 다시 열처리되기 위해 연소실로 들어가는데 이때는 산소가 사용돼요. 열분해로 발생하는 최종 생성물은 화석 연료 대신 사용될 수 있는 액체 오일과 가스가 되죠. 하지만 이는 또한 소각에서의 재 잔여물처럼 독소를 만들고 매립을 해야 하는 목탄 부산물을 남기죠.

Q01-4 The other thermal method I mentioned is gasification. Q03(C) It uses carbonaceous substances from waste and converts them into gaseous materials. Although it also requires high temperatures, the crucial difference is it doesn't involve combustion. Q03(B) Instead, it involves heating in a low-oxygen atmosphere to obtain its result called synthesis gas. Synthesis gas is considered a more desirable energy source and is used mainly for heat and electricity.

Now, there are also non-thermal technologies like anaerobic digestion, which uses microorganisms to destroy the biodegradable content in the waste. What happens during this process is that it taps the energy within the bio-content and releases energy in the form of biogas. Q01-5 Q04 The biogas from anaerobic digestion creates energy on a smaller scale, such as for running a gas engine. Yet it may be a feasible and certainly environmentally friendly option for replacing fossil fuels.

제가 언급한 또 다른 열처리 방식은 가스화예요. 이는 폐기물로부터 탄소질의 물질을 사용하고 이를 가스 물질로 전환시켜요. 높은 온도가 필요하지만, 결정적인 차이점은 연소 과정을 거치지 않는다는 거예요. 대신 합성 가스라 불리는 결과물을 얻기 위해 산소량이 낮은 대기에서 열처리를 하죠. 합성 가스는 더 바람직한 에너지원으로 여겨지며 주로 열과 전기를 얻기 위해 사용돼요.

자, 혐기성 소화와 같은 비열처리 기술도 있어요. 이는 미생물을 사용하여 폐기물에서의 생물 분해성 물질을 분해하는 거예요. 이 과정에서는 생물 물질 내의 에너지를 사용해서 생물 가스의 형태로 에너지를 방출시킵니다. 혐기성 소화로 발생한 생물 가스는 가스 엔진을 작동시키기 위한 에너지 같이 소규모의 에너지를 발생시키죠. 하지만 이는 화석 연료를 대체시키기 위한 실현 가능하고 분명히 환경친화적인 선택사항이 될 수 있어요.

01 강의의 주된 목적은?

(A) 폐기물에너지 과정의 여러 영향을 검토하기 위해
(B) 폐기물에너지 생산의 장점을 설명하기 위해
(C) 인간의 쓰레기를 활용하려는 다양한 노력을 설명하기 위해
(D) 폐기물에너지에서의 열처리법과 비열처리법을 비교하기 위해

해설 | Main Idea 교수는 강의 초반에 "Today, we'll examine another means of securing energy, namely, Waste-to-Energy …"라고 말하며 폐기물에너지를 얻는 과정에 대한 강의를 진행할 것임을 보여준다. 그 후에 여러 방식과 그에 따른 영향 및 결과물들에 대해 논의한다.

02 교수에 따르면, 다음 중 소각 기술을 사용하는 것에 대한 논쟁의 원인이 되는 요인들은?

3개의 답을 고르시오.

(A) 절차의 안전성
(B) 속도 및 비용 효율성
(C) 모순되는 기술
(D) 절차상의 잔여물
(E) 환경과 관련된 문제들

해설 | Detail 교수에 의하면, 소각 기술은 안전성과 환경적 영향에 대한 문제를 일으키고, 중금속, 다이옥신, 산성 가스, 재 등의 잔여물을 남기기 때문에 논란이 되고 있다.

03 강의에서 교수는 폐기물의 열처리 방법으로서 열분해와 가스화를 설명한다. 다음 각 과정이 열분해나 가스화와 관련 있는지 표시하시오.

각 사항에 대해 알맞은 항목에 표시하시오.

	열분해	가스화
(A) 주재료로 바이오매스와 플라스틱을 사용한다.	✔	
(B) 산소량이 낮은 대기에서의 열처리를 포함한다.		✔
(C) 폐기물로부터 탄소질의 물질을 사용한다.		✔
(D) 유독성일 가능성이 있는 목탄 부산물을 남긴다.	✔	

해설 | Connecting Content 교수에 의하면, 열분해는 바이오매스와 플라스틱 폐기물을 주재료로 사용하고, 독소를 발생시키는 목탄 부산물을 남긴다. 가스화는 합성 가스를 얻기 위해 산소량이 낮은 대기에서 열처리를 하며, 폐기물로부터 탄소질의 물질을 사용하여 이를 가스 물질로 전환시킨다.

04 교수가 혐기성 소화의 사용에 대해 암시하는 것은?

(A) 속도가 느린 과정은 에너지 생산량을 증가시킬 수 있다.
(B) 이 과정에서 생산된 생물 가스의 품질은 일관성이 없다.
(C) 이 과정의 생산물인 에너지 사용은 제한적일 수도 있다.
(D) 미생물의 사용은 소화 작용의 속도를 높일 수 있다.

해설 | Inference 교수에 의하면 혐기성 소화로 발생한 생물 가스는 가스 엔진을 작동시키는 데 쓰이는 에너지와 같이 소규모의 에너지를 발생시킨다. 즉, 혐기성 소화 과정에서 생산된 에너지 사용은 제한적일 수도 있음을 나타낸다.

05 강의의 일부를 다시 듣고 질문에 답하시오.
교수가 다음과 같이 말할 때 의미하는 것은?

"Well, there are no alternatives cost-effective enough to compete with incineration yet."

(A) 소각은 폐기물에너지 과정으로서의 인기를 점점 잃고 있다.
(B) 다른 폐기물에너지 기술들은 비용적인 측면과 관련해서만 발전하였다.
(C) 소각의 부산물은 비용 효율성을 향상시킬 수 있다.
(D) 소각 기술은 비용 효율성이 훨씬 더 높다는 특징이 있다.

해설 | Function 교수는 소각과 경쟁할 만큼 충분히 비용 효율이 높은 대안이 없다고 말하므로 소각 기술의 비용 효율성이 매우 높다는 것을 의미한다.

어휘 | **implication** 영향, 결과 **fossil fuel** 화석 연료 **renewable** 재생 가능한 **solar** 태양열을 이용한, 태양의 **geothermal** 지열의 **Waste-to-Energy** 폐기물에너지 **implementation** 실행, 이행 **incineration** 소각 **incinerator** 소각로 **combustion** 연소 **heavy metal** 중금속 **dioxin** 다이옥신 **landfill** (쓰레기) 매립(지) **byproduct** 부산물 **pyrolysis** 열분해 **gasification** 가스화 **charcoal** 목탄, 숯 **carbonaceous** 탄소질의 **synthesis** 합성, 종합 **anaerobic digestion** 혐기성 소화 **microorganism** 미생물 **biodegradable** 생물 분해성의, 자연 분해성의 **feasible** 실현 가능한

Mini Test 1
p.134

01 (D) **02** (C) **03** (A) **04** (D) **05** (C)

Listen to part of a discussion in an astronomy class.

Professor (F): As you all know, stars emit light at different wavelengths, and we observe these various wavelengths as colors. The particular range of colors that a star emits is called its spectrum, and to astronomers this spectrum is a very important feature of a star. Does anyone know why?

Student 1 (M): Q01 Well, I know that a star's spectrum gives details about its size and its distance from the Earth, but I don't really understand how.

Professor: That's OK, because that is actually what we are going to talk about today. Alright, let's start with how we can determine a star's size from its spectrum. Q05-1 The colors emitted by a particular star are determined by two things: the internal chemistry of the star, and its temperature. Q02-1 Hotter stars emit more light in the blue end of the spectrum, and cooler stars emit more light in the yellow and red areas. How does that relate to the size of a star? Anyone?

Student 2 (F): Oh! I know! Like, two classes ago, you told us that Q02-2 larger stars burn at hotter temperatures than smaller stars. So if a star is emitting a lot of blue light, you can probably guess that it is pretty big.

Professor: Good. In fact, there is a whole class of stars called blue super giants for exactly that reason.

Student 1: I'm confused. I remember reading in our book about stars called red giants, too. Based on what you just told us, how can you have a star that is big and red? You just said that all big stars are blue.

천문학 수업 중 토론의 일부를 들으시오.

교수 (여): 여러분 모두 알다시피, 별은 다양한 파장으로 빛을 내고 우리는 이러한 다양한 파장을 색으로 보게 됩니다. 별이 내는 특별한 색의 범위를 별의 스펙트럼이라고 하는데, 천문학자들에게 있어 이 스펙트럼은 별의 아주 중요한 특징이랍니다. 그 이유를 아는 사람 있나요?

학생 1 (남): 음, 별의 스펙트럼이 별의 크기와 지구로부터의 거리를 알려준다는 것은 아는데, 어떻게 그런지는 잘 모르겠어요.

교수: 괜찮아요, 사실 오늘 알아볼 내용이 바로 그것이거든요. 좋아요. 스펙트럼으로 어떻게 별의 크기를 알 수 있는지부터 시작하죠. 특정 별에서 나는 색은 두 가지로 결정됩니다. 바로 별 내부의 화학 물질과 별의 온도죠. 뜨거운 별은 스펙트럼의 파란 끝부분에서 빛을 더 많이 내고, 차가운 별은 노란색 및 붉은색 부분에서 빛을 더 많이 내죠. 이것이 어떻게 별의 크기와 관련이 있을까요? 누구 아는 사람?

학생 2 (여): 오, 저 알아요! 지지난 수업 때 교수님께서 더 큰 별은 더 작은 별보다 높은 온도에서 탄다고 말씀하셨잖아요. 그러니까 만약 별이 파란빛을 내면 그 별은 꽤 크다고 추측할 수 있겠죠.

교수: 맞아요. 사실 바로 그 이유로 청색 초거성이라고 불리는 종류의 별이 있죠.

학생 1: 저는 좀 헷갈려요. 교재에서 적색 초거성에 대해서도 읽은 기억이 나거든요. 교수님께서 방금 말씀하신 것에 근거하면, 어떻게 크면서 붉은 별이 있을 수 있죠? 방금 모든 거성은 파란색이라고 말씀하셨잖아요.

Professor: Q03 I'm being a little careless with my terminology. Let me clarify. Q04 When I talk about big stars, what I really mean is stars with a lot of material, uh, with a lot of mass. All of those stars are blue stars. When we talk about red giants, we are talking about stars at the end of their lives. These stars swell in size, but they don't gain any more mass. So while they're physically big, they are low in mass, and this is why they emit red light. Does that help?

Student 1: Yeah. I think I get it now. So how does a star's spectrum tell us about its distance?

Professor: That is a bit more complex. The first thing you need to know is that the universe is expanding, and that the parts of the universe that are farther away from us are expanding at a faster rate than the parts that are close to us. So distant stars are moving away from us faster than closer stars. Q05-2 Now, when a light source moves away from us, its entire spectrum gets shifted to the red, and objects moving away at higher speeds experience more red shift than objects at lower speeds. So by observing the spectrum of a star and determining the amount of red shift, we can determine the speed at which it is moving away from us. And from that we can determine its distance.

교수: 제가 용어 선택에 있어 조금 부주의했군요. 명확하게 설명하죠. 제가 말한 거성은 물질이 많은 별, 그러니까, 질량이 큰 별을 의미해요. 그 별들은 모두 푸른 별이죠. 적색 초거성에 대해서 말할 때는 수명이 거의 다한 별을 말해요. 이 별들은 크기에서는 팽창하지만, 질량은 늘어나지 않는답니다. 그래서 물리적으로는 커도 질량이 낮기 때문에 붉은빛을 내는 거예요. 이 설명이 도움이 되나요?

학생 1: 네, 이제 알겠어요. 그러면 어떻게 별의 스펙트럼으로 거리를 알 수 있죠?

교수: 그건 좀 더 복잡해요. 우선 여러분이 알아야 할 사실은 우주가 팽창하고 있으며, 우리와 멀리 떨어진 곳은 우리에게 가까운 곳보다 더 빠른 속도로 팽창하고 있다는 거예요. 그래서 멀리 떨어져 있는 별은 가까운 별보다 더 빠르게 멀어져 가고 있답니다. 자, 광원이 우리에게서 멀어지면 그에 따른 스펙트럼 전체가 붉은색으로 바뀌고, 빠른 속도로 멀어져 가는 물체일수록 천천히 움직이는 물체보다 더 붉게 바뀌죠. 그래서 별의 스펙트럼을 관찰하면서 붉게 바뀌는 양을 파악하면, 우리에게서 멀어져 가는 속도를 계산할 수 있답니다. 그리고 그로부터 별의 거리를 측정할 수 있지요.

01 화자들이 논의하는 주된 내용은?
(A) 거리가 먼 별의 스펙트럼을 관찰하는 방법
(B) 스펙트럼으로 별의 등급 구별하기
(C) 별의 색으로 별의 온도 알아내기
(D) 별의 스펙트럼을 통해 별에 대해 알 수 있는 것

해설 | Main Idea 별의 스펙트럼으로부터 별의 크기와 거리를 알 수 있음을 설명하고 있다.

02 더 큰 별이 더 파란빛을 내는 이유는?
(A) 더 많은 핵연료를 연소한다.
(B) 더 빠른 속도로 움직인다.
(C) 내부 온도가 더 높다.
(D) 직경이 더 크다.

해설 | Detail 크기가 큰 별일수록 높은 온도에서 연소하고, 높은 온도의 별일수록 파란빛을 낸다고 했다.

03 적색 초거성에 대해 헷갈린 학생에 대한 교수의 의견은?
(A) 학생이 헷갈린 것은 자신의 부적절한 용어 사용으로 인한 잘못이다.
(B) 학생은 기본 용어를 이해하지 못하고 있다.
(C) 학생은 논의 초반에 집중하지 않았다.
(D) 문제를 제기한 학생의 용기는 칭찬받아야 한다.

해설 | Attitude "I'm being a little careless with my terminology"라는 교수의 말을 통해 자신이 용어에 대한 오해의 소지를 제공했다고 생각하고 있음을 알 수 있다.

04 교수가 청색 초거성과 적색 초거성에서 비교하는 것은?
(A) 각각의 나이
(B) 내부 화학 물질
(C) 우주에서의 분포도
(D) 전체 질량

해설 | Detail 학생이 어떻게 적색 초거성이 있을 수 있는지 묻자, 교수는 청색 초거성은 질량이 높지만, 적색 초거성은 물리적으로만 클 뿐 질량은 높지 않다고 설명하고 있다.

05 별에 대해 추론할 수 있는 것은?

(A) 청색 별은 적색 별보다 항상 더 가까이 있다.
(B) 우주에는 청색 별보다 적색 별이 더 많다.
(C) 별의 스펙트럼의 색깔에 영향을 미치는 데는 한 가지 이상의 요인이 있다.
(D) 별의 크기를 알아야만 별 스펙트럼으로부터 유익한 정보를 얻을 수 있다.

해설 | Inference 별의 스펙트럼은 내부 화학 물질, 별의 온도, 거리 등의 영향을 함께 받으므로 이 중 어느 한 가지에 의해 색이 결정되는 것은 아니다.

어휘 | **emit** (빛·열·향기 등을) 내다, 방출하다 **wavelength** 파장 **terminology** (전문) 용어 **mass** 질량 **swell** 팽창하다, 증가하다 **expand** 팽창[확장]하다 **shift** 바뀌다, 변화

Mini Test 2   p.136

01 (D)   02 (C)   03 (B)   04 (A)   05 (C)

Listen to part of a lecture in a geology class.

Professor (M): OK, everyone. We talked about several types of glaciers last time. The types are based on their shape, where they are, or where they come from.

Q01 Now, today, we are going to continue our discussion of glaciers, focusing specifically on how they move. Understanding this aspect of glaciers is important for a number of reasons. First, the better we understand glacier movement, the better we can model the ways in which glaciers deform and alter the local geography over time. Second, understanding the dynamics of glacier movement allows us to better monitor their health and make accurate predictions about their future growth or degradation. We'll get into both of these concepts a bit later, but first we need to go over the two factors that affect glacier movement.

Q05 The engine behind the movement of glaciers is the force of gravity. The immense weight of the glacier pushes it downhill following the path of least resistance. Think of the way a mountain stream follows the course of a valley. Now, on the surface that sounds fairly simple, but there are quite a number of factors that complicate the picture.

First, it's somewhat inaccurate to think of a glacier as simply a big hunk of ice. Because of the immense weight and pressure exerted on the ice in a glacier, it has different properties than those we usually associate with ice. The ice in a glacier behaves more like plastic, as it can stretch and bend. As a result, different parts of a glacier may move at different speeds. **Q03-1** For example, the ice at the bottom of a glacier rubs against the ground, and the resulting friction slows it down a bit. The ice at the top of the glacier isn't exposed to this friction, and consequently moves faster than that at the bottom. The same thing happens at the sides of the glacier. **Q02** As a result, the fastest moving part of the glacier tends to be the ice in its upper center portion.

Q03-2 Another factor that complicates the movement of glaciers is the melting of its ice. As some of the ice in a glacier melts, it trickles down through cracks in the glacier and begins to build up underneath. **Q04** This layer of water at the bottom of a glacier acts as a lubricant, allowing the glacier to slide across the bedrock more easily.

지질학 강의 중 일부를 들으시오.

교수 (남): 자, 여러분. 지난 시간에 여러 종류의 빙하에 대해 얘기했어요. 빙하의 종류는 그것의 모양, 어디에 있는지, 어디서 왔는지에 따라 다르죠.

자, 오늘은 빙하에 대한 이야기를 계속하면서, 특히 빙하가 어떻게 이동하는지에 대해 집중해서 알아보겠어요. 빙하의 이러한 측면을 이해하는 것은 많은 이유로 중요합니다. 첫 번째로, 빙하의 이동을 더 잘 이해할수록, 빙하가 지역의 지리를 어떻게 변형시키고 바꾸는지에 대해 더 잘 연구할 수 있어요. 두 번째로, 빙하 이동의 역학을 이해함으로써 빙하의 상태를 관찰하고, 향후 증대 또는 붕괴 여부에 대해 정확한 예측을 할 수 있어요. 이 두 가지에 대해서는 조금 후에 이야기하기로 하고, 우선 빙하의 이동에 영향을 끼치는 두 가지 요인부터 알아보도록 하죠.

빙하 이동의 원동력은 바로 중력입니다. 빙하의 거대한 무게로 인해 빙하는 저항력이 가장 작은 경로를 따라 내려가게 됩니다. 계곡을 따라 내려오는 산골짜기 시냇물을 생각해 보세요. 자, 겉보기에는 아주 간단해 보이지만, 이 일을 복잡하게 만드는 꽤 많은 요인이 있습니다.

우선, 빙하를 그저 아주 큰 얼음 덩어리로 보는 것은 다소 부정확합니다. 빙하의 얼음에 가해지는 거대한 중력과 압력으로 인해, 빙하는 우리가 보통 연상하는 얼음과는 다른 특성을 보이고 있어요. 빙하의 얼음은 늘어질 수도 있고 구부러질 수도 있어서, 플라스틱과 더 비슷하게 작용합니다. 그 결과, 빙하의 여러 부분은 다른 속도로 움직일 수 있게 되죠. 예를 들어, 빙하의 밑부분은 땅과 마찰하게 되는데, 이로 인해 생기는 마찰력 때문에 빙하의 속도는 약간 줄어들게 됩니다. 빙하 윗부분의 얼음은 이런 마찰력에 노출되지 않기 때문에 결과적으로 밑부분보다 더 빨리 움직이게 되죠. 빙하의 옆 부분도 마찬가지예요. 그 결과, 빙하에서 가장 빠르게 움직이는 부분은 위쪽 중앙 부분이 됩니다.

빙하의 이동을 복잡하게 만드는 또 다른 요인은 얼음이 녹는 현상입니다. 빙하의 얼음 일부가 녹으면서 빙하 안의 틈새로 조금씩 흘러 밑부분에 쌓이기 시작하죠. 이렇게 생긴 빙하 바닥의 물 층은 윤활제 역할을 해서 빙하가 기반암을 더 쉽게 미끄러져 나갈 수 있게 해줍니다.

You can perform a basic experiment at home to see this in action. Take an ice cube out of your freezer and place it on a flat wooden board. Then tilt that board at an angle, say 30 or 40 degrees. At first, nothing should happen. The friction between the ice cube and the board should keep the ice cube right where it is. However, if you leave the ice cube there long enough, it will start to melt. The melting water will act as a lubricant between the board and the still-frozen portion of the ice cube, and it should begin to slide down towards the bottom of the board. This is roughly what happens with glaciers.

집에서 간단한 실험을 통해 이것의 활동을 볼 수 있어요. 냉동고에서 각 얼음을 꺼내 평평한 나무판자 위에 올려놓으세요. 그리고 판자를 30도나 40도 정도로 기울여 보세요. 처음에는 아무 일도 일어나지 않아요. 각 얼음과 판자 사이의 마찰력으로 얼음이 제자리에 있을 겁니다. 하지만 얼음을 그 자리에 충분히 오랫동안 놓아두면 녹기 시작할 거예요. 녹은 물이 판자와 아직 얼어 있는 얼음 사이에 윤활제 역할을 해서 얼음이 판자 밑으로 미끄러져 내려가게 될 겁니다. 이것이 대략 빙하에서 생기는 현상이라고 보면 돼요.

01 교수가 빙하의 이동에 대한 논의를 도입하는 방식은?
(A) 주제와 관련한 최근 발견 내용을 설명함으로써
(B) 학생들이 빙하에 대해 이미 배운 것을 복습함으로써
(C) 빙하의 이동과 관련한 기본 원동력을 개략적으로 설명함으로써
(D) 빙하의 이동을 이해하는 것이 왜 유익한지를 강조함으로써

해설 | Organization 교수는 강의 도입부에서 빙하의 이동에 대해 배우겠다고 말하고, "Understanding this aspect of glaciers is important for a number of reasons"라고 말하며 빙하의 이동을 이해하는 것이 중요한 이유를 강조하고 있다.

02 빙하에서 가장 빠르게 움직이는 부분은?
(A) 측면
(B) 중심
(C) 위쪽 중간
(D) 밑바닥

해설 | Detail 빙하의 밑부분은 땅과의 마찰로 인해 속도가 느리며, 마찰이 없는 위쪽과 측면은 밑부분보다 속도가 더 빠르다. 결국, 마찰의 영향을 받지 않으며 바닥에서 가장 멀리 떨어진 위쪽 중간 부분의 속도가 가장 빠르게 된다.

03 교수가 빙하의 이동에 대해 암시하는 것은?
(A) 빙하의 무게에도 불구하고 중력은 빙하가 아래로 더 쉽게 내려갈 수 있도록 해준다.
(B) 빙하의 얼음이 녹는 것은 기반암과 빙하 사이의 마찰력을 줄여주어 이동을 쉽게 해준다.
(C) 빙하의 이동은 각 얼음과 성질이 다르므로 각 얼음의 이동과 비교될 수 없다.
(D) 빙하 하부의 얼음은 얼음이 녹는 영향으로 인해 가장 빠르게 이동한다.

해설 | Inference 교수는 빙하의 밑부분이 땅과 마찰하면서 생기는 마찰력으로 인해 빙하의 속도가 줄어든다고 말한다. 또한, 빙하의 얼음 일부가 녹으면서 빙하 안의 틈새로 물이 조금씩 흘러 밑부분에 쌓이고 이것이 윤활제 역할을 해서 빙하가 더 쉽게 미끄러져 나갈 수 있도록 해준다고 말한다. 교수는 이 두 가지 내용을 통해 빙하의 얼음이 녹는 것은 기반암과 빙하 사이의 마찰력을 줄여주어 이동을 쉽게 해준다는 것을 암시한다.

04 교수가 각 얼음을 언급하는 이유는?
(A) 녹은 물이 빙하의 이동을 어떻게 촉진시키는지 예를 들어 설명하기 위해
(B) 빙하의 구조를 설명하기 위해
(C) 빙하가 왜 저항력이 가장 작은 경로를 따라가는지 나타내기 위해
(D) 빙하가 이동할 때 어떻게 갈라지고 쪼개지는지 설명하기 위해

해설 | Organization 교수는 빙하 속에서 녹은 물이 어떻게 윤활제 역할을 해 줄 수 있는지를 설명하면서 각 얼음과 나무판자 실험을 언급하였다.

05 강의의 일부를 다시 듣고 질문에 답하시오.
교수가 다음과 같이 말하는 이유는?
"Think of the way a mountain stream follows the course of a valley."
(A) 빙하와 유수와의 관계를 제시하기 위해
(B) 빙하 이동의 복잡성을 강조하기 위해
(C) 빙하가 어떻게 이동하는지를 결정짓는 원리를 명확하게 설명하기 위해
(D) 빙하의 이동에서 중력의 역할을 언급하기 위해

해설 | Function 교수는 빙하의 이동을 유발하는 원리를 보다 친숙한 경우, 즉 계곡과 산골짜기 시냇물로 비유해 학생들이 이해하기 쉽도록 명확하게 설명하려 하고 있다.

어휘 | **glacier** 빙하   **deform** 변형시키다   **degradation** (지층·암석 등의) 붕괴   **on the surface** 겉보기에는, 면상으로는   **hunk** 큰 덩어리   **exert** (압력을) 가하다, (힘·영향력 등을) 쓰다   **property** 특성   **associate** 연상하다   **friction** 마찰(력)   **portion** 부분, 일부   **trickle** 조금씩 흐르다, 똑똑 떨어지다   **lubricant** 윤활제   **bedrock** 기반암   **tilt** 기울이다

iBT Practice

01 (A) 02 (D) 03 (B) 04 (B) 05 (D) – (A) – (C) – (B) 06 (C)

Listen to part of a lecture in an astronomy class.

Professor (F): One of the most prominent features of the lunar surface is the presence of numerous craters created by asteroid impacts. The Moon is covered with literally thousands of such impact craters, some of which are so large that they can be seen from the Earth without a telescope. The craters are especially visible when the Moon is full. Look up at the full moon and you'll see a number of shadows across its surface. Each of these is a crater, and some of them are more than a thousand miles across.

Anyway, the dating of rock samples taken from lunar craters during NASA's Apollo missions suggests that, um, the vast majority of these craters were formed between 4.1 and 3.8 billion years ago. Similar crater formations can be found on the surfaces of Mars and Mercury — although these have not been dated, since no samples have ever been brought back from either planet. Still, when taken together, the existence of all of these craters provides pretty convincing evidence that something extraordinary occurred during the earliest stages of the solar system's history.

Astronomers call this event the Late Heavy Bombardment. It was a period in which the Moon as well as the inner planets fell under a near-constant barrage of asteroids, comets, and small planetoids, with impacts occurring at perhaps 100,000 times the rate at which such impacts occur in the modern era. **Q02** At this rate, the Earth would have been hit by an object 1 kilometer in size once every 5 years on average, and impacts involving objects larger than 5 kilometers would have occurred an average of once every 100 years. Think about that, 5 kilometers. That's about half the size of the object that is thought to have hit the Earth and killed off the dinosaurs. Something that big and that destructive hit the Earth every 100 years. The other inner planets would have received a similarly severe beating.

Q01 Q06 So, today we're going to look at two questions. First, what could have been responsible for this intense period of planetary bombardment, and second, what was its impact on the history of the solar system?

The first of those two questions is the one more open to debate. Simply put, we're not sure what set the Late Heavy Bombardment in motion . . . uh, primarily because our picture of the early solar system is still incomplete. It's basically hard to say anything with certainty about this period. **Q03** However, the scenario that I favor — and a lot of other astronomers do as well — is the planetary migration scenario. Under this theory, the orbits of Saturn and Jupiter were originally closer to the Sun than they currently are. **Q05(D)** At some point, uh, probably just prior to the beginning of the Late Heavy Bombardment, Saturn and Jupiter rather quickly drifted out into farther orbits.

천문학 강의 중 일부를 들으시오.

교수 (여): 달 표면의 가장 두드러진 특징 중 하나는 소행성 충돌로 생긴 수많은 분화구가 있다는 점입니다. 달은 말 그대로 수천 개의 충돌 분화구로 뒤덮여 있는데, 어떤 것들은 너무 커서 지구에서 망원경이 없어도 보일 정도랍니다. 분화구는 특히 만월 때 잘 보이죠. 보름달을 보면 표면에 많은 그림자가 보일 거예요. 이것들이 다 분화구인데, 어떤 것들은 직경이 천 마일 이상입니다.

미국 항공 우주국의 아폴로 탐사 기간에 달 분화구에서 채취한 암석 표본의 연대에 따르면, 이 분화구의 상당수가 41억 년 전부터 38억 년 전 사이에 형성되었다고 합니다. 화성과 수성 표면에서도 이와 비슷한 분화구의 형성을 찾아볼 수 있지만, 그 행성들로부터 가져온 표본이 없기 때문에 그것들의 연대는 추정되지 않았습니다. 하지만 종합해 볼 때, 이러한 분화구의 존재는 태양계 역사의 초기 단계에 어떤 엄청난 사건이 일어났을 거라는 것에 꽤 설득력 있는 증거를 제공해주고 있습니다.

천문학자들은 이 사건을 후기 운석 대충돌기라고 부릅니다. 이는 지구형 행성들과 달이 소행성, 혜성, 그리고 작은 미행성의 거의 끊임없는 연발에 놓인 시기이며, 근대기에 일어난 충돌보다 약 10만 배나 많이 일어났죠. 이러한 상태는 마치 지구가 평균 5년마다 한 번씩 1km 크기의 물체와 충돌하고, 100년마다 한 번씩 5km가 넘는 물체와 충돌한다고 가정하는 것과 비슷합니다. 5km의 크기를 생각해 보세요. 그것은 지구와 충돌해 공룡들을 멸종시켰다고 여겨지는 물체의 약 반 정도 되는 크기입니다. 그렇게 크고 파괴력이 강한 것이 지구와 평균 100년마다 부딪치는 것이죠. 다른 지구형 행성들도 이와 비슷한 심한 충격을 받았을 겁니다.

그래서 오늘 수업에서는 두 가지 문제를 다루고자 합니다. 첫 번째는 이 행성 충돌의 원인이 무엇인가이며, 두 번째는 이것이 태양계의 역사에 어떤 영향을 주었나입니다.

그 두 가지 중 첫 번째 질문은 좀 더 논란의 중심에 놓여 있어요. 간단히 말해, 무엇이 후기 운석 대충돌기를 움직이게 했는지 확실치 않다는 거지요… 어, 왜냐하면 우리가 아직 초기 태양계에 대해 완벽히 알지 못하기 때문입니다. 기본적으로 이 시기에 대해 확실하게 말하는 것이 어렵죠. 하지만 제가, 아니 저뿐만 아니라 많은 천문학자도 함께 지지하고 있는 설은, 바로 행성 이동설이에요. 이 설에 따르면, 토성과 목성의 궤도는 본래 현재의 위치보다 태양에 더 가까웠다고 해요. 그러다 어느 순간, 어, 아마도 후기 운석 대충돌기가 시작되기 바로 전쯤 토성과 목성이 더 먼 궤도로 밀려나게 된 것이죠.

Now, being the two largest planets in the solar system, Saturn and Jupiter exert a lot of gravitational influence on the others. Q05(A) So when their orbits migrated outwards, that in turn disrupted the orbits of Neptune and Uranus. Q05(C) These two planets spun into highly unstable orbits that sent them crashing through the asteroid belt, and the remaining material left over from planetary formation — Q04 uh, there was a lot more of this material back then, by the way. In fact, our current asteroid belt only contains an estimated 3 percent of the material it contained at the beginning of the Late Heavy Bombardment. So you can see that this was a very crowded, uh, high-traffic environment that Neptune and Uranus had to pass through.

Q05(B) Anyway, the result of all of this was that a good portion of the original asteroid belt was either flung out of the solar system or sent hurtling in toward the inner planets. By 3.7 billion years ago, the orbits of the planets had begun to stabilize once again, and the period of the Late Heavy Bombardment had come to a close.

Now again, remember that this is just one scenario for how all this came about. And while it currently matches most closely with what we know about the early solar system, there are other scenarios, which are described in Chapter 11 of your textbook. You'll be expected to know these as well for the final.

Are there any questions so far? *[pause]* No? Then let's move on to our second question of the day.

자, 태양계에서 가장 큰 두 행성인 토성과 목성은 다른 행성에 매우 크게 중력에 영향을 끼칩니다. 그래서 두 행성의 궤도가 바깥쪽으로 이동했을 때, 그것은 해왕성과 천왕성의 궤도에 큰 혼란을 일으켰죠. 이 두 행성은 매우 불안정한 궤도로 빨려 들어가서 행성이 형성될 때 남은 잔여물과 소행성대 사이를 통과하면서 그것들과 부딪치게 되었어요. 어, 그런데 그 당시에는 지금보다 이런 물질이 더 많이 있었습니다. 사실, 현재 소행성대에는 후기 운석 대충돌기 초기에 있었던 물질의 약 3%만이 남아 있어요. 따라서 해왕성과 천왕성이 지나가야 했던 그곳은 굉장히 복잡하고, 어, 많은 것들이 군집해 있는 환경이었습니다.

하지만 이 모든 것의 결과로 본래 소행성대에 있던 상당 부분은 태양계 밖으로 내던져지거나 지구형 행성 안쪽으로 돌진해 들어오게 되었어요. 37억 년 전에 행성의 궤도가 다시 안정되기 시작했고, 후기 운석 대충돌기도 끝이 났죠.

다시 말하지만, 이것은 그저 이 모든것이 어떻게 일어났는지에 대한 하나의 가설에 불과하다는 것을 기억해두세요. 또한, 이 가설은 현재 우리의 초기 태양계에 대한 지식과 가장 잘 들어맞기는 하지만, 다른 가설들도 있으며 이것들은 교과서 11장을 보면 나와 있어요. 기말시험을 위해서는 이것들도 알고 있어야 해요.

질문 있나요? *[잠시 후]* 없어요? 그럼 두 번째 질문으로 넘어갑시다.

01 강의의 주된 내용은?
(A) 후기 운석 대충돌기의 가능성 있는 원인
(B) 후기 운석 대충돌기의 증거
(C) 후기 운석 대충돌기의 격렬함
(D) 후기 운석 대충돌기의 영향

해설 | Main Idea 교수는 후기 운석 대충돌기의 원인과 그것이 태양계 역사에 끼친 영향에 대해 다루겠다고 언급하고, 그 중 첫 번째 내용에 대해 설명하고 있다.

02 교수가 후기 운석 대충돌기의 격렬함을 설명하는 방식은?
(A) 그것이 어떻게 다른 행성들에 생명체가 존재하지 않게 만들었는지 설명함으로써
(B) 그것이 지구의 경관을 어떻게 그렸는지 설명함으로써
(C) 그것을 다른 천문학적 사건들과 비교함으로써
(D) 지구의 소행성 충돌 빈도에 대한 정보를 제공함으로써

해설 | Organization 교수는 후기 운석 대충돌기를 지구에서 일어난 운석 충돌의 정도와 비교했을 때 그것이 얼마나 자주 발생할 수 있는 정도인지 수치로 제시해가며 당시 충돌의 위력을 설명하고 있다.

03 행성 이동설에 대한 교수의 의견은?
(A) 후기 운석 대충돌기와 아무런 관계가 없다.
(B) 후기 운석 대충돌기에 대해 가장 그럴듯한 설명이다.
(C) 후기 운석 대충돌기의 결과로 일어났을 가능성이 크다.
(D) 한때 가장 설득력 있는 후기 운석 대충돌기의 원인이라고 여겨졌다.

해설 | Attitude "However, the scenario that I favor — and a lot of other astronomers do as well — is the planetary migration scenario"라는 교수의 말을 통해, 자신을 포함한 많은 천문학자들이 그 가설을 지지하고 있음을 나타내고 있다.

04 교수가 후기 운석 대충돌기가 시작되기 전의 소행성대에 대해 말하는 것은?
(A) 태양과 훨씬 더 가깝게 궤도를 그리며 돌았다.
(B) 훨씬 더 많은 물질이 존재했다.
(C) 지구형 행성에 물체를 거의 보내지 않았다.
(D) 해왕성과 천왕성의 충돌에 자주 연루되었다.

해설 | Detail 교수는 후기 운석 대충돌기 이전의 소행성대에는 더 많은 물질이 있었으며 오늘날에는 그 당시의 3%만이 남아 있다고 설명하고 있다.

05 교수는 후기 운석 대충돌기의 역사를 설명한다.
다음 각 사건들을 올바른 순서대로 나열하시오.
각 문장을 해당되는 곳으로 옮기시오.

1	(D) 토성과 목성이 태양에서 더 먼 궤도로 이동하였다.
2	(A) 해왕성과 천왕성의 궤도가 불안정해졌다.
3	(C) 천왕성과 해왕성이 소행성대를 지나갔다.
4	(B) 지구형 행성에 더 많은 소행성 충돌이 일어났다.

해설 | Connecting Content 태양계에서 가장 큰 행성인 토성과 목성이 태양에서 더 먼 궤도로 밀려나면서 다른 행성들에 중력적인 영향력을 행사하였고, 그 영향을 받은 해왕성과 천왕성은 궤도가 불안정해지면서 소행성대로 들어가게 되었다. 이로 인해 그곳에 있던 물질들과 소행성들이 지구형 행성 안으로 들어오거나 태양계 바깥으로 밀려나면서 후기 운석 대충돌기가 일어나게 된 것이다.

06 강의의 일부를 다시 듣고 질문에 답하시오.
교수가 천문학자들에 대해 암시하는 것은?
(A) 그들은 후기 운석 대충돌기가 실제로 언제 일어났는지 잘 모른다.
(B) 그들은 초기 태양계가 훨씬 더 컸을지도 모른다고 생각한다.
(C) 그들은 후기 운석 대충돌기의 원인보다 영향에 대해 더 많이 알고 있다.
(D) 그들은 후기 운석 대충돌기에 대한 정보가 부족하기 때문에 추측하기를 꺼린다.

해설 | Inference "The first of those two questions is the one more open to debate"라는 교수의 말을 통해 후기 운석 대충돌기의 원인과 영향 중 그 원인에 대해서는 아직 확증된 상태가 아님을 알 수 있다.

어휘 | **lunar** 달의 **crater** 분화구 **asteroid impact** 소행성 충돌 **Mars** 화성 **Mercury** 수성 **convincing** 설득력 있는 **extraordinary** 엄청난, 비범한 **Late Heavy Bombardment** 후기 운석 대충돌기 **inner planet** 지구형 행성(= terrestrial planet) **barrage** 연발 **comet** 혜성 **planetoid** 미행성 **era** 시대 **set something in motion** ~을 움직이게 하다 **Saturn** 토성 **Jupiter** 목성 **Neptune** 해왕성 **Uranus** 천왕성 **asteroid belt** 소행성대 **fling** 내던지다 **hurtle** 돌진하다 **stabilize** 안정되다, 안정시키다

Chapter 13 Social Science

Intensive Drill 1   p.142

01 (B)   **02** (D)   **03** (D)   **04** (A)   **05** (B)

Listen to part of a discussion in an archaeology class.

Professor (F): Good morning. Today we're going to discuss the ancient city of Mohenjo-Daro, built four to five thousand years ago in the Indus River Valley. Q01 Mohenjo-Daro was first excavated in the 1920s, and the discoveries there helped shed some new light on the ancient civilizations that once inhabited what is now Pakistan and northwestern India. Um, who can name one such discovery for me?

Student 1 (M): Well, a lot of researchers are impressed by the city's gridded layout and sanitation system, from what I've heard.

Professor: Right, those are two of the most impressive features, demonstrating a magnificent knowledge of city planning, architecture, and engineering. Q02 The city itself is divided into rectangular blocks, which are formed by crisscrossing streets. This is still definitely one of the earliest examples anywhere of regular city planning. Further evidence of such advanced planning and construction is seen in the city's sanitation system. Q03 Within most of the city's houses, archaeologists found clay pipes connecting a bathroom drain to a main pipe, and residents were even able to dispose of waste through holes cut in their walls.

Furthermore, throughout all this, one can see a definite social organization in Mohenjo-Daro. There are numerous buildings that serve specific purposes. There's a central fortified area that was used for all religious and political purposes, and there's a city granary that's positioned and designed to conveniently store crops brought in from surrounding rural areas to feed the city's population. The presence of a few larger houses with courtyards shows that there were different classes in the city, due to the mixture of trade and agriculture. Q05 So, from determining the nature of all these buildings, we get a sense of the social and economic life of the people and their culture.

Now there were also many interesting artifacts uncovered here. I know that someone can give me some more information.

Student 2 (F): I think there was a famous statue of a dancing girl from Mohenjo-Daro, right?

Professor: Ah, well, that is one of the most famous relics excavated there. I think it is more stylistically interesting and mysterious than anything else, as the statue of the girl has a commanding and somewhat haughty pose. It does raise some interesting questions about women's social status then, so hold that thought for a few minutes.

고고학 수업 중 토론의 일부를 들으시오.

교수 (여): 안녕하세요. 오늘은 4천 년에서 5천 년 전에 인더스 강 계곡에 세워진 고대 도시인 모헨조다로에 대해 논의해 볼게요. 모헨조다로는 1920년대에 처음 발굴되었고, 그곳에서 발견된 것들로 인해 한때 지금의 파키스탄과 인도 북서부에 살았던 고대 문명에 대한 새로운 정보를 주는 데 도움이 되었어요. 음, 누가 그런 발견물을 말해보겠어요?

학생 1 (남): 그게, 제가 들은 바로는 많은 연구자들이 도시의 격자 모양 설계와 위생 시설에 큰 인상을 받았다던데요.

교수: 맞아요, 그 두 가지는 가장 인상적인 특징으로, 도시 계획, 건축, 공학에 관한 뛰어난 지식을 보여주고 있어요. 그 도시는 열 십자 모양의 도로로 형성된 직사각형 구역으로 나뉘어 있어요. 여전히 이것은 분명 정규 도시 계획의 가장 초기의 예에 속한다고 할 수 있죠. 그런 발전된 도시 계획과 건설에 대한 더 많은 증거는 그 도시의 위생 시설에서 볼 수 있어요. 도시 내 대부분 주택에서 고고학자들은 욕실 배수로와 본관을 연결하는 흙으로 만든 관을 발견했고, 거주자들은 심지어 벽에 뚫려 있는 구멍을 통해 폐수를 버릴 수도 있습니다.

더 나아가, 이 모든 것을 통해 모헨조다로의 명확한 사회 조직을 알 수 있어요. 이곳에는 특정 목적으로 쓰인 수많은 건물들이 있습니다. 중앙 요새로 만들어진 곳은 모든 종교적, 정치적 용도로 사용되었고, 곡물 창고는 주변 지방으로부터 도시 사람들에게 공급하기 위해 가져온 작물들을 편리하게 저장할 수 있도록 배치되고 설계되었어요. 안뜰이 있는 몇몇 대저택의 존재는 상업과 농업의 혼재로 인해 도시에 여러 계층이 있었다는 것을 보여줍니다. 그래서 이 모든 건물의 특성을 파악해보면, 사람들의 사회적, 경제적 생활 및 그들의 문화를 알 수 있습니다.

그런데 이곳에서는 흥미로운 유물도 많이 발견되었어요. 여러분 중 누군가 더 많은 정보를 줄 수 있을 것 같은데요.

학생 2 (여): 모헨조다로의 유명한 춤추는 소녀상이 있었죠, 맞나요?

교수: 아, 음, 거기서 발굴된 가장 유명한 유물 중 하나지요. 사실 저는 그 소녀상이 당당하고 다소 거만한 자세를 취하고 있다는 점에서 다른 어떤 것보다 양식 면에서 더 흥미롭고 신비하다고 생각합니다. 이 상은 당시 여성의 사회적 지위에 대해 몇몇 흥미로운 문제들을 제기하고 있어요. 그러니 이것에 대해 잠시 후에 더 알아보도록 하죠.

Now, another group of artifacts that I think are very interesting are the stone seals that were found. These are square pendants with inscriptions and, usually, pictures of different animals. They were mainly used for trading and administrative purposes, as they marked who owned what goods and how much they owned. **Q04** These give us an idea of how the cities in the region traded with one another. Also, they can help us learn about how these people traded with other cultures, including ones as distant as Mesopotamia.

자, 개인적으로 매우 흥미롭다고 생각하는 또 다른 유물의 집단은 돌 도장입니다. 이것은 사각형 모양의 펜던트로, 새겨진 글과 보통 여러 동물 그림이 있어요. 이것은 주로 상업적 또는 행정적 목적으로 사용되었는데, 이 돌 도장에 누가 어떤 물건을 얼마나 소유하고 있는지 표시되어 있었기 때문이죠. 이것들은 그 지역 도시들이 서로 어떻게 거래했는지도 알려줍니다. 또한, 이 사람들이 메소포타미아만큼이나 먼 곳을 포함해, 다른 문화권과 어떻게 거래했는지도 알 수 있게 해주죠.

01 화자들이 논의하는 주된 내용은?
(A) 어떻게 모헨조다로가 1902년대에 처음 발굴되었는지
(B) 모헨조다로는 인더스 문명에 대해 무엇을 알려주는지
(C) 모헨조다로에서 발견된 유물들의 예술적 가치
(D) 모헨조다로 사회의 기술 발전

해설 | Main Idea 교수는 모헨조다로에서 발굴된 유적과 유물들을 소개하고 이를 통해 인더스 문명을 살펴보고 있다.

02 교수가 도시의 격자 모양 설계에 대해 암시하는 것은?
(A) 더 이상 도시 계획의 방식으로 사용되지 않는다.
(B) 도시의 위생 시설을 구축하는 것을 더 쉽게 만들었다.
(C) 주로 종교적이고 정치적인 목적으로 발명되었다.
(D) 일반적으로 정규 도시 계획에 사용됐다.

해설 | Inference 강의에서 교수는 격자 모양 설계는 여전히 분명 정규 도시 계획의 가장 초기의 예에 속한다고 말하며, 이것이 일반적으로 정규 도시 계획에 사용됐다는 것을 암시한다.

03 모헨조다로 주택들의 흥미로운 특징은?
(A) 도시의 곡물 창고와 연결되어 있었다.
(B) 모두 커다란 안뜰과 정원이 있었다.
(C) 장식을 위해 조각상을 갖는 경향이 있었다.
(D) 욕실에 폐수 처리를 위한 관이 있었다.

해설 | Detail 교수는 모헨조다로의 주택 대부분이 욕실 배수로와 벽의 구멍을 통해 폐수를 처리하게 되어 있었다고 설명하고 있다.

04 모헨조다로의 돌 도장으로 알 수 있는 것은?
(A) 그 사회가 어떻게 상업 활동을 행했는지
(B) 어떻게 그 사회에 상류층과 하류층이 존재했는지
(C) 도장에 새겨진 각 동물이 무엇을 의미했는지
(D) 어떻게 조각 기술이 발달했는지

해설 | Detail 돌 도장은 누가 어떤 상품을 얼마만큼 소유하고 있는지를 보여줌으로써 그 지역 도시들 또는 다른 문화권들과의 거래가 어떻게 이뤄졌는지를 알려준다.

05 강의의 일부를 다시 듣고 질문에 답하시오.
교수가 다음과 같이 말하는 이유는?
"I know that someone can give me some more information."
(A) 학생들이 이 주제에 대해 연구해보도록 하기 위해
(B) 학생들로부터 대답을 끌어내기 위해
(C) 학생들의 소극성에 대한 실망감을 나타내기 위해
(D) 현재 부족한 정보를 얻기 위해

해설 | Function 교수 자신이 답을 제시하지 않고 "I know that someone can give me some more information"이라고 말한 것은 학생들에게 그 답을 끌어내기 위함이다.

어휘 | **shed light on** 새로운 정보를 주다, 밝히다　**inhabit** 살다, 거주하다　**gridded** 격자 모양의　**sanitation** 위생, 위생 설비　**crisscrossing** 십자인, 교차하는　**drain** 배수로(관), 하수구　**dispose of** 버리다, 치우다　**fortified** 요새로 만들어진　**granary** 곡물 창고　**feed** 공급하다, 먹이다　**courtyard** 안뜰, 마당　**artifact** (인공) 유물　**relic** 유물　**stylistically** 양식(문체)상　**commanding** 당당한, 명령조인　**haughty** 거만한　**seal** 도장　**inscription** (책·금석에) 새겨진 글, 새기기　**distant** (거리가) 먼

Intensive Drill 2
p.144

01 (A)　　02 (C)　　03 (B)　　04 (A), (D), (E)　　05 (E) – (A) – (C) – (B)

Listen to part of a lecture in an anthropology class.

Professor (M): Q02 Q03 All of you probably already know that the Maya empire is considered by many to have been a highly sophisticated civilization for its time. Study of its architecture and artifacts has shown signs of decidedly progressive thinking and technology. From the meticulously designed temples and pyramids to their intricate understanding of astronomy, and from developing the world's first written language to the creation of a calendar system, the Maya were able to thrive not only in a time period that did not have modern machinery, but also in a geographical location and climate that traditionally was not conducive to inhabitation during ancient times.

Q01 So what happened to this Maya civilization that was so advanced for its time? The decline of the Maya empire has been the topic of research and discussion for decades among researchers, archaeologists, and historians. Many theories have been formulated as to the reason that the Maya seemed to have suddenly abandoned their marvelous cities. Most theories are realistic; Q04(E) that they fell victim to foreign invasion, Q04(A) that they overhunted the animals in their habitat and thus had to move on for continued sustenance, that there was a revolt by the peasants from within their social system. However, there are occasional theories that seem to have come straight out of a science fiction story. One such theory is that they were overrun by an alien invasion, and another that the Maya were aliens themselves who had secretly come to study the Earth, as depicted in the last Indiana Jones movie.

Q04(D) Evidence from more recent studies lends credence to a new kind of theory, one that suggests the Maya decline had something to do with an extended drought and persistent deforestation. One of the unique aspects of Maya civilization was that it was able to establish itself and thrive in a tropical area, right in the middle of a rainforest, when other civilizations in that time period mostly settled in drier areas. Ironically, researchers now think that this was a big reason for their undoing. Q05(E) In order to clear land for cultivating crops as well as to use wood for fuel, the Maya consistently chopped down trees in the forest that surrounded them. Unfortunately, a prolonged drought befell the area and began to affect their water supply, and the continued deforestation only added to the lack of rainfall. Q05(A), (C) Scientists have run experiments that simulated this situation and were able to surmise that fewer trees would have resulted in less evaporation of water, thus causing the creation of fewer rainclouds and, consequently, less rainfall. Q05(B) Of course, this can only lead to the failing of crops and depletion of food supplies. The only choice they would have had would have been to pick up everything and search for a friendlier environment. In this way, a reshaping of the natural environment resulted in unintended, and perhaps catastrophic, consequences.

인류학 강의 중 일부를 들으시오.

교수 (남): 아마 여러분 모두 많은 사람들에게 마야 제국이 당시 고도로 발달한 문명이었다고 여겨진다는 것을 알 거예요. 마야 제국의 건축과 인공 유물에 대한 연구는 확실히 혁신적인 사고와 기술에 대한 흔적을 보여줬어요. 꼼꼼하게 설계된 사찰과 피라미드부터 천문학에 대한 복잡한 이해까지, 그리고 세계 최초의 문자 언어를 발달시킨 것부터 달력 시스템을 만든 것까지, 마야인들은 현대적 기계가 없던 시기에서뿐만 아니라, 고대에는 생활에 도움이 되지 않았던 지리학적인 위치와 기후에서조차 번성할 수 있었던 거죠.

그럼 당시 매우 발달하였던 이 마야 문명에 어떤 일이 벌어졌던 걸까요? 마야 제국의 몰락은 수십 년 동안 연구원, 고고학자, 역사학자 사이에서 연구와 토론의 주제가 되어 왔어요. 마야인들이 그 놀라운 도시를 갑자기 떠나버린 것처럼 보였던 이유에 대해 많은 이론들이 만들어졌어요. 대부분의 이론은 현실적이에요. 외세 침략의 피해자가 되었다든지, 그 지역의 동물들을 너무 많이 사냥해서 생계를 지속하기 위해 이동해야 했다든지, 사회 제도 내에서 소작농들의 반란이 있었다든지 하는 이론들이요. 하지만 가끔 공상 과학 소설에서 나온 것처럼 보이는 이론들도 있죠. 그런 이론의 하나는 외계인의 침공을 당했다는 것이고, 또 다른 이론은 마야인들 스스로가 예전 인디애나 존스 영화에서 묘사된 것처럼 지구를 연구하기 위해 비밀리에 온 외계인들이었다는 것이에요.

최근 연구들에 의한 증거는 새로운 이론에 신빙성을 부여하는데, 한 이론은 마야 몰락이 지속된 가뭄과 삼림 파괴와 관련이 있다고 주장해요. 마야 문명의 독특한 면 중 하나는 바로 열대우림 한가운데의 열대 지방에 문명을 세우고 번성할 수 있었다는 거예요. 그 시기의 다른 문명들은 대부분 더 건조한 지역에 정착했었거든요. 아이러니하게도, 현재는 연구원들이 그것을 실패의 큰 원인으로 생각하기도 해요. 연료로 나무를 사용하기 위해서 뿐만 아니라 곡식을 경작하기 위한 땅을 개간하기 위해, 마야인들은 계속해서 그들을 둘러싼 숲의 나무들을 잘라냈어요. 불행하게도, 장기적인 가뭄이 그 지역에 발생했고 물 공급에 영향을 미치기 시작했어요. 그리고 지속된 삼림 파괴는 강우량 부족으로 이어졌죠. 과학자들은 이 상황을 모의 실험하였고, 줄어든 나무가 수분 증발량을 줄어들게 하였고, 이는 결국 비구름이 감소하여 더 적은 강우량으로 이어졌다는 추측을 할 수 있었죠. 물론, 이는 흉작과 식량 공급량 감소로 이어질 수 있죠. 그들이 유일하게 선택할 수 있었던 것은 모든 짐을 싸서 더 도움이 되는 환경을 찾아가는 것이었을 거예요. 이렇게 해서, 자연 환경을 개조하는 것은 의도치 않은, 그리고 아마도 비극적이기까지 한 결과를 낳았어요.

01 강의의 주된 목적은?
(A) 마야 문명 몰락에 관한 가능성 있는 이론에 대해 논의하기 위해
(B) 마야인들의 기술적 성과와 건축적 성과를 개략적으로 설명하기 위해
(C) 마야인들이 그들의 도시를 떠나지 않았다는 것을 증명하기 위해
(D) 삼림 파괴가 어떻게 장기간 가뭄으로 이어질 수 있는지 보여주기 위해

해설 | Main Idea 교수는 "So what happened to this Maya civilization that was so advanced for its time?"이라고 말하며 마야 문명 몰락의 원인에 대한 여러 가지 이론에 대해 논의한다.

02 교수가 마야 제국에 대한 설명을 도입하는 방식은?
(A) 그 시기의 다른 문명 중 하나와 비교함으로써
(B) 지난 강의에서 그가 논의한 내용을 학생들에게 상기시켜줌으로써
(C) 다양한 방면에서의 우월성을 보여주는 예들을 제공함으로써
(D) 알맞은 주변 환경으로 인한 발달을 강조함으로써

해설 | Organization 교수는 강의 초반에 마야 제국의 건축, 인공 유물, 문자, 달력 시스템 등에 대해 얘기하면서, 다양한 방면에서 우월했다는 점을 보여주며 마야 제국에 대한 설명을 시작한다.

03 마야인들의 다양한 업적에 대한 교수의 의견은?
(A) 역사에서 마야인들의 업적과 상대가 될 수 있는 문명은 없다.
(B) 그들의 업적은 놀랍고 의미 있다.
(C) 발명품들에 대해 독점적으로 공적을 인정받아서는 안 된다.
(D) 마야인들의 업적은 다른 지역 사람들로부터 도움을 받은 결과이다.

해설 | Attitude 교수는 강의 초반에 마야 제국의 다양한 업적에 대해 설명하며, 마야인들은 현대적 기계가 없던 시기뿐만 아니라 도움이 되지 않았던 지리학적인 위치와 기후에서조차 번성하였다고 말한다. 즉 그들의 업적은 놀랍고 의미 있다는 의견을 내비친다.

04 강의에 따르면, 마야 제국의 몰락을 설명하는 이론들은?
3개의 답을 고르시오.
(A) 마야인들은 식량 부족으로 거주지를 떠나야만 했다.
(B) 내전이 군대를 약화시켰고 마야인들의 사회적 질서를 통제할 수 없도록 만들었다.
(C) 마야인들이 정착했던 지역은 너무 열대 지방이었다.
(D) 장기간의 가뭄은 계속된 벌목으로 인해 악화되었다.
(E) 다른 지역 집단이 침략했고 마야인들을 장악했다.

해설 | Detail 교수가 강의에서 언급한 마야 몰락의 이론들에 의하면, (A) 사냥을 너무 많이 해서 식량이 부족하게 되어 다른 지역으로 이동해야 했다는 이론, (D) 계속된 벌목으로 인해 가뭄이 심해져서 흉작이나 식량 부족으로 다른 지역으로 이동해야 했다는 이론, (E) 외세 침략으로 인해 몰락했다는 이론 등이 있다.

05 교수는 마야 몰락에 대한 최근 이론의 과정에 대한 단계들을 설명한다. 이 단계들을 올바른 순서대로 나열하시오.
각 문장을 해당되는 곳으로 옮기시오.
선택지 중 하나는 사용되지 않는다.

1	(E) 계속된 벌목
2	(A) 비구름 형성을 위한 수분 증발량 감소
3	(C) 강우량 부족
4	(B) 식량 부족

(D) 다른 지역 사람들로부터의 침략

해설 | Connecting Content 강의에 의하면, 마야인들은 연료 및 개간을 위해 계속해서 벌목을 진행하였고, 이로 인해 수분 증발량이 줄어들어 비구름이 감소하였다. 그 결과로 강우량이 줄어들었고 이는 흉작과 식량 공급량 감소로 이어졌다.

어휘 | **Maya empire** 마야 제국 **sophisticated** 발달한, 세련된 **artifact** 인공 유물, 공예품 **decidedly** 확실히, 분명히 **progressive** 혁신적인, 진보적인 **meticulously** 꼼꼼히, 세밀하게 **intricate** 복잡한 **conducive to** ~에 도움이 되는 **decline** 몰락, 감소 **abandon** 떠나다, 버리다 **invasion** 침략, 침공 **sustenance** 생계, 생명을 유지하는 것 **peasant** 소작농 **credence** 신빙성 **persistent** 지속성의, 끊임없는 **deforestation** 삼림 파괴, 삼림 벌채 **tropical** 열대 지방의 **rainforest** 열대우림 **undoing** 실패의 원인 **prolonged** 장기적인, 오래 계속되는 **surmise** 추측하다, 추정하다 **depletion** 감소, 고갈, 소모 **catastrophic** 비극적인

Intensive Drill 3

p.146

01 (B)   02 (B)   03 [Included – (C), (D)], [Not Included – (A), (B)]   04 (A)   05 (B), (D)

Listen to part of a discussion in an archaeology class.

Professor (F): Understanding the development of a writing system can provide a sound guide to the growth of the civilization. Likewise, the study of ancient Egyptian writings is just as vital, if not more, as solving the mystery of the Pyramids in Egyptology. Q01 So, today, we'll have an overview of ancient Egyptian writing and examine how its evolution shows transitions in the ancient civilization. By the way, someone mentioned about a translation website of ancient Egyptian language . . . Ted, was that you?

Student 1 (M): Um, actually, it's a mobile app being developed by the company I worked for last summer. They say that this app can translate the hieroglyphic language written or carved in the ancient sites into several modern languages.

Professor: Hmm . . . you know, if they use the term hieroglyphic language, I'd suggest they verify their scholastic sources before going public. In fact, that is one of the surprisingly widespread inaccuracies when referring to the ancient Egyptian language. Hieroglyphs are not a language, but one of four different scripts or writings of the ancient Egyptian language.

Student 1: Q03(A) Uh . . . aren't hieroglyphs at least the principal script used by the ancient Egyptians, though?

Professor: Well, you need to remember that ancient Egyptian writing evolved in four successive stages. Hieroglyphs were the first, and therefore were the oldest scripts developed by the Egyptians to write their language. Q03(B) Although these pictorial scripts were used for all purposes of communication, they were mostly inscribed on the walls of sacred places like temples or tombs.

As the society became more complex, there was also the increasing need for documentation, especially for administrative purposes. This led to the development of more simplified and cursive writing, known as hieratic. Q03(C) Then, by around 650 BCE, hieratic script was replaced by demotic, which is much more cursive and simplified. Well, it had to be so to suit the growing complexity and diversity of social affairs and for everyday use.

Student 1: Professor Warren, aren't both hieratic and demotic scripts just simpler forms of hieroglyphs? They seem to be pretty much the same symbolic writing system with slightly different appearances.

Professor: Q02 Actually, many Egyptologists put them into the same category of hieroglyphs. However, if you consider how these scripts evolved in each stage along with respective social changes, I believe each of them deserves its own status.

Student 2 (F): Q03(D) Um, this may be off track, but didn't the Egyptians also use a modified Greek alphabet for a long time?

고고학 수업 중 토론의 일부를 들으시오.

교수 (여): 문자 체계의 발달을 이해하는 것은 그 문명의 성장을 이해하는 데 믿을 만한 도움을 줄 수 있어요. 마찬가지로, 고대 이집트 문자를 연구하는 것은 더는 아니더라도 이집트학 피라미드의 미스터리를 푸는 것만큼이나 중요합니다. 자, 오늘 우리는 고대 이집트 문자에 대해 간략히 얘기하고, 이것의 진화가 고대 문명의 변천을 어떻게 보여주는지 살펴볼 거예요. 그런데, 누군가 고대 이집트 언어의 번역 웹사이트에 대해 말했었는데… Ted였나요?

학생 1 (남): 음, 사실, 그건 제가 지난 여름에 일했던 회사에서 개발하고 있는 모바일 어플리케이션이에요. 그들이 말하길, 이 어플리케이션은 고대 유적지에 쓰여 있거나 새겨진 상형 문자를 여러 가지 현대 언어로 번역해줄 수 있다고 해요.

교수: 흠… 있잖아요, 상형 문자라는 용어를 사용한다면, 그것을 대중화시키기 전에 학문적인 자료를 먼저 확인하는 것이 좋겠어요. 사실, 그게 바로 고대 이집트 언어를 나타낼 때 발생하는 놀라울 정도로 널리 퍼진 오류 중 하나예요. 상형 문자는 언어가 아니라, 고대 이집트 언어의 네 가지 문자 중 하나예요.

학생 1: 아… 그래도 최소한 상형 문자는 고대 이집트인들이 사용한 주요 문자가 아닌가요?

교수: 음, 고대 이집트 문자는 네 가지 연속적인 단계로 진화했다는 것을 기억해야 해요. 상형 문자가 첫 단계라서 이집트인들이 그들의 언어를 쓰기 위해 발달시켰던 가장 오래된 문자인 거죠. 그림을 이용한 이 문자들이 소통을 위한 모든 목적으로 사용되었지만, 주로 사원이나 묘비와 같은 신성한 장소의 벽에 새겨졌어요.

사회가 좀 더 복잡해지면서, 특히 행정상의 목적으로 기록의 필요성이 커졌어요. 이는 신관 문자라고 알려진 좀 더 간단하고 흘려 쓴 듯한 문자로의 발전으로 이어졌어요. 그러고 나서, 기원전 650년쯤에는 신관 문자가 민용 문자로 대체되었는데, 이는 훨씬 더 흘려 쓴 듯하고 간단한 문자예요. 음, 사회적 문제의 복잡성 및 다양성과 일상적인 사용에 부합하기 위해 그렇게 돼야 했었죠.

학생 1: Warren 교수님, 신관 문자와 민용 문자 모두 단지 상형 문자가 더 간단해진 형태 아닌가요? 모양만 살짝 다르고, 매우 똑같이 기호를 쓰는 문자 체계 같이 보이는데요.

교수: 사실, 많은 이집트학자들은 그 문자들을 상형 문자와 같은 범주로 보긴 하죠. 하지만 이 문자들이 각각 다른 사회적 변화에 따라 어떻게 한 단계씩 진화했는지 생각해보면, 각 문자 체계는 각자 고유의 중요성을 가질 만하다고 생각해요.

학생 2 (여): 음, 벗어난 얘기일 수도 있는데요, 이집트인들이 오랫동안 수정된 그리스 문자도 사용하지 않았나요?

Professor: Q04 Yes, and that is Coptic, which developed after Alexander the Great invaded Egypt in 332 BCE and imposed the Greek alphabet on its people. Q05(B) As a consequence, Coptic holds a greater significance in the study of the Egyptian language because it is the first in Egyptian history to include written vowels. Q05(D) Also, with its simpler form, Coptic made written language more accessible to ancient Egyptians than it was before. Coptic is regarded as the final development in Egyptian writing, and it was used for over a thousand years.

교수: 맞아요, 그건 콥트어인데, Alexander 대왕이 기원전 332년에 이집트를 침략하고 이집트인들에게 그리스 문자를 도입하게 한 이후에 발달된 문자예요. 그 결과, 콥트어는 이집트 언어 연구에서 상당히 중요해졌어요. 왜냐하면, 이것이 이집트 역사에서 최초로 모음을 포함했기 때문이죠. 또한 콥트어의 더 간단한 형태로 인해, 이집트인들이 사용하는 문자를 그 전보다 더 이용하기 쉽게 만들었어요. 콥트어는 이집트 문자 체계 중 가장 마지막으로 발달된 문자로 여겨지고 있고, 천 년 이상 사용되었어요.

---

01 토론의 주된 목적은?
(A) 두 고대 문화의 성장과 변화를 비교하기 위해
(B) 고대 문자의 발달에 대해 학습하기 위해
(C) 고대 이집트 문자의 다양한 목적을 조사하기 위해
(D) 고대 기호와 문자의 차이점을 설명하기 위해

해설 | Main Idea 교수가 강의 초반에 "So, today, we'll have an overview of ancient Egyptian writing and examine how its evolution shows transitions in the ancient civilization"이라고 말한 것으로 보아 고대 문자의 발달에 대한 강의를 진행할 것임을 알 수 있다.

02 신관 문자와 민용 문자에 대한 교수의 태도는?
(A) 상형 문자의 또 다른 형태라고 생각한다.
(B) 각각의 문자가 서로 다른 범주로 여겨져야 한다고 생각한다.
(C) 그 문자들을 기호 문자로 취급하기를 꺼린다.
(D) 그 문자들에 대한 관심이 부족한 것을 유감스럽게 생각한다.

해설 | Attitude 교수는 신관 문자와 민용 문자가 진화한 방식을 생각해보면, 각 문자 체계는 각자 고유의 중요성을 가질 만하다고 말한다. 즉 교수는 각각의 문자가 서로 다른 범주로 여겨져야 한다고 생각한다.

03 토론에서 학생들과 교수는 다양한 고대 이집트 문자 체계에 대해 이야기한다. 다음 각 사항이 설명하는 내용에 포함되는지 표시하시오.
각 사항에 대해 알맞은 항목에 표시하시오.

	포함	미포함
(A) 상형 문자는 고대 이집트의 가장 오래된 주요 문자 체계이다.		✔
(B) 신관 문자는 주로 사원과 묘비에서 신성한 문자로 사용되었다.		✔
(C) 민용 문자는 사람들의 일상사를 기록하기 위해 매우 흘려 쓴 듯한 문자이다.	✔	
(D) 고대 이집트인들은 수정된 그리스 문자를 사용해야만 했다.	✔	

해설 | Connecting Content 상형 문자가 가장 오래된 문자 체계인 것은 맞지만, 주요 문자 체계는 아니었으며, 사원과 묘비에서 신성한 문자로 사용된 것은 신관 문자가 아니라 상형 문자였다. 또한, 민용 문자는 상형 문자보다 훨씬 더 흘려 쓴 듯한 형태의 문자이며, 사회적 문제의 복잡성 및 다양성과 일상적인 사용에 부합했던 문자였으며, 고대 이집트인들은 Alexander 대왕에 의해 수정된 그리스 문자를 사용해야만 했다. 즉, (A)와 (B)는 교수의 강의 내용과 어긋나고, (C)와 (D)는 교수의 강의 내용에 포함된다.

04 교수가 Alexander 대왕을 언급하는 이유는?
(A) 그리스 문화가 고대 이집트에 끼친 영향에 대해 언급하기 위해
(B) 고대 이집트 언어의 정치적 중요성에 대해 설명하기 위해
(C) 그의 통치 기간에 이뤄진 그리스 문자의 발달에 대해 묘사하기 위해
(D) 그가 콥트어의 일반적인 사용을 어떻게 조장했는지 나타내기 위해

해설 | Organization 교수는 이집트인들이 수정된 그리스 문자인 콥트어를 사용하게 된 배경을 설명하기 위해, 그리스의 Alexander 대왕이 이집트를 침략하고 이집트인들이 콥트어를 사용하도록 만들었음을 설명한다.

05 교수에 따르면, 콥트어의 중요한 측면은?
2개의 답을 고르시오.
(A) 이집트 언어의 주요 문자 체계가 되었다.
(B) 이집트 역사 최초로 모음을 사용하였다.
(C) 그리스의 점령하에서도 수년 동안 살아남았다.
(D) 문자가 좀 더 대중적으로 사용될 수 있도록 만들었다.

해설 | Detail 교수는 콥트어가 이집트 문자 연구에서 상당히 중요해졌다고 말하며, 그 이유는 최초로 모음을 포함했기 때문이라고 한다. 또한, 콥트어의 형태가 더 간단해짐으로써 이집트인들이 그 전보다 더 사용하기 쉬워졌다고 한다.

어휘 | **Egyptology** 이집트학 **app(application)** 어플리케이션 **hieroglyphic** 상형 문자의 **scholastic** 학술적인 **hieroglyph** 상형 문자 **successive** 연속적인, 연이은 **pictorial** 그림을 이용한 **sacred** 신성한 **administrative** 행정상의, 관리상의 **cursive** 흘려 쓴, 필기체의 **hieratic** 신관 문자(의), 성직자의 **demotic** 민용 문자(의), 일반 대중의 **Coptic** 콥트어, 콥트 말 **invade** 침략하다, 침입하다 **impose** 도입하다, 시행하다 **vowel** 모음 **accessible** 이용 가능한, 접근 가능한

Mini Test 1   p.148

| 01 (B) | 02 (C), (D) | 03 (A) | 04 (C) | 05 (D) |

Listen to part of a discussion in a psychology class.

Professor (M): Q01-1 Today we are going to be looking at the issue of conformity, and specifically we will be discussing some of the sociologists and psychologists who did pioneering work on the subject. First, however, let's define exactly what we mean by conformity. Q05 So, in a sociological or psychological context, what do we mean by conformity?

Student 1 (M): That's easy. Q01-2 Q02(C) Conformity is when a person changes his opinions or actions so that they match those of a larger group.

Professor: Is everyone satisfied with that definition? *[Jokingly]* Are we all going to conform to it?

Student 2 (F): Actually, I think that definition needs to be refined a little bit.

Professor: How so, Stacy?

Student 2: Well, sometimes people change their beliefs or actions because of some kind of direct threat. Like if you told me to give you my purse or you would punch me in the nose, and I gave you my purse to avoid being punched, that wouldn't seem like an example of conformity. Q02(D) To me, conformity is the willingness to change one's attitudes or actions even when there is no direct threat. You, uh, do it not to avoid punishment, but just to be part of the group . . . to, uh, fit in.

Student 1: I think Stacy is right. That's a better definition.

Professor: Alright. So, now we have a general definition of conformity. Let's look at some studies on the issue. We'll start with the earliest and move on to more recent ones.

One of the earliest studies was conducted by Muzafer Sherif, a Turkish researcher. Sherif was interested in social psychology . . . he, uh, was actually one of the pioneers of the field. Anyway, he wanted to look at the issue of conformity and to know if it was a truly universal . . . uh, if it was inherent to our nature. So he put a group of people into a darkened room and asked them to look at a white dot on the wall for a while. Then he asked them to estimate how much the dot had moved during that time.

Now here's the thing. The dot hadn't moved at all, but the muscles of our eyes make hundreds of involuntary, tiny movements every minute. And these create the illusion of movement. Anyway, when the subjects were asked to estimate how much the dot had moved, they came up with very different estimates, because the illusion is slightly different for each person.

Q03 The interesting part is what happened when the experiment was repeated over a number of times. The estimates of each individual in the group gradually converged on a single agreed-upon number. The more times the experiment was repeated, the more closely the estimates of the individual subjects matched. **Q04** Now, here's the part that just really blows my mind whenever I think about it. This happened without any discussion between the individuals in the group. Over time, they just naturally adjusted their opinions to form a consensus. Pretty interesting, huh?

흥미로운 점은 실험이 여러 번 반복되었을 때 일어난 현상이에요. 집단에 있던 각 개인의 추정치가 점점 일치된 단일 숫자로 모였다는 점입니다. 실험이 계속 반복될수록, 실험 대상자 개개인의 측정치는 더욱 더 가까워졌어요. 자, 생각할 때마다 저를 놀라게 한 부분은 바로 이거에요. 이 현상이 그 집단의 개개인간에 아무런 논의도 없이 일어났다는 점이죠. 점차, 그들은 자연스럽게 자신의 의견을 조정해 의견의 일치를 형성했습니다. 꽤 흥미롭지 않나요?

01 화자들이 논의하는 주된 내용은?
(A) 집단에서 의견의 불일치를 해결하는 방법
(B) 사람들이 다수의 의견을 따르는 경향
(C) 사람들이 권위자에게 복종하는 경향
(D) 개인에 따라 환영을 다르게 인식하는 이유

해설 | Main Idea 교수는 더 큰 집단의 의견에 따라 자신의 의견을 조정해가는 동조(conformity)에 관한 실험 내용에 대해 이야기하고 있다.

02 토론에 따르면, 동조의 기본 요소들은?
2개의 답을 고르시오.
(A) 대규모 집단에서만 일어난다.
(B) 인식의 차이를 해결하는 방법이다.
(C) 의견이나 행동의 변경을 수반한다.
(D) 물리적 위험이 없는 상황에서 수행된다.

해설 | Detail 강의 초반에 제시된 동조의 정의에 대한 두 학생의 대답을 통해, 동조는 집단의 의견에 따라 자신의 의견이나 행동을 바꾸는 것을 의미하며, 이때 직접적인 물리적 위험이 없어야 한다는 것을 알 수 있다.

03 Muzafer Sherif의 실험 결과에 대해 추론할 수 있는 것은?
(A) 사람들은 집단에서 전반적인 합의에 이르도록 동조하는 경향이 있다.
(B) 동조는 사회적 집단이 오랜 기간 존재할 때만 발생한다.
(C) 사람들은 자신의 의견에 대해 믿을 만한 증거가 없을 때 동조를 선택한다.
(D) 동조는 그 집단의 의견을 이끄는 지도자에게 달려 있다.

해설 | Inference Muzafer Sherif는 동조가 보편적인 문제인지, 우리 본성의 고유한 것인지에 대해서 알아보기 위해 실험을 진행하였고, 그 결과 집단에 있던 각 개인의 의견이 처음에는 매우 달랐지만, 실험이 반복될수록 개인의 의견이 서로 비슷해졌다고 설명한다. 즉 이 실험을 통해 사람들은 집단에서조차 전반적인 합의에 이르도록 동조하는 경향이 있다는 것을 추론할 수 있다.

04 Sherif의 실험에 대해 교수가 흥미롭게 생각하는 점은?
(A) 사람들이 집단에 동조하기 위해 자신의 인식은 무시한 것
(B) 사람들이 명백한 위험이 없을 때도 일치를 형성하는 경향을 보인 것
(C) 사람들이 집단 간의 논의가 없었는데도 일치를 끌어내기 위해 동조한 것
(D) 사람들이 자신의 의견을 즉시 바꾸지 않고 오랜 시간에 걸쳐 천천히 바꾼 것

해설 | Detail 강의 마지막 부분에서 교수는 실험 대상자들이 어떠한 논의도 없이 의견의 일치를 위해 자신의 의견을 조정한 것에 대해 놀라워하고 있다.

05 강의의 일부를 다시 듣고 질문에 답하시오.
교수가 다음과 같이 말하는 이유는?
"Are we all going to conform to it?"
(A) 학생의 정의가 용인되지 않음을 암시하기 위해
(B) 가벼운 비평을 통해 학생이 내린 정의를 정정하기 위해
(C) 그 정의가 좋다는 것을 암시하기 위해
(D) 가벼운 농담을 통해 다른 의견을 찾아보기 위해

해설 | Function 교수는 질문에 강의 주제인 conformity라는 단어를 사용해 학생들에게 가벼운 농담을 던지며 다른 의견을 찾아보려고 하고 있다.

어휘 | **conformity** [심리] 동조 **pioneering** 선구적인 **subject** 실험 대상(자) **refine** 다듬다, 개선하다 **fit in** 어울리다, 조화하다 **inherent** 고유의, 타고난 **estimate** 추정(치) **converge** (공통의 결과에) 모이다 **blow one's mind** 놀라게 하다 **consensus** (의견 등의) 일치

Mini Test 2

p.150

01 (A)　　02 (A), (C)　　03 (D)　　04 (C)　　05 (B)

Listen to part of a lecture in an economics class.

Professor (F): Over the next few weeks we are going to be talking about the Bretton Woods Agreement. Uh, for those of you who don't know what this is, it is basically the agreement reached at the end of World War II that set up our modern financial system. **Q02** Many of the components of our system of international finance arose directly out of this agreement, including the formation of the International Monetary Fund, better known as the IMF, and the International Bank for Reconstruction and Development, part of today's World Bank, and most importantly, the proposed introduction of an adjustable pegged foreign exchange rate system. All of these were the major outcomes of the Bretton Woods Conference. Now, in later classes we will be talking in detail about the specific structure of the agreement and what it meant for the world economic system. **Q01** For today, however, we're going to focus on background information, uh, that is, what exactly the Bretton Woods Agreement was supposed to fix.

The motivations for the Bretton Woods Conference can be broken down into two broad areas. The first was a desire to never repeat the economic chaos that had followed the stock market crash of 1929 and the onset of the Great Depression. The second was to create a system that would facilitate the rebuilding of Europe's shattered economies after World War II.

Alright, so let's look at these two individually. The stock market crash and the depression that followed it quickly spread from the U.S. to infect the economies of Europe as well. **Q03** Under the intense financial strains of the depression, each nation pursued its own selfish ends, without much regard for the welfare of other nations. Countries devalued their own currencies in order to pay back debts or trade deficits at lower rates. Not only did this cause havoc to international trade, it created a great deal of distrust between nations. Some countries refused to trade with others, for fear that they would simply devalue their currencies when payments became due. This resulted in the formation of trade blocs, or groups of countries that dealt in equivalent currencies and were willing to trade with one another. **Q04** The lack of truly free and open trade limited the possibilities for cash flow and foreign investment, and generally made it harder for the world to pull itself out of the economic crisis of the 1930s. The Bretton Woods Agreement was, in part, intended to put an end to such problems.

Another major reason for the Bretton Woods Conference was that World War II was about to end. **Q05** The economies of Europe had been shattered by five years of war, and were in dire need of rebuilding and reconstruction. The problem was who was going to pay for it. Well, the only nation in a position to do so was the United States, which had avoided much of the war's destruction. So in a sense, the Bretton Woods Conference was held to get the U.S. to agree to finance reconstruction after the war in exchange for a dominant position in the new world order.

경제학 강의 중 일부를 들으시오.

교수 (여): 다음 몇 주 동안, 브레턴우즈 협정에 대해 이야기하도록 하겠습니다. 어, 이것이 무엇인지 모르는 사람들을 위해 이야기하자면, 이것은 제2차 세계대전 말에 체결된 현대 금융 제도를 세운 협정입니다. IMF라고 더 잘 알려진 국제통화기금과 오늘날 세계은행의 일부인 국제부흥개발은행의 설립, 그리고 가장 중요한 조정 가능한 고정 환율 제도의 도입을 제안한 것을 포함해, 우리가 사용하고 있는 국제 금융 제도의 많은 부분이 이 협정에서 직접적으로 생겨났습니다. 이 모두가 브레턴우즈 회의의 주요 산물인 거죠. 자, 다음 수업 시간에 걸쳐, 이 협정의 구체적인 구조와 이것이 세계 경제 체제에서 무엇을 의미하는지에 대해 자세히 알아볼 것입니다. 하지만 오늘은 브레턴우즈의 배경, 즉, 바로 브레턴우즈 협정이 정확히 무엇을 해결하려 했는가에 초점을 맞추어 보기로 하죠.

브레턴우즈 회의의 동기가 된 것은 크게 두 가지 영역으로 나눌 수 있습니다. 첫 번째는 1929년 주식 시장 붕괴 및 대공황의 시작에 뒤이은 경제 혼란을 되풀이하지 않으려는 바람이었습니다. 두 번째는 제2차 세계대전 이후 산산이 부서진 유럽 경제의 재건을 촉진시키기 위한 제도를 만들려는 것이었죠.

좋아요. 이 두 가지를 하나씩 살펴보도록 하죠. 주식시장의 붕괴와 곧 뒤따른 공황은 미국으로부터 확산되어 유럽 경제에도 영향을 주었습니다. 공황으로 인한 극도의 금융 부담 아래, 각 나라는 다른 나라의 안녕은 고려하지 않은 채 자신들의 이기적인 목적만을 추구하였어요. 나라들은 더 낮은 환율로 빚을 갚고 무역 적자를 만회하기 위해 자국의 통화를 평가 절하했습니다. 이는 국제 무역에 대혼란을 초래하였을 뿐만 아니라, 나라들 간의 거대한 불신을 낳았죠. 어떤 나라들은 상환 기일이 되면 상대국이 통화를 평가 절하하는 것은 아닐까 하는 두려움에 다른 나라들과의 무역 자체를 거부하였습니다. 이 결과로 무역권, 즉 동등한 가치의 통화로만 거래하고 서로 무역을 하려 했던 국가들의 집단을 형성하게 되었습니다. 진정한 의미의 자유 개방 무역이 없어지면서 현금의 흐름과 해외 투자 가능성이 제한되고, 전반적으로 세계가 1930년대의 경제 위기를 탈피하기가 더욱 힘들어졌습니다. 브레턴우즈 협정은 이러한 문제점들을 부분적으로나마 종식시키고자 했던 것이었습니다.

브레턴우즈 회의의 또 다른 주요 요인은 제2차 세계대전이 종전을 눈앞에 두고 있었다는 점입니다. 유럽 경제는 5년간의 전쟁으로 산산이 부서져 있었고, 재건이 시급히 필요했죠. 문제는 그 비용을 누가 부담하느냐였습니다. 글쎄요, 그럴 수 있는 위치에 있었던 나라는 전쟁으로 인한 대규모 파괴를 면했던 미국밖에 없었어요. 그래서 어떤 면에서, 브레턴우즈 회의는 미국이 새로운 세계 질서의 지배적인 위치를 얻는 대가로 전후 경제 재건에 동의하도록 하기 위해 열렸다고 볼 수 있습니다.

01 강의의 주된 내용은?
(A) 브레턴우즈 협정이 해결하고자 했던 경제적 문제들
(B) 브레턴우즈 협정에서 만들어진 금융 제도의 구조
(C) 미국이 어떻게 1930년대 경제 위기를 해결할 수 있었는지
(D) 브레턴우즈 회의 개최에 IMF가 한 역할

해설 | Main Idea 브레턴우즈 협정의 형성 배경, 즉 그것이 당시 무엇을 해결하기 위해 체결되었는지에 대한 내용이다.

02 브레턴우즈 협정의 산물로 언급된 기관은?
2개의 답을 고르시오.
(A) IMF
(B) 주식 시장
(C) 세계은행
(D) APEC

해설 | Detail 교수는 오늘날 많은 국제 금융 제도들이 브레턴우즈 협정으로 생겨났다고 하면서, IMF, 세계은행, 외국환 제도를 그 예로 들고 있다.

03 1930년대 통화의 평가 절하를 일으킨 요인은?
(A) 1929년의 주식 시장 붕괴
(B) 제2차 세계대전의 발발
(C) 외국 투자를 위한 자본의 부족
(D) 각 국가의 이기적인 정책

해설 | Detail 교수는 주식 시장 붕괴와 대공황으로 인해 금융 부담을 안게 된 나라들이 결국 더 낮은 환율로 빚을 갚고 무역 적자를 만회하기 위해 자국의 통화를 평가 절하했으며, 이는 모두 자신들의 이기적인 목적에서 비롯된 결과라고 설명하고 있다.

04 1930년대 무역권의 성립으로 인한 궁극적인 결과는?
(A) 세계 경제의 점진적 향상
(B) 국제 금융 제도의 발달
(C) 전반적인 경제 회복의 장애
(D) 국가 간의 증오심 증가

해설 | Detail 무역권의 형성은 현금의 흐름, 해외 투자 가능성 등을 제한시키면서 결과적으로 1930년대 경제 위기의 탈피를 전반적으로 어렵게 만들었다.

05 강의의 일부를 다시 듣고 질문에 답하시오.
미국에 대해 추론할 수 있는 것은?
(A) 전후에 재건 비용을 대기 위해 많은 돈을 빌려야 했다.
(B) 브레턴우즈 협정의 주요 수혜자였다.
(C) 제2차 세계대전에서 비교적 작은 역할을 했다.
(D) 브레턴우즈 협정에 서명하도록 속았다.

해설 | Inference 미국은 경제 재건 비용을 지급하는 대가로 세계 경제의 패권적 위치를 보장받게 되었으므로 이 협정의 주된 수혜자라고 볼 수 있다.

어휘 | component 부분, 구성 요소   International Monetary Fund(IMF) 국제통화기금
International Bank for Reconstruction and Development 국제부흥개발은행   pegged 고정된, 안정된   chaos 혼란
onset 시작, 엄습   Great Depression 대공황   facilitate 촉진하다, 쉽게 하다   shattered 산산이 부서진   infect 영향을 주다
intense 극도의   strain 부담, 압력   pursue 추구하다   devalue (통화의) 평가를 절하하다   deficit 적자   havoc 대혼란
equivalent 동등한, 같은 가치의   in dire need of ~을 시급히(절실히) 필요로 하는   in exchange for ~의 대가로

iBT Practice
p.152

01 (B), (C)   **02** (D)   **03** (A)   **04** (C)   **05** (C)   **06** (B)

Listen to part of a lecture in a sociology class.

Professor (M): Take your seats, everyone. OK, today we are going to continue our discussion about social interaction on the Internet. Let's focus on the size of certain social networking websites. We'll explore questions like, "What happens when these online networks get too big?" and "Are smaller networks inherently more intimate?" One theory that helps answer these questions is Dunbar's number, proposed by British anthropologist Robin Dunbar in the 1990s.

사회학 강의 중 일부를 들으시오.

교수 (남): 여러분, 자리에 모두 앉으세요. 좋아요. 오늘은 인터넷상에서의 사회적 상호 작용에 대한 이야기를 계속해보겠습니다. 특정 사회 네트워크 웹사이트들의 규모에 대해 중점적으로 살펴봅시다. 다음과 같은 질문들, 즉 '이러한 온라인 네트워크가 너무 커지면 어떤 일이 발생하는가?', '규모가 작은 네트워크들은 본질적으로 더 친밀한가?'와 같은 질문들에 대해 살펴보겠습니다. 이러한 질문들에 답하는 데 도움이 되는 한 이론은 'Dunbar의 수'로, 1990년대 영국의 인류학자인 Robin Dunbar에 의해 제안된 이론입니다. 웹사이트들에 대해 알아

Let's look at this theory really quickly before we move on to the websites.

Q02 In his studies of over 40 primate species, Dunbar noticed that certain species tended to gather together in groups that were consistently the same size. He saw that these groups were based around social grooming, where monkeys clean each other. For instance, the number of chimps that regularly groomed each other always remained a certain size. Dunbar theorized that this grooming was partially a way of building strong relationships among primates. Because a group could only spend so much time grooming each other, it usually didn't grow beyond a certain size. Q05-1 If it did, the chimps tended to become more hostile to each other and split into factions.

Q01(B) Dunbar further theorized that this maximum amount was primarily determined by the brain size of primates — in particular, the neocortex area. By measuring a species' neocortex area and comparing it with the maximum amount of relationships it could maintain, Dunbar essentially discovered a ratio between the size of primates' brains and the size of the groups in which they socialize. So, naturally, he applied this ratio to human beings — the primates with the biggest brains – and calculated that we could effectively socialize in groups no larger than 150 persons.

Now, you're probably all wondering why the neocortex area is so important for Dunbar's number. Well, for primates, it controls higher functions like spatial reasoning and conscious thought. For humans, it contains our capacity for language. See, language serves the same purpose as social grooming for primates, but it is far more time-efficient. After all, one can speak while doing other activities and speak with multiple people at one time, things primates can't accomplish through social grooming. Dunbar also discusses its importance in relaying information about how to act in a social group, usually through what he classifies as gossip. This helps people learn more social behaviors than is possible through mere observation. Q03 Essentially, the development of language helped early humans maintain larger social groups than the primates we evolved from.

Q01(C) Finally, Dunbar had to see how this number of 150 figured in human societies. He looked at many ancient long-standing tribal societies in Asia, Africa, the Americas, and all across the planet. He focused particularly on hunter-gatherer societies, most likely the earliest form of human society, and saw that the most stable and effective groups had between 100 and 200 people. He then examined modern social groupings. This included small agricultural communities in North America, academic communities, office staffs, and military organizations.

The last one is especially interesting because it shows a consistent pattern throughout various cultures and various time periods. Q04 Dunbar noticed that many groups of independent and effective military units range from 100 to 200 soldiers. They never get any larger. Dunbar speculated that his 150 average was so consistent in groups like military squads, small farming communities, and hunter-gatherer societies because these groups rely on banding together for survival. In such desperate conditions, everybody needs as much help as they can get, so they maximize their number of meaningful relationships. Q05-2 If it exceeds the maximum, there would be too much discord for it to function effectively and independently.

보기 전에, 이 이론에 대해 아주 간단히 살펴보도록 하죠.

40종 이상의 영장류를 연구하면서, Dunbar는 특정 종들에게 계속해서 같은 규모의 그룹으로 모이는 경향이 있다는 사실을 발견했어요. 그는 이 그룹들이, 원숭이들이 서로를 깨끗하게 해 주는 사회적 털 손질에 기초하고 있다고 보았습니다. 예를 들어, 서로 규칙적으로 털 손질을 해주는 침팬지의 수는 항상 특정 규모를 유지했죠. Dunbar는 이러한 털 손질이 영장류들 사이에서는 부분적으로 강한 유대 관계를 쌓는 방법이라는 이론을 세웠습니다. 서로 털 손질을 하는 데에는 상당한 시간이 쓰이기 때문에, 항상 일정 규모를 넘지 않는 것이죠. 만약 규모가 커지면, 침팬지들은 서로에게 더욱 적대적이 되어 파벌로 분열되는 경향을 보였어요.

Dunbar는 더 나아가서, 이 규모의 최대치는 주로 영장류 뇌의 크기, 특히 신피질 부위의 크기에 의해 결정된다는 이론을 세웠습니다. 어떤 종의 신피질 부위의 크기를 측정해 그것을 그 종이 유지할 수 있는 관계의 최대치와 비교함으로써, Dunbar는 영장류 뇌의 크기와 사회화하는 집단의 규모 간의 관계를 설명하는 하나의 비율을 발견해냈어요. 그래서, 그는 자연스럽게 가장 큰 뇌를 가진 영장류인 인간에 이 비율을 적용해, 우리가 150명 미만의 집단에서 효과적으로 사회화할 수 있다는 계산을 끌어냈죠.

그럼, 지금쯤 여러분은 신피질 부위가 Dunbar의 수에 있어서 왜 그렇게 중요한 것인지 궁금해하고 있을 것입니다. 글쎄요, 영장류의 경우, 신피질 부위는 공간 추리나 의식적인 사고와 같은 고차원적인 기능을 조절합니다. 인간에게 있어서 그 부위는 언어 능력을 포함하고 있죠. 그러니까, 언어는 영장류의 사회적 털 손질과 같은 목적을 수행합니다. 다만 시간적인 면에서 훨씬 효율적이죠. 결국, 사람은 다른 활동을 하면서 말을 할 수 있으며, 한 번에 여러 사람과 말을 할 수 있으니까요. 이는 영장류가 사회적 털 손질을 통해서 달성할 수 없는 것들이죠. Dunbar는 또한 사회 집단 내에서 어떻게 행동해야 하는지에 대해, 보통 그가 가십이라고 분류하는 것을 통해 정보를 전달하는 것의 중요성을 논의합니다. 가십은 사람들이 관찰만을 했을 때보다 더 많은 사회적 행동을 배울 수 있도록 도와줍니다. 근본적으로 언어의 발달은 초기 인류가 우리의 진화적 조상인 영장류보다 더 큰 사회 집단을 유지할 수 있도록 도와주었죠.

마지막으로, Dunbar는 이 150이라는 수가 인간 사회와 어떻게 관련이 있는지 알아보아야 했습니다. 그는 아시아, 아프리카, 아메리카 대륙 및 전 세계에 걸쳐, 오랫동안 지속된 여러 고대 부족 사회들을 살펴보았어요. 그는 특히 인간 사회의 초기 형태일 가능성이 큰 수렵·채집인 사회에 초점을 맞추었고, 가장 안정적이고 효과적인 집단은 100명에서 200명 사이의 규모였다는 것을 발견하였습니다. 그는 그런 다음에 현대 사회의 집단들을 살펴보았죠. 여기에는 북아메리카의 작은 농업 사회에서부터 학계, 사무직원, 군 조직까지 포함되었습니다.

여기서 마지막 집단은 다양한 문화와 시대에 걸쳐 일관된 양상을 보인다는 점에서 특히 흥미롭습니다. Dunbar는 독립적이고 효과적인 군부대 중 다수가 100명에서 200명에 이르는 군사들로 조직되었다는 사실을 알아냈습니다. 이보다 큰 경우는 결코 없었죠. Dunbar는 150이라는 평균치가 군 분대나 작은 농업 사회, 수렵·채집인 사회에서 너무도 일관성 있게 나타나는 이유가 이 집단들이 생존을 위해 서로 단결해야 했기 때문이라고 추측하였습니다. 이러한 필사적인 상황에서는 모두가 그들이 받을 수 있는 최대한의 도움이 필요하기 때문에 중요한 관계의 수를 최대화하는 것이죠. 그리고 만약 이 수가 다시 최대치를 초과하면 불화가 생겨 효과적이고 독립적으로 기능할 수 없게 되는 것이죠.

Q06 Now, there are a few issues with this whole theory. For instance, what actually qualifies as socialization or a relationship? This is open to interpretation and debated, mainly because there are different degrees of intimacy. So whether or not 150 represents some kind of upper limit for human relationships really depends on how you define the term.

Also, understand that Dunbar's number only reflects the very maximum. Dunbar admitted that not every human social group reaches this upper limit, and that other environmental and social conditions could restrict the size of a social unit.

Finally, the value itself is in dispute, as other anthropologists have proposed alternative maximum values, some twice as high as Dunbar's. Anyway, what we're interested in is not the numerical value, but how this concept of a limit to social interactions applies to the online world.

자, 그런데 이 이론 전반에는 몇 가지 문제가 있답니다. 예를 들어, 무엇을 사회화 또는 관계라고 부를 수 있을까요? 주로 친밀함의 정도가 다르기 때문에, 이 점은 해석에 따라 다를 수 있으며 논쟁의 여지가 있습니다. 그러니까 이 150이라는 수가 인간 관계에 일종의 상한선 역할을 하는지 아닌지는 사실 그 용어를 어떻게 정의하느냐에 달린 거죠.

또한, Dunbar의 수는 최상한선을 나타내는 것임을 알아두세요. Dunbar는 모든 인간의 사회적 집단이 이 상한선에 이르는 것은 아니며, 다른 환경적, 사회적 조건들이 사회 단위의 규모를 제한시킬 수 있다는 점을 인정하였습니다.

마지막으로, 다른 인류학자들이 다른 상한선을 제안했고, 어떤 학자들은 Dunbar의 수의 두 배가 되는 수를 제시하기도 하면서, 이 숫자 자체도 논쟁거리입니다. 어쨌든, 우리에게 흥미로운 부분은 수치적인 가치가 아니라, 이 사회적 상호 작용의 제한선 개념이 어떻게 온라인상에서 적용되는지에 관한 것이죠.

---

01 강의의 주된 내용은?
2개의 답을 고르시오.
(A) 인간과 영장류의 대표적인 사회적 상호 작용
(B) 어떻게 뇌의 크기가 사회적 네트워킹과 관련되어 있는지
(C) Dunbar의 수의 인간 사회 적용
(D) 사회적 네트워킹 관행에 대한 인터넷의 영향

해설 | Main Idea 교수는 뇌의 크기, 특히 신피질 부위와 사회적 네트워킹이 관련된 방식에 대해 설명하고, Dunbar의 수가 인간 사회에 어떻게 적용되는지 설명한다.

02 Dunbar가 처음에 그의 이론을 발전시킨 방식은?
(A) 인간의 뇌 구조를 연구함으로써
(B) 역사상 군대의 규모를 조사함으로써
(C) 사회적 네트워킹 웹사이트의 규모에서 드러나는 양상을 인식함으로써
(D) 여러 영장류 집단의 규모를 관찰함으로써

해설 | Detail Dunbar는 영장류 집단이 특정 종에 따라 같은 규모로 모이는 경향이 있다는 것을 발견하고 그 원인과 관련해 이론을 발전시키기 시작했다.

03 Dunbar에 따르면, 인간이 영장류보다 친밀한 관계를 더 많이 맺을 수 있는 이유는?
(A) 인간에게는 언어 능력이 있다.
(B) 인간은 생존을 위해 더 큰 집단을 형성해야 한다.
(C) 인간은 사회적 상호 작용을 위한 시간이 더 많다.
(D) 인간은 영장류만큼 많이 싸우지 않는다.

해설 | Detail 인간은 언어 능력을 통해 더 효과적으로 관계를 유지할 수 있고, 가십은 더 많은 사회적 행동을 배울 수 있게 하므로, 영장류보다 더 큰 집단 내에서 관계를 유지할 수 있다.

04 교수가 역사상 군대 조직을 언급하는 이유는?
(A) Dunbar의 수에 대한 타당성을 반증하기 위해
(B) 언어가 여러 다른 그룹에서 어떤 다른 역할을 하는지 설명하기 위해
(C) 생존을 위한 집단이 어떻게 비슷한 상한선에 다다르는지 보여주기 위해
(D) Dunbar의 이론과 이후의 이론들을 비교하기 위해

해설 | Organization 교수는 역사를 통해 나타난 많은 군부대들이 일관된 수로 조직되었다고 말하고, 생존을 위해 관계의 수를 최대로 유지해야 했던 집단들이 왜 그렇게 비슷한 상한선을 가진 것인지를 설명하고 있다.

05 Dunbar의 이론에 기초하여 사회적 집단들에 대해 추론할 수 있는 것은?
(A) 150명 이하의 사람들을 포함한 집단에서는 더 효과적인 소통이 가능하다.
(B) 집단이 속한 상황이 절박할수록 그 집단은 더 효과적으로 기능한다.
(C) 집단이 200명 이상의 사람들로 구성된다면 불화가 생겨 그 집단이 제대로 운영되지 못한다.
(D) 사람들은 심각한 위험에 처했을 때, 관계의 수를 최소화시키려는 경향이 있다.

해설 | Inference 교수는 원숭이와 군대를 예로 들며, 규모가 커지면 원숭이들은 서로 적대적이 되어 파벌로 분열되고, 군대에서는 규모가 최대치를 초과하면 불화가 생겨 효과적이고 독립적으로 기능할 수 없게 된다고 설명한다. 즉, 그룹이 최대치 이상인 200명 이상으로 구성되어 있다면 불화로 인해 효과적으로 운영되지 못함을 암시한다.

06 강의의 일부를 다시 듣고 질문에 답하시오.
교수가 다음과 같이 말하는 이유는?

"For instance, what actually qualifies as socialization or a relationship?"

(A) Dunbar의 이론에 허점이 있다는 점을 강조하기 위해
(B) 방금 언급한 요점을 더 자세히 설명하기 위해
(C) 이 주제에 대한 학생들의 의견을 구하기 위해
(D) 학생들이 이와 비슷한 질문을 하지 못하게 하기 위해

해설 | Function 앞서 언급한 이 이론이 가지는 몇 가지 문제(a few issues)에 대해 예를 들어 더 자세히 설명하고 있다.

어휘 | **intimate** 친밀한 **anthropologist** 인류학자 **primate** 영장류 **grooming** (동물의) 털 손질, 몸단장 **faction** 파벌, 당파 **neocortex** (대뇌의) 신피질 **ratio** 비율 **spatial** 공간의 **gossip** 가십, 소문 **hunter-gatherer** 수렵·채집인 **stable** 안정적인 **speculate** 추측하다 **squad** (군대의) 분대 **desperate** 필사적인 **exceed** 초과하다 **discord** 불화 **restrict** 제한시키다

Actual Test 1

Passage 1
01 (C) 02 (D) 03 (B) 04 (A), (B) 05 [Included – (C), (D)], [Not Included – (A), (B)]

Passage 2
06 (B) 07 (D) 08 (A) 09 (D) 10 (B) 11 (B)

Passage 3
12 (C) 13 (D) 14 (C) 15 (D) 16 (A) 17 (B)

Passage 1   p.156

01 (C) 02 (D) 03 (B) 04 (A), (B) 05 [Included – (C), (D)], [Not Included – (A), (B)]

Listen to a conversation between a student and a professor.

Student (M): Q01-1 Professor Gabriel, is it all right if I get some help from you on the film I'm making on climate change?

Professor (F): Hey, Robin, of course. Let me just take care of this e-mail first.

Student: Oh, I can come back another time if you're busy at the moment.

Professor: No, no, it's actually a perfect time right now. Just have to press send . . . there we go. Now, what can I help you with?

Student: Q01-2 I just wanted some much-needed advice on the film I'm going to be making on the effects that climate change has on birds.

Professor: Oh, right! I remember you told me about that a couple of months ago. How's that coming along?

Student: It's driving me up the wall! I've been planning and preparing for a long time, and yet I still can't seem to get everything together cohesively.

Professor: I understand. Q02 Filming is definitely a painstaking process, whether it's your first time or you're a well-seasoned veteran.

Student: Tell me about it! Oh, where do I even start . . . oh right! For example, even filming an interview seems to be so complicated! Q03 Coming up with thought-provoking questions that'll elicit insightful answers isn't that difficult, but I'm not sure if I need to capture the responses from multiple angles. Q05(D) When you film your interviews, do you usually shoot the same interview multiple times or do you just use multiple cameras for different angles?

학생과 교수의 대화를 들으시오.

학생 (남): Gabriel 교수님, 제가 기후 변화에 대해 찍을 영화에 대해 교수님으로부터 도움을 좀 받아도 괜찮을까요?

교수 (여): 안녕, Robin, 물론이지. 우선 이 이메일 좀 처리하고.

학생: 아, 지금 바쁘시면 나중에 다시 올 수 있어요.

교수: 아냐, 아냐. 사실 바로 지금이 완벽한 때란다. 발송 버튼만 누르고… 됐다. 자, 뭘 도와줄까?

학생: 기후 변화가 새들에게 미치는 영향에 대해 찍을 영화에 관해 조언이 몹시 필요해요.

교수: 아, 맞아! 네가 몇 달 전에 그것에 대해 얘기했던 걸로 기억한단다. 어떻게 되어가니?

학생: 절 궁지로 몰아넣고 있어요! 오랫동안 계획하고 준비해왔는데, 아직도 모든 것을 하나로 결합할 수가 없어요.

교수: 이해한다. 영화를 찍는 것은 네가 처음이든 노련한 전문가든 상관없이 분명 힘든 과정이지.

학생: 제 말이요! 아, 어디서부터 시작해야 할지… 아 맞아요! 예를 들면, 인터뷰를 찍는 것조차 너무 복잡해 보여요! 통찰력 있는 답변을 끌어낼 만한 시사하는 바가 큰 질문들을 생각해내는 것은 그리 어렵지 않지만, 답변을 여러 각도에서 찍어야 하는지 잘 모르겠어요. 교수님께서는 인터뷰를 찍으실 때 같은 인터뷰를 여러 번 찍으시나요, 아니면 그냥 다양한 각도를 위해 여러 카메라를 사용하시나요?

Professor: Well, it actually depends. There's no real correct answer. Q04(A) Sometimes, depending on the location and the set, you may have to film the same interview multiple times. For example, if you're filming in a small area where you can't fit in all of the equipment needed for multiple cameras, you'll obviously have to do it a few times. Q04(B) Also, you have to take into consideration the sound quality, as doing it outdoors can affect how the sound comes out in one cut.

Student: Those are great points, Professor Gabriel. How about inserting the interviews into the film? I keep rethinking about how I should structure it. Q05(C) Like, would I split the interview up into parts and insert small snippets into each topic section I'm including in the film? Or would it be better to go with larger chunks so that viewers can get a better feel for the general opinion of each of the experts?

Professor: Once again, it'll be different in each situation. But if it were me, since your piece is on birds and how climate change affects them, I would include short snippets of the interviews that are relevant to each topic you are covering. What you are producing is an informative piece that seeks to explain a certain phenomenon . . . If you were shifting it to an opinion piece, such as gathering the general consensus of whether the negative effects of climate change are worth enduring for the benefits that we enjoy, then it would be better to include larger chunks of interviews.

Student: I see. All of this advice is worth its weight in gold! There is so much more I feel like I need to contemplate before shooting this film. Honestly, my confidence is slowly waning more and more as each day passes by.

Professor: We all have our doubts and difficulties when our backs seem like they're up against the wall, but never let those doubts get the best of you! You're more than welcome to come seek my advice and help at any time. I'm really pulling for you.

Student: Really? Thank you so much for the vote of confidence.

교수: 글쎄, 사실 때에 따라 다르단다. 완전히 맞는 답은 없어. 가끔은 위치와 촬영장에 따라 같은 인터뷰를 여러 번 찍어야 할 때도 있지. 예를 들면, 여러 카메라를 위해 필요한 모든 장비를 놓을 수 없는 작은 장소에서 영상을 찍고 있다면, 분명 여러 번 찍어야겠지. 또한 야외에서 찍는 것은 하나의 장면에 음향이 어떻게 나오는지에 영향을 주기 때문에, 음질까지 고려해야 한단다.

학생: 좋은 지적을 해주셨네요, Gabriel 교수님. 영화에 인터뷰 장면을 넣는 것은 어떻게요? 어떻게 구성해야 하는지에 대해 계속 다시 생각하거든요. 인터뷰를 나눠서 그 작은 부분들을 제가 영화에 포함하려고 하는 각 주제 부분에 넣어야 하나요? 아니면 시청자들이 각 전문가의 일반적인 견해를 더 잘 이해할 수 있도록 더 큰 분량으로 넣는 게 나을까요?

교수: 다시 한 번 말하지만, 각 상황에 따라 다르단다. 하지만 나라면, 너의 영화가 새들과 기후 변화가 그들에게 미치는 영향에 관한 것이기 때문에, 네가 다루는 각 주제에 관련된 짧은 인터뷰 부분들을 포함할 것 같구나. 네가 제작하는 것이 특정한 현상을 설명하려는 정보 제공 작품이기 때문이지… 만약 우리가 누리는 이익들을 위해 기후 변화의 부정적인 영향들을 참아낼 만하다는 것에 대한 전반적인 합의를 모으는 것과 같이 견해 위주의 작품으로 바꾼다면, 더 긴 분량으로 포함하는 것이 좋겠지.

학생: 그렇군요. 모든 조언이 대단히 유용하네요! 이 영화를 찍기 전에 생각해봐야 할 것들이 훨씬 더 많은 것 같아요. 솔직히 말씀드리면, 날이 갈수록 제 자신감이 점점 더 줄어들고 있어요.

교수: 우리 모두 궁지에 몰리는 것 같을 때는 확신하지 못하고 어려움을 겪지만, 그런 의문들이 너를 사로잡도록 놔두지 마. 내 조언과 도움이 필요하다면 언제든 와서 물어보렴. 너를 정말로 응원한단다.

학생: 정말이요? 지지해주셔서 정말 감사합니다.

01 대화의 주제는?
(A) 기후 변화에 관한 작품을 촬영하는 것에 대해 교수에게 이메일 보내기
(B) 기후 변화의 여러 부정적인 영향을 대중에게 알리는 방법
(C) 새들이 기후 변화로부터 어떤 영향을 받는지에 대한 영화를 찍는 가장 좋은 방법
(D) 정보 제공 영화에서 전문가들을 인터뷰하는 가장 좋은 방법

해설 | Main Idea 학생은 교수를 찾아가 기후 변화가 새들에게 미치는 영향에 대해 영화를 찍을 것인데, 이에 관해 도움이 필요하다고 말한다.

02 영화 제작에 대한 교수의 의견은?
(A) 신중히 계획한다면 아주 어렵지는 않다.
(B) 영화 전공자들의 감독이 필요하다.
(C) 모든 세부사항이 계획되기까지 시작되어서는 안 된다.
(D) 힘들고 도전적인 과정이다.

해설 | Attitude 교수가 "Filming is definitely a painstaking process, whether it's your first time or you're a well-seasoned veteran"이라고 말하는 것으로 보아, 영화 제작이 힘들고 도전적인 과정이라고 생각한다는 것을 알 수 있다.

03 학생의 영화 프로젝트에 대해 추론할 수 있는 것은?
(A) 영화 주제에 대한 유용한 정보를 찾는 데 시간이 더 필요하다.
(B) 인터뷰에 사용할 좋은 질문들을 이미 생각해냈다.
(C) 인터뷰를 위한 적절한 전문가들을 찾는 데 어려움을 겪고 있다.
(D) 기후 변화가 새들에게 미치는 긍정적인 영향과 부정적인 영향 모두를 포함할 계획이다.

해설 | Inference 학생이 통찰력 있는 답변을 끌어낼 만한 시사하는 바가 있는 질문들을 생각해내는 것은 그리 어렵지 않다고 말한 것으로 보아, 이미 몇몇 좋은 질문들을 생각해냈다는 것을 추론할 수 있다.

04 같은 인터뷰를 여러 번 찍을지 결정하기 위해 고려해야 할 요인들은?

2개의 답을 고르시오.

(A) 촬영장의 규모
(B) 오디오 품질
(C) 인터뷰가 작은 부분으로 나뉘어 사용될지 여부
(D) 인터뷰 대상자 수

해설 | Detail 교수는 위치와 촬영장에 따라 다르고, 야외에서 찍을 때는 음질 또한 고려해야 한다고 말한다.

05 대화에서 교수와 학생은 학생의 영화에 관한 여러 측면에 대해 논의한다. 다음 각 사항이 포함되는지 표시하시오.

각 사항에 대해 알맞은 항목에 표시하시오.

	포함	미포함
(A) 촬영 장비를 준비하는 방법		✔
(B) 주제에 관한 참고 자료를 찾을 장소		✔
(C) 인터뷰를 삽입하는 효과적인 방법	✔	
(D) 인터뷰를 촬영할 때 여러 카메라를 써야 하는지 여부	✔	

해설 | Connecting Content 학생은 교수에게 인터뷰를 찍을 때 같은 인터뷰를 여러 번 찍는지, 혹은 다양한 각도에서 찍기 위해 여러 카메라를 사용하는지 묻는다. 또한 인터뷰를 영화에 삽입할 때 작은 부분으로 나눠서 넣는지, 혹은 좀 더 큰 분량으로 넣는지 묻는다.

어휘 | **climate change** 기후 변화   **much-needed** 몹시 필요한   **drive someone up the wall** 누군가를 궁지에 몰아 넣다, 누군가를 몹시 화나게 하다   **painstaking** 힘든, 공들인   **well-seasoned** 노련한   **veteran** 전문가   **thought-provoking** 시사하는 바가 큰, 진지하게 생각하게 하는   **insightful** 통찰력 있는   **snippet** (작은) 정보, 토막   **chunk** 상당히 많은 양, 덩어리   **worth one's weight in gold** 대단히 유용한

Passage 2

p.158

| 06 (B) | 07 (D) | 08 (A) | 09 (D) | 10 (B) | 11 (B) |

Listen to part of a lecture in a linguistics class.

Professor (F): Now, as you all should remember, we had an in-depth discussion about how Middle English developed from Old English. Again, recall that Middle English began after the French conquered England in the eleventh century and imposed the French language upon British subjects. As we discussed, Middle English saw many dramatic changes to its grammar, pronunciation, and orthography. Q06 Well, today we are going to move on to what we call the Early Modern English phase, when the language formed into what we recognize today.

Now, there were some major adjustments made over a few hundred years, and they affected just about every aspect of the language. The most important and dramatic change was to pronunciation, and this was due to the Great Vowel Shift. This is undoubtedly the most important development in the transition of Middle English to Modern English. It was a shift in the pronunciation of most vowels. Let's see, what is a good example?

OK, for instance, before the shift, the vowel sound in the word "boot" was pronounced "oh." [Pronounce as the vowel sound in "boat"]. So, basically, the word was pronounced "boat." Now, after the shift, this vowel sound changed to "oo." [Pronounce as the vowel sound in "boot"]. This led to our modern pronunciation of "boot."

언어학 강의 중 일부를 들으시오.

교수 (여): 자, 여러분 모두 기억하고 있듯이, 중세 영어가 고대 영어로부터 어떻게 발전했는지에 대해 심층 토론을 벌였어요. 다시 한 번 상기해보자면, 중세 영어는 11세기에 프랑스인들이 영국을 점령하고 영국 피지배자들에게 프랑스어 사용을 강요하면서 시작되었죠. 우리가 논의했듯이, 중세 영어에는 문법, 발음, 맞춤법에서 많은 극적인 변화가 있었어요. 음, 오늘은 영어가 오늘날 우리가 알아볼 수 있는 형태로 형성된 때인 소위 초기 현대 영어 시기에 대해 알아보겠어요.

자, 몇백 년에 걸쳐서 일부 중대한 조정이 일어났고, 그것은 언어의 거의 모든 면에 영향을 미쳤답니다. 가장 중요하고 극적인 변화는 발음에 있었는데, 이는 '대모음 추이' 때문이었습니다. 이는 중세 영어가 현대 영어로 전환하는 데 있어 확실히 가장 중요한 발전이죠. 대부분의 모음에 발음 변화가 있었어요. 그럼, 좋은 예로 무엇이 있을까요?

자, 예를 들어, 변화 이전에는 단어 '부트(boot)'의 모음은 '오우(oh)'로 발음되었어요. ['보우트(boat)'의 모음처럼 발음하며], 그러니까 기본적으로 그 단어는 '보우트(boat)'처럼 발음이 된 것이죠. 하지만 변화 이후에는 이 모음이 '우(oo)'로 바뀌었어요. ['부트(boot)'의 모음 발음처럼 발음하며], 이로써 우리의 현대식 발음인 '부트(boot)'가 나오게 된 것이에요.

Another notable change was the creation of new diphthongs. Q07 These are vowel sounds that result from the combination of two pre-existing vowels. Take the word "time," for instance. In Middle English, it used the same vowel sound found in "tree" — so it was pronounced as "teem." The Great Vowel Shift caused this vowel sound to be merged with the "ah" vowel, though. As these two combined, the new vowel was pronounced "ah – ee." When said quickly, it sounds like "ai," the sound we now hear in the word "time."

Now, no one knows exactly what brought about the Great Vowel Shift, although many theorize that it came about through the interaction of people of various dialects. I should also point out that some of these vowel sounds continued to evolve up until Later Modern English. What's also interesting is that some speakers have retained pronunciations found before the Great Vowel Shift. For example, the people of Scotland still pronounce some vowels as they were pronounced before the shift. Q08 Anyway, the important thing to remember is that the French pronunciation of vowels used in Middle English disappeared, making Modern English very dissimilar to French.

Q11 Another major development we should discuss is how written English became standardized. Remember that there were still many dialects being used at this time, so a single word could have multiple pronunciations. Well, when people wrote words, they would spell them according to the way they pronounced them. Can you imagine the kinds of problems that caused? Obviously a standard spelling was needed. There were two driving forces that brought this about.

The centralization of England's government in the fifteenth and sixteenth centuries was the first one. The government originally used French and Latin, but as it became stronger and more bureaucratic, it found that it needed a single, official language — preferably in the common tongue, English.

Around the early fifteenth century, the English government began using a common standard based on the East Midland and London dialects for official business. This made necessary tasks like record-keeping, issuing proclamations and decrees, and other official legal tasks much easier.

Q09 The advent of the printing press was the second factor. Books and other texts became more plentiful, and publishers found the inconsistencies to be a problem. The best example of this is William Caxton, the first publisher in England. When Caxton began printing books in 1476, he wasn't certain of which dialect to use. So he was probably one of the first people to realize the need for standardized spelling.

Q10 Now, uh, it's not exactly clear how far Caxton went in correcting these problems. However, most scholars agree he had an immense influence, at least on later publishers. In time, they began to settle on a standard form of writing in order to lessen the confusion of various dialects. And in the end, Samuel Johnson's dictionary, published in 1755 in England, was influential in establishing a standard form of spelling, and Noah Webster did the same in the U.S., publishing his dictionary in 1828. However, before them, there were some side effects of the attempts to settle on a standard form of writing, but we'll get into that in a minute.

06 강의의 주된 내용은?
(A) 중세 영어 단어의 발음
(B) 현대 영어의 등장과 함께 생긴 변화들
(C) 인쇄기가 중세 영어 철자법에 끼친 영향
(D) 대모음 추이가 현대 영어에 끼친 영향

해설 | Main Idea 교수는 초기 현대 영어 시기에 영어에서 나타난 주요 변화들에 대해 설명하고 있다.

07 이중 모음이란?
(A) 대모음 추이 기간에 변화된 영어의 모음
(B) 특정 방언의 발음에 기초한 단어의 철자법
(C) 하나의 철자를 쓰는 단어의 여러 발음법
(D) 서로 다른 두 개의 모음이 결합해서 형성된 모음

해설 | Detail 이중 모음이란 이미 존재하던 두 개의 모음이 결합해서 형성된 모음을 일컫는다.

08 교수가 중세 영어에 대해 암시하는 것은?
(A) 현대 영어보다 프랑스어에 더 가까웠다.
(B) 인쇄기의 발명으로 인해 많은 변화에도 불구하고 살아남았다.
(C) 화자들 사이에 방언이나 지역적 차이가 거의 없었다.
(D) 단어의 철자가 현대 영어 단어들보다 더 헷갈렸다.

해설 | Inference 초기 현대 영어 시기 동안 중세 영어에서 쓰이던 프랑스 모음 발음이 사라지면서 두 언어가 달라졌다고 했으므로 중세 영어는 프랑스어와 더 유사했음을 알 수 있다.

09 교수가 William Caxton에 대해 논의하는 이유는?
(A) 영국 정부가 영어 표준화를 도운 방식을 설명하기 위해
(B) 르네상스가 영국에 인쇄술을 도입시킨 방법을 보여주기 위해
(C) 출판에서 쓰인 여러 다른 영어 방언들을 비교하기 위해
(D) 출판업자들이 영어 표준화의 필요성을 느낀 이유를 입증하기 위해

해설 | Organization 교수는 인쇄기의 출현으로 출판물이 증가하면서 출판업자들이 영어의 불일치로 인한 표준화의 필요성을 느꼈다고 설명하며, 그 인물 중 하나로 William Caxton을 언급하고 있다.

10 William Caxton에 대한 교수의 태도는?
(A) 영국에서 가장 영향력 있는 출판인이었다고 생각한다.
(B) 표준화된 철자법을 확립하는 데 있어서 그의 역할을 높이 평가한다.
(C) 표준화된 철자법을 결정하려는 그의 노력이 많은 문제점을 일으켰다고 생각한다.
(D) 여러 방언의 혼선을 줄이는 데 있어서의 그의 영향을 부인한다.

해설 | Attitude 교수가 "… most scholars agree he had an immense influence, at least on later publishers"라고 말하는 것으로 보아 표준화된 철자법을 확립하는 데 있어서 그의 역할을 높이 평가한다는 것을 알 수 있다.

11 강의의 일부를 다시 듣고 질문에 답하시오.
교수가 다음과 같이 말하는 이유는?
"Can you imagine the kinds of problems that caused?"
(A) 학생들로부터 답변을 끌어내기 위해
(B) 문제의 심각성을 강조하기 위해
(C) 표준화된 철자법의 문제점을 지적하기 위해
(D) 학생들이 대체 철자법을 시도하도록 격려하기 위해

해설 | Function "Can you imagine the kinds of problems that caused?"라고 물은 것은 학생들이 그 문제의 심각했던 상황을 마음에 떠올려 보도록 유도하고자 한 말이다.

어휘 | **impose** 강요하다　**phase** 시기, 단계　**Great Vowel Shift** 대모음 추이(중세 영어에서 현대 영어로의 역사적인 음운 변화)　**notable** 주목할 만한　**diphthong** 이중 모음　**dissimilar** 다른　**centralization** 중앙 집권화　**bureaucratic** 관료적인　**preferably** 가급적이면, 되도록　**proclamation** 성명서　**decree** 법령　**advent** 출현, 도래　**plentiful** 많은, 풍부한

Passage 3

p.160

12 (C)   13 (D)   14 (C)   15 (D)   16 (A)   17 (B)

Listen to part of a discussion in an environmental science class.

Professor (M): Well, it looks like everyone has come in, so, shall we get started? Alright, then. Today we're going over desalinization, the process of removing salt from seawater or marsh water.

Now, I know you guys have been taking excellent notes from your reading, right? So what can you tell me about desalinization?

Student 1 (F): I know that dumping previously removed salt back into the ocean has caused some environmental problems. It upsets the balance of salt and water, potentially killing off species of plants and fish that eat them.

Student 2 (M): That's pretty easy to fix, though. Just find other places to dump it.

Professor: That's possible. Anyway, if you ask me, a bigger problem we face is a growing global population with only so much naturally occurring fresh water. Q13 Desalinization is definitely the best solution to providing the drinking water we all need, especially in increasingly unstable weather and environmental conditions.

But let's talk about the problems of desalinization later. Q12-1 Today we're going to get into the technical details of desalinization. Q14 Most desalinization processes actually utilize a phenomenon commonly found in nature: evaporation. Now, everyone knows that heat in nature comes primarily from the sun, and it will cause water to undergo a phase shift and turn into water vapor. When salt water undergoes evaporation, the salt contained in the water gets left behind. Now, when that evaporated water cools, it condenses and forms liquid water, but liquid water that is now free of salt.

Our atmosphere does this naturally every day. It's called the rain cycle. But most desalinization plants use the same principle. They essentially boil the water until it evaporates, leaving the salt behind. Then they cool down the vapor to form fresh liquid water. This is not the only possible method, but it is the most widely used, so we'll begin our discussion with this. What problems do you think there might be with this method of desalinization?

Student 1: It sounds like it requires a lot of energy.

Professor: Yeah, you're on target. Boiling millions of gallons of seawater all day and cooling it down requires a lot of energy. So much so, in fact, that most desalinization plants are built right next to a power station. Q12-2 However, there have been some steps taken to reduce the energy needed. They rely on two principles.

The first principle is recycling heat. This is done through heat-exchange technology in desalinization plants that combines the evaporation and condensation processes. In a desalinization plant, you usually have a series of several evaporation chambers.

In the first chamber, some energy source, either electricity or a fossil fuel, is used to create the heat to boil salt water. Q17 The steam that results needs to be cooled down so that it will condense into fresh water. Now, you could use a cooling system to do that, but that's pretty wasteful. Instead, most desalinization plants route the steam through a series of pipes, and they spray more cold salt water on those pipes. The result is that the heat from the steam is transferred to the salt water. As you can see, this kills two birds with one stone. It conserves energy by using steam to heat up seawater, and it cools down the steam enough to condense into fresh water.

Of course, this doesn't solve everything. Naturally, a little heat is lost in each chamber, so chambers that come later in the series are cooler and below water's boiling point. So how do you boil saltwater in each chamber without heating up each and every single one? This is where the second principle comes into play: using low-pressure evaporation chambers. Who can tell me why this is important?

Student 1: Well, if water is at a lower pressure, it evaporates at a lower temperature, right?

Professor: Precisely. Q15 So by moving the salt water to chambers with progressively lower pressures, you conserve energy, because the evaporation temperature is lower, meaning less energy is needed to heat the water. In fact, if the pressure change from one chamber to the next is great enough, the water will evaporate almost instantly. This is known as flash evaporation, and the series of lower pressure chambers used in this process are known as flash generators. Q16 When using a combination of flash generators and heat-exchange technology, a desalinization plant can be powered by just a single, central heat source. That's why this method is so effective, and it produces more than half of the world's desalinized water.

위해서는 냉각이 되어야 합니다. 자, 이를 위해 냉각 시스템을 사용할 수도 있겠지만, 에너지 낭비가 꽤 심하겠죠. 대신, 대부분의 담수화 발전소에서는 일련의 관을 통해 그 증기를 보내면서, 이 관들 위에 차가운 해수를 더 많이 분사시켜요. 그 결과로 증기에서 발생한 열이 해수로 옮겨가죠. 알다시피 이는 일거양득인 셈이에요. 증기를 이용해 해수를 가열해서 에너지를 보존하고, 해수는 증기를 충분히 냉각시켜 담수로 응축시키는 것이죠.

물론 이로써 모든 문제가 해결되지는 않아요. 자연히 열은 각 방을 지나면서 조금씩 손실되고, 그렇기 때문에 뒤에 있는 방은 온도가 더 낮아져 물의 끓는점 아래로 내려가게 됩니다. 그러면 각 방의 해수를 각각 개별적으로 가열하지 않고 어떻게 끓이냐고요? 여기서 바로 두 번째 원리가 작동하기 시작합니다. 바로 저압력 증발실을 사용하는 것이죠. 이것이 왜 중요한지 누가 말해줄 수 있나요?

학생 1: 글쎄요, 물이 낮은 압력에 놓이면 더 낮은 온도에서 증발하지 않나요?

교수: 바로 그거에요. 그래서 해수를 계속해서 저압력실로 옮김으로써 에너지를 절약할 수 있는데, 바로 증발 온도가 더 낮아져서 물을 가열하는 데 필요한 에너지가 줄어들기 때문입니다. 사실상 두 방 간의 압력 변화가 충분히 크다면, 물은 거의 즉시 증발해버릴 거예요. 이것은 플래시 증발이라고 알려져 있으며, 이 과정에서 사용되는 일련의 저압력실을 플래시 발전기라고 합니다. 플래시 발전기와 열교환 기술을 결합해서 사용하면, 담수화 발전소는 단 한 개의 중앙열원으로 동력을 공급받을 수 있게 되는 거예요. 그게 바로 이 방법이 매우 효과적인 이유이며, 전 세계의 담수화된 물 절반 이상을 생산합니다.

---

12 화자들이 논의하는 주된 내용은?
(A) 담수화에서 낮은 압력의 사용
(B) 열교환 기술의 발전
(C) 에너지를 절약하는 담수화 기술
(D) 담수화가 환경에 끼치는 영향

해설 | Main Idea 강의는 담수화의 기술적인 측면 중에서도 담수화 발전소에서 에너지를 절약하기 위해 쓰이는 열교환 기술과 플래시 증발 원리를 설명하고 있다.

13 담수화에 대한 교수의 입장은?
(A) 너무 많이 의존해선 안 된다고 생각한다.
(B) 환경에 긍정적인 영향을 줄 거라는 것에 대해 의구심을 갖는다.
(C) 더 효율적이지 않음을 유감스럽게 생각한다.
(D) 필요성이 증대되고 있다고 생각한다.

해설 | Attitude 교수가 "Desalinization is definitely the best solution to providing the drinking water we all need …"라고 언급했듯이, 교수는 늘어나는 인구의 식수 공급을 위해서는 담수화가 최선의 방법이라고 생각하고 있다.

14 교수가 현대의 담수화 과정을 소개하는 방식은?
(A) 초기의 담수화 방법과 비교함으로써
(B) 자주 사용되는 곳을 나열함으로써
(C) 기초를 둔 자연 현상을 설명함으로써
(D) 전통적인 담수화 방법의 문제점을 비판함으로써

해설 | Organization 교수는 담수화의 기술적인 면에 대해 알아보겠다고 하면서 먼저 담수화 과정의 기초가 되는 자연 현상인 증발 원리를 설명하고 있다.

15 플래시 발전기가 담수화에 유용한 이유는?
(A) 증기를 담수로 더 빨리 응축시키도록 도와준다.
(B) 물에서 더 많은 양의 소금을 없앤다.
(C) 해수를 미리 가열해 더 쉽게 용해시킨다.
(D) 물이 더 낮은 온도에서 증발하게 한다.

해설 | Detail 물은 압력이 낮을 때 더 낮은 온도에서도 증발하며, 이 원리를 이용한 담수화 발전소의 저압력실을 플래시 발전기라고 한다. 즉, 플래시 발전기는 압력을 낮추어 물이 더 낮은 온도에서도 증발할 수 있게 해준다.

16 교수가 열교환 기술과 플래시 발전기에 대해 말하는 것은?
(A) 결합해서 사용되는 때가 많다.
(B) 아직 완성되지 못한 기술이다.
(C) 전통적인 담수화 방법보다 더 많은 양의 에너지를 필요로 한다.
(D) 많은 환경 문제를 일으킨다.

해설 | Detail 강의 마지막 부분에서 교수는 이 두 기술을 결합하면, 담수화 발전소는 단 한 개의 중앙열원으로 동력을 공급받을 수 있어 매우 효과적이며, 전 세계 담수화된 물의 절반 이상이 이 방법으로 생산된다고 설명하고 있다.

17 강의의 일부를 다시 듣고 질문에 답하시오.
교수가 다음과 같이 말할 때 의미하는 것은?
"As you can see, this kills two birds with one stone."
(A) 열교환은 환경에 특히 이롭다.
(B) 열교환은 하나 이상의 문제를 해결한다.
(C) 열교환은 다른 방법들보다 두 배 더 빨리 작용한다.
(D) 열교환은 두 개의 에너지원에 의존한다.

해설 | Function 여기서 일거양득이란 말은 열교환 기술을 통해 해수의 가열과 증기의 냉각에 필요한 에너지를 한 번에 해결할 수 있음을 의미한다.

어휘 | **desalinization** 담수화 **marsh** 늪, 습지 **dump** 버리다 **evaporation** 증발(작용, 상태) **vapor** 증기
condense 응축하다, (기체를) 액화하다 **on target** 정확한 **progressively** 계속해서 **instantly** 즉시 **generator** 발전기

Actual Test 2

Passage 1
01 (D)　02 (C)　03 (C)　04 (A)　05 (A)

Passage 2
06 (A), (D)　07 (B)　08 (C)　09 (A)　10 (C) – (A) – (B) – (D)　11 (B)

Passage 3
12 (D)　13 (A)　14 (B), (C)　15 [Blue Whale – (B), (C)], [American Shad – (A), (D), (E)]　16 (A)　17 (D)

Passage 1
p.162

01 (D)　02 (C)　03 (C)	04 (A)	05 (A)

Listen to a conversation between a student and an employee at the Housing Department.

Student (M): Excuse me, ma'am, is this the Housing Department?

Employee (F): Yes it is. How can I help you?

Student: My name is Hank Lean, and I live over in Claymore Hall on the third floor. Q01 I'm, uh, not terribly comfortable talking about this, but it's gotten to the point where I have to say something. It's about my RA. I don't think that I can't take much more of him.

Employee: [Concerned] Oh, well, this sounds serious. So, what seems to be the trouble?

Student: Um, it's really not one major event. It's actually a lot of little things that have been building up over time. OK, the first thing was that there was this problem with someone on my floor playing their stereo really loud, like all the time, even at night, and the walls in my dorm are paper thin. So, I politely ask this student to turn the radio down, but he starts playing it even louder. Q05 Then I asked my RA to talk to the guy. Well, he went and talked to him, and the guy still played the stereo loud. I told my RA about it, and he said I should take it easy and not let the music bother me. As if it's my fault!

Employee: And that's just one example, I take it.

Student: Exactly! I mean, people are always running through the halls, throwing footballs in the middle of the hallways, throwing loud parties, acting really rowdy — this kind of stuff goes on all the time. Q02 I used to complain about it all the time to my RA, and he never did anything about it. Then I found out that he is actually really tight with a lot of these guys, and he even joins in on these activities, too.

Employee: Yeah. He might have become an RA because he thought he and his pals could do whatever they wanted. Or maybe they are just taking advantage of him.

Actual Test 2　A139

Student: Well, either way, this is way out of control. I can't believe I'm actually paying money to live like this.

Employee: Q03 Here, I'm going to register this and see if other people have had similar problems on this floor. If so, then this is definitely a violation of school rules, and we can remove him from his position. We have to investigate it, though, and we may need you to speak with us again.

Student: OK. But there's one other thing. I don't want to be over-dramatic, but what if he gets in trouble and his friends begin harassing me? I really don't want that.

Employee: Of course not, and you should report any such incidents to campus security. Also, report any more behavior like this to them. Their authority overrides any RA. Now, if you are just uncomfortable living there, then I can probably arrange a switch to another floor or dorm. We have a lot of vacancies, and once you fill out the paperwork, we can have you moved out of there as soon as, say, the end of the week.

Student: Really? Yeah, I think that would be a great idea.

Employee: Now, keep in mind that we might also have to remove some of the troublemakers, too. Q04 Depending on what we find out, you might not be the one moving out.

Student: Well, thanks, but I'd rather not take that chance.

Employee: OK, let's get on to the paperwork, then.

학생: 글쎄요, 어떤 쪽이든 너무 통제 불능이에요. 제가 정말 이렇게 살기 위해 돈을 낸다는 사실이 믿기 힘들어요.

직원: 그럼, 제가 이 사안을 등록하고 그 층에 사는 다른 사람들도 비슷한 문제를 겪고 있는지 알아볼게요. 만약 그렇다면 이건 분명 학칙 위반이니까 그를 직위에서 해고할 수 있어요. 그렇지만 어쨌든 조사를 해야 하고, 어쩌면 우리는 학생과 다시 이야기해야 할 수도 있을 거예요.

학생: 알겠어요. 하지만 한 가지 더 있어요. 저도 과잉 반응을 하고 싶지는 않은데요, 만약 그에게 문제가 생겨서 그의 친구들이 저를 괴롭히기라도 하면 어쩌죠? 전 그렇게 되는 것은 정말 싫어요.

직원: 물론 아닙니다. 그리고 이런 일은 당연히 학교 경비 사무실에 신고하는 게 옳아요. 또한 이와 같은 다른 행동도 거기에 신고하세요. 그들의 권한이 어떤 사감보다도 우선하니까요. 그리고 만약 학생이 거기 사는 것이 불편하다면, 제가 아마도 다른 층이나 다른 기숙사로 옮기도록 조정해줄 수 있을 거예요. 빈 방들이 많으니까 서류만 작성하면, 어, 이번 주말 정도만큼 빨리 옮기게 해 줄 수 있어요.

학생: 정말이에요? 네, 좋은 생각이에요.

직원: 그리고 말썽을 일으키는 사람들 또한 내보낼 수 있다는 사실도 기억해 두세요. 조사 결과에 따라서는 나가야 할 사람이 학생이 아닐지도 모르죠.

학생: 글쎄요. 말씀은 고맙지만, 그렇게는 하지 않는 편이 좋겠어요.

직원: 알겠어요. 그럼 서류 작업을 해보죠.

---

01 학생이 기숙사 사무실을 찾아간 이유는?

(A) 새 기숙사 방으로 바꿔달라고 요청하기 위해
(B) 조사들 중 하나에 응하기 위해
(C) 기숙사에서 다른 학생들을 내보낼 것을 요청하기 위해
(D) 기숙사 생활에 대한 불만을 제기하기 위해

02 사감이 기숙사에서 잘못된 행동을 허용하는 이유는?

(A) 그것을 그만두게 할 권한이 없다.
(B) 누군가를 괴롭히고 있다는 것을 모른다.
(C) 잘못된 행동을 하는 다수의 사람들과 친구이다.
(D) 잘못된 행동을 하는 사람들을 무서워한다.

03 직원이 학생의 상황에 대처하려는 방식은?

(A) 사감이 유능하다고 주장함으로써
(B) 기숙사 규칙을 점검함으로써
(C) 문제를 조사하겠다고 약속함으로써
(D) 학비 일부를 환급해준다고 제안함으로써

04 학생이 다음에 할 행동은?

(A) 기숙사 방을 바꾸려고 한다.
(B) 사감에게 기숙사 거주자들을 통제하라고 부탁한다.
(C) 기숙사 거주자들을 학교 경비 사무실에 신고한다.
(D) 사감이 조사받기를 기다린다.

해설 | **Main Idea** 대화 초반 "It's about my RA. I don't think that I can't take much more of him"이라는 학생의 말을 통해 기숙사 사감에 대해 불만이 있어 온 것임을 알 수 있다.

해설 | **Detail** 학생은 사감이 아무런 조치도 취하지 않은 것에 대해 그가 그런 행동을 하는 사람들 다수와 매우 친하기 때문이라고 설명하고 있다.

해설 | **Detail** 직원은 그 층의 다른 학생들도 같은 문제를 겪고 있는지 알아보겠다고 말했다.

해설 | **Inference** 학생은 다른 기숙사 방으로 옮겨주겠다는 직원의 제안에 응했고, 이후 다시 직원이 조사 결과에 따라 학생이 나가지 않을 수도 있다고 하자 "Well, thanks, but I'd rather not take that chance"라고 거절한 것으로 보아, 학생은 처음 직원의 제안에 따라 방을 옮기려고 할 것이다.

05 대화의 일부를 다시 듣고 질문에 답하시오.
직원이 다음과 같이 말할 때 의미하는 것은?
"And that's just one example, I take it."

(A) 다른 비슷한 사례들이 많다는 것을 알아챘다.
(B) 잘못된 행동의 단 한 가지 예는 대수롭지 않게 여긴다.
(C) 학생이 더 자세히 설명해주기를 원한다.
(D) 학생이 안 좋은 일을 겪어서 기분이 나쁘다.

해설 | **Function** 그것이 단지 하나의 예일 뿐이라고 말한 것은 그러한 사건들이 더 많이 있었음을 알아차리고 한 말이다.

어휘 | **RA**(Resident Advisor) (기숙사) 사감 **rowdy** 떠들썩한 **tight** 친한, 단단한 **harass** 괴롭히다 **override** 우선하다

Passage 2   p.164

| 06 (A), (D) | 07 (B) | 08 (C) | 09 (A) | 10 (C) – (A) – (B) – (D) | 11 (B) |

Listen to part of a discussion in a drama class.

Professor (M): Good morning, class. **Q06** Today we're going to discuss the rise of what is popularly known as "method acting," and we're going to go into a lot of detail.

Student (F): Method acting? Like the kind that really great actors like Robert De Niro and Dustin Hoffman use?

Professor: Uh, yes, that's one manifestation of method acting. But its history extends far beyond the film and stage actors of the past few decades. In fact, we have to go all the way back to nineteenth-century Russia in order to trace the roots of method acting. It all begins with the famous Russian thespian Konstantin Stanislavsky.

Q07 In the 1890s, Stanislavsky began developing an alternative method to the common style of stage acting. He felt that the acting he often witnessed in the Moscow theater was too shallow. The actors were more concerned with mimicking physical gestures, copying speech affectations, and relying too much on specific instructions from the director. In other words, the actors were representing all the external traits of their characters, but they were lacking the genuine thoughts and feelings that such characters should have. Stanislavsky believed that capturing this genuine emotion was the main goal of acting, so he developed his own distinct set of techniques for doing just that.

See, Stanislavsky basically tried to turn acting into a science, with an emphasis on experimentation. He insisted that the first thing an actor must do is view his character as real and not just a role in a play. In fact, the actor should be so immersed that he forgets that the audience is there. One technique that helps is emotional memory. The actor uses this to recall his thoughts and feelings in situations similar to those of his character. Instead of creating a mere performance, the actor creates a deep and complex character for himself and interacts with his environment as if he were the character.

Q10(C) Anyway, one of Stanislavsky's most triumphant moments with this new method was his historic production of *The Seagull* in 1898. This play essentially introduced his new style of acting to the world of theater, and Stanislavsky acquired many talented and influential followers.

연극 수업 중 토론의 일부를 들으시오.

교수 (남): 안녕하세요, 여러분. 오늘은 흔히 '메소드 연기'라고 알려진 연기법의 등장에 대해 논의하고 상세히 알아보도록 하겠습니다.

학생 (여): 메소드 연기요? Robert De Niro와 Dustin Hoffman 같은 명배우들이 사용하는 방법 말인가요?

교수: 맞아요. 그것은 메소드 연기의 한 가지 명시이죠. 하지만 메소드 연기의 역사는 지난 수십 년 동안 배출된 영화 및 연극배우들보다도 훨씬 전이에요. 사실, 메소드 연기 근원의 자취를 추적하기 위해서는 19세기 러시아까지 거슬러 올라가야 합니다. 그것은 러시아의 유명 비극 배우인 Konstantin Stanislavsky에서 시작되지요.

1890년대에 Stanislavsky는 평범한 무대 연기 스타일을 대체할 방법을 개발하기 시작했어요. 그는 모스크바 극장에서 본 연기는 너무 깊이가 없다고 생각했어요. 배우들은 신체 동작을 흉내 내고 언어의 허식을 모방하는 데 더 신경을 쓰며, 감독의 구체적인 지시에 너무 의존했거든요. 다시 말해서, 배우들은 극 중 배역의 외면적인 특성을 표현하고 있었지만, 그 배역이 지녀야 하는 진정한 사고와 느낌은 부족했었죠. Stanislavsky는 연기에 있어서 가장 중요한 목표가 이러한 진정한 감정을 잡아내는 것으로 생각했습니다. 그래서 그 목표를 이루고자 자신만의 독특한 기술들을 개발했어요.

우선, Stanislavsky는 실험을 강조하면서 기본적으로 연기를 과학으로 간주하고자 했어요. 그는 배우가 가장 먼저 해야 할 것은 극 중 인물을 작품의 인물이 아닌 실존 인물로 보는 것이라고 주장했어요. 사실, 연기자는 관객이 지켜보고 있다는 것을 잊을 정도로 몰입해야 합니다. 여기에 도움이 되는 기술 중 하나는 정서적 기억입니다. 연기자는 이 방법을 사용해 자신이 맡은 배역이 처한 상황과 비슷한 상황에서의 생각과 느낌을 상기시키죠. 배우가 단지 연기만 하는 것이 아니라 심오하고 복잡한 등장인물을 스스로 만들어 내고 주위 상황에 마치 실제로 자신이 극 중 인물인 것처럼 반응하는 것입니다.

어쨌든 이 새로운 방법으로 Stanislavsky가 가장 성공한 경우 중 하나는 바로 1898년 그의 역사적인 작품인 『갈매기』였습니다. 이 연극은 근본적으로 Stanislavsky의 새로운 연기 스타일을 연극계에 소개했으며, 그는 많은 재능 있고 영향력 있는 추종자들을 얻게 되었어요.

One particularly remarkable student was Michael Chekhov, whom Stanislavsky regarded as his most brilliant pupil. Even though Chekhov was the most astute observer of the method, he tended to put his own spin on it and rejected some of Stanislavsky's rules. Q08 Chekhov developed techniques that required actors to be more imaginative and physically active than they would be under Stanislavsky's method.

Q10(A) Unfortunately, Chekhov fled from Soviet authorities and ended up working and teaching in Europe throughout the 1920s and 1930s, even setting up his own theater school in London in 1936. But his bad luck continued when World War II broke out and forced the school to dissolve after just a few years. He finally settled in Hollywood, primarily serving as an acting coach before passing away in 1955.

Student: Well, that's a shame. From what I understand, method acting had already been well established by Lee Strasberg.

Professor: That's true, but it is also a little misleading. Chekhov's teachings had a tremendous impact on many famous actors. Some studied with him directly, such as Clint Eastwood, Ingrid Bergman, and Gary Cooper. Others learned from his writings, such as Anthony Hopkins and Johnny Depp. Q09 While not famous in his lifetime, Chekhov's overall impact is second to none.

You do bring me to my next focus, though, which is the enormous influence of Lee Strasberg. For those of you who are unfamiliar with him, he was a legendary American stage actor who played the biggest role in making method acting popular in the United States. Q10(B) Q11 Upon joining the Actors' Studio in New York in 1948, Strasberg became one of the most renowned teachers of method acting. His students include screen legends such as Marlon Brando, James Dean, Paul Newman, Jane Fonda — I mean, really, I could list off names all day. You get the picture. This approach would be the most dominant acting style for the next two decades, and it forever transformed film and stage acting.

Another important teacher I want to mention is Uta Hagen. Q10(D) In fact, her book *Respect for Acting* is on your syllabus. This book was published in the 1970s, when method acting was perhaps at its strongest, and I think it's good for beginning actors. It really breaks down the method into the most basic fundamentals and makes the whole process easy to understand.

---

06 강의의 주된 내용은?
2개의 답을 고르시오.

(A) 메소드 연기의 역사에서 중요한 인물들
(B) 미국에서 메소드 연기의 출현
(C) 메소드 연기 양식들의 차이점
(D) 메소드 연기의 역사적 발전

07 Stanislavsky가 그의 연기법을 개발한 이유는?

(A) 배우들의 움직임이 충분치 않다고 생각했다.
(B) 배우들이 자신들의 배역을 완전히 이해하지 못한다고 생각했다.
(C) 그의 명성이 모스크바 극장에서 더 유명해지기를 원했다.
(D) 배우들이 관객들의 영향을 받는다고 생각하지 않았다.

08 Chekhov의 기법이 Stanislavsky의 방법과 다른 점은?

(A) 대사를 정확히 전달하는 것에 초점을 둔다.
(B) 극적인 효과를 위해 무대 장치를 더 많이 사용한다.
(C) 배우는 정신과 신체를 더 많이 사용해야 한다.
(D) 배우는 감정의 표현을 절제해야 한다.

해설 | Detail Chekhov가 개발한 기술에서는 배우들이 상상력과 신체적 움직임을 더 많이 사용해야 했다.

09 Michael Chekhov에 대한 교수의 의견은?

(A) 메소드 연기의 가장 중요한 선생 중 하나라고 생각한다.
(B) 불행한 환경으로 인해 비교적 알려지지 못했다고 느낀다.
(C) 메소드 연기에 대한 그의 해석이 다른 이들보다 뛰어나다고 믿는다.
(D) 더 많은 연기 교사들이 수업에서 그의 방법을 채택하길 희망한다.

해설 | Attitude 교수는 그의 영향을 받은 유명 배우들을 언급하며, 그의 영향력이 누구에게도 뒤지지 않는다고 설명하고 있다.

10 강의에서 교수는 메소드 연기의 역사에 대해 논의한다. 다음 사건들을 올바른 순서대로 나열하시오.

각 문장을 해당되는 곳으로 옮기시오.

1	(C) Stanislavsky가 작품 『갈매기』를 상연했다.
2	(A) Michael Chekhov가 런던에 그의 학교를 설립했다.
3	(B) Lee Strasberg가 액터스 스튜디오에 들어갔다.
4	(D) Uta Hagen의 저서 『산 연기』가 출간됐다.

해설 | Connecting Content 메소드 연기를 맨 처음 도입한 인물은 Stanislavsky였고 1898년에 이 방법을 도입한 그의 작품 『갈매기』가 성공을 거두었다. 그의 제자였던 Michael Chekhov는 이 방법을 이어받아 1936년에 런던에 연극 학교를 설립했다. 이후 1948년에 미국에서는 Lee Strasberg가 액터스 스튜디오에 들어가면서 메소드 연기의 가장 저명한 지도자 중 한 명이 되었고, Uta Hagen은 1970년대에 메소드 연기의 기본 원리와 전 과정을 쉽게 설명한 『산 연기』라는 책을 출간하였다.

11 강의의 일부를 다시 듣고 질문에 답하시오.
교수가 다음과 같이 말할 때 의미하는 것은?

"I mean, really, I could list off names all day."

(A) 이런 이름들을 열거하는 것은 시간 낭비다.
(B) 제시할 수 있는 예가 정말 많다.
(C) 교수는 자신의 지식을 뽐내고 싶어 한다.
(D) 교수는 강의에서 모든 내용을 다뤘다.

해설 | Function 이름을 열거하자면 하루가 걸릴 것이라는 말은 Lee Strasberg의 영향을 받은 배우들이 그만큼 많다는 것을 보여준다.

어휘 | method acting 메소드 연기(맡은 배역에 완전히 몰입하는 연기법) **manifestation** 명시, 표명 **trace** 추적하다 **thespian** (비극) 배우 **shallow** 깊이가 없는, 얕은 **affectation** 허식, 가식 **trait** 특성 **genuine** 진정한, 진짜의 **immerse** 몰입하다 **triumphant** 성공한 **acquire** 얻다 **pupil** 제자, 학생 **astute** 기민한, 눈치 빠른 **spin** 특정한 견해 **misleading** 오해가 있는, 오해하게 만드는 **tremendous** 엄청난 **enormous** 거대한 **renowned** 저명한

Passage 3

p.166

| 12 (D) | 13 (A) | 14 (B), (C) | 15 [Blue Whale – (B), (C)], [American Shad – (A), (D), (E)] | 16 (A) | 17 (D) |

Listen to part of a lecture in a biology class.

Professor (F): **Q12** OK. Today, we're going to be continuing our discussion of evolution, uh, specifically how the forces of natural selection and environmental pressures interact. Last time, we said that for any species, the most important urge is to reproduce and ensure survival of the species. Now any organism also has a set amount of energy it can devote to the task of reproduction, to uh, produce eggs, find a mate, rear its offspring, etc. But different species have different strategies for how they use that energy. Let's look at two examples to clarify this. For this purpose, we'll compare two aquatic animals: the blue whale and the American shad, which is a type of school fish.

생물학 강의 중 일부를 들으시오.

교수 (여): 좋아요. 오늘 우리는 진화에 대해 계속 이야기해보도록 하겠습니다. 특히, 자연 선택의 힘과 환경적인 압력이 서로 어떻게 영향을 끼치는지에 대해 이야기하겠습니다. 지난 시간에는 어떤 종이든 가장 중요한 욕구는 번식하고 종의 생존을 보장하는 것이라고 이야기했었죠. 모든 생물은 알을 낳고 짝을 찾고 새끼를 기르는 등의 번식 활동에 쏟을 수 있는 에너지가 정해져 있습니다. 하지만 이 에너지를 사용하는 전략은 종마다 달라요. 이를 명확하게 설명하기 위해 두 가지 예를 들어볼게요. 두 수생 동물인 흰긴수염고래와 떼를 지어 다니는 물고기 종인 아메리칸 청어를 비교해 보겠습니다.

Q15(B) Alright, now if you look at the blue whale, it reproduces quite slowly. Females don't reach sexual maturity until they are about ten years old. They take an entire year to give birth, and then the calf — that's the term for a baby whale, by the way — is dependent on its mother for at least the next six months. So that means at maximum, blue whales can reproduce once every two years, and it's often more like every three years. In the context of this low birth rate, every calf is valuable, and a considerable amount of energy is devoted to caring for the calf and ensuring its survival.

Now, contrast that with the American shad. **Q15(A)** These fish reach sexual maturity in as little as three years. They breed every single year, and in one breeding season, a female American shad may lay as many as 300,000 eggs. Of course, only a tiny fraction of these will survive to become mature shad themselves. After the female shad lays her eggs, she moves back out into the ocean, leaving her young to fend for themselves. **Q15(E)** She devotes no energy to the rearing of her young. Instead, all her reproductive energy is focused on producing huge numbers of eggs in the hope that at least some will survive.

So you can see that blue whales and American shad employ entirely different reproductive strategies that kind of lie on opposite ends of the spectrum. **Q14(B)** Blue whales invest all of their energy into a small number of offspring, while American shad put their energy into reproducing in huge numbers but with a very low chance of survival into maturity.

Now, many other species follow one of these two reproductive strategies. Those that fit into the pattern of the blue whale and reproduce in low numbers are known as K-strategists, and those that reproduce in large numbers with low chances of survival for individual offspring are known as r-strategists. **Q13** So what determines whether a species evolves to be a K-strategist or an r-strategist? Well, it largely has to do with the environmental pressures that the species faces and how they fit into their overall habitat. Let's again go back and look at blue whales and American shad.

Q15(C) Blue whales are the largest organisms in the ocean, and as such they have no natural predators. What's more, their large bodies allow them to build up large reserves of fat to sustain them when food is scarce. **Q17** As a result, a mature blue whale has a very good chance of surviving from year to year. **Q14(C)** In fact, if a blue whale manages to survive its childhood and reach maturity, it will most likely continue to live until it either dies of disease or old age. What all this means is that the blue whale population tends to be pretty stable. It generally doesn't experience massive or sudden declines, or at least it didn't until humans started disrupting its habitat.

American shad, on the other hand, lead a much riskier existence. **Q15(D)** Even when they reach maturity, they are preyed upon by a number of larger fish. Moreover, their population is much more susceptible to food shortages and mass starvation. But this is balanced out by the shad's ability to reproduce quickly and in large numbers. Every once in a while the shad population will suffer a significant decline, but it can always bounce back because of its high reproduction rate.

Let's take some more examples of K-strategists and r-strategists. Elephants and most birds are K-strategists, developing slowly, caring for only a few young over multiple births, and being strong competitors. Some reptiles, like alligators and crocodiles, are also K-strategists, living for a long time and laying eggs multiple times. **Q16** Mice, however, are mammals that are better described as r-strategists because they are small, able to reproduce early, and have many offspring with a high mortality rate.

K-전략가와 r-전략가의 예를 좀 더 살펴봅시다. 코끼리와 대부분 조류는 느리게 발달하고, 여러 출산 동안 오직 몇몇 새끼들만 돌보며, 강력한 경쟁자가 된다는 점에서 K-전략가예요. 앨리게이터나 크로코다일과 같은 파충류 또한 오랫동안 살고 여러 번 알을 낳는다는 점에서 K-전략가죠. 하지만 쥐는 크기가 작고 빨리 번식하며 높은 폐사율을 가진 많은 새끼를 낳기 때문에 r-전략가로 더 잘 설명되는 포유류예요.

---

12 강의의 주제는?
(A) K-전략가와 r-전략가의 환경적 경쟁
(B) 다양한 해양 생물 종의 번식 전략
(C) 환경이 생존 가능성에 영향을 미치는 방식
(D) 번식에 사용하는 에너지 할당과 그것에 영향을 끼치는 요인

해설 | Main Idea 교수는 생물의 종에 따라 번식에 쏟는 에너지 분배와 그러한 번식 전략에 영향을 끼치는 요인들에 대해 설명하고 있다.

13 교수가 여러 종이 r-전략가 또는 K-전략가로 진화한 이유를 설명하는 방식은?
(A) 그들이 처한 환경적 압력을 설명함으로써
(B) r-전략가와 K-전략가의 생활 주기를 설명함으로써
(C) 몇몇 종의 진화적 근원을 설명함으로써
(D) r-전략가와 K-전략가의 생존 가능성을 비교함으로써

해설 | Organization 교수는 흰긴수염고래와 아메리칸 청어가 처한 환경적 상황을 설명하며 그것이 두 종의 번식 전략에 어떠한 영향을 주고 있는지를 설명하고 있다.

14 다음 중 K-전략가에 대해 옳은 것은?
2개의 답을 고르시오.
(A) 일반적으로 작은 종을 잡아먹는 몸집이 큰 포식자이다.
(B) 대부분 에너지를 소수의 새끼를 기르는 데 쓴다.
(C) 일단 다 자라면 대체로 생존 가능성이 크다.
(D) 보통 먹이가 풍부한 서식지에서 산다.

해설 | Detail 흰긴수염고래와 같은 방식으로 번식하는 종을 K-전략가라고 하며, 대체로 적은 수의 새끼를 낳아 기르는 데 모든 에너지를 쏟고, 일단 성장을 하면 계속 살아남을 가능성이 크다.

15 강의에서 교수는 흰긴수염고래와 아메리칸 청어의 여러 가지 특징들을 언급한다. 다음 각 사항이 어떤 종에 해당되는지 표시하시오.
각 사항에 대해 알맞은 항목에 표시하시오.

	흰긴수염고래	아메리칸 청어
(A) 성적 성숙기에 빨리 도달함		✔
(B) 번식률이 낮음	✔	
(C) 천적이 없음	✔	
(D) 개체 수가 빨리 감소하기 쉬움		✔
(E) 새끼를 기르는 데 에너지를 쓰지 않음		✔

해설 | Connecting Content 흰긴수염고래는 성적 성숙기에 이르는 기간이 길고 2~3년에 한 번씩 출산할 수 있기 때문에 번식률이 낮으며, 바다에서 가장 큰 생물체로 천적이 없다. 반면에, 아메리칸 청어는 성적 성숙기에 이르는 기간이 3년으로 짧은 편이고, 다른 물고기에게 먹히거나, 먹이 부족, 굶주림 등의 영향으로 개체 수가 감소하기 쉬우며, 따라서 개체 수를 유지하기 위해 번식 에너지 대부분을 새끼를 기르는 데 쓰기보다는 알을 낳는 데에 집중적으로 쓴다.

16 강의에 따르면, 다음 중 r-전략가인 종은?
(A) 쥐
(B) 새
(C) 앨리게이터
(D) 코끼리

해설 | Detail 교수에 의하면, 쥐는 크기가 작고 빨리 번식하며 높은 폐사율을 가진 많은 새끼를 낳기 때문에 r-전략가인 포유류로 볼 수 있다.

17 강의의 일부를 다시 듣고 질문에 답하시오.
교수가 다음과 같이 말하는 이유는?

"or at least it didn't until humans started disrupting its habitat."

(A) 인간이 동물의 번식에 어떠한 영향을 주는지에 대한 논의를 시작하기 위해
(B) 인류 발전이 세계 환경에 끼치는 악영향을 시사하기 위해
(C) 인간이 K-전략가 종의 진화에서 맡는 역할을 강조하기 위해
(D) 외부 요인이 흰긴수염고래 개체 수의 정상적인 안정성에 영향을 줄 수 있음을 인정하기 위해

해설 | Function 교수가 '적어도 인간이 서식지를 파괴하기 전까지는 말입니다'라고 조건을 붙인 것은 앞서 언급한 흰긴수염고래 개체 수가 상당히 안정적으로 유지된다는 말에 대해 외적인 요인이 있을 수 있음을 나타내기 위함이다.

어휘 | evolution 진화 **natural selection** 자연 선택 **urge** (강한) 욕구, 충동 **ensure** 보장하다, 확실히 하다 **devote** (노력·시간·돈 등을) 쏟다 **mate** 짝, 배우자 **offspring** 새끼, 자식 **aquatic** 수생의 **shad** 청어 (무리) **school** (물고기·고래 등의) 떼 **maturity** 성숙(기) **calf** (하마·물소·고래 등의) 새끼 **breed** (새끼·알을) 낳다, 번식하다 **fraction** 소수, 파편 **employ** 쓰다, 사용하다 **reserve** 비축(물) **massive** 대규모의 **susceptible** 영향을 받기 쉬운 **shortage** 부족 **starvation** 굶주림

MEMO

MEMO

New Edition
i TOEFL iBT® LISTENING

- Thorough analysis of up-to-date information on the TOEFL iBT® Test
- Step-by-step listening practice through short, middle, and long passages
- Easy-to-learn and easy-to-teach with a detailed reference material
- Plenty of practice questions about frequently used topics

LinguaForum's Prep Book Series for the TOEFL iBT® Test

- **Beginners**
  TOEFL iBT® e Basic Series, TOEFL iBT® e Series
- **Pre-intermediate**
  TOEFL iBT® b Series, TOEFL iBT® b+ Series, TOEFL iBT® Basic Vocabulary
- **Intermediate**
  TOEFL iBT® M Series, TOEFL iBT® M+ Series, TOEFL iBT® Intro Vocabulary
- **High-intermediate**
  TOEFL iBT® i Series
- **Advanced**
  Hooked On TOEFL® Series, Frequency #1 TOEFL® Vocabulary
- **Reading for Building Background Knowledge**
  Core Topic Guide vol. 1-4

Online Downloadable Materials (www.linguaforum.com)
MP3 Files · Online TOEFL iBT® Mock Test · Vocabulary · Vocabulary Test · Dictation

LinguaForum is a research institute that specializes in the research and development Of preparation kits for all kinds of English proficiency tests including the TOEFL iBT® Test.

TOEFL® is a registered trademark of Educational Testing Service.
This publication is not endorsed or approved by ETS.